Entrepreneurial Cuba

ENTREPRENEURIAL CUBA

The Changing
Policy Landscape

Archibald R. M. Ritter
Ted A. Henken

FIRST**FORUM**PRESS
A DIVISION OF LYNNE RIENNER PUBLISHERS, INC. • BOULDER & LONDON

Published in the United States of America in 2015 by
FirstForumPress
A division of Lynne Rienner Publishers, Inc.
1800 30th Street, Boulder, Colorado 80301
www.rienner.com

and in the United Kingdom by
FirstForumPress
A division of Lynne Rienner Publishers, Inc.
3 Henrietta Street, Covent Garden, London WC2E 8LU

© 2015 by Lynne Rienner Publishers, Inc. All rights reserved

Library of Congress Cataloging-in-Publication Data
A Cataloging-in-Publication record for this book
is available from the Library of Congress.
ISBN: 978-1-62637-163-7

British Cataloguing in Publication Data
A Cataloguing in Publication record for this book
is available from the British Library.

Printed and bound in the United States of America

∞ The paper used in this publication meets the requirements
of the American National Standard for Permanence of
Paper for Printed Library Materials Z39.48-1992.

5 4 3 2 1

Contents

List of Tables and Figures vii
Preface ix

1 Cuba's Changing Policy Landscape 1
2 The Small Enterprise Sector 21
3 Revolutionary Trajectories and Strategic Shifts, 1959–1990 51
4 The "Special Period," 1990–2006 79
5 Policy Reform Under Raúl Castro, 2006–2014 127
6 The Movement Toward Non-Agricultural Cooperatives 181
7 The Underground Economy 203
8 The Rise, Fall, and Rebirth of the *Paladar*, 1993–2014 245
9 The Future of Small Enterprise in Cuba 297

Appendix 1: Timeline of Small Enterprise Under the Revolution 315
Appendix 2: 201 Legalized Self-Employment Occupations 327
Glossary 337
Bibliography 339
Index 365
About the Book 373

Tables and Figures

Tables

2.1	Types of States by Regulatory Capacity and Regulatory Intent	26
2.2	Characterization of the Components of an Economy	34
3.1	Cuba's Major Economic Reforms, 1959–1961	56
3.2	Percentage Distribution of Cuba's Labor Force by Institutional Forms, 1970–1989	68
4.1	The Top Self-Employment Occupations, June 1999	88
4.2	The Self-Employment Licensing Process, Havana, 1996–2001	97
4.3	Decree 174: Microenterprise Rules, Contraventions, and Punishments	104
4.4	Taxation Rates for *Paladares* and Other Food Services	110
4.5	Tax Scale Worksheet Applied to Personal Income, 1997	112
4.6	Tax Regimes for Cuban Microenterprise and Foreign Enterprise Operating in Joint Ventures, 1995–2010	118
5.1	Taxation Calculation for a *Paladar*, Three Cases	153
5.2	Comparison of the Tax Regimes for Small Enterprise and Foreign Mixed Enterprise After the 2014 Foreign Investment Law	157
5.3	Major Public Policy Areas for Microenterprises as of August 2014	175
6.1	Cooperative Agricultural Organizations in Cuba, 2010	186
6.2	Non-Agricultural Cooperatives in Operation or in Process of Formation	198
7.1	A Categorization of Economic Activities in the Cuban Context	205
7.2	Economic Illegalities and Their Social and Economic Impacts in Summary	223
8.1	Distribution of Self-Employment Licenses by Economic Activity, Plaza Municipality, 1999	254

Figures

3.1	Economic Assistance from the Soviet Union to Cuba, 1960–1990	63
4.1	Cuban Exports by Product Shares, 1990	82
4.2	Non-Agricultural Self-Employment as a Percentage of Total Employment, 1970–2006	89
5.1	GDP per Capita, 1989–2012	131
5.2	Cuba: Real Inflation-Adjusted Wages, 1989–2009	132
5.3	Cuban Sugar Production, 1985–2013	135
5.4	Cuban Exports and Imports of Foodstuffs, 1989–2010	136
5.5	Non-Agricultural Employment as a Percentage of Total Employment, 2000–2014	170

Preface

This book is the product of the authors' many years of investigation of and fascination with small enterprise and the informal, underground, and second economies of revolutionary Cuba. We hope that it reflects the unending resourcefulness, as well as the innumerable *inventos* (inventions), often technically illegal, that most Cuban citizens have long had to undertake in their daily struggle to *resolver* or "make ends meet." As with the countries of Eastern Europe, this part of the economy—long hidden, but everywhere in plain sight—has been of major importance in the everyday lives of the Cuban people, playing a role in the provision of needed goods, services, and employment.

Prior to 2010, serious study of this sector was taboo because state policies had consistently stigmatized it as illegitimate and banished it to the shadows. Even since 2010, small private enterprise has been relatively under-analyzed within Cuba, a trend partly remedied by the important work of Omar Everleny Pérez Villanueva and Pavel Vidal Alejandro (2010, 2012) and Juan Triana (2012, 2013). Elsewhere, the earliest and most rigorous work on the subject is easily that of Cuban-American economist Jorge Pérez-López, whose insightful 1995 volume, *Cuba's Second Economy: From Behind the Scenes to Center Stage*, set a high bar for those who might follow him. In the ten years following that book's publication, an increasingly antagonistic public policy toward microenterprise pushed self-employment (*trabajo por cuenta propia*) behind the scenes once again, culminating in its practical extinction by 2005. During those years, as well as more recently, the work of Joseph Scarpaci (1995, 2009, and 2014), Richard Feinberg (2011, 2013), and especially Phil Peters (1997, 1998, 1998 with Scarpaci, 2006a, 2012a, 2012b, and 2014) has been exemplary both for its rich ethnographic reportage and its original, dispassionate analysis of Cuba's now reemerging small enterprise sector.

The main thrust of the present volume is to analyze why self-employment has returned once again to the center stage in Cuba—and to what effect. Our objective is to analyze the policies of the Cuban government toward the legal small enterprise sector, always recognizing that a continual counterpoint is played out between legal private enterprises and "extra-legal" or informal ones operating clandestinely, out of reach of the regulatory and fiscal controls of the state. Our central focus is on the varying policy approaches (including implementation and consequences) toward small- and microenterprise on the part of the government of Fidel Castro in contrast with the subsequent dramatic reforms of Raúl Castro's presidency.

• • •

Arch Ritter was first introduced to Cuba's underground economy and to its rich variety of illegal economic activities during his many research visits to the island beginning in the 1960s. Some of these activities are chronicled in his 1974 book, *The Economic Development of Revolutionary Cuba: Strategy and Performance*. His subsequent trips to the island in the late-1980s and especially the 1990s, when he was the co-coordinator of a Cuban-Canadian academic program at the University of Havana, revealed that such practices had only intensified during the intervening years. He was fortunate to have a number of good Cuban friends who provided insightful if informal exposure to the sector first in the 1960s and again in the 1990s, 2000s, and through 2014. On repeated lengthy visits to Cuba, he was able to observe the travails and successes of various legal and extralegal microenterprises firsthand. These trips have only deepened his interest in Cuba's resilient small- and microenterprise sector, especially now that state policy seems to have definitively shifted away from ideology, placing Cuba's second economy once again at the "center stage" of Raúl's economic reform program.

Ritter is indebted to many people for insights into the small enterprise sector and the underground economy. Many legal *cuentapropistas* provided him with valuable information on their activities. Many microentrepreneurs in the shadow economy were also helpful in illuminating how that part of the Cuban economy functioned and interacted with the legal self-employment sector. Most of those who provided such assistance in the 1990s and 2000s cannot yet be named. However, he can thank some of his friends and guides from the 1960s, namely Modesto Alcalá and the brothers Nieves and José de la O—now deceased—who took him under their collective wing during some of his visits and guided him around the economic underside of Havana. Ritter is likewise indebted to many analysts and scholars who shared their ideas on Cuba's economy over many years. Among these are the late Evaldo Cabarrouy, Francisco León, Richard Carson, Carmelo Mesa-Lago, Jorge Pérez-López, Sergio Díaz-Briquets, Juan Antonio Blanco, Luis René Fernández, Alberto Díaz, Ana Julia Faya, Óscar Espinosa Chepe, Adrián Denis, Jorge Mario Sánchez, Juan Triana, Omar Everleny Pérez, and Pavel Vidal, as well as analysts and scholars at the Centro de Estudios Sobre la Economía Cubana in Havana and, of course, his co-author, Ted Henken. He is also indebted to David Clift for valuable editorial work.

Ted Henken first traveled to Cuba as a graduate student in the summer of 1997, with follow-up trips in the spring and summer of 1999. Initially, he was studying the social costs, economic benefits, and political contradictions of Cuba's then reemerging international tourism industry. However, a number of vivid encounters during those initial three trips to the island shifted his focus away from tourism as a government development strategy and toward microenterprise as an individual and family survival strategy. The first encounter took place as he left Terminal 2 of José Martí International Airport on his first visit to the island on a hot summer night in 1997. Met by a throng of boisterous, expectant Cubans and inundated with offers of help with his bags and transportation into the city, Henken was particularly struck when a slight Cuban man brushed quietly past him whispering, "*¿Taxi particular?*" (Private taxi?). The man soon reappeared, standing at the far back of the now thinning crowd and giving a sly glance that seemed say, "Well, what'll it be?"

After nodding casually in the cabbie's direction, Henken spied him slowly make his way out to the parking lot, stopping periodically to check if anyone else had taken notice of the "deal." Following the cabbie's lead, Henken gathered up his belongings and headed toward the parking lot too, taking care not to make it obvious whom he was following—even as he attracted more than a few quizzical looks as he walked away from the waiting state-run cabs. Minutes later, the cabbie pulled up, sprang out of his car (a small, Russian-made Lada), and began hastily throwing Henken's bags into his trunk, saying, "*Rápido, rápido, para que no nos vean*" (Quick, quick, so that they don't see us). After bundling hurriedly into the car with him in tow, the driver came out onto the main road (deserted except for an occasional car or, more commonly, a bicycle) and breathed a sigh of relief as he had once again successfully avoided detection and an exorbitant fine for transporting foreigners without a government license. His relief was mingled with a kind of happiness, he explained, since his $15 fare (paid in U.S. dollars) was more than he made monthly (in Cuban pesos) working as an air-traffic controller at that same airport.

Two years later, during an unforgettable visit to the renowned tourist resort Varadero Beach in summer 1999, Henken stumbled upon a whole range of informal entrepreneurial activities run out of the private home where he stayed. Despite the fact that *paladares* (private, home-based restaurants), bed-and-breakfasts, and private taxis—three of the most common and lucrative self-employment activities at that time (and once again since 2010)—were all prohibited in a place almost completely given over to international tourism, underground activity thrived. Arriving without a place to stay, he was offered efficient and personalized assistance in finding lodging by a waiter in a state-run restaurant. Like a man on a mission, the waiter took a "smoke break" from his official job and led him on foot to six different private bed-and-breakfasts within just 15 minutes. After settling on a place and leaving his belongings in his room, Henken was advised by the owner not to return until after 9 p.m.

Though initially baffled at such a request, on returning he discovered that his intrepid hosts ran a clandestine seafood restaurant out of what was to become his bedroom. They also used their aged Russian-made Lada sedan to transport their guests around the island and were even then in the process of expanding their operation by adding a second floor to their home, all without much effort to conceal these activities from their neighbors or the local housing inspectors. Eventually, he would learn that even his friendly waiter and guide was paid a $5 commission for each night he spent in the home. In other words, like the air-traffic controller cabbie from two years before, this waiter's official job was not necessarily his real job. This odyssey and innumerable subsequent experiences like it all across the island caused Henken to reevaluate the focus of his research, and he ended up spending much of his time in Cuba on his yearly visits over the following decade investigating Cuba's unique brand of self-employment and visiting and interviewing scores of *cuentapropistas* to learn about their survival strategies. That is, he sought to discover how private microentrepreneurs (both legal and extra-legal) stay afloat and turn a profit in a still nominally revolutionary socialist society.

Henken has also incurred many debts over the course of his research. He would first like to acknowledge the trust, honesty, and generosity of scores of private entrepreneurs who opened their lives to an unknown and often overly inquisitive outsider. Thanks are also due to *Havana Times* blogger Erasmo Calzadilla, who expertly transcribed all of Henken's 2011 follow-up interviews with Cuban *cuentapropistas* (barbers, cabbies, bed-and-breakfast proprietors, and *paladar* owners-operators). Excerpts from these interviews and other stories collected over the course of his many visits between 1997 and 2011 appear in Chapters 4, 7, and 8. Henken has also received vital feedback and encouragement on this project from a host of scholars, mentors, and colleagues both in Cuba and abroad, including Carmelo Mesa-Lago, Jorge Pérez-López, Óscar Espinosa Chepe, Miriam Leiva, Lisandro Pérez, Julio Carranza, Pedro Monreal, Marc Frank, Julio César González Pagés, Armando Chaguaceda, Miriam Celaya, Dimas Castellanos, Yoani Sánchez, Reinaldo Escobar, Alejandro Portes, Damián Fernández, Neili Fernández Peláez, Elena Sacchetti, Adrian Hearn, Javier Corrales, Peter Roman, Phil Peters, Joseph Scarpaci, Richard Feinberg, J. Timmons Roberts, Eloise Linger, and Holly Ackerman. Some of these colleagues are also fellow members of the Association for the Study of the Cuban Economy (ASCE), a true *caldo de cultivo* for this book. In fact, it was at one of ASCE's annual gatherings in the summer of 2002 that Henken first met the person to whom he owes his greatest debt in bringing this project to fruition, Arch Ritter.

Indeed, years earlier, in the fall of 1995, while living in Mobile, Alabama, and working as a resettlement coordinator for recently arrived Cuban refugees from Guantánamo Bay Naval Base, Henken came across a discounted 50¢ (!) copy of Ritter's first book while rummaging through a cart of remainders at the Mobile Public Library on Government Street. Five years later, in the summer of 2000, they stayed in private bed-and-breakfasts just a block away from each other in Havana; although they did not meet, Ritter was kind enough to leave behind one of his penetrating articles on Cuba's underground economy for Henken to read ("El régimen impositivo para la microempresa en Cuba," *Revista de la CEPAL* 71, pp. 145–162, August 2000). These near misses culminated in their meeting finally at ASCE's annual conference, followed by more than a decade of subsequent visits between New York City and Ottawa, their respective homes.

Henken also thanks the many good folks at the Roger Thayer Stone Center for Latin American Studies—Gene Yeager, Richard Greenleaf, James Huck, Suyapa Inglés, Thomas Reese, Valerie McGinley Marshall, and Ana López—and the associated Cuban-Caribbean Studies Institute at Tulane University (his alma mater) for their funding and support, which enabled him to make various trips to the island between 1997 and 2001. He also gratefully acknowledges an initial seed grant from Johns Hopkins University's Cuba Exchange Program (then directed by Wayne Smith) for travel and research in Cuba in the summer of 1999. Subsequent travel grants between 2003 and 2011 were provided by the City University of New York's (CUNY) Caribbean Exchange Program and the Research Foundation of CUNY's Professional Staff Congress. Financial support from Baruch College's Weissman School of Arts and Sciences and Provost's Office also helped to fund travel to both Cuba and Canada during the many years of this project's gestation. Henken also tips his hat to Virginia Sánchez-Korral, the senior faculty facilitator of a CUNY Faculty Fellowship Publication Program peer writing group where early drafts of Chapters 2 and 8 were critically (and very kindly) scrutinized by her and by Henken's faculty colleagues, including Amy Chazkel, John Collins, Tomás López-Pumarejo, Gilbert Marzán, Carolina Bank Múñoz, and Eva Vásquez. Finally, Henken gives a thankful shout out to Elias, Sarina, and all the other good folks at Café Buunni for bringing a few drops of Ethiopia to their micro roasted oasis in Washington Heights, allowing him the space and caffeinated stimulation necessary to complete a good portion of the final manuscript.

Both Ritter and Henken express their sincere thanks to Lynne Rienner, Alex Wilcox, and the always intrepid and ebullient Jessica Gribble, former acquisitions editor at Lynne Rienner Publishers and FirstForumPress. Their presence and solid advice at the Latin American Studies Association conferences over a period of years acted as an always encouraging reminder that our at times nebulous and seemingly never-ending book project on the fascinating world of Cuba's "underground" would eventually find a publishing home (with them) and a receptive audience (with you). Our colleague Gabriel Vignoli and two anonymous reviewers selected by the publisher were kind enough to read our entire manuscript at vital stages in its development. Their generous and critical feedback has made the final book much stronger and more clearly focused. We also thank our multitalented research assistant, copyeditor, and overall formatting guru, Derek Ludovici, for his assistance on the final stages of this project, along with Jeffrey Peck, dean of Baruch College's Weissman School of Arts and Sciences, for the funding that allowed us to bring Derek on board for the last leg of this journey.

In the summer of 2010 as Raúl Castro began to publicly embrace the very thing that his elder brother, Fidel, had long vilified and stigmatized—small, private enterprise—as a key part of the solution to Cuba's economic woes, we knew that the time was ripe to finish our book comparing these differing policy approaches and chronicling the intense struggles and inventive strategies of Cuba's *cuentapropistas*. This is that book.

1
Cuba's Changing Policy Landscape

We have to erase forever the notion that Cuba is the only country in the world where one can live without working.
—*Raúl Castro, to delegates of the National Assembly, August 1, 2010 (Peters 2012a)*

The Cuban model doesn't even work for us anymore.
—*Fidel Castro, responding to U.S. journalist Jeffrey Goldberg's question about whether the Cuban model was still something worth exporting, September 8, 2010 (Goldberg 2010)*

The aim is to distance ourselves from those policies that condemned self-employment to near extinction and stigmatized those who decided to join its ranks legally in the 1990s.
—*Granma, Official Organ of the Communist Party of Cuba, September 24, 2010 (Martínez Hernández 2010)*

While it is perhaps a fool's errand to guess at the internal dynamics of the relationship between the Castro brothers, a breathtaking series of announcements coming out of Cuba during September 2010 shed new light on how their different economic orientations intersect with Cuba's changing power dynamics. First, on September 8, 2010, the U.S. journalist Jeffrey Goldberg posted details on his blog from a series of interviews he had done with Fidel Castro in late August, when Cuba's aging but newly active and vocal former leader invited him to Havana to discuss Goldberg's recent article about Iran and Israel in the *Atlantic* magazine. During a break in one of their marathon conversations, Goldberg wondered aloud whether Castro believed that the Cuban model was still something worth exporting abroad. Stunningly, the elder statesman responded with the telling quip, "The Cuban model doesn't even work for us anymore."

Though Castro later claimed that Goldberg had misinterpreted his statement, an announcement published in the Communist Party daily *Granma* less than a week later on September 13 confirmed Goldberg's original interpretation. Addressed to Cuban workers and signed by the national secretary of

Cuba's official trade union, the *Central de Trabajadores Cubanos* (CTC, or Union of Cuban Workers), the astounding *"Pronunciamiento"* declared that half a million state sector jobs would be eliminated over the next six months (October 2010–March 2011) with hundreds-of-thousands more layoffs to follow in the coming years. The statement went on to indicate that the state sector was bloated by more than a million redundant workers, reducing the productivity and efficiency state enterprises. Ironically, this planned "updating" (*actualización*) of Cuba's economic model was justified as a way to "continue to build socialism" (*"Pronunciamiento"* 2010).

At the same time, the announcement sought to communicate to workers a new understanding of socialism and a new relationship between Cuban workers and the state. "We must revitalize the principle of socialist distribution," declared the communiqué. Salaries should be based on "paying each worker according to the quantity and quality of the work performed." This same principle was used to justify a strict new policy for state enterprises. The *"Pronunciamiento"* made clear:

> Our state cannot and should not continue maintaining enterprises and productive and service entities whose inflated payrolls and losses weigh down the economy, turn out to be counterproductive, generate bad work habits, and deform the conduct of workers. It is necessary to increase production and the quality of services, reduce bulky social spending and eliminate improper gratuities, excessive subsidies, study as a source of employment, and early retirement. (*"Pronunciamiento"* 2010)

This announcement confirmed what Raúl Castro had already forcefully declared in a session of Cuba's National Assembly in August: "We have to eliminate forever the notion that Cuba is the only country in the world where one can live without working." In that same speech Raúl spoke of imminent economic changes that would

> eliminate the paternalistic attitudes that dis-incentivize the need to work for a living, and thereby reduce the unproductive expenditures represented by the equal payment [...] of wage guarantees during long periods to people who do not work. (Castro, R. 2010b)

While taking many casual Cuba watchers by surprise, such a contraction in the state sector along with a shift away from his elder brother's more rigid application of socialist ideology was the culminating event in a series of moves aimed at eliminating what Cuba's new Commander-in-Chief had long described as an unsustainable group of heavily subsidized "gratuities." Indeed, as part of a set of "guidelines" (*Lineamientos* 2010) first published in November 2010 in anticipation of the Sixth Communist Party Congress in April 2011, Cubans were informed that the island's long-standing *libreta* or ration booklet would be gradually phased out, with future subsidies targeted on the needy only. The same document also echoed Raúl's oft-repeated argument that socialism does *not* mean egalitarianism. Instead, the "guidelines" indicated that under the new understanding of Cuba's political economy "socialism is equality of rights and opportunities for all citizens, not egalitarianism. Work is simultaneously a right and a duty, a motivation for personal realization for each citizen, and should be rewarded according to its quantity and quality" (*Lineamientos* 2010: 7).

Rounding out the month's series of dramatic announcements was a September 24 *Granma* article declaring that self-employment was "much more than an alternative" to the state sector, detailing changes in legislation intended to revive the microenterprise sector and begin to increasingly rely on it as a way to fill the employment shortfall created by the coming layoffs in the state sector (Martínez Hernández 2010). Though quite dramatic as a comprehensive new policy toward entrepreneurship, the announcement reviving microenterprise was the culmination of a series of experiments and pilot programs allowing Cuban workers greater economic autonomy in agriculture, public transport, food sales, home construction, barber shops, and beauty salons begun in 2008 (Peters 2008, 2009, 2010; *CubaEncuentro* 2008; Weissert 2009; Pérez Navarro 2009; Gettig 2013; Miroff 2010; Robles 2010; Ferrer 2010). Breaking with a past policy that never viewed microenterprise as anything more than a stop-gap measure to halt the economic crisis of the early 1990s, the article now described self-employment as:

> a solution that, far from being improvised or ephemeral, will make possible an increase in the supply of goods and services while simultaneously assuring income to those who decide to engage in it. It will also allow the state to shake off a good portion of its excessive subsidies while leaving in non-state [private] hands productive activities that had been the responsibility of the state despite the difficult economic juncture. (Martínez Hernández 2010)

Openly repudiating President Fidel Castro's half-hearted approach to self-employment during the 1990s (without naming him, of course), the article went on to outline new microenterprise regulations ahead of the new October self-employment law, stating unequivocally:

> The measure of making self-employment more flexible is one of the decisions taken by the country as it redesigns its economic policy, in order to increase levels of productivity and efficiency. The aim, in addition to providing workers with another way to feel useful with their personal effort, is to *distance ourselves from those policies that condemned self-employment to near extinction and stigmatized those who decided to joint its ranks legally in the 1990s*. (Martínez Hernández 2010, our emphasis)

The months following these dramatic September announcements saw the release of the new laws that would guide state layoffs and regulate the expanded self-employment sector (*Gaceta Oficial* 2010a, b). Most significantly, though the self-employed would be required to pay a number of new taxes (including a mandatory new social security tax), a broader range of 178 licensed occupations was now included on the legal list of self-employment options; entrepreneurs would also be allowed to deduct a greater percentage of their expenses before paying taxes; for the first time, businesses would have the ability to hire non-family employees; and they would be permitted to rent out private locales to set up shop. Later announcements also recognized the need for the development of credit systems and wholesale markets while admitting that putting these in place would take some time. In subsequent years (2011-2014), these initial changes would be coupled with other symbolically monumental economic, civic, and political reforms such as the legalization of the buying and selling of automobiles and real estate on the open, if still highly regulated domestic market (Haven 2011; Sánchez 2011), the imposition of term limits for top political leaders, the liberalization of foreign travel (Cancio Isla 2012; Decree-Law 302, 2012; *Granma* 2012c), and an opening—however small and prohibitively expensive—in public access to the Internet via 118 new state-run cybercafés (Café Fuerte 2013a; Del Valle 2013).

Cuban Microenterprise and Changing Public Policy

This book critically examines revolutionary Cuba's changing public policy toward the private sector, microenterprise, non-agricultural cooperatives, and the underground economy. The core of our analysis contrasts the halting and tentative experiments with self-employment (*trabajo por cuenta propia*) under Fidel Castro during the 1993-2006 period with the more thoroughgoing and likely more permanent economic reforms and structural adjustments so far enacted under Raúl Castro from 2006 to 2014.

We argue that President Raúl Castro's approach to the non-state sector and microenterprise is decidedly more pragmatic and potentially more economically productive than that of his more ideologically-minded brother Fidel. We also identify a number of continuities that characterize both policy periods and leadership styles. We argue that these remaining bureaucratic restrictions, ideological obstacles, and political fears prevent the optimal development of microenterprise. Without more fundamental reform that expands occupational categories to include professionals, further minimizes (and more narrowly focuses) the remaining prohibitions and regulations, and supports entrepreneurs with access to credit and wholesale supplies, many of Cuba's new breed of microentrepreneurs will not be able to exit the underground and contribute more effectively to the Cuban economy. Furthermore, without a second round of well-implemented reforms that cede space to small- and medium-sized enterprises (SMEs) as well as to the new non-agricultural cooperatives, the microenterprises within the current framework will not alone be able to create productive employment for workers displaced from the state sector.

Thus, we address the following central questions in this book:

1. How can we best characterize public policy toward entrepreneurship, small and microenterprise, and the informal sector under the Revolution; what have been the developmental consequences of past policies; and can Raúl Castro's current more pragmatic if still guarded approach produce positive, economically significant results?
2. What are the main characteristics that differentiate the current policy approach toward entrepreneurship, microenterprise, and informality under Raúl Castro from the policies under Fidel?
3. How have Cuban entrepreneurs responded in the past to similar changes in public policy toward microenterprise and how have they reacted to the most recent reforms enacted since 2010? Is their general orientation vis-à-vis the pace, scope, and depth of the current reforms one of skepticism, doubt, hopefulness, or enthusiasm? Thus far, as a result of the economic opening have they experienced a positive impact on their own enterprises and standards of living?
4. What problems remain with Cuba's current approach toward entrepreneurship and how might those problems be mitigated with a second round of more through-going reforms?

Continuities between Fidel's and Raúl's approach to small private enterprise include the priorities of maintaining centralized political control, preserving a dominant role in the economy for state enterprises and the central plan, and a continuing ideological and rhetorical commitment to state socialism. Indeed, while Raúl's tenure as president has seen an increasingly ambitious series of changes in the rules that govern the functioning of the country's moribund economy, there have been virtually no accompanying changes in its authoritarian political system apart from a declared intention to impose a limit of two terms of five years each on top political posts. Moreover, despite making a significant ideological break from his elder brother's antagonistic approach to the private sector, Raúl has been careful to stress that his changes to the Cuban economy constitute an "updating" or "perfecting" of the island's socialist economic model, not wholesale economic "reform" or a transition to capitalism. It is notable, for example, that references to the "market" or the "private sector" are absent from government discourse, which consistently uses the euphemistic term "non-state sector" whenever referring to self-employment. "Only socialism," declares the major planning document issued by the Cuban Communist Party in November 2010, "is capable of overcoming the difficulties and preserving the conquests of the Revolution" (*Lineamientos* 2010: 7). Whatever one may think of the authenticity of such seemingly obligatory declarations, the Cuban government continues to insist to its people and to the world that it will continue to place the very visible hand of the socialist "plan" above what Adam Smith famously called the invisible hand of the "market."

Regardless of whatever the government prefers to call this new stage in the island's political economy, the real question we seek to address in this book is: Will it work? Thus, this study seeks to compare the country's previous experience with self-employment during the 1990s with this emerging one, and to evaluate how changes in licensing, the number and type of occupational categories, the tax regime, and measures incentivizing legality (such as access to credit and wholesale markets) might impact the Cuban economy and the viability of microenterprise in the future. Although it is still in its infancy, we also aim to give a preliminary evaluation of Cuba's recent expansion of non-agricultural cooperatives (the implementation of which only began in summer 2013) since they could be the legal basis for a move beyond the current, marginally productive, service and subsistence kinds of self-employment toward a more dynamic small- and medium-sized cooperative enterprise sector.

The Past is Prologue: Legal, but Still Illegitimate?

In response to the economic meltdown that Cuba faced in the early 1990s as a result of the lethal combination of the collapse of the former Soviet Union, the strengthening of the U.S. embargo, and the island's own economic rigidity and mismanagement, the Cuban government liberalized microenterprise, or "self-employment" (*trabajo por cuenta propia*) in September 1993. Microenterprise—in both its licensed, legal and underground, informal, and extra-legal variants—has long existed in Cuba, even after the extensive nationalizations and near-abolition of the private sector by the revolutionary government starting in 1959 and culminating in the notorious "Revolutionary Offensive" of 1968 (see Appendix 1 for a chronology of Cuban policy toward private enterprise under the Revolution). However, the liberalization of 1993 led to a flowering of legal microenterprise as new self-employment activities burst forth into the open from the underground economy.

Small and microenterprise is of great importance in virtually all countries. It generates such important economic and social benefits that most governments have constructed a variety of programs to support it. Cuba is indeed exceptional in that it has long limited such activities in so draconian a manner. However, despite the strict controls placed upon it, legalized microenterprise or "self-employment" has produced a variety of benefits for Cuba during the past twenty years (1993-2014). These include job creation, income generation, the provision of goods and services with a high domestic value added content, and significant tax revenues for the government. These taxes in turn provide support for social expenditures and productive investment. The government of Raúl Castro is even betting the future of the Revolution itself on the ability of microenterprise—together with an expanded cooperative sector—to absorb hundreds-of-thousands of workers laidoff from state jobs.

Self-employment has generated foreign exchange earnings from the provision of goods and services to the tourism sector and the replacement of imports. Microenterprise has also contributed to the unique and vibrant Cuban culture through a flowering of different offerings in the areas of music, art, craft production, and food services, all of great value to Cubans themselves and in the tourism sector. Legalized microenterprise also unleashes the ingenuity, inventiveness, initiative, and industriousness of the self-employed and promotes the widespread development of entrepreneurial talents and experience that may be of immense benefit to Cuba in the future. The legalization of microenterprise has also likely reduced the numbers of underground economic activities. Finally, it encourages the development of a potential "culture of legality" in place of the much vilified but omnipresent "culture of illegality" that currently prevails in Cuba's rampant and extensive underground economy (Orsi 2013a; Burnett 2013), the subject of Chapter 7.

On the other hand, many of the negative, even noxious features of the functioning of the sector in fact arise from public policy. The limitations on microenterprise force enterprises to remain artificially small in size, create distortions arising from attempts at regulation evasion, and provoke higher prices and incomes due to limitations on the numbers of such activities in each field. Furthermore, in order to avoid onerous regulations, microenterprises can slip into the underground economy since the "costs of formality" are often greater than those of informality (de Soto 2000; Centeno and Portes 2006). From the perspective of the Cuban government, the legalization of microenterprise has led to negative consequences. Indeed, it has fought a long battle—though perhaps a losing one—against the growth in socioeconomic inequality and concentration of wealth that the expansion of the private sector has brought. Moreover, by definition granting more legal space for private entrepreneurs would weaken state control over the economy and political control over Cuban citizens who would begin to gain substantial independence from party and labor controls through independent economic activity. Finally, the government's hostility toward microenterprise also springs from the belief that it encourages a "shop-keeper's mentality" and the flourishing of behaviors, attitudes, and values incompatible with the development of socialism (Sacchetti 2011; Vignoli 2014), though Raúl Castro's new understanding of socialism seems to differ substantially from his elder brother's on this point (Peters 2010).

Revolutionary Cuba's public policy toward microenterprise since 1993, switching from legalization, to containment, to virtual asphyxiation, and now back to legalization and broad-based promotion for the first time, highlights one of the Revolution's central socioeconomic dilemmas. As it enters its sixth decade, in order to survive and prosper economically Cuba needs to increase economic efficiency, improve productive employment and overall economic productivity, and compete internationally, while simultaneously seeking to maintain relative equality of income distribution and strong social programs for all its citizens. However, the existence of self-employment is perceived to involve a significant sociopolitical cost, namely the ceding of economic and political space to the private sector, a risk the Cuban government is decidedly ambivalent about.[1] Despite the significance of Raúl Castro's reforms so far in the area of self-employment, it is wise to note that they are still limited to just 201 exceedingly specific and largely subsistence-oriented microenterprise occupations, not yet reaching the level of small- and medium-sized enterprises (SMEs). Indeed, the long-awaited regulations on an expanded non-agricultural cooperative sector were only issued in December 2012 and thus have yet to have any measurable impact on employment or the economy. Perhaps this is due to the fear that, as one of our self-employed informants put it to us succinctly in an interview: "Economic independence equals political independence." Thus, while the growth of microenterprise holds significant economic potential for Cuba, it also generates new challenges and dilemmas.

Specifically, Cuba is faced with the challenge of releasing the entrepreneurial energy of its citizens, while simultaneously avoiding the enhancement of a culture of illegality. As examples from the Eastern European transitions briefly examined in Chapter 2 indicate, a large underground economy can give way to a "marginalized" informal sector (as already exists in many other Latin American and Caribbean nations) and lead to the intensification of the underground economy, with some groups of entrepreneurs morphing into powerful mafias as has been the case in Russia and other parts of the former Soviet Union. In sum, Cuba's "second economy" consisting of legal microenterprises and the current underground economy has both positive and negative implications. It poses great challenges as well as offering many potential opportunities to the government's current economic regime. It also creates useful potential for greater economic prosperity and the future evolution towards a more thoroughly mixed or full market economy.

Public policy in Cuba towards legalized self-employment reflects the ambiguous economic contributions of microenterprise as well as evident incompatibilities with the Cuban government and its vision of the "good society." While various microenterprise activities were legalized in 1993, public policy in the areas of licensing, taxation, regulation, state competition, employment, social security, publicity, and prohibitions regarding the formation of cooperatives or associations seemed aimed at shrinking the sector as a whole, as well as constricting the size of individual microenterprises. This approach contrasts sharply with the approach of other countries, where the contributions of microenterprise are well understood, encouraged, and appreciated. In fact, through its attempt to maintain total control over the economy, the government's past policy approach to microenterprise neutralized most of its potential benefits and inadvertently enhanced the development of the underground economy.

Before proceeding, a brief note on our use of the terms self-employment, microenterprise, and small enterprise is in order. The standard definitions of these terms[2] differ slightly from our use of the terms here, which are the outgrowth of the Cuban situation. In the Cuban context, *cuentapropistas* are persons who work for themselves (thus, the terms "self-employed" or "own-account" workers). However, in actual practice on the island the term has been broadened to refer to persons who work for themselves but may also employ up to five additional workers or in some cases, such as private *paladar* restaurants (analyzed in detail in Chapter 8), even more. We also use the term "microenterprise" synonymously with the Cuban use of the term *trabajo por cuenta propia* to refer to those who may work alone as well as those who employ additional workers either as informal friend or family workers or as officially or informally hired employees. In contrast, we use the term "small enterprise" to include microenterprises but also to encompass larger types of enterprise that may employ more than 10 persons. So far, Cuba does not have private sector "medium-sized" enterprises, though it has many medium and large-sized state and joint state-foreign enterprises and is in the process of developing a new SME cooperative sector outside of agriculture for the first time.

A number of economists, sociologists, anthropologists, and political scientists both on the island and in the diaspora (Pérez-López 1995a; Carranza, Gutiérrez, and Monreal 1995; Togores González n.d.; Togores González and Pérez Villanueva 1996; Núñez Moreno 1997; Peters and Scarpaci 1998; Fernández Peláez 2000; Peters 2006a; Scarpaci 2009; Sacchetti 2011; Mesa Lago 2011; Espinosa Chepe 2011; Vidal Alejandro and Pérez Villanueva 2010, 2012; Peters 2012a, 2012b; Piñeiro Harnecker 2012a, 2013; Mesa-Lago and Pérez-López 2013; Feinberg 2013; Scarpaci 2014; Vignoli 2014; González-Corzo and Justo 2014)) have recognized the potentially positive impact and contribution of the self-employed sector, especially if allowed to develop into a full-fledged, if carefully regulated SME and cooperative sector. Many of these studies explicitly focus on harnessing the potential of the self-employed sector as a compliment to and collaborator with what would remain a dominant state sector of a "restructured" and "updated" socialist economy under the Revolution. Another interesting study (Pérez Izquierdo, Oberto Calderón, and González Rodríguez 2003) explored and analyzed the self-employed sector, undertaking a survey, which drew together useful statistical materials. However, it appears that relatively few other analysts have yet carried out extensive ethnographic research and qualitative analysis on the island in order to understand the possible contributions of the microenterprise sector, the most appropriate public policy towards the sector, and the implications of the evolution of the sector on Cuba's future. This is what we aspire to do in this book.

Objectives, Central Themes, and Methods

The central objectives of this study are to analyze the evolution of Cuba's microenterprise sector during the revolutionary period but especially since the legalization of self-employment in 1993, to analyze and evaluate the current policies of the government of Cuba towards the sector (comparing them to past policies), and to explore the potential evolution and impacts of the sector under a number of possible future scenarios. This work is conducted from an historical perspective, analyzing the development of the sector in the context of Cuba's unique past. It is also set in a comparative perspective, considering the international experience and literature on microenterprise and public policy together with the Latin American experience and literature, as well as that of the countries of the former Soviet Union. Finally, given the distinct disciplinary perspectives of the co-authors, this study brings together both economic and sociological analyses and insights on the current impact and future potential of microenterprise in Cuba.

Cuba's legal microenterprises and the underground activities in Cuba's "second economy" interact in a complex counterpoint. This is the first theme of this study. A common saying in Cuba is "*todo está prohibido, pero vale todo*" (everything is prohibited, but anything goes).[3] In other words, despite (or perhaps because of) rigorous prohibitions, regulations, and controls and in the face of strict enforcement and severe penalties for non-compliance, illegal economic activities in Cuba are widespread and highly diverse. Thus, while a portion of Cuba's underground economy was legalized in 1993 and has been incorporated into the official, formal economy through taxation and regulation, much self-employed activity remains "underground" and beyond government control. Many microentrepreneurs have little option but to remain legal if their particular activities are high profile and must be conducted publicly.

On the other hand, other Cuban entrepreneurs prefer to remain unlicensed and extra-legal in order to avoid onerous government regulations, taxes, and controls. By definition, clandestinity also allows these entrepreneurs to operate in secret, thereby ensuring that they continue to survive despite the potential toughening of public policy or the future outright prohibition of their activities. At the same time, legal microenterprises interact closely with the underground economy and participate in a wide variety of interactions with it, in part through the purchase of stolen supplies via the black market, the sale of their products and services, the hiring of labor, the renting of facilities, the hiring of transport, etc.

In fact, the acquisition of a self-employment license can occasionally be used in practice as a cover, protecting its holder from suspicion while he or she engages in other profit-oriented activities not explicitly permitted under their license. In the introduction to her collection of essays on the interaction of the informal economy with the Latin American state, *Out of the Shadows*, sociologist Patricia Fernández-Kelly argues that just such nuance is a more common characteristic of this complex and dynamic relationship than the dichotomous, adversarial stereotype would have us believe. "In other words," she concludes, "a mounting body of evidence made clear that a porous membrane, not a rigid boundary, separates the formal and informal sectors" (2006: 4). It is precisely this nuanced relationship and porous boundary that we have found in Cuba between the supposedly separate worlds of the island's first, official economy and its once stigmatized but now bourgeoning second economy.

A second theme is that the policy approach of the Cuban government toward legal microenterprise has produced major disadvantages both for the Cuban people and for the Cuban government as well, despite its understandable rationale and certain benefits arising from its measured, deliberative, "*sin pausa, pero sin prisa*" (without pause, but without haste) approach (The Economist 2012). While the "*Fidelista*" policy approach to legal microenterprise seemed designed to eliminate the sector, this is certainly not the case under his brother Raúl. At the same time, there is great reluctance to grant Cuban entrepreneurs the full ability to operate as private businesses with interests and defensible property rights of their own. On the one hand, Raúl Castro has repeatedly demanded a through-going "change of mentality" among Cuba's communist cadres—even including himself among those who need to "change their way of thinking" (Castro, R. 2010b; Peters 2010d). On the other hand, official documents and speeches emphasize the continued dominance of the central plan over the market, the leading role of state enterprises, and ownership by the state of the primary means of production, while fulminating against the private concentration of wealth ("*Lineamientos*" 2010, 2011).

This emphasis of "order, discipline, and control" over the flexible promotion of small enterprise was clearly evident during the second half of 2013 when the government moved to clarify existing legislation and explicitly outlaw a number of creative business strategies that had developed among the island's *cuentapropistas*. This included banning the resale of household products acquired in the island's retail stores as well as the sale of imported clothing under the legal licenses of "seamstress" or "tailor" (*Gaceta Oficial* 2013a). Further explicit limits were placed on Cuba's entrepreneurs in early November when *Granma* published a "*Nota informativa sobre el trabajo por cuenta propia*," which demanded "a strict compliance with the law and payment of taxes." The article, which was signed by the Executive Committee of Cuba's Council of Ministers, went on to call for the liquidation of private inventories of imported clothing by December 31 and require the immediate closure of all private 3D cinemas and game rooms which had been operating under "operator of children's recreational equipment" or "*paladar*" licenses (*Granma* 2013).

Finally, perhaps in response to a sustained pushback from Cuba's entrepreneurs and some of its leading intellectuals as well (*Espacio Laical* 2013; Cárdenas Lema 2013), Raúl Castro himself included a lengthy reference to this issue in his annual National Assembly speech in December 2013, where he repeated almost word-for-word the language used in *Granma*'s earlier "*Nota informativa*," leaving no doubt as to where he stood on the question of regulation vs. prohibition:

> Recent events have revealed a lack of control on the part of government institutions leading to illegalities in the exercise of self-employment, which were not confronted with the necessary resolve creating an environment of impunity and stimulating the accelerated growth of activities that have never been authorized. [...] Problems should be identified before they appear and, if they raise their heads, we must act immediately and without vacillation [...] which is always preferable to paying the political cost that comes from inertia and passivity in requiring compliance with the law. (Castro, R. 2013)

Under the "*Raulista*" approach, the legalization of formerly unregulated economic activities allows the government to increase tax revenues in order to better finance social services and the public sector generally and it also helps to reduce income inequalities through taxation and the regulatory framework. Moreover, licensing allows the government to track microentrepreneurs and control their activities more effectively. However, the current policy framework still seems based on a fundamental distrust of entrepreneurs. It leads to serious disadvantages from the perspective of both efficiency and equity at a number of levels: for individual enterprises, for the microenterprise sector, and for the necessary building of mutual trust and the rule of law between the citizenry and the state.

Even though the current "*Raulista*" approach has constructed a more enabling environment than ever existed during the long tenure of Fidel Castro, the approach has still not gone far enough. It continues to limit job creation in professional areas, thereby reducing the generation of real income and blocking the production of a diverse range of goods and services. For this reason, it continues to impair savings and productive investment. It wastes the entrepreneurial talents of the Cuban people on low productivity endeavors and wastes Cuba's scarce human, natural, and capital resources. For example, though slowly expanding to include more productive and professional activities, the existing list of 201 occupations—a translation and analysis of which is provided in Appendix 2—continues to be populated largely by survival-oriented activities low in the productivity or dynamism required by a modern economy (Orozco and Hansing 2011).

A third theme of the book is that while the licensed microenterprise sector is "legal," it has lacked true "legitimacy" judging from the often arbitrary actions of the government bureaucrats charged with regulating it.[4] However, this is changing if the exhortations of President Raúl Castro and the good intentions behind the new self-employment regulations are to be believed. As Raúl's words quoted above about the "political cost" of not enforcing existing laws indicate, the government is well aware that opening up space to the market and the private sector has political ramifications. Restrictions and high taxes on the private, non-state sector are therefore probably the result of a desire to retain political control, which may be threatened by the unconstrained growth of a private microenterprise and small enterprise sector.

Licensing requirements, taxes, regulations, fines and crackdowns on the self-employed may not be intended primarily as redistributive nor as tax collection instruments, but instead as a means of exerting political control over the population during an period of economic crisis and political uncertainty—especially given the recent death of Venezuelan President Hugo Chávez and the subsequent political unrest and street violence that has erupted there. However, the actual result of these measures makes much microenterprise so costly that it becomes difficult for self-employed workers to survive without occasionally going outside the law or into complete clandestinity. Have the reforms enacted under Raúl Castro done anything to change this balance? The latest statistics from late August 2014, after nearly four years under the new self-employment regulations, show a great increase in overall numbers from roughly 150,000 to nearly 500,000. However, as much as 82% of the new licensees have gone to either the formerly unemployed or retired (not to those laid off from state jobs) (Peters 2012a and b; Cuba Central Blog 2014; CubaDebate 2014b; Mesa Redonda 2014; Manguela 2014; 14ymedio 2014a). Thus, there has indeed been some success in bringing at least some of Cuba's microentrepreneurs "out of the underground."

However, Raúl's stated goal is more ambitious than that if we remember that the expansion of self-employment in October 2010 was accompanied (and justified) by a simultaneous decision to lay off hundreds-of-thousands of state employees ("*Pronunciamiento*" 2010). A better gauge of the success of the opening toward microenterprise would include both a determination of its record in absorbing newly idle state workers and its ability to contribute to greater productivity and efficiency in the economy as a whole. Remaining restrictions on the types of self-employed occupations allowed to date (almost none of which harness Cuba's highly-educated, professional workforce) make achieving this second goal doubtful.

While there have been important debates in Cuba over the pace and direction of economic reforms, the Cuban government under Fidel never saw the self-employed sector (or most of its other economic reforms enacted after 1993) as more than stop-gap measures, grudgingly employed during the economic crisis with the purpose of saving socialism. Furthermore, these limited economic reforms were certainly never intended to begin a transition toward capitalism. Thus, with relative economic stability achieved by the late 1990s, it was not surprising to find the government slowly, but inexorably containing self-employment through increasingly rigorous policies. The question now is whether Raúl's seemingly more pragmatic and encouraging approach toward microenterprise is fundamentally different. So far, the answer seems to be an encouraging but highly qualified "yes."

A fourth theme of this study is that Cuba could gain immensely (and from a variety of perspectives) by further liberalizing the microenterprise sector. Such liberalization would unleash the entrepreneurial energies of many Cubans, energies that are currently wasted on low-level subsistence activities, often in the underground economy, or that find their release outside of Cuba through emigration—which has reached record levels especially among the young and is likely to grow following the elimination of the exit visa in January 2013 (Peters 2012c; Morales 2013). In justifying its migration reform when it was first announced in October 2012, the government spoke of its right to defend the nation against "brain drain" and "*el robo de cerebros*" (literally, brain stealing) (Cancio Isla 2012; Decree-Law 302, 2012; *Granma* 2012c). However, if other countries like the United States are "guilty" of enticing Cuban professionals to "abandon ship" and invest their skills in a better labor market abroad, Cuba is equally guilty of what might be called "brain waste," given its often frustrating and counterproductive regulations on entrepreneurship (Blanco 2013).

A diverse set of research methods are used in this study. First, in order to place the examination of Cuban microenterprise in a broad context, we undertake an historical analysis of the evolution of microenterprise in Cuba, beginning with the prerevolutionary period and continuing through the first 30 years of the Revolution. This is complemented with an analysis of Fidel Castro's reluctant embrace of self-employment in the 1990-2006 period in contrast with the policy approach under Raúl.

Analyzing the structure, functioning, and size of Cuba's underground economy presented us with major methodological difficulties, as is the case for the underground economy of all other countries. Enterprises operating illegally are seldom willing to divulge any information on their activities for fear of being detected and prosecuted. In most countries, the main motive for remaining in clandestinity is likely tax evasion. However, if the enterprises themselves have been declared illegal, as is the case with the underground economy of Cuba, the fear may be of prosecution, fines, or outright closure and confiscation of relevant equipment, materials, or properties. How to acquire information on the underground economy of various countries has been the focus of steadily improving studies in recent years, as governments and international agencies have tried to learn more about the magnitude and functioning of the underground economies in their countries (Portes and Haller

2005; Losby et al 2002; Schneider and Enste 2002a, b). In this study, however, we make no quantitative attempt to measure the size of Cuba's second economy, opting instead to complement our comparative historical approach with a qualitative one that relies on extensive ethnographic observations and interviews with Cuban entrepreneurs themselves.

For this study, an initial series of interviews was conducted between 1999 and 2001 with a group of more than 60 microentrepreneurs operating both with self-employment licenses and in the underground economy. Roughly half of these entrepreneurs were interviewed in multiple follow-up visits between 2002 and 2009. Some of the difficulties of undertaking this kind of qualitative ethnographic and interview research in Cuba today are discussed in Chapters 4, 5, 7, and 8, which focus on the underground economy and economic illegalities on the one hand (Chapter 7) and Cuba's experiments with legal self-employment on the other (Chapters 4, 5, and 8). In order to acquire an in depth knowledge of the strategies, functioning, performance, and prospects for microenterprises in the most dynamic and potentially productive part of the emerging private sector (a sector we refer to in Chapter 7 as "legitimate underground economic activities," or LUEAs), we carried out these interviews with *cuentapropistas* (CPs) in food service (especially *paladar* restaurants), transportation (with a focus on private taxis, or *taxis particulares*), and guest-housing (or Cuba's burgeoning bed-and-breakfasts, known as *casas particulares*).

Interviews focused on the following three themes: (1) Ambition and expectations for the future, (2) survival strategies employed by entrepreneurs as they negotiate their nuanced relationship with the state, and (3) an exploration of the often overlapping, porous borders that distinguish licensed from informal operators. In other words, we first asked if interviewees expect that their enterprises in particular and the fledging microenterprise sector in general would be able and permitted to become a true small- and medium-sized enterprise sector in the future. Second, we sought to learn how they respond to the Cuban government's regulations, licensing requirements, and taxes. Third, we asked how licensed self-employment differs socioeconomically from clandestine private economic activity (LUEAs)? Follow-up interviews with many of these same microentrepreneurs took place in April 2011 and focused on their evaluation of Raúl Castro's post-2010 reforms in comparison with the previous microenterprise regulations. Respondents were also asked about changing perceptions of entrepreneurial activity in Cuban society and the difficulty they had managing various potential obstacles to the growth of their businesses, such as obtaining an initial license, credit, and raw materials, finding employees, paying taxes, and navigating regulations and inspections.

As mentioned above, in order to better focus the study and have a means of comparative analysis with which to approach the research questions outlined above, these interviews and observations focused primarily on three somewhat interconnected areas of what might be called Cuba's "informal tourism economy": small-scale, privately run restaurants (*paladares*), private transportation (*taxis particulares*), and private lodging (*casas particulares*). Among the more than 100 occupations legally opened up to self-employment in Cuba since 1993, these three were selected because they were then and still are today among the most lucrative, dynamic, and sizeable legal microenterprise sectors—both in terms of number of employees and amount of revenue generated.

In fact, in late March 2014, the Cuban television program "*Mesa Redonda*" aired a two-part series on self-employment reporting that of the total of 455,577 registered cuentapropistas as of the end of February 2014, the food service sector remains the largest single area of self-employment with 57,776 license holders (12.7%), followed by the 47,733 licensees in transportation (10.5%), and the 29,952 in private home rentals (6.6%). Moreover, an additional 91,978 licensees work as contractors for other enterprises (20.2%), themselves chiefly employed in the food service and transportation sectors. Thus, these four self-employed occupations comprise a full 50% of all *cuentapropistas* currently working in the small enterprise sector (Cuba Central Blog 2014; CubaDebate 2014b; Mesa Redonda 2014). It is also likely that these occupations hold the greatest potential of avoiding the curse and costs of informality and transforming themselves into SMEs either as private operations or formal cooperatives, when and if such larger-scale activities become politically feasible. Because of this, Chapters 4 and 8 draw extensively on our ethnographic interivews with *cuentapropistas* themselves, focusing specifically on the survival strategies of entrepreneurs in the transportation, bed-and-breakfast, and *paladar*/food service sector.[5]

Organization and Structure of the Book

In Chapter 2, we define and discuss the interrelated terms "informal," "underground," and "second" economies and describe their relationship with small and microenterprise, entrepreneurship, and economic and human development. The chapter takes a broad, global view of entrepreneurship and informality seeking to synthesize various public policy responses to these phenomena while also delineating the various social and economic consequences of distinct policy approaches. Given Cuba's unique profile as Latin America's only state socialist regime, the bulk of the chapter focuses on Latin America and Eastern Europe, as their histories, cultures, and political economies are most relevant to the Cuban case. We summarize the lessons from other studies of Latin America's "informal sector" and compare them to the related lessons from studies of the "second economy" in the former socialist countries of Eastern Europe. This comparison allows us to identify a number of theoretical concepts and models, as well as practical lessons and experiences that we employ throughout the remainder of the book to explain Cuba's shifting policies toward its own "non-state sector."

Chapter 2 ends by identifying the characteristics that make Cuba a unique, hybrid case. As a Latin American country, Cuba is heir to a tradition where the paternalistic state (whether under Spanish colonialism—prior to 1898—or as a nominally independent nation—between 1902 and 1958 –) has long played a central, commanding role in the economy, leaving little space or encouragement for entrepreneurship (Crabb 2001). Likewise, as a socialist country, Cuba has instituted an economic model defined by a state monopoly over employment, centralized economic decision-making, and a rigid central plan that together lead to chronic bottlenecks, inefficiencies, and low worker incentives, creating a perfect environment for rent-seeking behavior, theft of state resources for private use, corruption, and a thriving black market and underground economy (Díaz Briquets and Pérez-López 2006).

In Chapters 3 and 4, we describe the history and consequences of an antagonistic public policy toward microenterprise under the leadership of Fidel Castro (1959-2006). In our analysis, we place special emphasis on the lessons from the last round of "Special Period" reforms in the area of self-employment from 1990-2006. Specifically, Chapter 3 provides a history of socialist Cuba's fluctuating policy toward the private sector, microenterprise, and the underground economy, tracing a series of pendular swings between ideologically-driven socialist retrenchment followed by pragmatic market reforms between 1959 and 1989. In fact, this chapter argues that the revolutionary government's shifting policies toward the private sector and microenterprise can be understood primarily as a recurring tug-of-war between communist ideology on the one hand and economic pragmatism on the other (Mesa-Lago 2000; Mesa Lago and Pérez-López 2005, 2013).

In Chapter 4, we chronicle the emergence, evolution, increasing stigmatization, eventual asphyxiation, and near extinction of a legal microenterprise sector in Cuba between 1990 and 2006. We describe the sequential stages of this particular cycle of reform and retrenchment, beginning with the initial external economic reforms associated with the special period, followed by a series of internal economic reforms including the introduction of self-employment in 1993 as a response to the country's severe economic crisis. The chapter also provides a detailed analysis of Cuban state policies toward microenterprise licensing, regulation, and taxation during this period, discussing the rationale and implications of policies that were clearly designed to prioritize order and control over encouragement and expansion of the non-state sector. We augment this analysis with a series of brief vignettes that illustrate how the evolving regulatory environment of the late-1990s and early-2000s was experienced by some of Cuba's entrepreneurs themselves. We conclude the chapter by chronicling the phasing out of the self-employed sector between 2004 and 2006 as part of a crackdown on economic illegalities and a move toward economic recentralization, accompanied by a newfound emphasis on ideological campaigns of preaching, policing, and prohibition, such as Fidel Castro's now suspended ideological swan song, "the battle of ideas."

Chapter 5 begins with an analysis of the structural and conjunctural factors that came together between 2006 and 2009 to enable, or perhaps force, President Raúl Castro to institute a long-delayed and unprecedented series of economic reforms that highlighted the central role of microenterprise in economic recovery, when its economic potential had been seen in the past as marginal at best. The chapter then describes and evaluates these economic reforms emphasizing the central policy initiatives of layoffs in the state sector accompanied by a major expansion of self-employment. The chapter also chronicles and analyses the specific changes in Cuba's self-employment regulations.

We focus here on four elements. First, we analyze the changes in the regulatory framework for microenterprise, focusing on the type of occupations available for self-employment. Second, we evaluate the new tax system for private entrepreneurs and workers, comparing it to Cuba's previous tax regime for microenterprise and tracing changes in the tax legislation for microentrepreneurs since they were first announced in late-2010. Third, we chronicle and evaluate the various adjustments that have been made since 2010 to the original self-employment legislation as a result of the inability of the first round of reforms to achieve stated goals, with a particular focus on a handful of positive steps forward between 2011 and 2014 while highlighting a number of significant steps backward as well—including the fall 2013 banning of the resale of imported clothing by the private sector and the subsequent shuttering of private 3D cinemas and game rooms. Finally, we identify areas where further reform would be appropriate, especially in relation to access to credit, the availability of a wholesale market, and the incorporation of professionals into entrepreneurial activity.

In Chapter 6, we review the new cooperative regulations issued in December 2012 that legalized the creation of non-agricultural cooperatives for the first time under the Revolution. Chapter 7 describes the broad range of economic illegalities and underground enterprises that flourish in Cuba, seeking to distinguish illicit and therefore illegitimate activities from a subset of everyday survival practices we denominate "legitimate underground economic activities" (LUEAs). We do this with an eye toward the emergence of a wiser, more pragmatic public policy that would legitimize such activities in the future harnessing their potential to contribute toward greater productivity, efficiency, and employment. Based on our interviews and ethnographic work done with Cuban entrepreneurs between 1999 and 2011, Chapter 8 focuses on the most lucrative, sizable, and dynamic self-employment activity legalized after 1993: private food service, with a particular emphasis on private *"paladar"* restaurants. Tracing the storied evolution of the Cuban *paladar*, thorugh its various cycles of birth, death, and rebirth, allows us to understand and critically compare the experiences, opinions, and evaluations of the two most recent rounds of reform from the perspective of Cuban entrepreneurs themselves.

The concluding chapter attempts to gauge the achievements to date of the reform process, especially in terms of layoffs, employment, and productivity so far achieved. We also evaluate other, related aspects of the reform process. Some of these are quite tangible, such as the pace of layoffs, the phasing out of subsidies and rationing, and the legalization of the automobile and real estate markets. Others are less tangible but no less important, such as the depth of change in bureaucratic and cadre mentality and the extent to which mutual trust between entrepreneurs and the state has been consolidated. We end the book by presenting a series of possible future policy scenarios for small enterprise, some more skeptical and others more hopeful, including: (1) a return to small and microenterprise suppression, (2) a continued if exceedingly cautious liberalization of private enterprise together with the complementary growth of a new non-agricultural cooperative experiment, and (3) a more rapid, significant, and pro-market liberalization that would allow for the emergence of private small- and medium-sized enterprises, the concentration of wealth in private hands, full property rights for private entrepreneurs, and direct credit and foreign investment in small and microenterprise from abroad. We also highlight the potential impact that a reform of U.S. policy—shifting from isolating the Cuban government to principled engagement with the island's emergent civil society—could have for entrepreneurial Cuba.

Notes

[1] One possible consequence to the growth of an independent economic sector during the 1990s was emphasized by the late Max Azicri, who identified the source of government ambivalence this way: "Self-employment had allowed a significant portion of the population to become disconnected from the official labor network and to be more self-reliant economically. The possibility that this growing sector might become a political force with its own sectarian agenda is a political concern for the government" (2000: 147).

[2] According to the Commission of the European Union, these terms are defined according to their "staff headcount and turnover or annual balance-sheet total." A microenterprise employs fewer than 10 persons and has an annual turnover of less than EUR 2 million. A small enterprise employs between 10 and 50 persons and has an annual turnover of less than EUR 10 million. A medium-sized enterprise employs up to 250 persons and has an annual turnover between EUR 10 and 50 million (Europa 2013). These are not the definitions we use in this study.

[3] Another, more skeptical version of this same *choteo*, or ironic Cuban humor goes, "*En Cuba lo que no está prohibido, es obligatorio*" (In Cuba, whatever is not prohibited, is obligatory). While the first saying mocks the government's inability to exercise full authority over the country, the second indicates the pressure felt by individuals who find little or no space for independent activities not regulated or overseen by the state. Then there is the mocking reference to Cuba's notoriously low peso salaries and its workers resulting lack of enthusiasm on the job: "In Cuba we pretend to work and the government pretends to pay us."

[4] An example of this phenomenon is the successful restaurant and night club known as *El Cabildo*, run by Ulises Aquino and his popular theater group, *La Opera de la Calle*, which was closed down by regulators in the summer of 2012 and remains closed today (Frank 2012a, b; Ravsberg 2012a, b; 2013a; McAuliff 2012; Miroff 2012a, b; Fernández 2012a, b; Trip Advisor 2013; León 2013; DDC 2014). We summarize this case in the conclusion of Chapter 8, which focuses on the evolution of the Cuban *paladar*.

[5] A late-August 2014 article from the offical Cuban newspaper *Trabajadores* entitled, "Self-Employment: With the Foot on the Pedal," confirmed these trends, reporting a total of 471,085 registered self-employed workers by the end of July 2014. Sixty-nine percent of these *cuentapropistas* were previously unemployed, while food service, transportation, and housing rental remain the most common occupations (Manguela 2014; 14ymedio 2014a).

2
The Small Enterprise Sector

> In command economies, informalization is ironically a tool in the hands of urban workers to confront the all-powerful state.
> —*(Portes, Castels, and Benton 1989: 308)*

Governments have long struggled to balance the promotion and regulation of entrepreneurial activity, often failing to bring the bulk of informal entrepreneurs into the legal, regulated economy. Whether informal micro and small entrepreneurs can contribute to national development rests in part on how policy makers understand the origin and functioning of the informal sector. Some understand informality as the result of state regulations, overbearing costs, and unfair legal criteria that effectively shut most entrepreneurs out of the legal, formal economy—condemning them to informality and forcing them to operate "underground" (de Soto 1989, 2000). In contrast, others argue that governments and formal capitalist enterprises actually rely on and benefit from the existence of the informal sector as a way to ensure political stability while simultaneously driving down wages, denying worker benefits, and ensuring higher profits through sub-contracting (Portes, Castells, and Benton 1989). However, the case of microenterprise in socialist Cuba presents a challenge to these two dominant and largely irreconcilable conceptual paradigms. First legalized two decades ago in 1993, Cuban microenterprise in the form of self-employment (*trabajo por cuenta propia*) was brought back from near extinction in 2005 and placed at the center of President Raúl Castro's economic reform agenda starting in 2010.

Because Cuban entrepreneurs operate within (and often in opposition to) the peculiar institutional framework of state socialism, neither neoclassical theory nor neo-Marxist theory can adequately explain its origins and functioning. Nor can such theories adequately explain the Cuban government's traditionally hostile treatment of entrepreneurs. In light of this inadequacy, in this chapter we turn to a branch of "new institutional theory" which was originally developed to explain social change and the "second economy" within the state socialist systems of Eastern Europe, in order to better understand the peculiar and often paradoxical relationship between the Cuban state and the island's own informal or "second" economy.

Like other Latin American and Caribbean governments, the Cuban state has sought to exercise near total control over the informal sector. However, in those other contexts "extensive paper regulations [...] coexist with an inept and weak state" (Portes and Haller 2005: 410). As a result, the "frustrated" governments in Latin America and the Caribbean tended to favor only a small, well-connected elite cadre of formal enterprises with the benefits of state recognition, protection, and resources. Cuba, however, is a state that combines a "total" regulatory *intent* with a strong regulatory *capacity*, which has effectively equated informality with illegality and was at least initially successful in virtually eliminating the private sector and criminalizing all non-state economic activity. Despite this "totalitarian" preference for absolute control over the economy and the complete capture of civil society, over time such zeal has only provoked widespread resistance to cumbersome and endless regulations, inadvertently "multiplying the opportunities for their violation" (Portes and Haller 2005: 411). Though the supposed achievements of the socialist, formal, and "first" economy were heralded by the Cuban government at every opportunity, the bourgeoning "second" economy contradicts, undermines, and displaces it at every turn, gradually becoming the country's real economy (Centeno and Portes 2006: 31), just as employment in that "second" economy often constitutes many Cubans' *real* jobs even as they may continue to labor in official occupations in the first economy.

The three key and interlocking institutions of state socialism—the central plan, state ownership of the means of production, and near universal state employment—effectively protect the government's monopoly on legitimate economic activity (often called the "official" or "first" economy), thereby provoking a vast array of illegitimate, yet ubiquitous economic strategies that make up Cuba's second economy. At the same time, these state institutions have been relatively inefficient and unproductive both in the former socialist regimes of Eastern Europe and in Cuba's own state-centered economy, causing the government to tolerate and—now under Raúl Castro—even promote the legalization of informal microenterprises bringing them once again "from behind the scenes to center stage" (Pérez-López 1995a). President Raúl Castro's government has gone so far as to wager the future of the Revolution and, ironically, of socialism itself on the ability of the second economy—in the form of an expanded non-state, self-employment sector—to provide the island with sorely needed goods, services, and jobs, absorbing much of the unemployment created by a major downsizing of the state sector. In fact, in his own report to the Sixth Party Congress in April, 2011, the younger Castro argued that self-employment should be promoted as a "facilitating factor for the construction of socialism in Cuba," meaning that bringing informal entrepreneurs "out of the underground" and simultaneously allowing laid off state workers to legally enter the expanding non-state sector would allow the state to rid itself of such responsibilities so that it could concentrate on increasing the efficiency and productivity in more economically fundamental areas of the economy (Castro, R. 2011a).

This shifting relationship between the state and the informal sector—at times antagonistic and at others accommodating—highlights a fundamental paradox in the Cuban government's relationship with informal microentrepreneurs. In short, less is more. That is, as the state attempts to regulate the island's microenterprise sector as it emerges from the underground—always emphasizing control and discipline over openness and trust—it becomes increasingly ineffective in such regulation and succeeds only in creating more opportunities for the profitable violation of the rules. However, Cuba actually could use *less regulation* combined with better and *more* narrowly focused and efficient *enforcement*. "A state does not become weaker because it regulates less," write Centeno and Portes in a study of the relationship between the informal economy and the state in Latin America. "It is weakened by the inability to enforce its own rules" (2006: 41).

Following this logic, this chapter begins by summarizing economic thinking on the concepts of small and microenterprise and entrepreneurship, delineating their impact on economic and human development. Then we bring together two major historical experiences and theoretical traditions with unregulated economic activity, also known as the "underground economy," in order to develop a framework to understand similar activities in Cuba. First, we describe the "informal sector" debate that has emerged based on the economic realities of many developing countries, especially those of Latin America and the Caribbean. We then contrast this with the literature on the "second economy" of past and current state socialist economies, with special emphasis on those of central and eastern Europe during the existence of the Soviet Union. We conclude by applying these lessons and models to Revolutionary Cuba. A unique hybrid, Cuba is an underdeveloped Latin American/Caribbean nation that has adopted a state socialist economy modeled after those of the former Soviet bloc. Thus, Cuba's underground economy exhibits characteristics found in both the "informal" sectors of the developing world and in the "second" economies of state socialism.

Small Enterprise, Entrepreneurship, and State Policy Toward Informality

Before exploring the underground economy, a brief comment on the concept and nature of entrepreneurship—and its role in the process of development—is appropriate. Entrepreneurship has long been recognized as performing a central role in economic development. Yet entrepreneurship is largely ignored in the main body of economic theory and has received surprisingly little attention in the general literature on development. Originating from the Old French word *entreprendre*, "to undertake," an entrepreneur is essentially one who takes risks in order to achieve an objective. In 1730, the French resident Irishman, Richard Cantillion, first coined the term *entrepreneur* to identify the unique risk-bearing role that certain self-employed persons played in economic development by purchasing inputs and combining them with the intent of reselling them at uncertain (but hopefully higher) prices (Cantillion 1755 in Long 1983; Outcalt 2000). Indeed, Cantillion believed that because they were not working for wages in a stable job, self-employed workers were in a uniquely independent economic position. Thus, for Cantillion, "the Beggars and even the Robbers" were entrepreneurs *par excellence* given the constant uncertainty and risk under which they lived (Cantillion 1755: 55, quoted in Long 1983: 48).

To the idea of risk, other theorists added a uniting, coordinating, organizing, and supervising function (Say 1847). In this sense, an entrepreneur is one who combines various inputs (such as land, labor, and capital) in order to produce a product, retaining the profit as a reward. In the twentieth century, Frank Knight (1961) reiterated the concept of risk in the face of uncertainty as a fundamental characteristic of the entrepreneur. Joseph Schumpeter (1974) expanded our understanding of entrepreneurship further by stressing the innovative role of the entrepreneur as a "creative destroyer" leading to economic growth and development (Long 1983; Outcalt 2000; Brouwer 2002; Wu 2011). Leibenstein's seminal analysis of the role of entrepreneurship in ensuring efficiency and achieving economic development is particularly useful in explaining the challenge of being an entrepreneur under state socialism (1968). Leibenstein understood the importance of the entrepreneur as one who leads the struggle against the inefficiency that plagues most economic systems, especially ones which are characterized by legally enforced state monopolies.

In discussing the functions performed by an entrepreneur, Leibenstein (1968) argued that the entrepreneur was someone who because of special knowledge or positioning improves efficiency by playing:

1. A "market connecting role": linking up the potential market for the outputs with the markets for all the relevant inputs;
2. A "gap-filling role": doing what is not normally or easily done through markets;
3. An "input-completing role": improvising the provision of all the inputs necessary for the enterprise; and
4. An "enterprise creating role": bringing together the inputs for the production of an output over a period of time and in some sort of organization.

Thus, the entrepreneur is distinguished by his or her ability to perceive opportunities not noted by others and act with the goal of achieving an objective that has yet to be realized. An entrepreneur then visualizes and plans how the objective can be achieved and undertakes to do everything necessary to implement that vision. As such, seizing a new opportunity, visualizing and planning the various steps necessary to bring about a desired result, taking necessary risks, and actually carrying out a project or building an "enterprise" are the most common traits of the entrepreneur. While an entrepreneur may possess various skills and knowledge, his or her most important talent is likely that of organizer, connector, or "middle-man," bringing together the resources, inputs, and individuals necessary to implement a project.

The contribution of entrepreneurship to the process of economic development is clear from the above description. Entrepreneurs are a dynamic force in an economy, envisioning the possibilities of new types of economic activity and doing everything necessary to put into effect their visions. As a result, entrepreneurs give birth to new enterprises, new economic activities, and new sectors in an economy. They promote the process of learning and adapting to changing circumstances as technology changes, as markets evolve, and as policies change. In sum, an entrepreneur contributes to economic development through: (1) taking risks or bearing uncertainty, (2) acting as a coordinator who combines various inputs to produce a new product, (3) engaging in "creative opportunism" or innovation, (4) and ensuring the efficiency in economic exchange (Leibenstein 1968; Long 1983; Brouwer 2002; Outcalt 2000).

The foregoing depiction of entrepreneurship is all positive. However, for entrepreneurship to operate in this type of constructive, pro-developmental way, the proper institutional environment (a system of laws, a regulatory environment, and basic political and economic stability) has to exist. In pathological circumstances—in the absence of law and order, a reasonable judicial system, and political stability, or in a context where economic monopolies (state or private) and corruption predominate—entrepreneurship may become deformed, criminalized, or simply impossible. In systems with vast and complex regulations and restrictions, entrepreneurs may become preoccupied with "rent-seeking" of various sorts, all of them relatively unproductive, and they may dissipate their entrepreneurial energies in endless bureaucratic maneuvering and red-tape manipulation. When law and order break down or when government policy makes entrepreneurial activities illegal or stigmatizes them as illegitimate,[1] entrepreneurship may be forced underground and become criminalized through mafia-like racketeering organizations or through official corruption.

Therefore, entrepreneurship alone is a necessary but insufficient factor in the generation of economic development. Instead, it must operate within a supportive, legal, and orderly institutional and regulatory environment. Writing with reference to state policies toward the informal sector, much of which

Table 2.1: Types of States by Regulatory Capacity and Regulatory Intent

		State Regulatory Intent		
		Minimal	Limited	Total
State Regulatory Capacity	Weak	Cell #1 The "Frontier" or "Absent" State (Somalia, Congo)	Cell #2 The "Enclave" State (Bolivia, Kenya, Angola)	Cell #3 The "Frustrated" or "Mercantilist" State (Mexico, Peru, Ecuador)
	Strong	Cell #4 The Liberal State (United States, United Kingdom)	Cell #5 The Social Democratic Welfare State (France, Germany, Sweden)	Cell #6 The Totalitarian State (Cuba, North Korea, former Soviet Union)

Sources: Slightly modified from Portes and Haller 2005 and Centeno and Portes 2006.

is "proto-entrepreneurial," Centeno and Portes (2006: 27-31) posit that governments often have different *intents* (how rigid or permissive the scope of laws are) and varying *capacities* (the strength or ability of the state to enforce those laws) in their regulation of informal entrepreneurs as presented in the typology of Table 2.1. Some weak states combine little ability to enforce laws with an equally minimal intent. With the state regulatory function largely "absent," informal entrepreneurs are left to fend for themselves in a kind of self-regulating state of "frontier" justice (cell #1).

Weak states that attempt to exert a limited degree of economic regulation, however, often succeed in creating only an "enclave" of formal jurisdiction restricted to the capital city and a few industrial, agricultural, or mining zones (cell #2). Traditionally, however, many Latin American countries have sought to exert a still greater level of control over the national economy without the necessary capacity to do so leading to "frustration," or what the influential economist Hernando de Soto has characterized as a "mercantilist" state (1989) in the case of Peru (cell #3). This often leads to "the rise of a predatory pattern in which only a small elite benefits from state protection and resources" (Portes and Haller 2005: 410). This "frustration" is poignantly captured by Centeno and Portes:

These states may be described as "frustrated" because of the permanent contradiction between the voluminous paper regulations that they spawn and their inability to enforce them in practice. They give rise to a vast informal sector precisely because ever expanding rules force economic actors to find ways around them and because a weak and frequently corrupt state apparatus

Strong states also vary in their approach to informal entrepreneurial activity, with the three ideal types being the "liberal" state (the U.S. and UK), the "welfare" state (Western Europe and Canada), and the "totalitarian" state (North Korea, the former USSR, and Cuba).[2] The laissez-faire approach to informality popular with neoclassical or neoliberal theorists (liberal in the sense of limited government) posits that if regulations are low in a context where a strong state effectively enforces the few, targeted "rules of the game" that do exist, the resulting level of informality will also be low (cell #4). The welfare states of Canada and much of Western Europe, however, take a somewhat more proactive, interventionist approach to the economy justified by their priority of creating a more equitable distribution of wealth and a set of social guarantees such as health care and education which are available to all (cell #5). Such "welfare" states often have more regulations and higher taxes than their liberal counterparts, coupled with greater levels of security, equality, and general welfare (thus their name). However, they also typically offer their citizens fewer economic opportunities and less lucrative pay offs to entrepreneurial risk takers who may be stymied by high taxes, onerous labor regulations, and other rules.

Cuba is indeed a Latin American/Caribbean country with a "mercantilist" tradition of an overbearing patrimonial state during both its colonial and republican periods—similar to the frustrated states mentioned in cell #3 above (Crabb 2001). However, given its demonstrated *intent* and long-time (but now diminishing) *ability* to control virtually all economic activity on the island, it better fits into the "total intent" and "strong capacity" cell in the above typology: the totalitarian state (cell #6). Such states—like the many now defunct socialist "republics" of the former Soviet Union—seek to subsume civil society and eradicate the private sector, equating all informal activity with criminality. However, despite the Cuban government's relative strength and effectiveness in enforcing its laws against underground activity as compared to the *frustrated* or *mercantilist* states typical of much of the rest of Latin America (cell #3), for the past two decades Cuba has increasingly faced a two pronged paradox common to many of its fellow (and now former) totalitarian socialist states.

On the one hand, by very definition the extent of state regulation determines the potential scope of informal activity. That is, state regulation can create informality simply by declaring some activities legitimate while actively suppressing others. It logically follows then that attempts at complete regulation common under state socialism proportionally expand the potential universe of informal activity. On the other hand, states with such total regulatory intent inevitably face the law of diminishing returns. At first, as a state's regulatory intent increases so does its effective regulation of economic activity. However, attempts to exercise absolute control "inevitably trigger resistance." Beyond a certain mid-range "sweet spot" balanced between regulatory intent and effectiveness, more regulations or greater enforcement does not yield more control and can even have the unintended consequence of "reducing the very scope of control that proliferating rules seek to achieve" (Portes and Haller 2005).

This is the reason why the underground economy within totalitarian socialist states is properly understood as constituting something *more* than mere "informality" (economic activity taking place outside the state's regulatory framework) as might exist in the weak, frustrated states described in cell #3 above. Instead, its inherent entrepreneurial logic often sets it in direct—if often disguised—*opposition to* the command and control logic that drives the key institutions of state socialism: the central plan, state monopoly ownership of the means of production, and universal state employment. This dynamic has given rise to the term "second economy" to characterize underground economic activity in socialist states given that it operates not only outside but also often *against* the official, "first" economy. Writing prior to the collapse of the Soviet Union, the Polish criminologist Maria Los recognized this corrosive impact of the second economy in socialist states arguing that it "represents a counter-economy and not just a sub-economy" (Los 1987: 55). As such, the second economy is a source of systemic change, constantly applying pressure to remake the economic institutions of socialism.[3]

Highlighting Cuba, Centeno and Portes echo this conviction in their own study of the relationship between the state and the informal economy in Latin America, writing:

> The attempt by a totalitarian government to suffocate any manifestation of popular entrepreneurship ends up, over time, encouraging its proliferation. The result, evident in every case where this path has been attempted, is a bourgeoning "second economy" which contradicts and undermines at every turn that subject to official rules. [...] In the end stages of this process, as it happened in defunct socialist states of Eastern Europe and is currently happening in Cuba, the "second economy" becomes the real economy of the country, effectively displacing the economy subject to official planning. (2006: 31)

Lest we think that Centeno and Portes are engaging in some eye-catching sociological hyperbole or well-worn Cuban-American wishful thinking (they were both born in Cuba) by using the term "end stages," we should remember the dire warnings both Fidel and Raúl Castro have repeatedly given to the Cuban people when referencing state policy toward entrepreneurship. For example, in one of his last marathon six-hour speeches delivered on November

17, 2005 to students at the University of Havana, President Fidel Castro called for nothing short of a cultural revolution, the strict control of self-employment—especially singling out Cuba's renown home-based private restaurants (*paladares*) for criticism—and a return to an egalitarian society. "The abuses will end," railed Castro, "many of the inequalities will disappear, as will the conditions that allowed them to exist." Stressing the mortal threat of economic crime and corruption, he also declared, "In this battle against vice, nobody will be spared. Either we will defeat all these deviations and make our Revolution strong, or we die" (Castro, F. 2005a).

With the very same urgency, five years later Raúl Castro made almost exactly the *opposite* point about what was needed to "save the Revolution" to delegates to the National Assembly in December, 2010. Because the gathering was largely dedicated to implementing economic reforms intended to *do away with* egalitarianism and *promote* entrepreneurial self-employment, Raúl demanded that cadres change their mentality toward private work. "What the party and government must do in the first place is to facilitate this form of work and not to generate stigmas or prejudices against them, much less demonize them," he demanded. "For this, it is fundamental to change the negative views that more than a few of us hold toward this form of private work," he concluded. In the same speech, Raúl also underlined the seriousness of the current situation, demanding that this time the decisions made and laws passed must be put into practice. "If we want to save the Revolution," he warned, "we have to comply with whatever we agree. We should not allow that, after the Congress is over [...] documents go into desk drawers to sleep the eternal sleep." He then forcefully if dubiously linked his call to arms *in favor of* an expanded entrepreneurial sector with the revolutionary sacrifices of past generations. "Either we rectify our errors," he warned, "or time will run out on us at the edge of the precipice and we will sink, taking down with us the efforts of entire generations" (Castro, R. 2010a; Peters 2010d).

Thus, in the Cuban case, even Raúl Castro has come to accept that the entrepreneurship exemplified by the legal self-employed microenterprise sector, along with the various burgeoning activities in the informal sector (many of which we define as "legitimate underground economic activities" in Chapter 7), constitutes a potential economic resource that could be of immense value for the Cuban economy. Of course, such reforms are not without their risks in undermining state socialism itself. Still, the fact is that even the unprecedented self-employment reforms enacted between 2010 and 2014 are still hobbled by a web of intricate regulations that limit the size and type of enterprise, as well as hampering their potential wealth generation and employment potential, in turn discouraging more potential entrepreneurs from obtaining licenses and/or exiting the underground. Furthermore, many forms of entrepreneurship—especially in the professional and technical fields—remain illegal in Cuba and thus subject to intense repression under the assumption that they are synonymous with exploitation, criminality, and the supposedly noxious concentration of wealth. This approach only intensifies their pathological potentialities contributing to the prevailing culture of illegality.

Indeed, for most of the revolutionary period government leaders and the official Cuban press have routinely resorted to ideological stigmatization of entrepreneurs as parasitic *macetas*.[4] In a stunning rebuke of these past policies *Granma* itself declared that granting greater legal space to microentrepreneurs was aimed at "distancing ourselves from policies that condemned self-employment to near extinction and stigmatized those who decided to joint its ranks" (Martínez Hernández 2010). This was only a prelude to the even stronger and more categorical statements made later by Raúl Castro cited above. The on-again, off-again denial of the positive economic contribution that entrepreneurs can make, as well as the refusal to recognize any distinction between productive, innovative entrepreneurs and destructive, corrupting parasites, has had the effect of transforming much private economic activity into anti-social behavior. Such a controlling and criminalizing approach to entrepreneurship is a self-fulfilling prophecy that only contributes to the generalized distrust of legal institutions and the prevailing culture of illegality in Cuba, also forcefully decried by Raúl Castro in a July 2013 speech (Orsi 2013a; Burnett 2013).

Of course, Adam Smith was one of the first to recognize the abnormal effect of overbearing laws in the creation of criminality. In *The Wealth of Nations* he wrote, "The smuggler would have been, in every respect, an excellent citizen, had not the laws of the country made that a crime which nature never meant to be so" (quoted in Grossman 1979: 844). Thus, the current character and future development of microenterprise in Cuba, as well as its own "informal" or "second" economy, arise from and exist in relation to specific government policics (active eradication under Fidel, benign neglect at different times, or now open encouragement under Raúl) and the general economic system in place in the country. What follows then is a comparison of the phenomenon of entrepreneurship and underground economic activity under the very different economic regimes of "frustrated" Latin American capitalism and "totalitarian" Eastern European state socialism.

The Informal Sector vs. the Second Economy: An International Phenomenon

What role and weight should the informal sector, the individual entrepreneur, the household, SMEs, large private industry, and the state play in the economy? What kind and degree of regulation best promotes economic growth? What is the state's role in mediating between the interests of capital and labor? Much of the 20th century was spent in an ideological battle over these questions writ large as the Cold War. Economically, the Cold War was a competition between two very different answers to these questions: the mixed market economy versus the centrally-planned economy. National development and personal well-being would be achieved through the relatively "invisible" hand of the market (giving free reign to the entrepreneur as an economic dynamo), or alternately, the very visible hand of the state (restricting or wholly outlawing the entrepreneur as an exploitative parasite).

On the labor front, workers under capitalism gradually won protection from market abuse in the form of labor unions and formal labor regulations—giving rise to the post World War II welfare state—while workers under socialism were guaranteed full employment and absolute equality and well-being as citizens. Neither of these promises held true over time and both systems have gradually recreated the unregulated, informal labor relations they had previously outlawed. Over the course of the century, a quiet rebellion for survival by unregulated workers took place within both systems, largely hidden from view or willfully ignored by both policy makers and academics alike. Existing in its majority outside (but not unconnected to) both the market and the plan, this quiet rebellion grew and became known alternately as the "underground economy," the "informal sector," or the "second economy."

Informal economic activity has turned out not to be an anomaly, but an integral feature of modern capitalism, just as the second economy is not an alien element within contemporary socialism, but one of its basic structural features. In both West and East, unregulated economic activity is best understood as a product of both modernity and bureaucracy. Informality is reproduced in direct counterpoint to the "rationalization" and "formalization" of the labor process that has taken place both under market capitalism and state socialism. However, these important parallels do not mean that the informal sector and the second economy are necessarily "functional equivalents or structural counterparts" (Stark 1989: 639). In essence, each one coexists with and arises from the contradictions of the dominant mode of production (the formal or official economy) within which it functions.

In study after study of the informal sector of Latin America, the Cuban case has been consistently, and at times justifiably, excluded (Alessandrini and Dallago 1987; Feige 1989; Portes, Castells, and Benton 1989; Schoepfle and Pérez-López 1993; Rakowski 1994; Portes et al 1997; Fernández-Kelly and Shefner 2006). After all, despite significant changes in its economic profile since 1990—and especially since Raúl Castro became president in 2006—Cuba does not share the economic structure or political system of its fellow Latin American nations (though it does share a common colonial history, culture, and language). Therefore, while taking some lessons from Latin America's experience with informality, we explain Cuba's second economy primarily within the theoretical and historical context of the former centrally planned economies (CPE) of Eastern Europe.

In our understanding of Cuba's "second economy," we combine aspects of the normally contrary neoliberal, state-centered and neo-Marxist, capital-centered approaches to informality, by using the new institutional approach to state socialism described below, and by making reference to the typology outlined above in Table 2.1. Because Cuba's is a hybrid, "post-socialist" economy undergoing a transformation from a fairly orthodox CPE to an uncertain future, with elements of capitalism, mercantilism, patrimonialism, and socialism mixed together (Kubalkova 1994; Radu 1995; Cabarrouy 2000; Crabb 2001; Corrales 2004; Burki and Erikson 2005; Erikson 2005a), no single theoretical approach fully explains the complexities of the Cuban case. However, each of these theoretical schools contributes essential understandings of the competing roles of the state, capital, and labor, as well as the importance of the socialist system itself in determining the nature and functioning of Cuba's second economy.

Defining the Informal Sector in Latin America

The informal sector can be defined as that part of the economy where the production and sale of legal goods and services manages to avoid labor and safety regulations, taxation, and official record keeping. Beginning with Keith Hart's study of small-scale enterprises in Ghana in 1971, economists originally saw the informal sector as a phenomenon unique to underdeveloped countries (Hart 1971; 1973). Observers often assumed that the many, often inventive, survival strategies used by informal workers were merely the reaction of poor urban migrants to the challenges of finding work in major Third World cities. When informal labor arrangements began to appear in immigrant destinations within the United States such as New York, Los Angeles, and Miami, there was a tendency to explain the phenomena as survival strategies brought by new immigrants themselves, not as something integral to advanced capitalism.

Challenging this preliminary assessment, sociologist Alejandro Portes led a multi-country comparative study of the informal economy (Portes, Castells, and Benton 1989), updating its definition and delineating a number of its common characteristics across different world regions. These researchers found that informal labor markets exist not only in the developing countries of the Third World but also in the advanced mixed economies of the West, as well as in the then socialist, centrally planned economies of the Soviet bloc. Effectively, this study "revealed the global scope of what was originally thought to be an exclusively Third World phenomenon" (Portes, Castells, and Benton 1989: 2).

The rich variety of activities within the sector share one central feature: they are "unregulated by the institutions of society, in a legal and social environment in which similar activities are regulated" (Portes, Castells, and Benton 1989: 2). The key criteria in identifying informality is not small size, low profitability, or even its common illegality, but the absence of state regulation. This conceptualization of informality identifies as its main characteristic the unregulated nature of its labor relations in contrast to the relatively protected environment in which formal workers operate. Thus, the informal sector's central characteristics can be enumerated as follows:

1. It is unregulated and not taxed;
2. It is a process, not a particular product or service;
3. It normally operates in cash, "under the table," and "off the books";
4. It includes some marginal, last-resort, survival activities as well as some middle- and higher-tech activities of a sophisticated nature;
5. It is deeply embedded in and connected to the formal, modern, capitalist economy;
6. Labor in the informal economy tends to be "downgraded," with informal workers typically receiving fewer benefits and protections than formal employees;
7. It possesses a great internal heterogeneity (including owners, entrepreneurs, managers, wage laborers, unpaid family workers, etc.);
8. The sector normally benefits from a government attitude of tolerance (alternating with periodic crackdowns);
9. Though frequently "hidden in plain sight," it is not apolitical and, in fact, often has a major if indirect impact on a country's politics and power relations (Fernández-Kelly 2006: 1; Losby et al 2002).

To these characteristics should be added one final caveat that follows from the second point above. The distinction that informality is a process and not a particular product or service allows us to distinguish between the informal economy on the one hand and the criminal or illegal economy on the other. The major types of economic activity are summarized in Table 2.2 below. They are defined according to the legality of the production process and the legality of the goods and services they produce.

The formal economy includes formal enterprises large and small that produce legal goods and services legally within the state's regulatory framework. Meanwhile, the informal economy produces legal goods and services, but does so in an unregulated, illegal manner. "The basic difference between formal and informal," therefore, "hinges not on the character of the final product, but on the manner in which it is produced or exchanged" (Centeno and Portes 2006: 26). The very important home-based economy produces legal goods and services but does so "extra-legally," outside the regulatory framework of the state. The criminal economy, on the other hand, is distinct from the informal economy since it produces goods and services defined as illegal in most contexts—such as illicit drugs or prostitution—while actively avoiding state regulation (licensing, taxes, and worker protections).

Table 2.2: Characterization of the Components of an Economy

Economic Type	Legality of the Production and Distribution Processes	Legality of Final Goods and Services
A. Household Economy	"Extra-legal"	Legal Goods and Services
B. Formal Economy	Legal: Within Tax and Regulatory Framework of the State	Legal Goods and Services
C. Informal Economy	Illegal: Outside Regulatory and Tax Regimes of the State	Legal Goods and Services
D. Criminal Economy	Illegal: Total Clandestinity	Illegal Goods and Services

In the Cuban case, the informal economy category disappeared after 1968, as all firms producing legal goods and services extra-legally were in effect criminal. Among the very few exceptions to this rule are pensioners reselling newspapers or cigarettes in the street, who may be technically illegal but are tolerated. However, in Chapter 7 we will distinguish between what we term "legitimate underground economic activities" (LUEAs) and the criminal economy, since the first produces legal products and has great potential for growth under a more inclusive and proactive public policy, while the second produces patently illicit goods and services and would remain illegal under all but the most laissez-faire economic system.

Debates over Informality in Latin America

Peruvian economist Hernando de Soto caused a paradigm shift of sorts when he published his treatise on Latin America's informal sector. Tellingly titled, *The Other Path: The Invisible Revolution in the Third World* (1989), de Soto's best-selling book characterized the informal sector as a popular revolutionary movement. Contrasting it with the Shining Path, Peru's own then powerful Maoist guerrilla revolutionary army, de Soto argued that Peru's non-violent informal army was led by the excluded masses of poor urban migrants to Lima. He further characterized the informal sector as a popular reaction to over-regulation of the economy by an essentially patrimonial, mercantilist (that is, not truly capitalist), and corrupt state. His effort in "applied economics" included the founding of the ILD (Institute for Liberty and Democracy) in 1979, a think-tank that aimed to turn his ideas into public-policy first in Peru and eventually all around the world. For this reason, de Soto can be credited with turning the informality debate on its head and bringing it out of the academy, into public view, and front-and-center in debates about public policy, entrepreneurship, and informality in the developing world.

In his work, de Soto argues that Marx himself would be surprised to find that, "In developing countries much of the teeming mass does not consist of oppressed legal proletarians but of oppressed 'extra-legal' small entrepreneurs with a sizeable amount of assets" (2000: 216). He therefore advocates transforming the "class struggle into a struggle for popular initiative and entrepreneurship" (1989: 255). Essentially, de Soto argues that the masses have united in a revolutionary front not as proletarians against capitalist exploitation, but as extra-legal, microentrepreneurs against a bureaucratic, state-directed economy and a patrimonial, "mercantilist" state that excludes them from becoming full and equal capitalists themselves (Apuleyo Mendoza, Montaner, and Vargas Llosa 1996). According to de Soto, it is their very marginalization that has transformed these migrants into entrepreneurs. Locked out of formal jobs and denied formal, legal title to their property, they proceeded to create their own microenterprises and institute their own set of extra-legal norms and regulations.

To his credit, de Soto does recognize and describe the many "costs of informality." Avoidance of detection, working on a small-scale, bribery, reliance on unskilled labor and low-technology production, and the inability to trust in investments or enforce contracts all act as indirect taxes in informal workers' quotidian struggle (1989: 131-187). Whereas his first book seemed to argue that all regulations should be thrown aside to accommodate informal entrepreneurs, his second book, *The Mystery of Capital*, makes the more realistic demand that erroneous and archaic legal regulations be changed to allow entry to informals—thereby making the "costs of formality" less than the "costs of informality" (2000: 154-170). In this sense, de Soto characterizes the status quo in many supposedly capitalist countries of the Third World and Eastern Europe as one of "capitalist apartheid": privileges are granted to a small, well-connected elite while the majority remain excluded from legal participation in the formal economy.

Other scholars have criticized de Soto for what they see as his simplistic portrayal of an adversarial relationship between informal workers on the one hand, and formal enterprises and the state on the other, arguing that he ignores the many ways that they work hand-in-glove. For example, it would seem that the state's goal of making everyone pay their dues and play by the same rules would come into inevitable conflict with the informal economy, which avoids the state's "protection racket" by facilitating "transactions where the state neither provides protection nor receives a 'cut'" (Centeno and Portes 2006: 26). Informal entrepreneurs do indeed seek to avoid all contact with the state as manifested in its three guises of the regulator (laws), the policeman (enforcement of laws), and the tax collector (paying dues). However, total avoidance is seldom possible and what started out as an "inevitable conflict" between the state's desire to exercise a monopoly on authority and the informal enterprise's attempt to subvert that authority results in actual practice in various forms of mutual accommodation, such as cooptation through bribes, benign neglect, and open tolerance (Centeno and Portes 2006: 26-27).

Such an accommodating relationship develops so often not only because of the active resistance of informal entrepreneurs so enthusiastically celebrated by de Soto, but also because both economic and political stability in developing countries often depends to no small degree on the role of the informal sector as a "buffer zone" that can absorb open unemployment, provide consumers with inexpensive goods and services, and even supply a ready and willing workforce to formal enterprises on a largely unregulated subcontracting basis. "Reality is more complex," argue Portes and Schauffler,

> Not only are many informal activities modern, [...], but they are often initiated with the support and sponsorship of formal firms. Instead of the Trojan Horse that will ultimately break down the fortress of "mercantilist" privilege, the informal sector in fact represents part of the routine operation of capitalism as it is presently organized in Latin America. (1993b: 47)

The single most important contribution of this understanding of informality is the contention that deep and necessary linkages exist between the informal sector and the larger capitalist economy, including both formal firms and state regulators. Portes and his colleagues have labeled their approach "structuralist" because they emphasize the complex and heterogeneous "structure of formal-informal relationships" (Portes and Schauffler 1993b: 48). Elsewhere, these same authors have gone further, saying:

> Formal and informal activities are simply *alternative facets of the same economy* and their articulation adopts a "variable geometry" depending on the scope of state regulations, the requirements of capitalist firms, and the size and characteristics of the labor force. This *articulation between both sectors* is the core of the structuralist approach (1993a: 25, our emphasis).

Informality is not simply the result of excess labor supply on the one hand and or over-regulation on the other. Instead, the central element of the structuralist approach is the idea that informality is in essence an alternate form of labor utilization (and often labor exploitation) by capital. Informal labor relations (like informal workers) are not "just there" by some accident or flaw in capitalist development. Instead, these relations (and workers) are actively "informalized" by capital under the logic of peripheral capitalist accumulation and profit maximization.

The structuralist approach explains informality as the result of the complex and ongoing class struggle between capital and labor, where capital has successfully evaded state regulations by actively creating and/or taking strategic advantage of a "new" type of labor: the unprotected informal worker. Though de Soto's neo-liberal and Portes' structural understandings of informality are usually seen as polar opposites, both share a focus on the power dynamic that exists between informal, underground workers on the one hand and the state/capital nexus on the other. As a political system, "totalitarian" state socialism is far from being a mirror image of the mercantilist nations of the past or of the "frustrated" states of modern Latin America. However, as systems of economic organization all have the same "total" regulatory intent (as illustrated in cells #3 and #6 of Table 2.1 above). That is, they seek to exercise the same bureaucratic and paternalistic control over all economic activities within their "domain."

This mercantilist, patrimonial tradition of state-led economic development continues to hamper entrepreneurial initiative throughout in Latin America. However, Centeno and Portes argue that this should not be taken to mean that complete deregulation is the answer to informality. Instead, "less regulation should be coupled with a state machinery capable of implementing existing laws" (Centeno and Portes 2006: 41). Still, there is a similar "vicious cycle" of attempts at total control of economic activity only provoking more popular resistance, diversification, and expansion of the informal sector and the second economy in both the "frustrated" and "totalitarian" described in the typology presented in Table 2.1 (ibid. 30-32).

Moreover, whereas the mercantilist nations of yesteryear and the weak, frustrated states of today have often monopolized international trade and severely limited the development of local markets—granting "state protection and resources [to] a minority, while the rest of the population is left to fend for itself through widespread violation of the law" (ibid. 31)—state socialism has exercised its control through establishing a rigid central plan, a monopoly of ownership of productive forces, and universal state employment (Rona-Tas 1997). Still, unsanctioned entrepreneurial activities run the same risks and provoke the same official condemnation under both systems. The ubiquitous informal private entrepreneurs that were once the lifeblood of the "hidden economies" of the Soviet Union and Eastern Europe bear a striking resemblance to both de Soto's informal "heroes" of today and the ubiquitous contrabandists that once populated the underside of the mercantilist economic structure during Latin America's colonial period. However, whereas de Soto's informal heroes frustrate the state through open defiance, workers in the second economies of socialist states deploy their "weapons of the weak" by foot-dragging and withholding vital information. "Since totalitarian planning of an entire economy depends on massive amounts of information," reason Centeno and Portes:

and since accurate information is not forthcoming as actors in civil society regularly conceal, cheat, and exaggerate, the formal "first" economy ends up trapped in a make-believe world of false statistics and illusory achievements. [...] In the case of [such] totalitarian states, the occupation of every crevice of economic activity by informal enterprise and the generalized withdrawal of information from official agents lead to the state-ruled economy to spiral into a fantasy world. (2006: 31)

Such is undoubtedly the case in contemporary Cuba where petty crime and high-level corruption within state firms is ubiquitous, and where swarms of *macetas* (middlemen) and *bisneros* (businessmen) struggle to *resolver* and *inventar* solutions to the multiple daily challenges even amid the marginally pro-entrepreneurial reforms being currently implemented under Raúl Castro.

Likewise, the systematic utilization of the informal sector by formal capitalist firms described above has a counterpart in state socialism's systematic reliance upon the second economy to make up for its own inefficiencies and contradictions. The existence of a flexible second economy (providing employment and efficient production) within the official planned economy provides state socialism with a very convenient, short-term subsidy, even if its long-term impact can be quite corrosive. Furthermore, this subsidy is provided through the active self-exploitation of a large part of the workforce (working in a state job as an air-traffic controller by day, while moonlighting as a clandestine airport cabbie by night, for example). In other words, an important, if largely unintended consequence of widespread private entrepreneurial activity is the preservation of an inefficient, bureaucratic, and unproductive state socialist system.

If we characterize Cuba's current economic system as passing from an orthodox form of state socialism based on a central plan, to one of "market socialism" or "state capitalism" based on a relatively "open" economy in terms of joint ventures and foreign investment (but still relatively closed in terms of restrictions on private citizens' full and equal participation in the economy), then the benefits to the state/capital nexus provided by an active second economy are clear. Though an active second economy may constitute a long-term threat to regime stability in socialist states (Portes and Böröcz 1988; Grossman 1989a; Sik 1992; Gábor 1994; Fernández 2000: 31-32), it also acts as a short-term regime stabilizer. Still, despite the general applicability of some elements of the above models in the Latin American case, they ultimately fail to grapple with the structural, systemic, and institutional realities that have provoked extensive underground economies and black markets in all historical examples of state socialism. For this reason, we now turn to this history—and the related theoretical literature—in order to synthesize a model that can better explain the Cuban case.

The Second Economy under State Socialism

While Portes and his colleagues reject de Soto's belief in the "revolutionary" potential of informal workers, they do recognize the special nature of informal work (the second economy) under state socialism. As cited in the epigraph that began this chapter, they contend that, "In command economies, informalization is ironically a tool in the hands of urban workers... to confront the all-powerful state." They continue, "In certain national instances, the informal economy has proven strong enough to compel state managers to gradually yield to its logic." Because the "triangular relationship between capital, labor, and the state" (Portes, Castells, and Benton 1989: 308-309) has been institutionalized under different terms in state socialist societies, unregulated activities in centrally planned economies arise from distinct causes and are not functional equivalents to the informal labor relations of the West. Now we describe the particular "logic" of the second economy in socialist states and apply that logic to the Cuban case.

Under the dependent capitalism that exists in much of Latin America, the Caribbean, and the developing world, informalization is primarily a strategy employed by formal firms in order to expand their profit margin by avoiding formal labor laws. Thus, in Latin America informality commonly "serves to strengthen the hand of the dominant class and to weaken labor's organizations" (Portes, Castells, and Benton 1989: 309). In contrast, under state socialism informalization is carried out *by workers themselves* in order to win a greater return on their labor output than is common under employment in the poorly paid state jobs of the official or "first" economy. Therefore, the functional equivalent in the West of socialism's "second economy" is not the informal sector but actually the trade union (Stark 1989). Though not institutionalized and legally protected as is the trade union (which in most historical examples of state socialism—including that of Cuba—is controlled by the state), the second economy functions to protect workers from arbitrary abuse by the "dominant class" (state firms and the party) and provide them with the supplemental wages they are denied as workers in the first economy.[5]

In his groundbreaking essay, "Bending the Bars of the Iron Cage: Bureaucratization and Informalization in Capitalism and Socialism," David Stark (1989) argues that while informality often manifests itself as an effort to circumvent regulations, it is *essentially congruent* with the same market principles (production for private profit) that coordinate the formal capitalist economy. In contrast, the second economy, while responding to the contradictions of socialist redistributive bureaucracy, responds to market mechanisms that are *fundamentally incongruent* with the redistributive principles of the state. As such, the second economy is an antagonistic source of systemic change, constantly applying pressure to remake the economic institutions of socialism.

In establishing state socialism in different countries throughout the world, Marxist leaders shared the common goal of replacing the alleged "anarchy" of the market with the alleged "rationality" of the plan. A single, visible authority, the state, would oversee and coordinate production and distribution for the entire society. Bureaucratization under state socialism is not just deeper than under capitalism, but of a different type. Stark points out that under capitalism the state issues regulations that market competitors must follow. Under socialism, however, the state issues directives, not as "interventions [...] but as the solely legitimate prescriptions for economic behavior." In other words, under socialism "the state does not influence [markets], it controls them" or at least attempts to (Stark 1989: 647).

In such a context, the second economy represents much more than a mere supplementary alternative to the state sector. In quiet revolt against the desire of the state to control all markets, the second economy represents an *antagonistic* alternative. Its existence expands the space available to workers beyond the state-controlled realm, effectively freeing them from exclusive dependence on state wages. Whereas under capitalism informal workers are often worse off compared to the officially employed and protected formal workers, under state socialism the earnings of underground workers have often been higher than those of state workers (Stark 1989: 655-656). This disadvantage of formal, state sector jobs is a key characteristic that distinguishes Cuba's "informals" from their counterparts in the rest of Latin America.[6]

Despite the fact that socialist states are threatened by the growth of private enterprise, economic reforms in chronically inefficient state socialist systems often include the expansion of private enterprise. In Cuba, the legalization of self-employment—first in the early 1990s under Fidel and again following Raúl Castro's 2010 expansion—exposed the contradiction between the promotion of entrepreneurship and the maintenance of socialist egalitarianism. At the same time, as Cuba's second economy grows the government risks losing its ability to punish and reward citizens through state jobs (just as workers lose access to the goods that can be "appropriated" when working for the government). Indeed, while Cuba's self-employed workers often take greater risks and work much longer hours than state workers, "Most are quite content to have the opportunity to liberate themselves financially from the economic and social restrictions of working for the state" (Jackiewicz and Bolster 2003: 375).

Examples of this type of low-level "liberation" through turning to the black market in Cuba are legion (and chronicled in Chapters 4, 7, and 8). While the state may be omnipresent and while the punishments for theft of state resources and corruption are heavy, so also are the opportunities for "escape" into the second economy, given the extremely low state salaries and accentuated need of most Cubans. In fact, analysts on the island (Vidal Alejandro and Pérez Villanueva 2010, 2012; Espinosa Chepe 2011; Espinosa Chepe and

Henken 2013; Castellanos 2013) often describe Raúl Castro's initial expansion of self-employment in 2010 as merely a public admission of the existence of a bourgeoning informal economy, which constitutes perhaps 40 percent of the national domestic product (Pérez Roque 2002; Portes and Haller 2005). Of course, the strategy of legalization can win the state increased revenue through taxation and control through licensing, while granting legal status could also inadvertently lead to greater demands for deeper, broader change. Writing in 2002 prior to Raúl's expansion of self-employment, an independent economist on the island noted:

> [T]here is a great variety of clandestine enterprises with a notable capacity of innovation and accumulation [...] When one enters the exclusive zone of Miramar in Havana, vendors call in a low voice "microwave," "air conditioner," "bedroom set," "satellite dish" [...] a great variety of products forbidden to Cubans. Where do they get them? Without a doubt from state supplies, but there are also clandestine networks departing from the special export processing zones. Here we find everything: theft, corruption, speculation, delivery of products by foreign firms to their Cuban workers for sale in the black markets. (Pérez Roque 2002: 10-11, quoted in Portes and Haller 2005: 408)

Defining the Second Economy

The term second economy is used here to describe those economic activities in socialist economies neither regulated by the state nor included in its central plan. While these unregulated activities often make up for the state sector's lack of economic efficiency, second economy activities have more than a merely economic meaning and as such are not normally encouraged (though they are sometimes tolerated). Even when legal, licensed, and taxed by the state, such activities are often seen as a threat to the monopoly of central planning since they provide a modicum of economic freedom to their participants and cut against the ideological grain of full state ownership, labor solidarity (and control), egalitarianism, and universal state employment. For this reason, the legitimacy of the small private sector is frequently under attack in state socialist regimes and entrepreneurs commonly find themselves caught in a cycle of periodic suppression and accommodation (a cycle clearly reflected in Cuba's own shifts in public policy, which we describe in Chapters 3, 4, and 5). Finally, unlike the informal sector under capitalism, the limits of which are set by legal criteria, the second economy under state socialism is defined by both legal and *ideological* criteria.

Grossman began giving systematic scholarly attention to the unregulated economic activity common in CPEs in the late 1970s with a seminal article on the second economy of the Soviet Union. He defined the second economy as those productive activities which meet at least one of the two following criteria: (1) they are to a large extent carried out in knowing violation of existing laws, and/or (2) they are directly conducted for private gain. Thus, the key difference between the *informal sector* as it exists in Latin America, and the *second economy* within CPEs like Cuba is one of *legality* versus *control*. In other words, the second economy expands the concept of informality to include not only economic activity that is illegal or unregulated by the state, but also all private profit-driven activities (legal or not), which contradict the socialist ideals of egalitarianism, the plan, state ownership of the means of production, and universal state employment.

Portes and Böröcz echo this basic distinction between informal and second economy activities. They argue that in both capitalist and socialist systems informal activity takes place "outside the scope of public regulation" (1988: 17). However, because informal activity in CPEs defies "the channels of central planning and direct state control" it becomes a "terrain of political struggle per se" (ibid: 19). Portes and Böröcz also make an important modification regarding the essentially *licit* nature of the goods and services produced in the second economy. Whereas Grossman needlessly includes all illegal activities, Portes and Böröcz make the necessary distinction that the second economy properly includes only the "production and distribution of licit products" (ibid) that take place outside the state's central plan. This is the same distinction we make between the informal and the criminal economies in Table 2.2 above.

In the introduction to her collection of articles, *The Second Economy in Marxist States* (1990), Los also rejects exclusively legal criteria as too narrow and moral criteria as too relative. She opts instead for an ideological definition: "the second economy includes all areas of economic activity which are officially viewed as being inconsistent with the ideologically sanctioned dominant mode of economic organization" (1990: 2). This ideological criteria would specifically exclude illicit goods and services such as drug trafficking and prostitution, but include both the illegal theft and resale of state goods and formally legal but ideologically suspect activities such as licensed self-employment (e.g., Cuba's private bed-and-breakfasts, taxis, and popular restaurants, known as "*paladares*") (Henken 2002; 2008).

Causes of the Second Economy:
State Ownership, Planning, and Employment

State socialist systems are characterized by the presence of three principal economic institutional structures: (1) *state ownership* of the means of production, (2) economic decisions being dictated by a *central plan*, and (3) the concentration of labor under *universal state employment*. Together, these three structural elements are present in all historical examples of state socialism and their rigidities provoke the necessary existence of a second economy (Rona-Tas 1997). State control over the means of production is one of the central elements of state socialism, even if absolute state ownership is an ideal rarely, if ever, fully achieved in any of the historically existing socialist nations. However, such an abstract notion of state ownership has led in practice to the misuse and theft of state supplies, often done with little social stigma. In fact, preferential access to state supplies is often understood as one of the few "informal rights" of state employment. Thus, under state ownership, workers are not inclined to remain in state jobs because of their wages, but rather they are more commonly motivated by the access those jobs give them to state goods (Díaz Briquets and Pérez-López 2006).

Likewise, the abolition of the market along with supply and demand gives rise to the need for an alternative form of product pricing, wage scales, and resource allocation and distribution: the central plan. However, unlike market allocations, central plans tend to be set administratively and arbitrarily. This leads to chronic shortages, production bottlenecks, and low quality products. The strict authoritarian and hierarchical structure of state socialist governments also makes production flexibility and information feedback difficult. Subordinate managers often simply tell planners what they want to hear in order to avoid reprimand, withholding information that could improve productivity and efficiency. Instead of aiming at efficient production based on profitability, the logic of central planning is the fulfillment of production quotas at any price and with little attention to efficiency, profitability, quality, or consumer preferences. As a result, use of the central plan often results in underemployment (workers employed, but underutilized), lack of motivation, absenteeism, and wastefulness. At the level of management, it is often necessary to resort to the periodic use of informal and even illegal mechanisms "outside the plan" by managers in order to meet production quotas. These common problems with central planning have given rise to the famous quip that, under socialism, labor and management have reached the peculiar agreement: "We pretend to work, and you pretend to pay us" (Pérez-López 1995a: 16-19).

Despite differences across the numerous manifestations of state socialism in Eastern Europe, communist regimes were unique in being the only strain of totalitarian or authoritarian systems, which "sought to hire its entire population" (Róna-Tas 1997: 5). Ironically, this distinctive feature of state socialism—universal state employment—has received little attention from Western scholars. Perhaps because universal employment (along with the universal provision of social services such as education and health care) is commonly seen as a desirable but unattainable goal under capitalism, most scholars have been slow to see it as a central structural feature of state socialism or to recognize its function as a fundamental *means of social control*. In fact, according to the Hungarian sociologist Ákos Róna-Tas, employment under state socialism is only secondarily concerned with the provision of wages and the achievement of production. Instead, state employment is primarily a means to ensure social order through "a complex, nationwide system of organized dependence whereby one's supervisors were entrusted not only with the enforcement of hard and productive work, but also with chores of imposing political control" (Róna-Tas 1997: 4).

Under the CPEs Eastern Europe, state employment was not just a universal right, but also a universal obligation. In order to protect the institution of universal state employment, nearly every state socialist nation has instituted extensive "vagrancy," "shirking," or "anti-loafing" laws, making willful unemployment a crime (Ritter 1974: 332-334).[7] Furthermore, the self-employed are inclined to remain connected to their official jobs since many social benefits are often unavailable outside the state employment sector. This complex system of effectively linking one's health, pension, and other social benefits to one's livelihood, and in turn linking that livelihood to participation in the socialist system "allow[s] the Party-state to exercise power through its ownership rights rather than through coercion" (Róna-Tas 1997: 4). Put another way, *when you receive everything from the state, you also owe everything to it.* However, when workers are able to break free from the system of universal state employment, one of the state's principal means of control is compromised. This explains why the socialist state feels constantly menaced by the growth of the private sector. Utilized as a stop-gap solution to the chronic scarcity and inefficiency in the first economy, the second economy represents a "Faustian pact" threatening the long-term stability of state socialism (Grossman 1979; 1989a; Díaz Briquets and Pérez-López 2006).[8]

The Consequences of Economic Reform within State Socialism

Whereas Western scholars largely assumed that the Soviet bloc's "suit of armor" was home to a fierce and fearsome knight, many economists and sociologists working in Eastern Europe itself were well aware that the knight inside had long since died. These social scientists were later joined by a group of Western academics, calling themselves the "new institutionalists," and together they placed the *economic institutions of state socialism* at the center of their analysis.[9] Essentially, in place of ad hoc explanations of the demise of state socialism, these researchers sought to develop an adequate theory of social order in state socialism. They were convinced that if they could explain how such a system was able to *hold together* over such a long period of time, they could also pinpoint the processes that led to its *ultimate undoing*. Their approach took into account the "institutional arrangements" particular to socialism, going beyond a focus on party-state elites to include the multiple interactions between subordinate groups and the state (Stark and Nee 1989).

Rejecting the idea of a sudden collapse and imminent "transition," these researchers recast the fall of the Soviet bloc as an ongoing transformation that had in fact begun long ago. Combining empirical research with historical analyses of socialist states, they (Seleny 1995; Róna-Tas 1995, 1997; Walder 1994, 1995) argued that the now quite visible transformation of state socialism was based on "forty years of [largely hidden] accommodation and compromise." In the end, the supposed "unchanging political structures [of socialism] hid as much as they revealed" (Seleny 1995: 27).[10] This approach argues that looking only at elite groups "unnecessarily restrict our analytic field of vision and precludes the possibility that social groups outside the state play a role in shaping society" (Stark and Nee 1989: 8). Instead, the proper focus to understand change within state socialist regimes is on the "weapons of the weak"— that is, on the activities of subordinate social groups within society such as informal entrepreneurs (Scott 1985).

By focusing on the three key *economic institutions* of state socialism described above, the new institutionalists pinpoint the locus of power within communist regimes. "Power comes from de facto party ownership of productive assets and organized monopoly over allocations of goods and career opportunities" (Walder 1995: 6). If near total state control over these resources is the key to political power, then it would follow that, "party loyalty and authority [are] founded upon citizen dependence upon officials for the satisfaction of material needs and access to career opportunities" (Walder 1995: 6). The stability of such a system arises not simply from the conviction, loyalty, or fear of citizens and cadres alike, but from individual self-interest in a controlled environment, reinforced by the scarcity of alternative sources of goods, services, employment, and income. Thus, any changes to or breakdowns in social order in such an environment would necessarily come about as a result of shifts in the economic dependence and incentive structures of different social groups. In other words, threats to regime stability originate in changes to the economic institutions of state socialism—state ownership, the central plan, and universal state employment.

Is the second economy ultimately a stabilizing or a subversive force for state socialism? Is it, as Grossman asked, a *boon* or *bane* for the first economy? And, if the second economy is indeed a wolf in sheep's clothing threatening the stability of the socialist system, why did nearly all pre-1989 socialist states of Eastern Europe enact economic reforms, creating legal space for the second economy that ultimately undermined their own power? If communist "cadre entrepreneurs" can learn to love the emerging market because it provides them with lucrative positions of power as "nomenklatura capitalists" (Walder 1995),[11] so too can private entrepreneurs learn to hate the market, preferring the former unregulated system where hard-won favors and special connections provide a stable source of protection and privilege (Gábor 1994).[12] Thus, two of the most significant unintended consequences of economic reforms within state socialism are the creation of a whole class of self-employed entrepreneurs who are less and less dependent on their state jobs for survival;

and the gradual corruption of state agents and party cadres for whom the opportunism and self-interest of the market came to predominate over and provide greater rewards than loyalty and commitment to the party.

Understanding the political role of universal state employment under state socialism allows us to identify the corrosive effect of the rise of the private sector (as an alternative labor market) in a socialist context. While the second economy compensates for the first economy's deficiencies, it also undermines the primary means of control and social order within a socialist system: universal state employment. When citizens cease to depend upon the state for their livelihoods, they are no longer complicit beneficiaries in the socialist system and therefore possess a potentially powerful form of freedom and independence.

Moreover, once reforms are begun, further reform is the product of pressures originating both outside and within the state apparatus "forc[ing] the state [...] to tolerate activities that were once illegal but not yet legalized, and to institutionalize reforms that were legal but were not yet legitimate" (Stark 1989: 652). Therefore, the growth of the second economy is not simply a case of state *against* society. It is also evidence of a lack of integration within the state itself. The state cannot scale back reforms if its main constituency, party cadres, benefit from and rely upon them. These cadres need not be consciously anti-government and are often far from being political dissidents. Instead, they are naturally self-interested in an environment of scarcity. It is often forgotten that the underlying goal of economic reforms in socialist states has everywhere been the same: to "update," perfect, and preserve socialism. Given this aim, economic reforms in Eastern European socialist states were a failure and the role of the second economy was clearly subversive.

Calling attention to the unique institutions of state socialism and tracing the linkages between state agents and private entrepreneurs affords us an insider's view of the corrosive effect of the second economy on state socialism. Such an approach also reveals a major historic instance of what Max Weber called "unintended consequences": the party-state's instrumental, if inadvertent role in its own demise. Therefore, Cuba along with the few other remaining outposts of state socialism face a difficult if not impossible dilemma: "[T]o survive in a world of competing states, they are compelled to institute and sustain market reforms. Yet the spread of markets erodes the commitment to the party and paves the way for regime change" (Nee and Lian 1994: 284).

Lessons for Cuba

Unregulated economic activity originates in relation to the dominant mode of economic organization in any given society (Light 2004). For this reason, models developed to understand the Latin American informal sector cannot fully explain the Cuban case. As was the case with the second economies of Eastern Europe, unregulated economic activity in Cuba takes place in a socialist context that prioritizes the state plan, state ownership, and state employment, and against that dominant ideal. The models developed to understand the phenomenon of informality the rest of Latin America shed some light on the Cuban case, especially given Cuba's common historical and cultural heritage. However, none captures the Cuban reality as precisely as do those models developed to explain the "second economy" of socialist states given the extent to which state socialism has been instituted in Cuba over the past half-century.

We can take from de Soto the idea that a major cause of informality is an overbearing, monopolistic state. This perspective parallels the new institutional theoretical paradigm developed out of Eastern Europe's experience with the even more rigid and overbearing socialist state, which aims to control all economic planning while monopolizing ownership and employment. Although it would seem to clash with these two state-centered approaches, the structuralist school's focus on capital's use of informal workers through subcontracting arrangements is analogous to the monopolistic socialist state's reliance on workers in the second economy to "resolve" the inefficiencies and bottlenecks common in centrally planned economies.

Only a handful of researchers have gone beyond description and attempted to tackle the Cuban conundrum within a comprehensive theoretical framework. Among these, Pérez-López (1995a) is unique in applying the models of the "second economy" as originally developed in the Eastern European context to Cuba. As Grossman (1977; 1979; 1989a) and Los (1987, 1990) did in their studies of the Soviet Union, Pérez-López makes *control* rather than legality or regulation the critical element in his definition of Cuba's second economy. Thus, the second economy concept is most appropriate for Cuba because it includes "all those economic activities which are inconsistent with the dominant ideology that shapes the official economy" (Pérez-López 1995a: 14), not simply those which have come under state regulation or been outlawed. Furthermore, Pérez-López contends that the second economy concept fits the Cuban context better than that of mere informality since in Cuba the rise in individual entrepreneurial activity takes place in a political context where societal gain is preferred over private gain and, though sometimes legal, is not considered legitimate. It is this particular understanding of the second economy that we will employ in the remainder of this study.

Notes

[1] Even under the current economic reforms enacted by Raúl Castro, which give unprecedented space to would-be Cuban entrepreneurs, one never hears the words *em-*

presario or *emprendedor* (entrepreneur) or *sector privado* (private sector) to refer to the island's nascent microenterprise sector. Instead, they are described with the euphemistic terms *cuentapropista* (self-employed worker) and *sector no-estatal* (non-state sector). Cuban blogger Yoani Sánchez recently noted this fact via her Twitter feed (2013), where she stated, "*Entre los eufemismos más llamativos de los últimos años está 'cuentapropistas' ... prohibido decir 'empresarios'*" ("Among the most glaring euphemisms of recent years is 'self-employed worker' ... it's prohibited to say 'entrepreneur'").

[2] The past 30 years has seen the emergence of economically vibrant and politically stable "state capitalist" or "market socialist" regimes such as Vietnam and China. While such economies exhibit some of the hybrid characteristics found in Cuba (mixing the "frustrated" regime type with the "totalitarian" one) the depth of their economic reforms combined with the maintenance of authoritarian political rule forces us to consider a seventh type: strong states with some restrictions on entrepreneurial activity that are not easily described as either "liberal," "welfare," or "totalitarian." This is a possible future path for Cuba. We thank Antonio Zamora for pointing this possibility out to us.

[3] The title of an anthology of the "new institutional" approach to change within state socialist regimes, *Remaking the Economic Institutions of Socialism: China and Eastern Europe* (1989), edited by Victor Nee and David Stark, reflects this.

[4] Literally meaning "flower pot," the term *maceta* originated through the practice of informal entrepreneurs hiding payments for goods and services under flower pots. In practice, *maceta* is a term of vilification used to refer to illicit intermediaries who "live off of the work of others."

[5] We understand Cuba's second economy both as "a tool in the hands of [...] workers to confront the all-powerful state" (Portes, Castels, and Benton 1989: 308) (informal collective bargaining and parasitic use of state supplies), and as a mechanism by which the socialist state receives an indirect subsidy from workers since what they produce in the hidden economy provides a functional flexibility normally absent in the rigid central plan. Given the fact that the second economy often acts simultaneously as a "boon and a bane" (Grossman 1989b) for the first economy, the complex, "mutually parasitic" (Pérez-López 1995a) relationship between the first and second economies in socialist states is a central focus of this work.

[6] Because access to most social services in Cuba is based on citizenship not employment status, self-employed workers there do not normally sacrifice their welfare benefits when they opt to work in the second economy. In fact, it is common for Cuba's self-employed workers to take advantage of state subsidies (such as low utility prices and rationed foods) to maximize profits in their private enterprises (socializing costs and privatizing income). Many entrepreneurs justify such actions as a response to the state's own more egregious attempts to control and exploit them through extremely low salaries, subcontracting their labor to foreign firms, high tax rates, and a monopoly on legal employment. Moreover, many self-employed insist that it is they who subsidize the state sector, since their "moonlighting" in the second economy enables them to continue to work in the grossly under-remunerated state sector.

[7] Cuba instituted its own "Anti-Loafing Law" in 1971 to combat absenteeism after the failed push to harvest 10 million tons of sugar in 1970.

[8] The legal principle behind such prohibitions is "everything is prohibited that is not explicitly allowed" (Stark 1989: 659). In fact, both cycles of the liberalization of Cuban self-employment, first in the early 1990s and after 2010, laid out a specific lists of licensable occupations (growing from 117 to 157 in the 1990s and from 178 to 201 after 2010). While these reforms represent an opening toward microenterprise, they are

based on a mentality of micro-management and control. This approach leaves citizens with little space to act independently, reducing acceptable economic activity to only what is explicitly authorized and practically forcing those who want to improve their standard of living to break the law. Thus, economic crime becomes so routine that it loses its moral stigma. See Chapter 7 below and Ted A. Henken, "*Vale Todo*: In Cuba's Paladares, Everything is Prohibited, but Anything Goes" (2008a).

[9] "What appeared to be the overnight crumbling of socialism in Eastern Europe and the Soviet Union," writes Damián Fernández with an eye to the Cuban case, "was in fact an incremental corrosion of the entire system in no small measure due to socioeconomic informality" (2000: 122).

[10] This tendency has been pronounced in studies of Cuban socialism. For example, it is common to hear of an imminent "regime change" or "transition," when changes that have already taken place on the island, especially since 1990, indicate that a transformation of Cuba's socialist system is already well underway (Bengelsdorf 1994). Many conceive of "transition" as an all-or-nothing event that will begin only after Cuba's maximum leader (or now his younger brother) is gone. Such wishful thinking persists even after the unmistakable continuity following Fidel Castro's illness and subsequent replacement. A better focus for students of Cuba's future would be on how everyday people have used "weapons of the weak" to pressure the state to enact economic reforms and on how those same people will respond to those reforms, expanding on them in myriad ways.

[11] As used in Cuba, "*nomenklatura*" is a pejorative term that refers mockingly to privileged government officials. It comes from the Soviet Union and other Eastern Bloc countries where it referred to a small group of officials—almost always Party members—who held key administrative positions and thus enjoyed special perquisites, essentially comprising a class unto itself.

[12] In Cuba, this has long been known as "*socio-lismo*," or the reliance on one's friends or "associates" over "*socialismo*," playing by the rules of egalitarian socialism (Ritter 1974).

3
Revolutionary Trajectories and Strategic Shifts, 1959–1990

Upon Fidel Castro's accession to power in January 1959, the policy of his revolutionary movement towards small private enterprise was unclear and indeed as yet undetermined. At this time, the Cuban economy consisted of numerous micro, small, middle-sized, and large enterprises, some foreign and some domestic, some formal and others informal, most legal but some underground. However, with the nationalizations of all large enterprises and most medium-sized enterprises between 1959 and 1963 and with the installation of central planning, the state socialist character of the Revolution was becoming increasingly clear.[1] Then during the "Revolutionary Offensive" of 1968, much of the remaining private sector was nationalized and virtually all non-agricultural microenterprises were confiscated or shut down. Nevertheless, some legal microenterprises as well as underground microenterprises continued to operate.

Public policy towards the remaining (and the handful of new) private sector enterprises fluctuated drastically during the subsequent 1969 to 1990 period. Following the quixotic effort to eliminate all small and microenterprises during the lead up to the failed 1970 effort to harvest 10 million tons of sugarcane came a shift between 1970 and 1985 toward relative tolerance and mild liberalization. However, policy reverted back again to containment and repression during the "Rectification Campaign" that took place between 1986 and 1990.

In this chapter, we analyze the evolution of public policy towards microenterprise during the Revolution's first three decades (1959-1990). We begin with a brief overview of the evolution of small enterprise from the colonial period up to the eve of the Revolution. The chapter's central analysis is framed around four distinct phases, each of which is defined by the character of public policy towards microenterprise. During the first phase, from 1959 to 1963, the radical ideology of the Revolution expressed itself through the confiscation of most of Cuba's existing private enterprise, large and small, foreign and domestic. Then, from 1963 to 1970, and most notably with the aforementioned "Revolutionary Offensive" of 1968, nearly all remaining legal, "above-ground" small and microenterprises were eradicated. In the third phase, from about 1971 to 1986, a more permissive approach towards microenterprise was gradually implemented within the context of the adoption of a more orthodox (that is, less radical) Soviet economic model. Following this, in a fourth, relatively brief phase from 1986 to 1990, public policy towards microenterprise was tightened once again as part of the short-lived "Rectification Campaign."

Cuba's Small Enterprise Sector Before 1959

Like most countries, Cuba has a long history of small and microenterprise, as well as medium and large enterprise dating back to the early colonial period. A large array of basic services and some manufacturing were carried out on a self-employment or very small enterprise basis, including a wide range of personal and business services in urban and rural areas, as well as transportation, construction and repair services, fishing and forestry-based activities, and the fabrication of basic manufactures such as cigars, clothing, footwear, and some furniture.

Cuba also has a long history of illegal economic activities beginning in the early colonial era and characterized by contraband trade in violation of the trade monopoly maintained by Spain. Indeed, the first major work of Cuban literature, namely *Espejo de Paciencia*, features *contrabandistas*, piracy, and kidnapping (de Balboa 1608). The chief cause of contraband trade for much of the colonial era was the enforced monopoly of trading with the colonies in the Americas granted to the merchants of Seville and Cádiz. These merchants, organized through the *Casa de Contratación* (Contracting House), were given exclusive control over trade between Peninsular Spain and all other parts of Europe on the one hand and the Spanish colonies of the Western Hemisphere on the other. Illegal trade in slaves (after the slave trade was outlawed by Great Britain in the early 19th century) was also an important element in the large-scale illegalities in the colonial era.

The enforced bilateralism of this artificial monopoly created strong incentives for illegal exchange between the Spanish colonies and other possible trading partners in Europe, in the Thirteen Colonies of North America, and in other colonies the Caribbean, where the British, Dutch, and French all had active trading relations. The intensity of this incentive is illustrated by the fact that in the 11 months of the British occupation of Havana from August 1762 to June 1763, over 700 British ships, sailing from Britain or from its colonies entered Havana harbor. This is in sharp contrast to the number of Spanish ships entering Havana in previous years, these averaging about 15 per year

(Stein and Stein, 1970: 97). Cuba's economic evolution was being stifled and deformed by the prohibitions against trading with natural trading partners in the New World and in Europe outside of Spain. The principal participants of the illegal trade were Cuba's far-flung provincial areas as opposed to Havana, which was the major beneficiary of the enforced trade bilateralism. The merchants of the city of Bayamo, for example, participated actively in the illegal trade by exchanging hides, meat, and other agricultural products with privateers and foreign merchant vessels. On the basis of this trade, the population of Bayamo approached that of Havana. Santiago de Cuba was also a major beneficiary of contraband trade.

Since its independence in 1902, Cuba evolved with a combination of private, cooperative, and public sectors. It relied upon the market mechanism as well as on planning at various levels of government and for various sectors of the economy. Private sector entrepreneurs, public sector managers or entrepreneurs, and various benevolent associations in the cooperative sector all contributed to the development of the country. Cuba also evolved with a wide range of enterprises in terms of size. By 1958, there was a mix of large, medium, small, and microenterprises throughout the economy. The large size of the sugar mills, electrical generating plants, telephone companies, railways, and some cigar manufacturers is well documented. However, there were also numerous small registered enterprises and also irregular tax-evading enterprises as in other countries. There were also many types of producers operating semi-legally or "extra-legally"—including small unregistered shoe makers, a similar small-scale industry in clothing, textiles, and furniture, as well as numerous informal and unregistered cigar and cigarette makers who worked at home producing for their own use and for that of their family and friends (Directorio Comercial del Municipio de La Habana 1958: 471-473).

In its 1950 report on its mission to Cuba, the International Bank of Reconstruction and Development (the IBRD, now better known as the World Bank) recognized that these microenterprises systematically evaded taxation but were often tolerated by the government (IBRD 1950: 913). Still, representatives of many larger-scale registered enterprises in these same industries complained that they had difficulty competing with them since the clandestine producers avoided taxes, paid wages below the minimum, and operated out of their own homes. Moreover, they were able to keep costs low and remain competitive vis-à-vis the larger firms by not providing benefits to workers nor having to contend with labor unions. Interestingly, the IBRD recognized the social benefits of these "cottage industries" from the standpoint of providing a livelihood and the usefulness of their low cost products, recommending continued government tolerance towards them (ibid.: 957-959).

Nationalization and the Installation of a Command Economy, 1959–1963

Before Castro's assumption of power in 1959 and even during the first six to nine months of the Revolution, the ideological orientation of the regime remained ambiguous. There were four distinct and competing possibilities regarding Cuba's economic future that coexisted during this early period. Which one of these would win out was difficult to foresee at the time. First was Fidel Castro's own radical (but not necessarily "revolutionary" and explicitly non-Communist) approach as presented in the written version of his well-known 1953 defense speech, "History Will Absolve Me" (Castro, F. n.d.). In the speech, he advocated such changes as an end to *latifundia* (large-scale landed estates) through limited agrarian reform, nationalizations in the utility sector, export diversification, and social-justice-oriented state investments in education, housing, and health care. However, he did not publicly advocate anything approaching the complete nationalization of the economy or wholesale elimination of the private sector, nor did he push for the state absorption of Cuba's many microenterprises (all of which eventually took place).

Secondly, there was the strategy laid out by Regino Boti and Felipe Pazos in their "Economic Thesis of the 26th of July Movement" (Boti and Pazos 1958), which was the official economic strategy of the revolutionary movement that Castro himself led. This document favored an increased role for the government in "democratically planning" the economy to ensure social justice, a greater redistribution of national income, and an increased participation of Cuban firms in the economy (Ritter 1974: 63-67, 226). A third path was associated with Ernesto "Che" Guevara, who later became the first revolutionary President of the Central Bank of Cuba and then the Minister of Industry. His approach called for the institution of revolutionary socialism on the island, including not only nationalization of major U.S. owned industries but also the collectivization of *all* the means of production under state ownership, the eradication of the private sector, and the replacement of the market by a central plan. A fourth option was the one likely anticipated by the majority of Cuba's moderate middle-class. It included a return to pre Batista "business-as-usual" with additional efforts to restore the 1940 constitution and bring honesty to public office, without attempting to significantly alter Cuba's economic base or external dependency (Ritter 1974: 68-70, 226).

As the first years of the Revolution proceeded, the policy orientation of Fidel Castro's government became clearer. Beginning in 1959 with modest and ad-hoc changes to deal with the inheritance from the Batista regime, policy thereafter became steadily more comprehensive and radical, peaking in mid-1960 with the nationalizations of many foreign and domestic properties and with the institution of central planning. Many of these new measures were instituted as part of an escalating confrontation with the United States and there is an as yet unresolved debate over whether Castro's government was pushed toward its radical, state socialist path by U.S. pressure or by Castro's own still hidden ideas, ambitions, and communist agenda (Farber 2011). A summary of the policies and actions is summarized in Table 3.1.

During 1959, hundreds of private businesses were seized under a new ministry set up to recover "ill-gotten gains" from fleeing *Batistianos*. Furthermore, legislation enacted from November 1959 to March 1960 permitted the Ministry of Labor to intervene in enterprises in which production had been disrupted by labor disputes, financial failure, abandonment by their owners, or by request of the labor unions (Ritter 1974: 76). In May 1959, the Revolution's first agrarian reform law was enacted, effectively eliminating large private land holdings and distributing them to small farmers. From June to October of 1960, Cuba's confrontation with the United States took on a dramatic quality, ultimately involving the nationalization of U.S. oil refineries, the suspension of Cuba's sugar quota by the U.S. on June 29, the nationalization of all U.S. properties in Cuba on July 6, and, later on that same day, the cancellation of the remainder of Cuba's 1960 sugar quota in the U.S. market. By the end of October, the regime had taken over all remaining U.S. property, all large foreign enterprises, as well as the property and businesses of many Cubans who had gone into exile (Ritter 1974: 76). Although there was more collectivization still to come in agriculture and retail trade, by early in 1961 the state had nationalized between 80 and 92 percent of the island's enterprises in industry, construction, and transportation. It had also acquired almost complete ownership and control in both wholesale and foreign trade, banking, and education (Mesa-Lago 2000: 347).

The nationalization of large-scale private enterprise was justified by the Cuban government as being both ideologically proper and economically necessary. The abandonment and/or sabotage of property and of key industries by U.S.-sponsored Cuban exiles became the pretext for some subsequent state takeovers. Castro could simultaneously defend the Revolution as a moral cause under attack and also reaffirm his own personal power by making drastic economic changes that would have a direct benefit for "the masses." In time, it was deemed necessary for planning purposes to eliminate as much of the private sector as possible to permit direct governmental controls to be used to run the economy "rationally," without the alleged "chaos" characteristic of market-oriented "capitalist" economies, and without the "exploitation of man by man" (Ritter 1974: 81).

The influence of the Soviet example was undoubtedly significant at this time as well. If Cuba was opting out of the U.S. dominated "capitalist" system, the obvious alternative was the "socialist" system of the Soviet Union. Moreover, the Soviet Union encouraged this geopolitical and economic shift with generous economic assistance and the provision of a sugar market even before the complete cut-off of the U.S. sugar market. Ultimately, Fidel Castro

Table 3.1: Cuba's Major Economic Reforms, 1959–1961

Date	Reform Measure	Specific Objectives
1959		
January	Creation of the "Ministry for the Recovery of Misappropriated Assets"	Confiscation of properties of Batista supporters, including 236 businesses
January–May	Elimination of foreign crime syndicates and prohibition of gambling	The Mafia departs; its properties are seized by the state
March	Urban Reform Law	Reduction of urban rents, to be based on renters' income levels
April	"Vacant Lot Law"; Establishment of the *Instituto de Ahoro y Vivienda* (INAV, Institute of Savings and Housing	Confiscation of unused urban lands; Promotion of housing construction
May	Establishment of the *Instituto Nacional de la Industria Turistica* (INIT, National Institute of Tourism); First Agrarian Reform Law	Promote tourism; Expropriation and redistribution of large estates, including 480,000 acres owned by U.S. interests
June	Establishment of the *Instituto Nacional de Reforma Agraria* (INRA, National Institute of Agrarian Reform)	Implementation of the agrarian reform; preliminary management of the state sector
July	Tax Reform Law	Rationalize tax structure and raise revenues
November	Law permitting Ministry of Labor to expropriate firms involved in labor disputes; "Oil Law," establishment of *Instituto Petrolera de Cuba* (Cuban Oil Institute)	Takeover of 50 enterprises by March 1960; Institution for managing the oil sector
1960		
March	Establishment of the *Junta Central de Planificacinón* (JUCEPLAN, Central Planning Board)	Institution preparatory for more centralized planning
June 29	Nationalization of oil companies	
July–Sept.	Law 851, "Nationalization of U.S. Properties"	Authorizing nationalization of all assets owned by U.S. citizens; Nationalization of all U.S. sugar mills plus telephone and electricity companies; Nationalization of U.S.-owned banks; Nationalization of foreign-owned enterprises

Continues

Date	Reform Measure	Specific Objectives
October	Law 890; Urban Reform Law	Nationalization of many Cuban owned enterprises; Nationalization of non-owner occupied housing and allocation to former renters under favorable terms
1961 January	"The Year of Education" Launch of Literacy Campaign; Expansion and structural change in education	Establishment of universal coverage for primary school; expansion of secondary and university education
June	Law for the Nationalization of Education	Takeover of all education by the state

adopted a radical anti-capitalist and communist position that involved the elimination of private economic activity. The establishment of central control over production and the allocations of resources buttressed central political control and the elimination of independent civil society as well (Castellanos, Henken, and Celaya 2013).

The collectivization begun in 1959 continued with the nationalization of all private schools and hospitals in 1961. In 1962, the rationing of consumer goods was instituted and most of the remaining retail trade stores were collectivized into a state-run network of "people's stores." In December of 1962, Law 1076 was decreed, nationalizing 4,600 Cuban-owned large- and medium-sized commercial enterprises, leaving only family and microenterprises under private ownership. The latter were defined by the government as "those [enterprises] in which all workers are family members or which have only a single worker" (Cabarrouy 2000: 6). In the following year private businesses continued to pass into state hands either because their owners were "absent," because they were linked with the black market, or because they had violated some new revolutionary law (Cabarrouy 2000). Also in 1963, the government enacted its second Agrarian Reform Law, eliminating middle-sized private farms, mandating the sale of all produce to the government at fixed, low prices, and requiring all remaining private farmers to become incorporated into ANAP (National Association of Small Farmers), the state-controlled mass organization for small private farmers (Mesa-Lago 2000: 181-182). Thus, within a five-year period collectivization of private enterprises was nearly total and by the end of 1963, only 30% of agriculture and 25% of retail trade (mostly street vendors) remained in private hands.

The "New Man," the "Revolutionary Offensive," and the "Ten Million Tons," 1963–1970

When the transition to central planning was well advanced and when the revolutionary leadership began to think about how to promote the development of the economy, they were influenced by three strains of thought. These were (1) the traditional criticism of the dependence on sugar production and the economic and social structures it engendered (often referred to as "dependency theory"), (2) the conventional wisdom in Latin America at the time that Cuba should industrialize behind protectionist barriers (called "import substitution industrialization"), and (3) the Soviet development approaches that emphasized state takeover of industry and economic autarchy. There was also uncertainty regarding future sugar prices and markets, notwithstanding the socialist countries' initial pledge to purchase 4.86 million tons per year from 1962 to 1965. A powerful and influential economic policymaker at the time, Che Guevara predicted a 12% annual growth rate from 1962 to 1965 and asserted that Cuba would be the most industrialized country in Latin America by 1965.

These strategies and predictions failed disastrously. The sugar harvest fell from 6.7 million tons in 1961 to 3.8 million tons in 1963, thereby greatly reducing foreign exchange earnings and generating a balance of payments crisis. At the same time, the industrialization program proved unviable, as it was import-intensive and required increased foreign exchange earnings for the purchase of imported machinery and equipment, raw materials, intermediate goods, managerial personnel, and repair and maintenance equipment. The end result was that Cuba became more dependent than ever on its sugar exports, on imported inputs of many kinds, and on a new hegemonic partner, the Soviet Union.

Following this failure, a strategic re-examination took place. If it had been erroneous to de-emphasize the sugar sector and its export earnings before, it was now decided that sugar should become the leading sector, earning the foreign exchange that would fuel future industrial and agricultural diversification. For this reason, Castro adopted the famous "10 million ton" target for the sugar harvest of 1970, up from an actual harvest of 3.3 million in 1963 (Ritter 1974: 167). Cuba's economic strategy had shifted from rejecting sugar dependence as an obstacle to development to embracing it as a partial solution, going from "sucrophobia" back to "sucrophilia."

The second feature of the new economic strategy of the second half of the 1960s was the development of the so-called "New Man" ideology as the principal mechanism for mobilizing human energies for the tasks of the economy spear-headed initially by Che Guevara. "Material incentives" were to be replaced by "moral incentives" so that people would work selflessly for the well-being of the Revolution but receive their income according to their need, not according to the quantity and quality of the work performed. The revolutionary leadership tried to foster this new public morality by reshaping institutions so that material incentives were reduced or eliminated and by ignoring the old structures of material incentives despite Cuba's inflationary situation.

The "New Man" was also supposed to be incubated through political education in schools and public exhortation in speeches and the press, as well as by encouraging and sometimes compelling people to behave as if they already were "New Men" thereby embodying "*conciencia*" (revolutionary consciousness) through a "learning by doing" process. One of the more notorious mechanisms of compulsion were the UMAP work and reeducation camps (*Unidades Militares de Ayuda a la Producción*) where supposedly "anti-social" elements—homosexuals, religious believers, counter-cultural individuals, etc.—were interned against their will between 1965 and 1968. Lastly, following Guevara's ideas as expressed in his influential essay, "Socialism and Man in Cuba," there was an effort to alter the bourgeois consciousness inherited from the Republican period by encouraging popular participation in the Revolution's periodic labor and political mobilizations (such as the 1961 summer Literacy Campaign and the annual sugar harvests), as well as by promoting participation in Cuba's many mass organizations, the Communist Youth League (UJC), and the Communist Party (PCC).

The third feature of Cuba's new economic strategy was institutional in character and crystallized with the "Revolutionary Offensive" in March and April of 1968. This offensive banned self-employment and eliminated or confiscated between 55,000 and 58,000 small private businesses that had remained after the first wave of nationalizations occurred between 1959 and 1963. The range and number nationalized firms included over 17,200 food retailers, 2,500 retailers of industrial products, 11,300 food and drink sellers, 14,000 service enterprises, and 9,600 small-scale industrial production enterprises. Ironically, while justified as a way of ridding the country of its exploitative, capitalist past, many of the enterprises targeted for closure or takeover were in fact founded during the mid-1960s. Small-scale private enterprises had been growing rapidly and earning substantial profits from 1963 to 1968, while filling the vacuum that had been created by the inefficient functioning of the state sector. With their greater degree of initiative and flexibility, these small enterprises produced goods and services that were preferred even by the state sector. The relationship between the private and the state sectors became well developed in this period. For example, a study of 45,548 small entrepreneurs found that 97% had sold merchandise or services valued at up to 10,000 pesos to the state. Indeed, three of them had earned over half-a-million pesos in the first semester in 1967 (Ayala Castro 1982).

President Castro elaborated his rationale for the nationalizations of the "Revolutionary Offensive" at length in his speech of March 13, 1968 (Castro, F. 1968: 2-7). Among the chief factors he mentioned to justify his government's closures and confiscations were:

1. The need to prevent the cultivation of egoistic attitudes that occurred in the private sector;
2. The low levels of support by the private sector owners for the Revolution;[2]
3. The "antisocial elements" that were thought to dominate the clientele for the enterprises;
4. The excessive profits and a need to eliminate excessively high incomes earned in many of the enterprises;
5. The purchases of inputs from illegal sources;
6. The alleged low quality of service to the public; and
7. The supposed unsanitary conditions in private sector enterprises.

In sum, President Castro also saw the Revolutionary Offensive as the necessary next stage in the movement toward Communism, now Cuba's ultimate objective. Only a total elimination of all manifestations of "capitalism" would permit the overcoming of those attitudes and values that accompanied it, allowing the selfless, revolutionary "New Man" to emerge. In Castro's own words:

> We cannot stimulate or permit the pursuit of egoistic attitudes by people and we do not want people to follow the instinct of egotism. [...] Capitalism must be ripped out by its roots. Parasitism must be ripped out by its roots. The exploitation of man must be ripped out by its roots.[3] (Ibid. p. 7)

The "Revolutionary Offensive" eliminated what had remained of Cuba's microenterprise and small-scale enterprise sectors. A wide range of these were confiscated, including foodstuffs, metal-working, chemical products, woodworking, tobacco products, leather-working, printing, and textiles. Many were then converted to state ownership, but many, including street vending, vegetable stands, bars, snack shops, and auto repair, were simply shut down, with their entrepreneurial owners driven underground or altogether out of business. However, an illegal but more-or-less tolerated "informal sector" continued to thrive, as did the "black market."

The adoption of a more extreme vision of socialist society between 1966 and 1970 is often explained as a case of Guevara's ideology overwhelming the more "economistic" approach that was favored by the pro-Soviet "pragmatists." However, what has been called the "radical experiment"—the combined effort to create the "New Man," carry out the "Revolutionary Offensive," and achieve a record "Ten Million Ton" sugar harvest—had complex political roots (Pérez-Stable 1999). First, the failure of Cuba's attempt at central planning and industrialization between 1961 and 1963 persuaded the more radical elements of the leadership that the "effervescence" of the Revolution must be maintained through radicalization. Second, as Castro finally began to consolidate the revolution under the Communist Party in mid-decade[4] there was a feeling that the models borrowed from the Soviets were undermining the true spirit of the Revolution. As a result, the "radical experiment" can be seen in part as an attempt to establish greater economic independence from the Soviets and political unity at home, while at the same time reintroducing *conciencia* into the economy (Pérez-Stable 1999).

With a new Central Committee in place and the Communist Party firmly under the control of the new communists by 1965, Castro had relatively free reign to implement his radical agenda. Though central planning was still theoretically operative under the Central Planning Board (JUCEPLAN), Castro took this opportunity to reinvigorate what he saw as the waning revolutionary spirit of the Revolution. Between 1966 and 1970, centrally planned budgets were often discarded in favor of Castro's own improvised mini-plans (Pérez-Stable 1999). The goal was to harness the self-sacrifice and collective consciousness that had enabled the guerrilla fighters to win the revolution and to defeat the invaders at the Bay of Pigs, by putting them to work in solving more mundane economic challenges. As Guevara had argued, the challenge was "to find the formula to perpetuate in day-to-day life the heroic attitude of the revolutionary struggle" because "in the attitude of our fighters, we could glimpse the man of the future" (Henken 2001: 257).

Essentially, between 1966 and 1970 the central plan itself was ignored and the economy was run as if the country were undertaking a second guerilla war (Mesa-Lago 2000: 209-211). President Castro declared that producing anything less than ten million tons of sugar in 1970 would be tantamount to a "moral defeat" of the revolution (Mesa-Lago 2000: 213). In a 1966 speech Fidel made such intentions clear and foreshadowed the eventual elimination of Cuba's "shopkeepers:"

> We will not create socialist consciousness, much less a communist consciousness, with the mentality of shopkeepers. We will not create a socialist consciousness with a dollar sign in the minds and hearts [...] of our people [...]. We will not reach communism by using the capitalist road. Using capitalist methods no one will ever reach communism. (Pérez-Stable 1999: 113)

President Castro's economic objectives were to be reached by mobilizing human energies through "moral incentives," that is through altruistic self-sacrifice—the "New Man" concept—which was to be created in a process that included political education, the supervised practice of hard labor following the example of the leadership, and working with the support of the Party and the mass organizations. "Voluntary" manual labor in agriculture for 45 days a year became a duty for all true revolutionaries as part of their consciousness training. Furthermore, this same hard work, combined with political education, was also seen as a cure for all types of "antisocial behavior," including homosexuality, laziness, and alternative Western youth culture, exemplified by long hair, blue jeans, and "rock n' roll." In the end, however, such methods tended to exacerbate antisocial and unproductive behaviors such as absenteeism, black market activities, loafing, and a general cynicism and distrust toward the revolution, all of which were the antithetical to *conciencia*.

As it became increasingly apparent, however, that *conciencia* alone was not enough to motivate the Cuban labor force, a process of "militarization" of the labor force was used to fill the void. Conscripts, students, prisoners, declared emigrants, and weekend volunteers were all put to work under quasi-militarized labor arrangements. "*Conciencia* did not inspire people to work for the collective well-being," notes Pérez-Stable. "Instead, [Cubans] chose to swell the ranks of absenteeism, waste the working day, and start their own small businesses" (1999: 118-119). In fact, Pérez-Stable indicates that absenteeism had become so rampant that it amounted to an uncoordinated strike and an informal protest against the state's mobilization methods. Essentially, the state continued to focus on fulfilling national production goals and priorities, Cuba's workers used their own "weapons of the weak" and remained primarily concerned about their individual needs, their family priorities, and their private consumption levels (Scott 1985).

In the end, this radical experiment failed in part because human nature was not as malleable as the leadership had believed. Cubans had to continue to be materially self-interested in order to maintain the "capital stock" embodied in themselves and their family members. The revolutionary fervor that energized the populace during the guerrilla struggle and the Bay of Pigs episode was not likely to continue as a motivating factor on a day-to-day basis. The failure to achieve economic independence, to create the "New Man," and to reach the ten-million ton goal originated in the government's belief that self-interest could and indeed should be completely eliminated (Ritter 1974). Certainly self-interest must be re-channeled to obtain voluntary cooperation among individuals. But any system of labor mobilization that completely ignores individual self-interest does so only at its own peril. Ironically, the best summation of the misguided 1964-1970 experience came from President Castro himself when he stated in his major 26th of July speech in 1970

> We have cost the people too much in our process of learning. [...] The learning process of Revolutionaries in the field of economic construction is more difficult than we had imagined. (Castro, F. 1970b)

Return to Soviet-style Orthodoxy: The "Golden Age" of Cuban Socialism, 1971–1985

The problems encountered with the economic approaches of the 1960s led to a reconsideration of Cuba's economic realities and development alternatives.

In view of the government's economic policy failures during the 1960s, the obvious course of action was to adopt wholeheartedly the tried and true approaches of the Soviet Union and its Eastern European satellites and to find a comfortable home within the economic system of the Soviet Bloc. The central feature of Cuba's economic destiny after 1970 therefore became its special relationship with the Soviet Union. Cuba joined the Council for Mutual Economic Assistance (CMEA, also referred to as CAME and Comecon) in 1972. A variety of trade, finance, and development aid agreements were reached covering the 1970 to 1990 period. Cuba's development became deeply intertwined with—even dependent on—that of the Soviet Bloc. The generosity of these agreements towards Cuba was impressive, as illustrated in Figure 3.1. Soviet assistance was disguised mainly in the form of above market prices for Cuban exports to the USSR and below market prices for Cuban imports of Soviet petroleum, together with trade credits from the Soviet Union that were never to be repaid. This assistance rose to extremely high levels in the early 1980s, reaching over 36% of Cuba's *Ingreso Nacional Creado* (a quasi-GDP measure) by 1982 (Ritter 1990: 126). The pay-off for this generous Soviet subsidization was Cuba's geopolitical support for the Soviet superpower in international relations including its military interventions in Africa.

Cuba's integration into the economic cooperation agreements with the Soviet Union required that the planning system become harmonized with the

Figure 3.1: Economic Assistance from the Soviet Union to Cuba, 1960–1990 (billions of U.S. dollars)

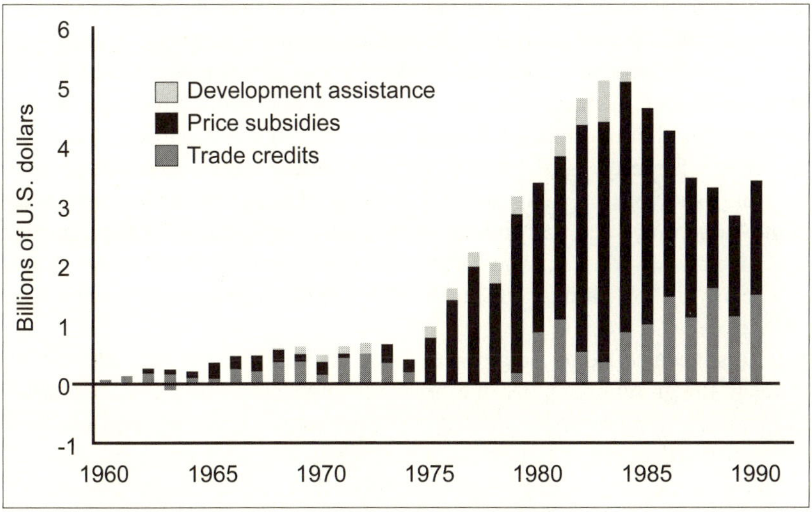

Source: Based on LeoGrande and Thomas 2002: 340–341.

Soviet system and planning cycle. Thus, at this time, a more market-oriented planning mechanism called the *Sistema de dirección y planificación de la economia* (System of Economic Direction and Planning, hereafter SDPE) was adopted. Although the new SDPE was introduced in 1976, by 1980 it had only been partly established. Included in the SDPE was an aspiration for self-financing by enterprises and a rational structuring of prices for inputs and outputs. It also granted greater relative autonomy to many state enterprises, eliminated voluntary labor, and allowed for the reintroduction of wage scales, work quotas, and material incentives within the state sector in order to stimulate production (Pérez-López 1995a).

Economistic labor and remuneration practices were brought back into the internal economy. Workers were to be paid according to the quality and quantity of work done and goods were allocated on the basis of labor productivity. As indicated by the 1971 Anti-Loafing Law, work came to be understood not simply as a "sacred right," but as a "social duty" and revolutionary obligation (Ritter 1974: 333). Furthermore, in this period, a large underground economy emerged consisting of self-employed persons who often worked with the assistance of friends and family members (León 1995).[5]

In the summer of 1978, the revolutionary government reversed its restrictive policy on private enterprise by approving Decree-Law #14, which permitted some 48 categories of self-employment (Pérez-López 1995a). Coming ten years after the collectivization of all private retail trade, this new law amounted to a legalization of parts of the underground economy. It was aimed at absorbing unemployment, improving the supply and quality of goods and services, and shrinking the size of the black market. Specifically, the new law allowed Cubans to engage in activities for private gain in the areas of services and handicrafts (small hand-made manufactures and goods sold in craft markets). The subsequent opening of private handicraft markets allowed for the legal production of many practical goods, such as utensils, brooms, clothing, and toys that the state sector had been unable to provide in sufficient numbers or quality. Three types of small-scale manufacture were especially popular: tailoring, shoemaking, and charcoal making. These microenterprises were home-based and often part-time activities. It is likely that a large proportion were operated by women, whose participation rate in the formal economy was still relatively low throughout much of this period (Pérez-López 1995a: 91-94).

This law also led to the growth of markets where artisans could sell their wares to the growing number of tourists visiting Cuba at this time. A monthly licensing fee ranging from 5 to 80 pesos per month was instituted for these self-employed artisans (ibid: 95). The number of officially registered non-agricultural microenterprises of this sort was placed in 1988 at 28,000 with 12,800 employees (Mesa-Lago 1988). It is impossible to know how large the underground economy was during these years. Various unrecognized and unregistered activities undoubtedly were carried out alongside the registered ones, eluding taxes and state regulations.

Although artisans were allowed to sell their products at free-market prices, they were also required to hold a full-time state-sector job elsewhere. They could engage in their private activity only after hours; they were prohibited from hiring any employees outside of unpaid family help; and they had to use only basic tools and were forced to manufacture their products in their own homes. Furthermore, while those who produced arts and crafts were allowed to retail their products in art markets such as the famous one in Cathedral Square in Old Havana, other small-scale manufacturers were not allowed to sell their products directly to consumers but instead had to use state stores as their official retailers.

Another problem encountered by the artisans was a lack of legal sources of raw materials with which to make their products. The scarcity of such materials was due to the fact that the state stores had first priority in allocations, often leading private artisans to rely on "irregular" sources of inputs (i.e. theft).[6] This link to the black market then helped to justify the governmental criticisms against these entrepreneurs and to validate their eventual elimination in the mid-1980s. Finally, the success of these small-scale artisans at providing basic niche goods to the Cuban public in an antagonistic legal environment reflected badly on the supposedly all-powerful state's inability to provide similar goods. Ironically, it was the very success of the private sector in outperforming parts of the state's manufacturing sector that helped bring about its eventual demise (Pérez-López 1995a: 91-93).

Among the 48 designated occupations legalized by Decree-Law #14 were a number of needed services including hairdressers, tailors, taxi drivers, photographers, plumbers, electricians, carpenters, and mechanics (Mesa-Lago 2000: 230). The law even permitted certain professionals including physicians, dentists, and architects to become self-employed with the important stipulation that they had to have been in private practice prior to 1959 (i.e., they were not trained by the Revolution) (Pérez-López 1995a: 95-96). Like artisans, these self-employed service providers were required to remain employed elsewhere in a state job, to work alone or only with unpaid family help, to have the proper qualifications and training to perform the indicated service, register with the government, and to pay the same monthly fee (*patente*) of between 5 and 80 pesos that other *cuentapropistas* paid, as well as income taxes if their monthly income exceeded 250 pesos. Furthermore, these CPs were required to obtain a certificate from their work center attesting to a history of "proper conduct, diligence, and work discipline" (Pérez-López 1995a: 93-96).

As a result of the chronic inefficiencies that plagued the state sector, the new law even included provisions for a new system of free labor hiring so that state enterprises could contract self-employed workers to perform needed tasks. This system allowed these state enterprises to provide private artisans and self-employed workers with the necessary inputs in exchange for 30 percent of their profits. Legal advertisements in Cuban trade publications appeared during these years publicizing the need for certain private contract workers (Mesa-Lago 1988; 2000: 230; Pérez-López 1995a: 93).

Despite this relative opening to the private sector, the government's efforts at legalization were constrained by its own repeated criticisms in the early 1980s of what it considered to be a "prostitution of the self-employment concept" (Mesa-Lago 2000: 230). High taxes, the crackdown on self-employment in 1982, and criticisms that lumped legal operators together with illegal profiteers sent confusing signals to potential entrepreneurs, thus dampening incentives and contradicting the goal of providing more goods and services of a higher quality to the population. The amount of criticism leveled against self-employment at this time is surprising given that in 1979 self-employed workers made up only 0.8 percent of the Cuban labor force (Mesa-Lago 1988: 78-81).[7]

Dovetailing with the legalization of self-employment, the most important reform measure aimed at the private sector during this time was the opening of "free" peasant markets or *Mercados Libres de Campesinos* (MLCs), free being a reference to the freely set prices in the markets and their produce, which came from private farmers. The passage of Decree-Law #66 on April 5, 1980 permitted the introduction of MLCs on the Cuban agricultural landscape. Allowing direct private sales of foodstuffs to consumers at market-determined prices was not an obvious choice for Cuba, given Castro's aversion to even modest amounts of private enterprise (Rosenberg 1992). Though both the legalization of self-employment and of the MLCs were carried out with Castro's approval, these reforms never had his active support and continued to be viewed as anachronistic and somewhat illegitimate despite their legality.

The new law allowed all private agricultural producers (private farmers and members of agricultural cooperatives) to set up retail agricultural markets throughout the island. Products like sugar, tobacco, coffee, and beef—which were thought to be vital in the state sector—were prohibited from these markets. Private farmers were required to first meet their *acopio* quota obligations to the state before being allowed to sell their surplus in these free markets. Finally, farmers were restricted to their local markets and prohibited from using intermediaries or hiring non-state trucks to transport their produce (Rosenberg 1992; Pérez-López 1995a).

While political motivations were predominant in the initial opening of the MLCs, according to Rosenberg (1992), their legalization was also a response to the dual problem of a domestic food crisis and the gradual rise of an underground food market in the late 1970s. In short, the decline of the availability of many foodstuffs between 1975 and 1980 provoked the development of an extensive network of black market food sources and led to an excess in monetary liquidity where consumers had more money than available goods on which to spend it.

The state first tried to tackle these problems by setting up "parallel (food) markets," new cooperatives in agriculture (CPAs), and stores selling non-rationed goods at high prices (often facetiously referred to at the time as "*las tiendas de los ricos*" or "stores of the rich") during the 1970s (Pérez-López 1995a; Rosenberg 1992). However, these strategies were unable to do away with the black market. Finally, between 1978 and 1979 the Cuban police began to crack down on the underground food market, arresting intermediaries, transporters, and even confiscating a number of private farms. This method of control did little to solve the root problem of food scarcity and led to a further contraction in the availability of foodstuffs. Thus, the opening of the MLCs in 1980 was enacted in part as recognition of and an attempt to regulate already existing underground activities (Eckstein 1994: 54).

Unfortunately for the future of the MLCs, their existence was fraught with a number of economic problems and political tensions. At the outset, the decision to open them was popular because the quantity, quality, and variety of foodstuffs expanded. However, common complaints included the sale of foods illegally diverted from state supplies, the use of middlemen and of illegal transport, and most important, the high prices common in the MLCs (Pérez-López 1995a). When expectations that the introduction of the markets would operate so as to reduce the high prices of foodstuffs on the black market were not fulfilled, government ambivalence toward the markets found growing support among the populace, especially with the many Cubans whose meager incomes severely restricted their access to them (Marshall 1998). The growth in income and consumption inequality that resulted from these private markets made them an easy target for popular frustration and governmental "scapegoating" (Marshall 1998). Consumers were more concerned with high prices than they were with continued illegality. However, the fact that the existence of the MLCs had not eliminated either high prices or the black market, undercut the position of those state elites who had originally advocated an opening of the small-scale private sector.

In 1982, there was an outpouring of government criticism of abuses in both the service and agricultural sectors together with an enactment of a number of new laws that placed more onerous restrictions on private activity. Private entrepreneurs were accused of using state stores as sales points for their own products, of secretly and illegally setting up their own shops, of diverting raw materials from the state sector, of hiring employees and middlemen, of selling goods for which they had no authorization and in places which were prohibited, and of making exorbitant profits (Mesa-Lago 1988: 78-81). As a result, raids were carried out against many workers in the MLCs, and in 1982, middlemen and some 250 self-employed workers were arrested and their allegedly illegal earnings were confiscated.

Decree-Law #106, passed in September 1982, excluded intermediaries from farmers' markets, revoking the right for workers on state farms to grow food on their family plots, and restricting participation in the MLCs to private farmers associated with ANAP. Furthermore, farmers were required to demonstrate the fulfillment of their obligations to supply the state before they would be allowed to market their goods, a 20 percent tax was levied on gross sales in the MLCs, and state-run "agricultural fairs" with competitive prices were introduced to further undercut the MLCs. These changes effectively spelled the end of the MLCs since after 1982 they did not account for more than 4 percent of total foodstuff consumer expenditures (Pérez-López 1995a; Marshall 1998).

The "Rectification Process," 1986–1989

President Castro first announced the "Rectification Process" (RP) at the Third Party Congress of the Communist Party in April of 1986. The RP was intended to "rectify the errors and negative tendencies" that Castro thought had occurred over the previous 15 years. The private sector received its *coup de grâce* with the shutdown of the farmers' markets and a tightening of restrictions on self-employment, which thereafter declined from 1.2% of total employment to 0.7% by 1989 (see Table 3.2).

The government abolished the free agricultural markets and accelerated the incorporation of small private farms into state cooperatives. It eliminated the activities of the small manufacturers, truck owners, and street vendors, and reduced independent employment. Furthermore, it restricted the construction, sale, rent, and inheritance of private residences. It was argued that farmers were making excessive profits from selling in the free markets, that they had

Table 3.2: Percentage Distribution of Cuba's Labor Force by Institutional Forms, 1970–1989

	1970	1979	1981	1985	1989
State Sector	86.3	93.6	93.4	93.1	94.1
Non-state	13.7	6.4	6.6	6.9	5.9
Agricultural Coops	0	0	0	2.1	1.6
Private Farmers	11.0	4.9	3.5	3.3	3.2
Private Salaries	1.5	0.4	0.7	0.4	0.4
Self-employed and Family Workers	1.2	1.1	1.5	1.2	0.7
Total	100	100	100	100	100

Source: Mesa-Lago 2000: 382.

resisted integration into cooperatives, that very of them few paid taxes, and that only some of them delivered the proper portion of their crops to the state. Private agricultural producers were also accused of having abandoned all-important sugar production in order to pursue the higher profits available by producing foods for sale in the MLCs.

Three lessons can be drawn from this first, short-lived experiment with private enterprise. First, the government's legalization of market production and exchange stimulated productivity and improved the quality and variety of goods and services. Second, the existence of these "islands of capitalism" within the larger socialist Cuban economy, led to increased inequality. Third, important shifts within elite coalitions of pro- and anti-market advocates led initially to the opening of the farmers' markets and later to their eradication. In fact, these policy shifts are prime examples of the state being torn between the competing claims of ideological legitimacy, political power, and economic growth. The next brief period of economic policy implementation would confirm the leadership's demonstrated desire to return to the radical experiments of the past when economics took a backseat to ideology, in the continuing efforts to centralize political control.

After 1986, attempts were made to modify the Soviet-type planning system with a less constraining "Economic Development System" (replacing the supposedly more cumbersome and bureaucratic SDPE) that would allow Castro more flexibility to intervene and alter the economy as he saw fit. These attempts were in varying stages of implementation by 1990 but they were not particularly successful in improving the planning system. In any case, after 1989, the termination of Cuba's special relationship with the Soviet Union and the end to Soviet subsidies plunged the country into a deep recession giving the new planning arrangements little chance to prove themselves.

The basic development strategy continued to emphasize sugar as the main source of foreign exchange earnings and good harvests continued to be achieved throughout this period. A major push was made into biotechnology and pharmaceuticals for both domestic consumption and export with a massive investment in state-of-the-art research facilities. Priority also was given to tourism and to nickel-mining for expanded foreign exchange earnings. A "Food Program" was begun in 1986, aiming at sugar harvests of 11 million tons as well as increased citrus fruit for export and increased production of foodstuffs for domestic use. Similar grandiose but unrealistic targets were set for irrigated acreage for rice and sugar, new cattle development centers, new dairies, etc.—all objectives that remained unfulfilled (Mesa-Lago 2000: 272-274). Work-place corruption and theft were also targeted by the government but with limited success, partly because the economic stagnation after 1985 operated against such an attempt.

The labor sector continued to be problematic during the RP. Castro once again emphasized the importance of moral incentives and criticized material incentives. Military-style brigades were established for the construction sector—and given special material compensation—as a means of absorbing the surplus labor in enterprises. Part of the problem was that to avoid rising unemployment, large numbers of low-productivity jobs had been created to absorb the large cohorts of young people from the baby boom years of 1960-1968 who were entering the job-market at this time.

The RP's increased emphasis on egalitarianism and the elimination of private supply networks (except for the ever-enduring black market) required an expansion of rationing (Mesa-Lago 2000: 264). As a result of the sociopolitical pressures associated with the RP, self-employment declined from an already miniscule 1.2 percent in 1985, to 0.9 percent in 1987, bottoming out at just 0.7 percent of the workforce in 1989 (Mesa-Lago 1990; 2000: 264). In the mid-1980s, the state admitted that a reason for the spread of the "second economy" was the fact that it was often the only source of many essential goods and services. Nevertheless, the government insisted that greater control and vigilance against such "anti-social" behaviors was the best solution and promised to increase state supplies to fill this gap.

Writing at the time the RP was being instituted in Cuba, Mesa-Lago expressed doubts about its potential success given the state sector's history of inefficiency and low productivity. He warned that the "severe attacks against private farmers, peasant markets, the self-employed, small independent manufactures and private house builders" would mean that state agencies notorious for their inability to provide quality goods and services would be unable to fill this gap. "Cuban socialist history teaches us," he argued, referring to the country's failed past experiments with radical ideology, "that when incentives to private farmers were cut by the state, the farmers' efforts and output were reduced." However, pointing to successful market experiments of the early 1980s, he contended that "when material incentives were added, their production increased" (1988: 84).

In fact, like the radical experiment that it resembled, the RP's overall performance was negative for the Cuban economy. Of course, its poor performance was exacerbated by the fact that it was attempted on the eve of what would prove to be the worst economic crisis faced by the Revolution. The depths reached by the 1990s crisis were primarily due to the collapse of the Soviet Union and the repercussions it had for an over-dependent Cuba through its loss of the generous though hidden financial support the USSR provided. However, the RP's ideological approach to economic problem-solving likely exacerbated the proliferation of the economic "crimes" that it was supposedly designed to eradicate. Moral and ideological exhortations (preaching, often combined with policing and punishment) are weak tools with which to motivate workers in a context of growing scarcity. Furthermore, such scarcity makes for a fertile ground for widespread illegalities, corruption, and the growth of the black market.

As with previous periods of retrenchment, the RP arose from competing political, economic, and ideological motivations. Most observers agree that the state's actions during the late 1980s can be explained by its continued desire to maintain political power and control, and to preserve Cuban socialism amidst the fundamental reforms taking place in the wider socialist world beyond. There is less unanimity regarding the relative weight of ideological and economic factors within the RP. Some analysts such as Zimbalist and Eckstein (1987) argued that Castro's ideological justifications for the RP were merely a pretext masking deeper economic exigencies; therefore they do give credit to Castro's public declarations regarding the ideological origin of the RP. Thus, for them the seemingly contradictory (and mostly unsuccessful) policies included in the RP, such as eliminating the internal private sector while simultaneously courting external private investment and tourism can be linked to underlying economic goals.

Others have argued that ideological factors were the decisive, though not the exclusive, cause behind the RP (Pérez-López 1995a; Mesa-Lago 1988; 2000). For example, Mesa-Lago persuasively argued that when times have been difficult, the Cuban leadership has been forced to prioritize rational, pragmatic economic policies over its preferred radical, ideologically motivated experimentation. Only in times of relative economic success could the leadership afford to act as economic ideologues (Mesa-Lago 1988: 83). Thus, the economic history of revolutionary Cuba has consisted of pendular swings between periods of relative pragmatism that adapted to the pressures of the market and allowed space for entrepreneurial experimentation (1961-1965, 1971-1985, 1990-1995, and again following Raúl Castro's ascension to power after 2006), and surges of ideology that aimed at achieving a more egalitarian distribution of goods, asserted centralized economic control, and targeted entrepreneurs as illegitimate exploiters (1966-70, 1986-89, and 1996-2005).

Developmental Consequences of the Suppression of Small Enterprise

There have been a variety of negative impacts resulting from the elimination of small and microenterprise starting in the 1960s. The state was unable to replace many of the activities that were nationalized and therefore they either ceased to exist or went underground, reducing the supply of goods and services, driving up prices, fueling the black market, and undermining respect for the law. The results were greater general inefficiencies, reduced quantity and quality of many goods and services, a reduced living standard for many citizens, and a forcing of economic activities into the underground economy.

For many types of small-scale producers of goods and services, entrepreneurs brought together inputs from informal supply networks and thereby provided goods and/or services in reasonable and competitive quality and price and in locations convenient for buyers (as discussed in Chapter 2). These entrepreneurs could not be replaced by bureaucratic structures in any reasonable way. In many cases, they had operated without formal accounts or statements of input sourcing or output marketing (e.g. street venders and handicraft producers). The state did not appear interested in ensuring full replacement of these activities by public enterprises and in any case would have had great difficulty doing so.

While this governmental action was justified partly with the aim of improving overall quality of services, the services eliminated were usually just lost for good. For example, of the roughly 56,000 stores and businesses that were shut down in 1968, only an estimated two-thirds continued operation under new state management—with the former owner occasionally allowed to stay on as a state employee (Pérez-López 1995a: 44). Furthermore, the elimination of some 3,700 street vendors in urban areas had the unfortunate effect of destroying informal systems that gathered food inputs from various sources, combined them, and sold them to clients in accessible and convenient locations. Such street vendors did not keep formal records or written accounts, nor did they spell out how, when, where, and from whom they purchased all the inputs that they acquired. The state could not have replaced these activities even if it had tried. The costs of acquiring the relevant information, of planning and of monitoring a replacement system would have been prohibitively high. Consequently, a valuable niche component of the economy was destroyed. Moreover, a greater burden was placed on the state stores and restaurants, and as a result, queues at stores and restaurants lengthened even further. The provisioning of food to citizens in urban areas deteriorated substantially and the result was first, a reduction in people's material levels of living, and second, increased absenteeism from work as they spent more and more time attempting to find food.

This cause and effect dynamic was undoubtedly multiplied many times over in other areas of the economy. Even where the state took over a small enterprise and tried to operate it within the state sector of the economy, it is unlikely that the performance of the state enterprise would have been effective. The nationalizations of the "Revolutionary Offensive" converted the former entrepreneurs in the "intervened" enterprises into employees. Rather than being self-activating and committed to the careful functioning of their enterprises, the state managers were simply employees, fulfilling orders from above. A range of problems intensified, including the ones involving "soft budget constraints" (the negligible price of labor feeding over-employment and inefficiency), weak management, disregard for the interests of purchasers, declining quality of goods and services, general coordination problems within the planning system, and worsening rigidities and sluggishness in responding to consumer demand and changing circumstances, as analyzed in depth elsewhere (Ritter 1974; Mesa-Lago 2000). The overall result of these problems was a downward pressure on real living standards, even as other factors such as improved education and health were benefitting them.

In contrast to the rest of Latin America where the streets are alive with commercial activity, the streets of the major cities of Cuba became commercially dead. Some non-agricultural private sector activity did continue legally after 1968, but as Table 3.2 above indicates, employment in this sector declined steadily to only 1.1% of the total by 1989. Ironically, it has since been shown that the elimination of some of these diverse, niche operations hurt the government sector as much as it did private entrepreneurs because the state had been one of the private sector's primary customers, especially in the industrial goods and services sector (Mesa-Lago 2000).

An additional consequence of the blockage of self-employment is the movement of many such enterprises into the underground economy, as will be discussed in Chapter 7. Indeed, many varieties of enterprise have been able to operate illicitly. As a result, the state loses potential sources of tax revenues. Moreover, various governmental regulations cannot be applied and a culture of illegality is promoted, making the shift of such activities above ground into legality more difficult. Clandestine operation is also contagious because such enterprises must obtain their inputs and sell their outputs clandestinely as well. This means that underground enterprises depend on illicit inputs, which consist in large part of items stolen from the state sector. To rebuild a culture of compliance and respect for public policy rather than avoidance and illegality is not easy.

An additional—as well as paradoxical and counter-intuitive—feature of Cuba's central planning system is that it inadvertently began to promote entrepreneurial behavior and attitudes in a large proportion of the population beginning with its initial installation in 1961. The most important single cause of this process was the rationing system, which was first implemented in 1961. This system was designed to provide everyone with a basic supply of foodstuffs, clothing, and household consumables in order to achieve a basic level of equality of consumption and real income. It replaced the market mechanism and individual or family choice with a rationed allotment of basic goods available at low prices relative to the average monthly income. This system provided every individual (or household for some products) with fixed monthly quotas of foodstuffs, toiletries, cigarettes, alcoholic beverages, and household consumables and with annual quotas for clothing and footwear.

Everyone received the same allocations of products at the controlled and generally low prices with the exception of children and those with special health problems such as diabetics, who received special food rations. Because everyone was provided with essentially the same rations, many people would receive some items that they did not want or which they did not need as much as other items. In the context of Cuba's generalized shortage and excess demand (which had existed with varying intensity since 1962, although it worsened after 1989), everyone had an incentive to sell those rationed items that they did not want or need, or to trade them for other products that they needed more urgently. For example, non-smokers would purchase their allotment of cigarettes and cigars through the rationing system but they would then give them to other family members or friends, resell them in unofficial markets, or trade them for other products. Thus, the rationing system itself converted virtually everyone, regardless of their levels of ideological enthusiasm, into mini-capitalists who were searching for opportunities to sell and to buy.[8]

The situation of excess demand and generalized shortage also meant that anyone with privileged access to a product at an official price could resell it at a higher free-market price or in the dollar economy. This meant that there was a strong incentive for "rent-seeking," or making a profit from buying and selling or exchanging many types of product between the fixed-price official sources and the unofficial or "black market" determined price. For example, a retiree vending the newspaper *Granma* to a tourist would have purchased it in the peso economy (where \$US 1 = 1 Cuban Peso) and resold it in the dollar economy (where \$US 1 = 22 CUPs in May 1997) thereby earning a "rent" or profit of around 95%. Indeed, everything available at official rationing prices could be resold for a higher market determined price.

Related to the above phenomenon was what quickly came to be known as *amiguismo* or *socio-lismo*, that is "friend-ism" or "partner-ism." These terms refer to the reciprocal exchange of favors by individuals. While such reciprocity probably occurs in all countries and in many different contexts, it has developed several additional important forms in Cuba. The form in which this expresses itself almost everywhere involves a process by which individuals in bureaucracies, in traditional village-level societies, or in modern market economies are pleasant with each other, providing gifts of goods, services and/or information in hopes of receiving reciprocal favorable treatment at some future date. This may be done either for direct personal benefit or to facilitate the achievement of work-related objectives.

In the Cuban case, however, this widespread practice developed new forms of expression. Basically any person with control over resources could exchange access to those resources for some current or future personal material benefit. This might involve a shoe store clerk reserving a pair of shoes at the low official price for a friend who could provide the clerk with reciprocal access to another product in the future. Or it could involve the exchange of an item or cash (a bribe) for access to some scarce product. In Cuba, developing friends or associates in this way quickly became vital during the 1960s for assuring access to the goods and services necessary for basic material well-being for oneself and one's family. Complex networks of reciprocal obligations therefore have become an important part of the functioning of the economy. Daily life involves continuing endeavors to develop, to extend, and to maintain the personal relationships necessary to ensure access to essential goods and services through the unofficial channels or through the official channels unofficially. This phenomenon occurred throughout the 1990s and the 2000s, and will likely continue for as long as the dual economy continues, with rationed goods sold at exceedingly low prices while excess monetary demand pushes black market prices up to large multiples of the rationed goods prices, and the dollar store prices also continue to be exceedingly high.

In summary, Cuban citizens either individually or in a family context, have had to behave much like entrepreneurs in their everyday material lives. They have been forced by circumstance, and using the lexicography of the 1990s and 2000s, to *resolver* (to "resolve" problems) and do whatever is necessary to achieve a specific survival need, to *inventar*, or to "invent" a solution to problem of survival, to *forrajear*, or to "forage" or "graze" in constant search for scarce goods and services,[9] and to *luchar*, or to "struggle" for survival by running an underground enterprise, exchanging pilfered products, evading taxes, or dodging regulations. In effect, they have used and strengthened their entrepreneurial skills to explore and evaluate new economic opportunities, to acquire the consumer goods that they and their families need, and to sell some other consumer goods or services that they need less. These phenomena are analyzed insightfully by Amelia Weinraub (2004) specifically in the context of the mid-2000s. However, they became widespread from almost the beginning of the Revolution.

A second area where entrepreneurial action has been necessary is ironically within the central planning system itself. In a perfectly functioning planning system, enterprise managers would have little to do besides obeying and implementing orders. However, because the planning system could not and cannot work perfectly, enterprise managers must sometimes take personal initiative in resolving unforeseen problems. Frequently, solutions to such problems are found only outside the normal channels of the planning system and require improvised responses by the enterprise managers. This type of improvisation also involves enterprise managers obtaining the required inputs through negotiations horizontally with other enterprises, vertically with superior officials, and/or diagonally with superiors or inferiors in other sectors or ministries. Political argumentation, political or Party *amiguismo* or *sociolismo* (i.e. the exchange of favors within the Party for political and material benefit) as well as economic criteria are central components of negotiating processes. Economic management has therefore been a highly political, even entrepreneurial process. Indeed, managers throughout Cuban society, including those in education and health as well as the economy, must invest large amounts of time and energy in resolving such input-supply problems.

In the Soviet system, a specific type of professional—the *tolkachi* or "fixer"—emerged to improvise solutions to such input-supply problems. In the Cuban case, however, enterprise managers (or officials who were responsible for the functioning of enterprises or units such as schools, hospitals, research institutes, or government operations) found it necessary to obtain necessary inputs, especially for their workers. Of particular importance in Cuba in the mid-1990s were enterprise officials with the label *Jefe de Servicios* or Chief of Services. These officials were responsible for the provision of meals, work clothes, gasoline, maintenance, vehicular parts, and goods and services in general for the workers. In the environment of scarcity during the 1990s these *Jefes de Servicios* played an important input-completing and gap-filling role, locating and arranging for the supply of inputs to the labor force, sometimes in exchange for services provided by the enterprise in question; many of the same qualities we identify as eminently entrepreneurial at the opening of Chapter 2.

Thus, as a result of the unavoidable imperfections of the planning system and in particular when unusually intense forms economic turbulence are occurring, with major disruptions in the flow of supplies, state sector managers must behave in entrepreneurial ways in order to improvise solutions to problems and to try to maintain levels of production. For this reason, the planning system itself, especially during periods of economic turmoil, can ironically promote some types of entrepreneurship—by default if not by design.

Notes

[1] Appendix 1 provides a detailed chronology of the Revolutionary government's shifting public policies toward small private enterprise.

[2] One report covering various Havana municipalities concluded that 66% of the customers of the remaining bars in those areas and 72% of bar owners were "antisocial and amoral" counter-revolutionaries. Cuban sociologist Haroldo Dilla notes that the research upon which this report was based – visits to 6,452 private businesses and 955 bars – was carried out by Communist Party members and Committee for the Defense of the Revolution heads clearly indicating that "the findings were constructed according to the conclusions that were needed to legitimize the operation" (Dilla Alfonso 2012; Domínguez Cuadriello 2008).

[3] In Spanish: "Nosotros no podemos estimular ni permitir siquiera actitudes egoistas en los hombres si no queremos que los hombres sigan an instinto del egoismo. [...] ...el capitalismo hay que arrancarlo de raiz, el parisitismo hay que arrancarlo de raiz, la explotacion del hombre hay que arrancarla de raiz."

[4] Before the refounding of a new Cuban Communist Party (PCC) under Fidel Castro's direct control in 1965, the Revolutionary government had already formed and disbanded two "unified" political party organizations between 1959 and 1964. These were, first, the Integrated Revolutionary Organizations (ORI, which combined the remnants of the old Popular Socialist Party, the July 26th Movement, and the Revolutionary Directorate) and then – after the Revolution took on a publicly socialist nature – the Unified Party of the Socialist Revolution (PURS).

[5] With success in underground microenterprise and the black market often determined by one's special relationships with family and friends, Cubans took to referring this alternate but often essential system of exchange as *socio-lismo*, the word *socio*

meaning a close friend or business associate. Much like the Soviet system of informal exchange or "economy of favors" known as *blat*, Cuban *sociolismo* was a mocking reinvention of the state's celebrated *socialismo* (socialism). For a discussion of *sociolismo* see León (1995) and of Soviet *blat* see Rehn and Taalas (2004).

[6] Cuban entrepreneurs colloquially refer to this practice as relying on their close "*socio*" (friend) "*Roberto*" for supplies, *Roberto* being a mocking if coded reference to "*robo*" or robbery.

[7] A total of 6.4% of the labor force worked in the private sector at the time, with private farmers making up the bulk at 4.9% (Mesa-Lago 1988).

[8] One of the authors was in the home of a high ranking and totally-committed government official one Saturday morning in 1995 when the *colero* (queue holder) or purchaser of the family's supplies from the rationed state sector market arrived with provisions. Among the products delivered were the full quotas of cigarettes and cigars for all the family members – none of whom smoked. They were destined for resale unofficially with the proceeds to be used for other needed products. Some of the cigars were kindly offered to the author present, who graciously accepted.

[9] Like their counterparts in the countries of Eastern Europe before the fall of the socialist bloc in 1989, many Cuban citizens would usually carry a *jaba* or bag of some sort with them throughout the day so that when they incidentally came upon a particularly scarce item for sale, they would be able to purchase it immediately.

4
The "Special Period," 1990–2006

When the Soviet Union ended its generous subsidy to the Cuban economy starting in 1989, Cuba slid inexorably into a deep economic crisis, with its economy shrinking almost 35% between 1989 and 1993. Cuba's foreign exchange earnings collapsed when the Soviet Union moved to world market prices in its trade with the island and ceased to finance Cuba's bilateral trade deficits. The crisis was exacerbated further when the markets for Cuban exports within the Soviet Bloc shrank due to the latter's transition-induced recession and to the ending of Cuba's special trading relationships with the other countries of Eastern Europe. The whole of Cuba's economy and society were deeply impacted by these new economic circumstances. In the face of this new situation, Castro announced a new phase of Cuba's historical trajectory in 1990, leaving behind the 1986-1989 "Rectification Process" and entering the newly-labeled "Special Period in Times of Peace."

The "Special Period" (SP) passed through three phases between 1990 and 2006. The first phase, from its initial declaration in August 1990 until the announcement of new economic reforms almost three years later on July 26, 1993, aimed to achieve an economic recovery by encouraging foreign investment, an expansion of the tourist sector, and export diversification. At the same time, Cuban citizens were both exhorted and required by circumstance to make greater personal sacrifices. In fact, the very name chosen for this new era, "Special Period in Times of Peace," indicated that to ensure survival the island would be placed on a special war footing even if they were technically still living in "times of peace." Emergency measures were implemented to reduce petroleum imports so that the economy could continue to function without significant change to its internal economic institutions and policies.

When these initial 1990 to 1993 adjustments failed to halt the decline and to generate an economic recovery, the government commenced a more fundamental process of restructuring Cuba's internal economy. This second phase of the SP began with Castro's July 26, 1993 announcement of internal economic reforms, including the acceptance of the U.S. dollar as a legal currency in the domestic economy and an expansion of the internal private sector in certain areas of agriculture (cooperative farming units and retail farmer's markets) and self-employment. These economic reforms were intended to decriminalize many of the activities that citizens had been resorting to in order to survive. However, these reforms were enacted in a reluctant, piecemeal fashion, neither integrated into a cohesive economic development plan nor aimed at any eventual market transition.

The third phase of the SP began around mid-1996, when the 1993-1995 reforms seemed to have halted the economic freefall of 1989-1993. As had been the case following earlier reform periods, further and deeper reforms were deemed unnecessary and those already in place were gradually scaled back. However, this time the terms of the debate between ideology and pragmatism had changed. It was no longer a question of choosing between plan and the market, rather it was a question of how far the market mechanism would have to be extended to ensure survival while simultaneously avoiding negative anti-egalitarian consequences along with the loss of political control. Because Cuba could no longer rely on Soviet support and because of the extent of the economic reforms (notably dollarization, tourism, remittances, foreign investment, and joint ventures), a return to a Guevarist-style retrenchment was out of the question.

Still, even those who favored a more rapid and complete opening to the market than the leadership had been willing to grant were hesitant in view of the problematic experiences of Eastern European countries. "They saw the private sector as capable of playing positive roles," observed Carmelo Mesa-Lago, "but feared a snowball effect as the sector demanded increasing inputs, accumulated wealth, and challenged the state. The disappearance or sharp reduction of the safety net was their major preoccupation" (2000: 290-291). Such fears included the unemployment that would follow a contraction in the state sector, the socioeconomic inequality that would accompany the growth of the private sector, the probable price increases of nearly all products, and a drop in Cuba's touted social services. Despite the strict limitations placed on market reforms and the anemic growth of the private sector since the early 1990s, many of these and other social problems have intensified anyway.

Cuba's microenterprise sector sprang to life quickly after its legalization in 1993. Its decriminalization occurred because the state sector was unable to manage the country's economic crises or ensure adequate provision of goods and services for the people's sustenance. The government came to recognize citizens were increasingly solving their own survival problems by undertaking entrepreneurial activities for themselves—essentially concluding that it would be easier to ask forgiveness if caught than permission before launching an enterprise. In legalizing self-employment, the state was in effect ratifying the economic activities in which most people were participating as producers and/or consumers and which, when it was illegal, placed most Cuban citizens formally outside the law.

The Context for Economic Liberalization, 1990–1993

The origins and nature of Cuba's economic crisis have already been well documented. Their ultimate cause was the decline in Cuba's foreign exchange receipts and in its capacity to purchase imports—by 75%—from 1990 to 1993, resulting from the termination by the USSR of the hidden subsidy inherent in its special trade and aid relations with Cuba. The true extent of this subsidy was obscured from the Cuban people and likely from Castro himself in a number of ways (Ritter 1990):

1. The above-market prices for Cuba's sugar and nickel exports to the USSR;
2. The below-market prices of Soviet oil exports to Cuba;
3. The middleman profits accruing to Cuba from the re-export of Soviet petroleum to other countries at higher than market prices;
4. The middleman profits arising from the re-export of sugar purchased from other countries at the lower market price to the Soviet Union at the higher price resulting from their special bilateral sugar trading arrangement;
5. The continuing trade deficit with the Soviet Union financed by credits from that country, credits that have not been repaid; and
6. Credits for military purposes.

These types of subsidies accounted for large proportions of Cuba's total output of goods and services as measured by *Ingreso Nacianal Creado* (INC) or "Created National Income," Cuba's measure of aggregate output at the time. Soviet assistance varied from 36.4% of INC in 1984 to 23.3% in 1986, averaging about 31.7% in the 1980-1987 period (ibid.: 126). Obviously, when the Soviet Union indicated that it was going to move to world prices for its trade with Cuba, it was clear that the subsidy would end and that a deep and lasting crisis would ensue for Cuba. Compounding the crisis was the reduction of export markets especially with the countries of Eastern Europe, arising from the break-up of the CMEA, the collapse of the Soviet Union, and the economic contraction in former Soviet bloc. Initially, however, Russia continued to purchase large amounts of Cuban sugar, but at the world market price as opposed to the previous subsidized price.

There were also other factors contributing to Cuba's economic crisis, of which the following are perhaps the more important. First, Cuba's economic structure was fragile and rigid and its export structure was undiversified by 1990, as illustrated in Figure 4.1. Cuba's exports were almost identical to what they had been in 1958, with continuing heavy reliance on the old staple agricultural and mineral products, namely sugar, nickel, cigars, citric fruit, seafood, and coffee; pharmaceuticals and tourism represented Cuba's only newly emerging foreign exchange-earning activities. Cuba's inability to diversify into other export products was caused by the extreme shortage of foreign exchange and by the economic contraction as well as the loss of Cuba's markets in the former Soviet Bloc.

Second, Cuba's central planning system itself compounded the inflexibilities and rigidities of the economy. Decentralized initiatives by independent enterprises were not possible within the centralized, sclerotic, and bureaucratized organizational system. Consequently there could be minimal exploration and discovery of new export niches. Third, Cuba lacked access to international credit in 1990. Because it had declared a moratorium on debt repayment and servicing in 1986, Cuba was not deemed credit-worthy by commercial banks, official bilateral sources, or suppliers. Moreover, because of the U.S. embargo, Cuba was not eligible for membership in the relevant international financial institutions, such as the International Monetary Fund, the World Bank, or the Inter-American Development Bank, all of which could have provided support

Figure 4.1: Cuban Export by Product Shares, 1990 (in millions of Cuban pesos, out of 5,658 total)

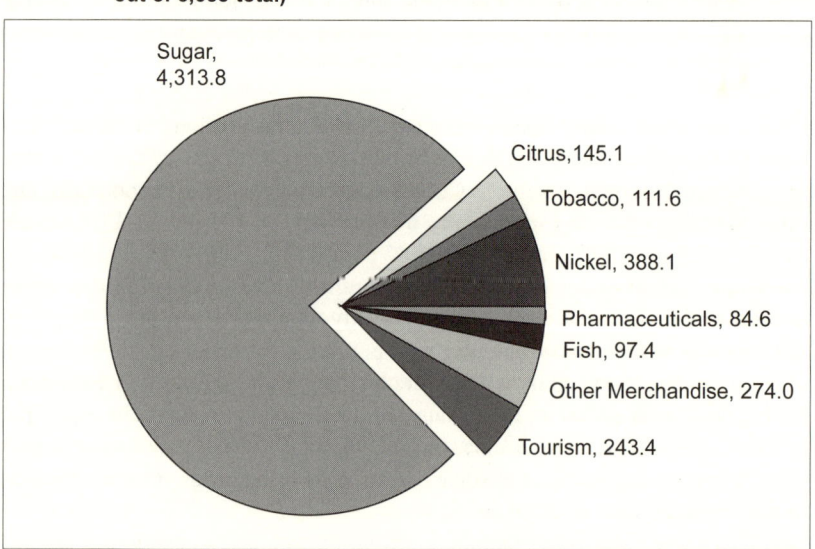

Source: *Naciones Unidas,* CEPAL 2000, Table A.38 and Mesa-Lago 2000: 366.

for Cuba's economic adjustment processes. Cuba was orphaned and on its own in economic terms.

Furthermore, Cuba's dysfunctional monetary system continued unchanged into the 1990s, with the official exchange rate for the old peso (CUP) in *Moneda Nacional* (national peso currency) becoming ever more overvalued as domestic inflation intensified—though suppressed by price controls for rationed products. At the old exchange rate, Cuba's exports became increasingly over-priced and the domestic purchasing power of peso earnings at the official exchange rate shrank steadily thereby reducing both the incentive and the capacity to produce for export. Finally, the continuing U.S. embargo, hardened by the "Torricelli Bill" of 1992 and the "Helms-Burton Bill" or "*Libertad*" Act of 1996, further blocked trade with the United States and complicated other aspects of Cuba's trade, foreign investment, and financial relationships. Foreign companies wanting to invest in Cuba had to make sure that they were not involving themselves with properties the ownership of which was being claimed by citizens or companies in the United States. Potential foreign investors that had exposure to the United States as exporters or as investors were also discouraged from engaging in closer economic interactions with Cuba.

The cumulative result of these factors was a severe foreign exchange shortage, which quickly generated a multidimensional economic crisis that was far worse than the situation of 1963–1964 following the failure of the "instant industrialization strategy" as well as the generalized disruptions caused by the unsuccessful attempt to produce 10 million tons of sugar in 1970. The other dimensions of the crisis included first, a macroeconomic crisis, with a 34% reduction in levels of income per capita from 1989 to 1993 (*Naciones Unidas,* CEPAL 2000). This was caused by shortages of imported inputs of all kinds, by difficulties in obtaining the necessary replacement parts, capital goods, and intermediate inputs from the former trade partners of Eastern Europe, and by the inadequate attempts to produce substitutes for these imported but no longer available products. There was also an energy crisis, in which petroleum imports for 1993 declined by almost 58% of the 1989 level (*Naciones Unidas,* CEPAL 2000). This in turn caused cut-backs in public transportation, reductions in electricity generation, a collapse of manufactured output especially in energy intensive products such as cement, and the substitution of tractors by oxen in the agricultural sector.

An additional dimension of this macroeconomic crisis was a dire shortage of food and widespread malnutrition. Imported foodstuffs accounted for 57% of Cuba's total human consumption of protein and for 50% of its caloric consumption according to the Central Planning Board (*Junta Central de Planificacion* 1992: 9). Moreover, large volumes of the inputs necessary for domestic agriculture and food production had been imported, including animal fodder, fertilizers, pesticides, machinery, and petroleum. Cuba's agricultural output for domestically consumed food products was therefore badly impaired by the foreign exchange shortage. Reductions in food imports and in domestic food production meant that Cuban citizens went hungry and were often malnourished. The painfully apparent evidence of this situation was the generalized weight loss that Cuban citizens experienced as well as the neuropathy or temporary blindness, which afflicted some 25,000 citizens between 1992 and 1993—thankfully reversed later on.

Further impacts of the foreign exchange shortage included major reductions of national savings and investment levels which fell to 3.7 and 4.9% of GDP respectively during 1994 in contrast to levels of 12 to 15% and 21 to 27% respectively from 1985 to 1988 (*Naciones Unidas,* CEPAL 2000). These reductions accelerated the deterioration of Cuba's capital stock including basic physical infrastructure such as housing, public facilities, and plant machinery and equipment. With this economic contraction came rising fiscal deficits, as tax revenues shrank. The government responded by financing public expenditures and state enterprise deficits with accelerated money creation, which in turn led to intensifying inflationary pressures. The suppression of these pressures due to the fixed prices on rapidly declining volumes of output in the state sector then led to pervasive shortages—too much money chasing too few goods—and an escalation of prices in the black market. In the illegal market for U.S. dollars, the unofficial exchange rate went up to 90 and briefly as high as 150 pesos per dollar between 1993 and 1994.

These interlinked crises lowered the Cuban people's material quality of life severely. Most serious was the decline of food availability through the rationing system. By 1994, the actual monthly supply of food per person available through rationing declined to perhaps 10 to 14 days. This forced people to purchase food on the black market at very high prices or in the even pricier dollar stores—if they were able. Indeed, the state system for agricultural production and for food distribution seemed close to collapse by mid-1994. It appeared to be incapable of adjusting successfully to the problems created by the lack of imported inputs for the agricultural sector and by the reduced quantities of imported foodstuffs. The ensuing decline in food availability reached crisis proportions by 1993. According to the Spanish aid agency, average daily caloric consumption in Cuba declined from 2,550 in 1970 to 1,780 in 1993 in sharp contrast to the level of 2,600 calories per day recommended by the World Health Organization (EIU 1994: 14).

In this situation, U.S. dollars became vital for Cuban citizens because the Cuban peso lost most of its purchasing power, given the low average monthly income (around 180 pesos per month in 1994) and the U.S. dollar to Cuban peso exchange rate (from 30 to 150 pesos per $1 U.S. in 1994). This situation alone produced a widespread demand for U.S. dollars for the purchase of food in dollar stores or on the black market, and a willingness to provide any goods or services which would earn dollars. The sale for dollars of cigars and rum, either stolen or of dubious source was one such activity quickly apparent to the foreign visitor. The private taxi services provided for dollars by almost anyone with a car—doctors, engineers, retired army officers, teachers, etc.—and the rental of private rooms and the establishment of private eating facilities popularly known as *paladares* became equally conspicuous manifestations of this intense need for U.S. dollars. At the same time, the reduced production of almost everything in the state sector created opportunities for people themselves to provide services or to fabricate products of various sorts for sale directly to others. Moreover, as people were laid off or continued to be paid without really working, they shifted to various types of self-employment.

Incomes in the illegal economy were very high relative to the deflating state employment sector, providing a further incentive for people to set up their own illegal enterprises. Similarly the flows of foodstuffs coming into the cities for illegal sale at black market prices also increased steadily for the same reasons, namely the need of the population for food and the need of food vendors for incomes. The black market prices for foodstuffs reached high levels because of the general inflationary pressures, which could not be released through the state sector where most prices were fixed at levels set long ago. In summary, what was happening from 1990 to mid-1993 was that people's family survival strategies were compelling them to participate in illegal markets, to establish small informal enterprises of all kinds, to resort to the emerging informal sector of the economy to obtain what the traditional socialist economy could not provide, and to engage in "rent-seeking" (buying and selling between the traditional socialist peso economy and the internationalized dollar economy as described in Chapters 3 and 7).

In the process, people were increasingly engaging in what was officially regarded as illegal activity. Moreover, with the worsening inflation of the peso and with a lack of confidence in the economic vision, strategy, and policy of the government and thence in the future value of the peso, Cuban citizens were increasingly holding U.S. dollars as both a "medium of exchange" and a "store of value." However, prior to 1994 this was still officially defined as a criminal activity and people were imprisoned for the offence. A set of policies, laws, or prohibitions which places a large proportion of the population outside the law jeopardizes the credibility or moral authority of a government and undermines people's respect for the rule of law. Thus, the move to liberalize self-employment can be seen as an administrative response to Cubans' economic survival strategies most of which were formally illegal. While the underground economy had always been a structural component of Cuba's centrally-planned economic system, such activities greatly expanded in the first few years of the SP as a response to generalized scarcity and the disintegration of state provisions of nearly all products, including food, gasoline, and even medical supplies.

The Reforms of 1992–1996

In the summer of 1992, the government decriminalized the possession and use of U.S. dollars thereby legalizing what large numbers of people were already doing. This measure accelerated the process of "dollarization" of the economy and further stimulated and legitimized the popular quest for dollars through activities in the underground economy. Then, on September 8, 1993 Decree Law 141 went into effect legalizing small-scale self-employment under the moniker *"trabajo por cuenta propia"* (own account work) (*Granma* 1993: 4-5). This represented a decisive policy shift permitting such microenterprises to exit the underground and operate more effectively, efficiently, and profitably.

Decree Law 141 and its accompanying resolution defined the legal framework for the character and functioning of self-employment activities. At first, those who could become self-employed were limited to retirees, housewives, people of "reduced work capacity," and workers who had lost their jobs due to the closure or to the "rationalization" (Cuba-speak for downsizing) of their enterprise. Specifically excluded were university graduates of all sorts, medical personnel, and enterprise managers. These restrictions were slightly modified in 1995, when professionals were allowed to become self-employed but only with permission from their work centers and in designated "low-tech" activities outside their areas of expertise.

Some 117 activities were permitted initially in six general areas, including transportation and support (16 in total); house repair (12); agricultural-related activities (16); family and personal services (39); housing services (12); and other activities (22). Activities not explicitly permitted were prohibited. A subsequent resolution on June 8, 1995 expanded the range of permitted self-employment activities by 19 (*Granma* 1995a: 2). It also announced increases in monthly licensing fee for some 25 activities. In order to qualify as a legal "self-employed" worker, individuals had to register officially with the Municipal Labor Administration and demonstrate that in their former employment they had complied with "labor discipline."

A range of other restrictions were placed on the self-employment sector, including the prohibition of hiring salaried workers (though unpaid family workers were acceptable in a small number of occupations); registered self-employment was to be charged a monthly fee, this being the only viable method of taxing them at the time; intermediaries were to be avoided "at all costs;" state sector enterprises were not permitted to purchase goods or services from the self-employed (with the exception of agriculture-related services and animal-powered transportation). Particularly important was the fact that the prices and conditions of sales were to be determined by the buyer and the seller, with self-employed workers themselves being the sellers. In effect, this constituted the price mechanism operating through markets. But the *Consejos*

Populares (Popular Councils) were also empowered to intervene with price regulations "in cases of abuses or clearly excessive prices" (ibid.: 4). The detail of how this would work was not spelled out.

The initial results of this policy were dramatic. Significant numbers of people registered their self-employment enterprises formally, either beginning new enterprises or bringing their formerly-illicit enterprises up out of the underground. On June 8, 1995 a resolution was signed permitting the establishment of food preparers and vendors in the street and in home-front cafeterias, as well as through what were formally labeled "gastronomic services"—better known colloquially as *paladares* or private, home-based restaurants (*Granma*, June 13, 1995, p. 2). The *paladares*, however, were famously limited to just 12 chiars in order to control their size and prevent their competing with state sector restaurants. By mid-1996 some 2,000 had sprung into existence across the entire island with perhaps 1,600 concentrated in Havana alone. (Chapter 8 provides a more detailed analysis of *paladares*.)

The self-employment law was originally intended to apply mainly to Cubans already providing services to other citizens so most licenses and fixed monthly taxes were paid in pesos. However, as tourism expanded at an accelerating rate throughout the island in the 1990s, some enterprises, especially in the areas of food service, transportation, and lodging, began to provide services to foreigners, charging in U.S. dollars. Partly as a result of this, modifications to the original legislation were added between 1995 and 1997, including expanded food service (1995), transportation (1996), and private home rental (1997) in the list of allowable occupations, since entrepreneurs in these three sectors often catered to foreigners and earned dollar incomes as a result.[1] Provision was also made requiring that taxes also be paid in dollars by such enterprises. Self-employment expanded rapidly following this wave of legalizations. From a level of 25,000 in 1989, numbers grew to 121,100 in 1994 reaching a peak of 138,100 in 1995. Following this, numbers began to decline falling to 112,900 in 1998 (*Naciones Unidas,* CEPAL 2000). However, these totals include neither private taxi service nor private lodging, which were administratively separate from self-employment at the time.

A breakdown of the most common self-employment activities in 1999 is presented in Table 4.1. While there were then 157 distinct occupations by this time in which one could become self-employed, over 70% of all active licenses for June 1999 were concentrated in just the 19 professions listed in Table 4.1. The most significant activities in terms of employment were vendors and preparers of food and drink (20.1% of the total); messengers (mainly purchasers of rationed products for others, 5.1%); carpenters (4.5%); tire repair (3.9%); hair stylist (3.2%); barber (2.9%); manicurists (2.2%); and shoe repair and shining (5.2%). Registered "family help" in other self-employed enterprises accounted for 16.1% of total employment in the sector. Again, Table

Table 4.1: Top Self-Employment Occupations (June 1999)

Occupation	Number of Self-employed	Percentage of Total
Prep/Sale Foods & Beverages "*al detalle*"	21,369	16.92
Family Help	20,326	16.09
Messenger	7,719	6.11
Carpenter	6,294	4.98
Flat Tire Repair	4,975	3.94
Prep/Sale Foods & Beverages "*punto fijo*"	4,846	3.84
Hair Stylist	4,081	3.23
Barber	3,668	2.90
Shoe Repair	3,529	2.79
Shoe Shine	3,009	2.38
Manicurist	2,786	2.21
Lighter Repair	1,335	1.06
Electric & Electronic Equipment Repair	1,302	1.03
Prep/Sale of Charcoal	1,135	0.90
Parking Attendant (Automobiles)	990	0.78
Air Compressor Operator	867	0.69
Parking Attendant (Bicycles & Motorcycles)	772	0.61
Mechanical & Combustion Equip. Repair	598	0.47
Prep/Sale of Home Use Articles	528	0.42
Total	90,129	71.35

Source: Ministerio de Trabajo, June 1999. This table has been translated from a statistical table produced by the *Dirección del Trabajo por Cuenta Propia* (Office of Self-Employment) of Cuba's Ministry of Labor, June 1999, provided by Neili Fernández Peláez's in her University of Havana thesis on self-employment in Cuba (2000).

4.1 does not include private transport (tracked by the Ministry of Transportation) or home rental (overseen by the Ministry of Housing), the inlcusion of which would significantly expand the totals.

These small enterprises emerged from a number of sources. Some sprang up from the underground economy when they became legal. However, many remained in the underground economy as will be discussed in Chapter 7. Some enterprises were started by individuals whose jobs had been eliminated during the depths of the 1993 depression. For example, an acquaintance of the authors with a Ph.D. in chemistry who was laid off from his scientific research center during this period became a sandal-maker to make ends meet. Other enterprises were started by individuals who saw a greater income-earning potential in self-employment than in their state sector jobs. In this case, they left their state employment voluntarily—using a certified disability of some sort as justification in order to start their small enterprise.

Figure 4.2 illustrates the rapid expansion of self-employment as a proportion of total employment between 1970 and the late 1980s, and then after

1989. From 1989 to 1995 the expansion was impressive, but was then followed by containment to the year 1998 followed again by an increase of about 30% in 1999. Thereafter, the proportion gradually fell once again into the mid-2000s. The public policies used to contain the sector are the subjects of subsequent parts of this chapter and are revisited again in Chapters 5, 7, and 8.

Though not formally part of the self-employment legislation, the reestablishment of agricultural markets (*mercados agropecuarios* or "*agros*," similar to the MLCs described in Chapter 3) on September 19, 1994 was an important step in the liberalization process for microenterprise. This measure produced rapid positive results: increased food supplies in urban areas, reductions in food prices to levels below those of the black market, the establishment of a more integrated national market for foodstuffs, a strengthening of incentives for food producers to expand supplies, and an increased use and hence demand for the Cuban peso with a positive impact on its value vis-à-vis the U.S. dollar. Although Castro had appeared to be a reluctant observer in the discussions leading up to the reestablishment of agricultural markets—with then Vice President Raúl Castro playing the leading role—it appears that Fidel had become supportive within three weeks of their reestablishment, taking it upon himself to explain how the markets were functioning to a meeting of the Presidents of the Provincial Assemblies (*Granma* 1994b: 4-5).

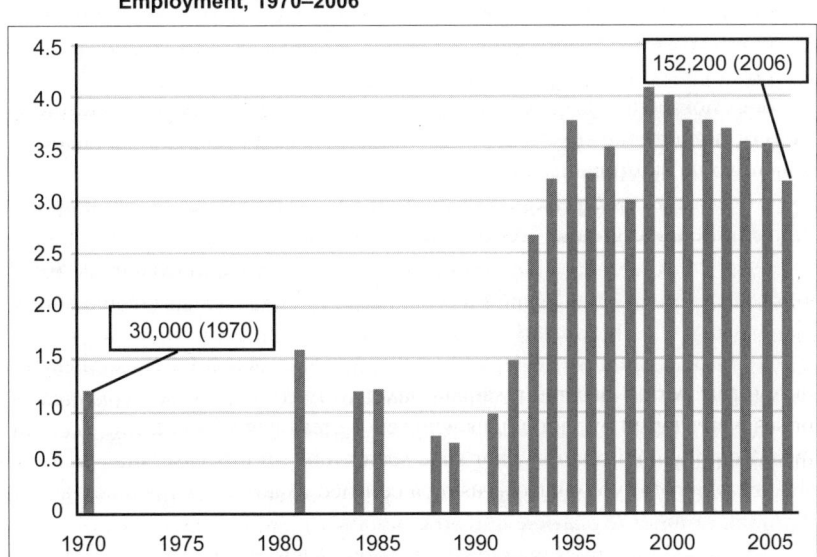

Figure 4.2: Non-Agricultural Self-Employment as a Percentage of Total Employment, 1970–2006

Source: ONE, *Anuario Estadistico de Cuba,* various issues.

The specific proposal for the reestablishment of agricultural markets following the disappearance of the MLCs in the 1980s emerged from discussions within the military followed by a series of three meetings of the Communist Party in different regions of the country in July 1994, all spearheaded by Raúl Castro. The party meetings were notable in the frankness with which the agriculture/food/nutrition problem was analyzed and in the attempt to go beyond the ritual blaming of the embargo and the collapse of the USSR and CMEA for the current difficulties. Decree No. 191 and the associated resolution were then passed on September 19 and 20 and published the next day (*Granma* 1994a: 3). The legislation was not discussed or approved by the National Assembly, indicating both the urgency of the legislation as well as the body's real lack of authority.

Markets for industrial and artisan products were legalized by Decree No. 92 of the Executive Committee of the Council of Ministers on October 21, 1994. This legislation permitted state enterprises, local enterprises, enterprises of the Ministry of the Interior, and self-employed producers to rent space in designated market areas for sales of their products. Additionally, prices in these markets were to be determined by supply and demand. Sellers would rent market stalls, paying rent to the market administration, which would be self-financing and independent in their operation. State farms could sell through representatives operating on consignment. However, self-employed workers would have to sell their own products themselves and could not legally use intermediaries as buyers or sellers.

Another area where entrepreneurial energies were unleashed was in rental accommodation for clients (often referred to in Cuba as *casas particulares*, or private homes) both in the peso economy and in the dollar economy for tourists. By 1993, many Cubans with well-located homes were investing in house repairs, furnishings, and air conditioning in order to rent them out. Such home and room rental was initially undertaken informally without any official permission and outside of any sort of regulation. By 1997, much accommodation of this sort was available at prices well below formal hotels. The consequences of this were that (1) more U.S. dollars flowed into the private economy at the expense of the state-owned hotels; (2) some Cubans received dollar incomes that were high relative to average incomes, thereby worsening the duality in the pattern of income distribution; and (3) a new variety of tourism developed, namely lower-end or student/backpacker type tourism dependent on low prices. Clearly, some sort of regulatory system and taxation was necessary for this sector.

Additionally, as microenterprises began to emerge from the underground during the 1990s, a hierarchy of sorts gradually became evident. This spectrum of scale and success was especially pronounced in the few larger-scale and more dynamic occupations—especially those such as bed-and-breakfasts, taxis, and *paladares* that had a connection to the burgeoning tourism industry.

Vignette: Milagros and the "Seven Seas *Paladar*"

One particular "untouchable" operation was run under the surprising name "Seven Seas *Paladar*," despite the fact that seafood was then prohibited in private restaurants. It turned out upon inquiry, however, that the operation was actually registered as a B&B, even if the business card Milagros, the restaurant manager, handed me (Henken) upon my entry identified the place as a "*paladar*." This strategy allowed the operators to take advantage of the fact that taxes and regulations were much less cumbersome for B&Bs than for *paladares*. Milagros happily offered to give me a full tour of the premises, leading me into two different 12-chair dining rooms, one of which contained a full bar. She also showed me two separate bedrooms (each with a double bed and its own air-conditioner) and one private apartment containing two beds. I was told that each room rented for $35 a night with breakfast included. There was also a space for parking a rental car and chauffer service if necessary. Milagros explained that the *paladar* had already been in business for 10 years (1991–2001) at the time of my visit and that the restaurant specialized in seafood, offering lobster, shrimp, fish, and even the delicacy *caguama* or Cuban sea turtle.

When I asked Milagros to show me the menu, however, she smiled saying that they only had an "oral menu," and began to describe their many dishes for me with pride and gusto. The lack of a menu was clearly not due to a lack of money with which to have them printed. Instead, it is likely that they did not wish to run the risk of printing menus that baldly declared their specialty in serving contraband seafood dishes. An oral menu was also convenient as it allowed them to raise or lower prices to accommodate commission-seeking hustlers.

After observing so many open violations of the self-employment regulations, I wondered if they had ever been made to pay a fine. Milagros quickly (and incredibly) responded, "never, here we always do things by the book." Furthermore, she explained that the self-employment laws are well enforced and that those who violate these laws create their own problems. She argued that the inspectors, when they have visited and found "inconsistencies," have only advised them how to better comply with the law accepting at face value their explanations that they had not fully understood the regulations. Milagros also stated that she wouldn't change existing laws since most Cubans were not yet ready for an open, uncontrolled economy, though she seemed quite ready herself.

Below—interspersed with our discussion of the increased enforcement and regulation of self-employment after 1995—we present illustrative vignettes from the emerging private bed-and-breakfast and transportation sectors.[2] Based on our ethnographic research and in-depth interviews with B&B operators, we developed an informal typology separating them into four somewhat distinct groups: (1) the "untouchables," (2) the "privileged operations," (3) the "family businesses," and (4) the "clandestine operations." We also outline a similar typology below for taxi services during the 1996-2005 period, identifying state-run tourist and domestic taxis, as well as licensed private cabs and unlicensed "gypsy" cabs.

The first necessary point about the "untouchables" is that such a term is a relative one. In Cuba, no one, especially within the then illegitimate, if now legal private microenterprise sector is strictly out of reach from the long arm of the law. This has been demonstrated many times in the revolutionary government's shifting policies toward the sector as chronicled in Chapter 3. However, the term is used here to indicate a degree of unofficial state tolerance of the violation of self-employment laws for a select group of well-connected operations. The specific characteristics of this group of private renters include, first and foremost, the systematic violation of the most basic rental regulations. For example, during the 1999–2005 period when these interviews and observations were carried out food was commonly offered for sale to both houseguests and others without the owner paying the then required 30% surcharge.

In fact, most of these few untouchable B&B operations doubled as *paladares* in practice, offering a full menu of prohibited foods such as lobster to as many diners who could fit into their large, elegant dining rooms. These operations also typically employed many workers, including a doorman, a driver, a few waiters/waitresses, a kitchen staff, a live band, and a group of two or three managers who would take shifts so that one of them was always present. Of course, few if any of the employees were household members or relatives of the license holder.[3]

Untouchable rental operations also benefitted from prime locations, first-rate infrastructure, and economies of scale. Many featured extensive capital investments in the business with recently purchased equipment and clean, stylish surroundings. Due to their luxury offerings, these places had often gained a following among a wealthy foreign clientele. Given their level of success and seeming impunity, other more humble private rental and food service operations often surmised that these "untouchables" had either been co-opted by the state or were in fact "planted" by the government (either for the purpose of spying or driving others out of business). Finally, given both the extent and relative openness of the violations of self-employment laws, it is very likely that these operations benefitted from extensive protection from the inspector corps in exchange for the regular payment of bribes.

From Expansion to Containment: Public Policies towards Microenterprise, 1996–2005

The General Political and Policy Environment

Cuba's political leadership and the official Cuban media became increasingly critical of the legal microenterprise sector between 1995 and 1996. By early 1997, the leadership began to state with greater clarity that the sector had been necessary for a while but that in time a policy reversal would be desirable. (In official discourse, the underground economy basically did not exist at this time with underground operators often lumped in with licensed CPs as ideologically suspect). The legal microenterprise sector was criticized for a number of reasons. First, it ostensibly promoted a mentality that was considered incompatible with "socialism." The purpose of the 1993-1994 reforms was in fact declared to be saving "socialism and the Revolution" not to commence a transition to anything else. That is, the existence of microenterprise was understood by the leadership to be a contradiction of the fundamental character of Cuban society. In the words of then Vice-President Raúl Castro, when reading the Report of the Central Committee of the Party on March 23, 1996:

> The psychology of the private producer and the self-employed worker in general, as a result of the personal or family origin of their incomes—the private sale of the good or service they produce—generates individualism and is not a source of socialist *conciencia*.

Moreover, the leadership emphasized the negative consequences of the sector but ignored its positive features. Nor was an analysis made of why the negative features occurred. To understand the negative impacts of self-employment requires a comprehension of the context within which it operated rather than a general evocation of the "evils of capitalism." President Castro, for example, dwelt on the impact that the emergence of self-employment had on income distribution referring to incomes "ten times, twenty times, or thirty times those earned by a [state] worker" (*Granma* 1997a). However, he said nothing about the structural and monetary bifurcation of the economy produced by government policies, which permitted the inequalities to occur in the first place. In fact, most of the microenterprises to emerge during this period were modest undertakings providing goods or services in the peso economy for other average income Cubans generating average incomes for their operators.

Apart from President Fidel Castro, whose long-time ideological opposition to markets and private enterprise are well known and discussed in Chapter 3, other key political leaders on the island also made open declarations against an increased role for self-employment. For example, in an article in *Granma* in November 1997, Raúl Valdés Vivo, the then director of the Communist

Party's ideological school and a member of the Party's Central Committee, rejected claims that it was unfair to allow foreign investment while prohibiting domestic capitalists to participate more fully in the island's economy (Valdés Vivo 1998). Comparing the latter group to "piranhas [...] capable in a minimum of time of devouring a horse down to the bones," he stated that the leadership had been forced to resort to capitalist investments from abroad against its will and claimed that Cuban nationals could not have provided the necessary capital, technology, or markets brought by outsiders. At the same time, Valdés Vivo admitted that the reasons for the restrictions against domestic capitalists are not only economic, but political and ideological as well. Specifically, he wrote that allowing Cuban citizens to provide money to private microenterprises "would introduce a social force that sooner or later would serve the counterrevolution." Adding that Cuba does not desire the return of an exploitative national class propped up by foreign interests, he cited President Castro's words during the 5th Party Congress: "Cuba cannot afford the existence of a new class of rich that would later acquire great power and end up conspiring against Socialism" (ibid.).

In contrast to many other reports from the state media that had characterized the self-employed as "*millionarios*" or "*explotadores*" who lived off others' work, the article by Valdés Vivo recognized that "the Cuban population is generally thankful for the services provided by the self-employed, who work an average of between 10 and 12 hours daily." However, his article closed by emphasizing the need for "discipline" and declared that if the self-employed workers did not like the high taxes and existing regulations, they had no other options than to hand in their licenses. "Whoever cannot comply with the conditions of order and discipline," declared the state journalist Rodríguez Cruz in the pages of the newspaper *Trabajadores*, "will not be allowed to become self-employed" (1996: 5).

Furthermore, the regulatory framework implemented at the time was designed to control and discipline the self-employed, constantly reminding them of their responsibilities, yet included almost no provisions for the protection of their legal rights. This paternalistic tendency to emphasize "control over support" (Fernández Peláez 2000) was reiterated in a July 2000 report on the internal economy. Deputy Minister of Culture Abel Acosta (2000) declared that the solution to Cuba's economic problems "does not lie in [the proliferation of] *chinchalitos*" (small, private, informal businesses). At the same time, Cuban officials admitted that the growth of the self-employed sector had provided needed goods, services, and employment during a time of severe economic crisis.

This paternalistic, if somewhat appreciative attitude toward the self-employed was echoed on a number of occasions in speeches by President Fidel Castro. For example, in his speech of April 9, 1997, just before the regulation of private rental activity was announced, Castro reiterated the need for discipline and control in the microenterprise sector, declaring that not all self-employed workers were registered and paying taxes.

> We have to be capable of putting this activity in order. If we need 100 inspectors, 100 inspectors; 800, 800; 2,000, 2,000. If we need 200 inspectors for the inspectors [themselves], then [we will have] 200, but it is necessary that this activity have order, that it have discipline. (Castro, F. 1997)

President Castro went on to characterize some of the self-employed as lazy speculators, warning his listeners: "We must combat illicit enrichment, of course, but not only illicit [enrichment], but also the enrichment that results not as a result of hard work but as a result of the conditions in which we are living" (Castro, F. 1997).

A final example of the state's increasingly antagonistic attitude toward Cuba's *cuentapropistas* was expressed in a *Granma* article citing the need to mobilize the neighborhood Committees for the Defense of the Revolution (CDRs) in the battle against growing levels of economic crime. National Assembly President Ricardo Alarcón expressed the following sentiment toward the island's *paladares*:

> We mustn't be confused by the "miracles" which they attribute to [the microenterprise sector]. The richest ones, such as the *paladares*, would do well to ask themselves first, in what home if not the one given them by the Revolution would they have been able to set up shop and second, if in a capitalist society, the owner of those houses would have permitted one of his tenants to set up a restaurant in one of his properties. If capitalism were to return to Cuba, it would sweep them away. (Lee 1997c)

Alarcón's declaration vividly foreshadowed what would prove to be an insecure future for holders of private properties who converted them into small businesses. Essentially, Alarcón likens the Cuban state to a kind-hearted landlord who has permitted his tenants to open businesses on his property. Cuban citizens are treated like children who have taken unfair advantage of the gifts given them by their father: If the capitalists return, they will do away with your businesses with your father no longer able to protect you.

This tension between the state policies of toleration, legalization, and expansion of the private sector on the one hand, and moves toward greater control, containment, and repression on the other, reveal the revolutionary government's mistrust of Cuba's microenterprise sector. At this time, Cuban officials and journalists continually emphasized the "indiscipline, illegalities, and lack of order" that characterized the private sector, always coming to the same conclusion. Since the cause of indiscipline was considered to be the lack of strong regulation and the waning revolutionary consciousness brought on by "the individualist psychology of the private producer" (Lee 1997c: 3), the appropriate solution was greater top-down control combined with greater revolutionary fervor and vigilance.

Small-scale entrepreneurs also lacked a political voice. Article 3.14 of Decree Law 174 prohibited the organization of producer cooperatives or associations unless officially authorized. Any type of independent association on the part of *cuentapropistas* was ruled out by the Cuban Minister of Economy, José Luis Rodríguez, in a 1997 interview with the Argentine newspaper *El País*:

> We are not stimulating the creation of independent associations in that direction. [...] Now, I will state clearly that we will not permit a camouflage in organizations of that type which would question the system and the basic objectives of the Revolution. (Rodríguez 1997)

The self-employed thus had no organization that could voice their concerns or defend their interests, leaving them particularly vulnerable to a potential reversal of government policy. Under Fidel, public policy toward self-employment clearly did not conceive of it as a right that could be defended but as a temporary permission that could be revoked at will.

Finally, basic security for the private sector entrepreneurs was lacking. Old memories persisted of the confiscations of virtually all enterprises in the early 1960s and particualrly in 1968. These confiscations were without compensation and could not be appealed to an independent judiciary.[4] Policy reversals such as the elimination of the farmers' markets in 1986 also must have been well-remembered. Periodically, the government has changed the rules of the game in capricious and confiscatory ways reinforcing the public perception that there could be no fundamental and enduring security for their activities under current political circumstances. This in turn fed a deep mistrust and skepticism of government motives among Cuba's *cuentapropistas*. In sum, in their relationship with the state, microentrepreneurs were largely powerless, without rights and without a legal capability to appeal policy actions of the government. But this does not mean that they did not develop often ingenious strategies to survive, as our various ethnographic vignettes interspesed throughout this chapter show.

The Licensing Process

Official authorization of self-employment is based on licensing at the municipal level. Officials are empowered to grant licenses to operate according to their own criteria and judgment though with some guidelines and influence from above. However, during this period potential entrepreneurs were often denied licenses. This surely induced some of them to go (or remain) underground. Although relatively little statistical information on the provision of licenses has been made public, some information is presented in Table 4.2 for the Municipalities of Havana in the 1996 to 2001 period. As the table indicates, licenses granted for self-employment activities over this period declined by almost 39 percent. Meanwhile, requests for licenses increased by 110 percent, despite the obvious discouragement effect that high and continuing "failure rates" would presumably generate. From another perspective, and as can be calculated from the information in the table, the licensing "success rate," that is, licenses granted as a percentage of total applications declined from 82.3 percent in 1996 to about 24 percent in 2001. This reduction likely occurred in other parts of the country as well.

The declining success rate in obtaining licenses for self-employment over this period likely led the unsuccessful applicants to find other venues for their entrepreneurial activities or to develop other survival strategies. A good deal of these energies likely shifted to activities in the underground economy across Cuba. On the other hand, the denial of licenses that have to be renewed annually, could lead to the complete shut-down of those microenterprises in activities that could not be practiced in clandestinity. For example, if *bicitaxi* (pedicab) drivers in Central Havana could not renew their licenses, their operation would have been forced to close. If they continued to ply their trade without a license, they faced a hefty fine and the confiscation of the pedicab itself.

In the summer of 2003, new regulations were announced against bed-and-breakfast operators that included raising overall tax rates, requiring all operators to pay an additional 30% tax for providing meals to their guests, charging an additional tax on common areas of the home used by renters, limiting renting to a maximum of two rooms with just two guests per room, prohibiting the

Table 4.2: The Self-Employment Licensing Process, Havana, 1996–2001 (number of applications per year)

Category	1994	1995	1996	1997	1998	1999	2000	2001
In Process	4,193	21,963	n.a.	n.a.	n.a.	n.a.	n.a.	499
Granted (#)	169,098	208,786	38,057	34,984	31,587	28,380	24,719	23,351
Granted (%)	68.0	53.4	82.3	50.4	37.4	31.1	26.1	23.9
Refused	10,675	11,519	8,211	34,423	52,889	63,018	70,106	74,337
-Withdrawn	n.a.	n.a.	n.a.	n.a.	n.a.	n.a.	n.a.	11,332
-Failed	64,586	148,491	1,791	24,990	41,002	50,015	56,809	60,627
Total	248,552	390,759	46,268	69,407	84,456	91,398	94,827	97,687

Source: Ministerio de Trabajo y Segundad Social, CEPAL 1997, and Dirección Provincial de Trabajo y Seguridad Social, 2001: 1 and 5.

Vignette: Dr. Alejandra Morales's Bed-and-Breakfast

The semi-retired Dr. Alejandra Morales began renting rooms in her home before the activity was first regulated in summer 1997. Given this, she and her husband Armando explained their reaction to the 1997 legalization this way: "You must remember that the law was instituted because the activity already existed. It was not passed in order to encourage private renting, but to recognize and legalize what had already existed under cover." Despite her general positive assessment of the rental system, Alejandra did point to some illogical restrictions.

> As things are now, we commonly charge between $25 and $30, but report only between $15 and $20. If the law were different, we could be honest about our earnings. You have to understand that Cuba has not had an income tax for over 30 years and that there is no culture of paying tax here. People feel like their money is being taken away. The state knows this and has made the tax law strict. It is a cycle. They expect us to cheat so make a law that is harsh and that forces us to underreport our income to survive.

When asked about the change in attitude that involvement in self-employment brings to individuals, Alejandra smiled broadly, admitting that it changes one's mentality completely. "In the past the mentality was give me this and give me that. People are leaving behind a socialist mentality and acquiring a capitalist one. Some are turning into little potentates. They seem to have forgotten just in which country they are living!" I (Henken) tried to sum up this line of reasoning by quoting something I had heard from an earlier interviewee: "It's no longer thanks to the revolution, but now thanks to my own hard work." However, Alejandra rejected this interpretation, saying that it would be more accurate to say thanks to both.

> Some renters quickly forget that many of the infrastructural goods that they use in their businesses are provided at a big subsidy by the state—lights, water, gas, housing itself... All these things are paid for at high prices in any capitalist country. Just imagine with all the guests we have here and all the gallons of water we use, we only pay three pesos ($0.15) per month for water, ten pesos ($0.50) for power, and six pesos ($0.30) for the telephone! If the government ever changes these subsidies or we ever have a new government, life will suddenly become very hard because all this will disappear.

Armando agreed with the spirit of her point but also reminded her that this kind of reasoning allows the state to justify paying extremely low salaries, reasoning that since all the basics are practically free Cubans do not really need much salary to get by.

hiring anyone from outside the family, revoking the right to rent out an entire apartment, and requiring that a family member always be present in the home. This laundry list of new regulations against a type of self-employment only first legalized in 1997 (Henken 2002), was justified based on the conviction that "negative tendencies and behaviors have emerged in the exercise of this activity that distort the very essence of renting" (Resolución No. 270, 2003).

Unlike the "untouchable" bed-and-breakfasts described above, those we categorize here as "privileged" cannot be said to have systematically violated self-employment regulations. While privileged operators were forced to cut corners by the antagonistic legal framework, the use of illegal cost-cutting strategies was done with much more discretion than was common in untouchable operations. Furthermore, because they often lacked special connections within the country, had little political clout themselves, and because their access to capital was relatively limited, privileged B&Bs were forced to rely much more on the advantages they did have: size, location, infrastructure, international connections, and hard work mixed with business sense.

The combination of increasingly strict regulations and the arbitrary denial of license applications was an important mechanism for downsizing the self-employment sector—especially in the dynamic sectors of private cabs and bed-and-breakfasts. However in 2004 a more draconian measure was adopted. Resolution 11/2004 of the Ministry of Labor stipulated that no new licenses were to be issued for 40 of the 157 legalized self-employment trades. Those already with licenses in these activities could continue, but no new licenses would be issued and transferring existing ones to others was prohibited. Among these occupations were used book venders, masseuses, jewelers, restaurateurs, magicians, metal-workers, food venders, and auto mechanics.

By limiting the issuance of licenses and preventing the legalization of applicants who wished to start microenterprises, the number of firms in all such areas was reduced, in many cases significantly. This in turn led to a contraction in the volume of production of goods and services in these areas with prices becoming higher than they otherwise would have been. This hurt consumers who were now forced to pay higher prices for goods and services. It also permitted higher incomes for those microenterprises that had managed to obtain licenses. On the other hand, in some "low profile" activities, it was possible for those who were refused a license to "go underground." In this case, the illegal producers, who would have been able to evade taxes and avoid costly regulations, then constituted unfair competition for the legal producers and may have limited much of the advantage that the latter experienced from the limitation on the licensed competition.

In contrast, "high profile" microenterprises that had to practice their trade in the open would perhaps find it impossible to operate in clandestinity. For these producers, limitations on numbers would have permitted higher prices and incomes for legal microenterprises in the absence of competition from un-

Vignette: Carlos, Retired Revolutionary and Cabbie

A former clandestine fighter against the Batista dictatorship, Carlos was a retired pilot for *Cubana de Aviación*, Cuba's national airline, for more than ten years at the time he was interviewed in 2001. He earned a pension of 440 pesos each month (almost double the average Cuban monthly salary of 250 pesos at the time). He admitted that his pension was relatively high by Cuban standards, even if the peso had lost much of its value since 1989. He added proudly, "I'll receive this amount every month until I die. Then, my wife will continue to collect it until she dies." Prior to retiring, Carlos earned a monthly salary of 490 pesos. He explained that because his retirement did not provide enough to make ends meet, he became self-employed as a taxi driver in 1997. "I got involved in this in order to have an extra source of income. So that I could buy the basic things that weren't available at the *bodega*: clothes, detergent, meat, oil, etc."

Carlos explained that he initially took out two different licenses in 1997. One allowed him to serve dollar-paying tourists (paying a tax of $75 per month). The other license, for which he paid 450 pesos ($23) per month, allowed him to transport Cubans. He worked with both licenses for less than a year, however, since the monthly tax for the dollar license was raised more than three-fold in February 1998 to $250 per month. He added that this drastic rise in taxes forced nearly all private cabbies with dollar licenses to give them up (though many—including Carlos—continued to serve foreigners on the sly).

He explained that when he worked with the two licenses, he would normally park near the arts and crafts market on the Malecón (near the Meliá Cohiba Hotel) and look for fares among the foreigners there. After turning in his dollar license, Carlos began running a specific route 4 to 5 times a day. He would start at the Copellia ice cream park in Vedado at L and 23rd Streets, from where he would make a run down 23rd through Playa from where he would return to Vedado again. This route was 14 kilometers round trip and he could count on a total of eight passengers (four down and four more returning), giving him around 80 pesos per round trip (320 pesos per day). From this he estimated that he needed to spend roughly 60 pesos per day on gas, leaving him with 260 pesos in net earnings per day or 1,560 pesos per week (before taxes).

When asked how the government kept track of and could verify the earnings he declares, Carlos explained that he had to fill out a weekly passenger and earnings report. These 52 reports are turned in to the National Tax Office (ONAT) at the end of each year and a tax is then levied on his personal income. He clarified that he was allowed to deduct 20% off the top for expenses, but that his own expenses were far more than just 20% of his earnings. "You have to buy gas, oil, etc. in dollars, but I make enough to live decently without having to steal from anyone." Before paying his year-end tax, he subtracted what he had already paid in over the year in the monthly CFM (450 pesos x 12). Carlos estimated that he could earn between 30,000-32,000 pesos per year as his gross income. He could then subtract roughly 6,000 pesos for expenses and another 5,400 based on what he had already paid, leaving him with just under 20,000 pesos (between $800 and $1,000) as his yearly taxable income.

Without prompting, Carlos launched into an explanation of the reasoning behind the emergence of self-employment during the 1990s:

> Self-employment came about as a means of survival during the special period. You have to remember that instead of softening in reaction to the disappearance of the eastern bloc, the U.S. tightened up the blockade against us and we had no choice but to allow self-employment as one of the strategies designed to save socialism, to save the Revolution. We suddenly found ourselves alone and from one day to the next we lost all our major markets. Foreign investment and self-employment were the only means to save socialism.

Since self-employment came about as a response to an emergency situation, Carlos warned that it was nothing more than a stage ("*una etapa, nada más*"). "This is a socialist country and we will eventually get rid of self-employment. It doesn't fit here," he insisted (quite prophetically it turned out—at least in the short term). "Private employment has existed for a while, but you can't create class antagonisms in a socialist system. All this goes against the essence of the system. The opening needed to exist, but now the economy is recovering." With an ironic smile, he added, "We have strong rates of growth over the past few years [1997-2001] even if you Americans keep trying to ruin us. We will hold onto our principles come what may."

At the same time, the state's subtle policy of running cabbies who prefer to operate in dollars out of business was not lost on Carlos.

> The state has its own taxis and wants the tourist dollars for itself. But, of course, when I work, what I earn is for my own benefit. This is competition between the state and the private sector. However, the tourist is drawn to the private sector first because of the uniqueness of the old cars and second because of the cheaper price. The state taxis are new and more expensive. This is why the state raised the dollar license from $75 to $250 per month. It wanted to eliminate private taxis in dollars.

derground operations. If the restrictive licensing of microenterprises led many small scale entrepreneurs to practice their activity in the underground economy, the tax revenues of the government would have been reduced as they avoided taxation. Finally, if the licensing process pushed microenterprises underground, the energies and efforts of the operators would have been further wasted due to exceedingly small scale together with the inefficiencies generated by attention avoidance.

During the late-1990s and early-2000s, Cuba's licensed private cabbies were informally divided between those who participated in the "collective" 10-peso routes that used the parking area just east of the Capitol Building in *Centro Habana* as their informal terminal, and those who sought their fares in strategically located but informal taxi stands around the city. While there was originally the option to obtain a license to operate private cabs in dollars, this was rescinded in the mid-1990s. Therefore, licensed private cabbies were legally (but not very effectively) restricted from serving anyone but peso-paying Cubans.

Due to the formidable financial and legal obstacles to obtaining an automobile in Cuba, licensed drivers during this period were a special breed. For example, Cuban law long prohibited private individuals from buying or selling vehicles except for those that predated the Revolution (a restriction recently rescinded under Raúl Castro). Thus, at this time the state was the only legal buyer or seller of all post-1959 vehicles. This prohibition led to the ironic concentration of classic, pre-revolutionary American cars in the private taxi business. In fact, though most private taxis displayed a make-shift "taxi" sign in their windshield, the easiest way to identify them at the time was by simply scanning the street for one of the huge, unmistakable, early-model American cars.[5]

The many restrictions on obtaining a car, along with the aforementioned limitations on obtaining a license, led to a web of informal arrangements in the licensed taxi sector that often hid complex relations of ownership behind a façade of legality. Just as in the housing market where false marriages were long used as a means of achieving otherwise unobtainable homeownership, it was not uncommon for Cubans to arrange fictitious marriages with foreigners in order to purchase a car. For example, upon inquiring of the Cuban wife of a friend if her husband had succeeded in purchasing the car he had long been saving for, one of the authors was told with a chuckle, "Yes, he finally got the car. It's beautiful, but he had to marry a Russian in order to buy it!" These many limitations also resulted in the economic polarization of the various actors engaged in this activity. Due to the lack of available cars, the need for a large amount of initial investment capital, and the restrictions on legal ownership and purchase, an informal but quite common practice emerged where owners contracted their cars out to workers who appeared as the legal owners on all documents (Fernández Peláez 2000: 31).

The Regulatory Environment

During the Special Period, the self-employed operated in an increasingly difficult regulatory environment. Formally licensed, legal microenterprises in most countries operate within a framework of laws and regulations regarding labor standards, minimum wage laws, and health, safety, and environmental standards. Through their taxes, they also bear part of the burden of financing the functioning of communities and public goods of all sorts. In Cuba, however, the tax and regulatory environment has been particularly stringent. It was designed to limit the incomes that can be earned in the sector, to restrict the size of individual microenterprises, and to reduce the size of the private sector generally.

The major part of the legislative framework within which Cuban microenterprises must operate was defined in Decree Law 174 instituted in 1997. Some major provisions of that law along with the punishments for violations of the regulations are summarized in Table 4.3. In particular, Articles 3 and 5 provide a useful snapshot of the flavor of the regulatory environment for self-employment activities in Cuba at this time. The first limitation on the microenterprise sector was the restricted range of authorized activities (Article 3.1). While by early 2003, 157 activities were authorized (employing 153,000 persons), all other activities were prohibited. Among those excluded were virtually all professional activities such as engineering, accounting, architecture, interior decorating, landscaping, computer and informatics, real estate, advertising and employment agencies, legal services, etc.

Second, a license was required in order to exercise legal activities (Article 3.2). As noted above, licenses were granted restrictively, not automatically, and were used initially to contain and later to reduce the size of the sector. Third, locating a microenterprise anywhere except one's home was also prohibited (Article 3.4). This greatly reduced the potential viability of some types of enterprise such as *paladares* and other food vendors. The law also mentioned a variety of limitations on the size and diversity of microenterprises. Private restaurants, for example, were infamously restricted from having any more than just 12 chairs. They were also prohibited from selling seafood or beef, alcohol without food, and from setting up a bar or having live music. For cafeteria-style food vendors (often popularly referred to as *puntos fijos* or *merolicos* in Cuba), the use of chairs, benches, and tables was prohibited. Additionally, sales in dollars were prohibited unless specifically authorized.

A wide range of other restrictions denied microenterprises access to a variety of production inputs. The first of these was labor. Microenterprises were prohibited from hiring labor, though unpaid family members could work in the microenterprise (a loophole that would give rise to many faux-cousins in the food service and rental sector). Second, microenterprises lacked access to foreign exchange and imported inputs. Large scale state firms and mixed enter-

Table 4.3: Decree-Law 174: Microenterprise Rules, Contraventions, and Punishments

Contravention	Fines (pesos)	Seizure of Equipment, Products	Withdrawal of License[a]
Article 3: Contravention of Microenterprise Regulations			
1. Exercise of unauthorized activity	500–1,500	Yes	Not relevant
2. Unauthorized exercise of legal activity	400–1,200	Yes	Not relevant
3. Violations of regulations in a legal activity:			
(a) More than 12 chairs in *paladar*	500–1,500		2 years* min.
(b) Sale of seafood or beef in *paladar*	500–1,500	Yes	
(c) Sales in $US when not authorized	500–1,500		2 years* min.
(d) Sale of alcohol without food	400–1,200		2 years* min.
(e) Use of benches, tables in street vending	500–1,500		2 years* min.
(f) Use of other location than one's home	250–750		2 years* min.
(g) Inadequate receipts for input purchase	250–750	Yes	2 years* min.
(h) Use of family labor without licenses	400–1,200		2 years* min.
(i) Exhibiting unauthorized films	400–1,200	Yes	2 years* min.
(j) Sale or use of protected flora or fauna	400–1,200	Yes	1 year* min.
4. Use of one's home for another enterprise	250–750		
5. Use of intermediaries or specialized sellers	400–1,200		1 year* min.
6. Acting as an intermediary for another	400–1,200		2 years* min.
7. Not paying of rental fee for market space	150–500		
8. Sales to state entity without permission	400–1,200		
9. Safety violations	400–1,200		
10. Hiding or falsifying information	400–1,200		
11. Failure to show registration documents	400–1,200		
12. Employment of persons under 17 years	500–1,500		2 years* min.
13. Acting as a wholesaler to others	500–1,500	Yes	1 year* min.
14. Sales of one's products by others	500–1,500	Yes	Permanent
15. Organization of producer coops or associations unless specifically authorized	500–1,500	Yes	Permanent
16. Resale of industrial products purchased in state sector	400–1,200		
17. Use of prohibited materials or inputs	250–750	Yes	2 years* min.
18. Operation in other provinces	250–750	Yes	
19. Failure to update information provided to *Registros de Trabajadores de Cuenta Propia*	150–500	Yes	
Article 4: Contravention of Microenterprise Sanitary Regulations			
1. Non-compliance with hygiene-sanitary rules	500–1,500	Yes	1 year* min.
2. Inappropriate waste disposal	400–1,200		2 years* min.
3. Failure to show authorities sanitary license	400–1,200		
Article 5: Contravention of Tax Provisions			
1. Failure to make monthly or annual payments on time	150–500		
2. Failure to register or provide new information	150–500		
3. Failure to show documentation of any time	250–750		
4. Failure to keep revenue and cost information for one year	500–1,500		
5. Failure to provide information in the required form	400–1,200		
6. Failure to permit free access to designated inspectors	400–1,200		2 years* min.

Source: Decree-Law No. 174, "De las Contravenciones Personales de las Regulaciones del Trabajo por Cuenta Propia," *Gaceta Oficial*, No. 22, June 30, 1997: 337-352.

a. Some microentrepreneurs stated in interviews that the minimum two-year license suspension functioned in practice as a permanent suspension.

* The average monthly income in Cuba was 214 pesos in 1996. Thus, these fines range from 70% to 700% of the average monthly income and are higher for multiple offenses.

prises could use their peso earnings to acquire foreign exchange at the official exchange rate of $1.00 U.S. = 1 Cuban Peso (in *Moneda Nacional*/CUPs) and were able to obtain the required bureaucratic permission to import needed material inputs or machinery and equipment at this exchange rate. Microenterprises could not do this. They could purchase items at the dollar stores, but only what was available and at the going prices. This included a 140% sales tax. Moreover, the microentrepreneur had to purchase U.S. dollars at the quasi-official rate for Cuban citizens, namely 1.00 U.S. = 22 to 26 Cuban pesos in the early 2000s, or 1.08 "Convertible pesos" or "CUCs" = 26 CUPs after 2004.

Microenterprises had no access to credit from the banking system so that their investments had to be financed from savings, informal loans from friends, retained earnings, sales of other assets, or remittances (Orozco and Hansing 2011). The availability of credit to the state sector and to the mixed enterprise sector and the absence of credit to the microenterprise sector represented a form of discrimination, the main effect of which was to help stunt its development. A further limitation on the microenterprise sector was that its access to markets was restricted. Sales only to individual consumers were permitted. Sales to state enterprises, the public service, mixed enterprises, or formal organizations (for example, to quasi-NGOs) were prohibited. The objectives of this restriction seemed to be to limit the expansion of the private sector and to protect state enterprises from competition with microenterprise.

Restrictions on the location of microenterprises were also introduced soon after their legalization. For example, in 1995 new regulations were issued for the exercise of self-employment activities in the 15 municipalities of the "City of Havana" province. With 63,969 legal license holders at the time (August 1995), Havana was home to the most profitable and largest number of self-employed operations. Accord #84 (1997), as the new law was known, established detailed regulations over the use of Havana's public spaces, specifying the locations where self-employment would be prohibited. The law made it illegal to engage in self-employment activity on Havana's major streets and thoroughfares (including the *Malecón*, 23rd Street (also known as *La Rampa*), Salvador Allende, San Rafael, Neptuno, San Lázaro, Boyeros, Avenida "L," Línea, Avenida "G," Paseo, and Quinta Avenida in Miramar). Such activities were also prohibited near any major government institution (schools, hospitals, cemeteries, military zones, and embassies) and in the vicinity of any tourism-related building or enterprise (hotels, airports, museums, etc.) (Accord #84 1997: 490-495).

The stated intent of Accord #84 was to achieve a "greater discipline and efficacy" of self-employment in the capital, to avoid the "excessive proliferation of vendors," and to "neutralize and combat any and all actions against the positive development of the self-employed individual, avoiding the impunity of those who violate existing legislation" (Martínez 1995b: 2). However, such a list of prohibited areas in which to carry out one's work, on top of the host of earlier restrictions, must have seemed draconian to those microentrepreneurs hurt by the prohibition. These individuals, who were investing their time and life savings in the development of their activities, likely interpreted the ruling as a signal that the government was aiming to complicate and penalize them simply for becoming microentrepreneurs in the first place. Such a conclusion, in turn, probably led a good portion of them to doubt the government's fairness and good faith, provoking further "violations of existing legislation" in order for them to stay in business.

Microenterprises were prohibited from advertising their products or services through the media or through advertising "flyers," news-sheets, or handouts. One early initiative by an enterprising individual (a friend of one of the authors) was to publish a "flyer" or handout publicizing *paladares*—and financed by them—in the city of Havana and to make them freely available in the major hotels for tourists. This would have been useful for the tourists and for tourism, as well as for the *paladares* themselves. However, this initiative was abandoned when the individual was warned against this activity by officials. No reason was given for the prohibition. However, one might guess that prevention of private sector competition for state sector dollar restaurants and containment of the *paladares* were probably the main reasons.[6]

A final restriction on microenterprise was the prohibition of the use of "intermediaries" (Articles 3.5, 3.6, and 3.13). This required that the self-employed producer alone sell his or her output. It was also forbidden for specialized vendors to purchase the products of other producers for resale. This prohibition of the most fundamental degree of specialization condemned many self-employed persons to continued low productivity, inefficiency, and low incomes because producers must also sell their products. It makes little sense to require craftsmen and artisans, for example, to produce their work and also to sit in the market stall selling it. In practice, such a restriction likely lead to widespread illegality, disrespect for unreasonable rules, and distrust of a government that enacts enforces them.

For some activities such as arts and crafts products that earned substantial amounts of foreign exchange from tourists, the relevant inspectors and officials seemed to tolerate infractions on the "no intermediary" rule, presumably realizing that its strict enforcement would put most operators out of business. This type of prohibition also existed for small private farmers who were supposed to transport their own produce to market. Most had neither the time nor the means to transport their crops from country to town. However, the relevant officials turned a blind eye on this infraction, perhaps recognizing that compliance was both impossible and unreasonable.

For the specific microenterprise activities such as *paladares*, bed-and-breakfast operators, and taxis, there were numerous additional restrictions. For example, *paladares* were restricted to supplies purchased exclusively in dollar stores. To ensure that this was the case, receipts for all input purchases had to be obtained and made available to inspectors upon request. For B&Bs, there were regulations on the spaces that could be used by houseguests with taxes based on the size of these areas. To enforce these regulations, a small army of inspectors was employed. These inspectors wielded arbitrary power and could levy large fines for infractions on the part of entrepreneurs. They constituted an additional corruptible layer in the system. Anecdotal evidence suggests that the taking of bribes of various sorts for overlooking infractions of the regulations was commonplace.[7]

The funds raised by the fines levied for infractions have been significant. Apart from the amount of revenues collected in taxes both through the monthly lump sum tax payment and the year-end "sworn declaration" personal income tax (described below), fines collected from the self-employed workers in the first six months of 1999 amounted to 13,093,500 pesos. This was the yield from 18,628 fines that were levied on the basis a total of 462,628 inspections that were carried out (Fernández Peláez 2000). The government also waged an assault on some types of microenterprise with what appears to have been a form of "predatory competition." An example of this was the campaign of some of the state enterprises against *merenderos* or vendors of snacks, soft drinks, and various types of food in the streets to a modest clientele in pesos. In early 1997, state firms used fleets of bicycle-carts to sell similar snacks in the same locations where *merenderos* tended to locate. Scores of new state-run cafeterias were also opened in Havana and reports indicate that as many as 600 new state food vendors were put on the street offering light snacks in direct competition with the private cafeterias (Whitefield 1996a).[8]

Cuba's Budget Minister Elio Amat explained that the state had plans to set up a chain of luxury peso restaurants intended to give the popular *paladares* a run for their money. "Not for a second have we considered falling behind the *paladares*," Amat was quoted as saying at the time (Whitefield 1996a). This could be a mere case of fair competition except for the discrimination in input costs and taxation levels favoring the state firms. State firms were able to purchase their inputs through the state controlled sector at subsidized prices. These prices are a small fraction of the prices at the dollar stores where the microentrepreneurs must purchase their inputs.[9]

In a sense, the third category of B&B—what we call "family businesses"—were exactly the kind of small-scale, survival-oriented operations that the state intended to legalize when self-employment was first legalized in 1993. The regularization of such small, individually- or family-run enterprises would allow Cuban families the space in which to "resolve" their basic survival needs, without having to resort to the black market as they had been doing en masse up to then. Moreover, an expanded space for family businesses would create employment and provide goods and services without threatening the predominance of state ownership within the socialist-command economy

Vignette: Leonardo and Julia Rent a Room

Both Leonardo and his wife Julia are professionals, having graduated from the University of Havana together in 1983. The couple's rental apartment is located on the north side of San Lázaro Street near the University of Havana, just inside of the hotel zone and within the reaches of upscale *Vedado*. In the early 2000s, this prime location forced them to pay a much higher tax rate than others located just across the street in the working-class neighborhood of *Centro Habana*. Whereas the rate just across the street was $3 per square meter, their location just within the hotel zone made their rate double that. Therefore, $6 per square meter for their apartment of 60 square meters made their monthly tax $360 U.S. Doing some quick mental math, Leonardo explained that each day was worth $12 to him, given that this was the amount he had to pay to the government ($360/30days = $12). With this tight budget, he explained that he could usually only clear between $70 and $120 per month in profit, after paying the government its $360 share.

Given such high tax rates, Julia added that she and many other renters in her municipality have protested the tax system as unfair in public meetings with authorities. "The fact is that these laws oblige you to commit illegalities. Decent people don't like to go outside of the law." When asked why they did not simply rent legitimately, without any tricks or violations, they responded that they had tried the first time around and went bankrupt as a result. "What happens to those who try to follow the laws? They go broke," Julia argued.

> In order to stay above water one has to be flexible and make small exceptions even if you don't like it. Legality is a relative concept in this business. I'd prefer to pay high taxes, register the whole house, whatever, but base the tax I pay on the business I do, on my earnings. This fixed tax system is feudal.

When asked to name the most positive aspects of self-employment, Julia mentioned that it helped her resolve her family's economic problems. However, she rejected any larger benefits, arguing:

> There's an erroneous idea that economic independence brings freedom. Maybe in theory but that just doesn't fit here. It doesn't matter much in Cuba whether you make a lot of money or have a private business. We all have to live under the same limitations. Economic independence doesn't liberate you here because one never knows how long the tolerant policy will last. You can't plan for the future and nothing is sure since the laws can all change overnight.

model. Ironically, as taxes began to rise and as inspections were stepped up, it was just these kinds of small-scale, low-profit, relatively law-abiding family operations that were hit the hardest by the tax system and many additional regulations.

Like other groups, these family-run operations did resort to illegal strategies to turn a profit and stay afloat. However, unlike the untouchable and privileged categories described above, which had various mechanisms at their disposal to neutralize the abuses of the system, family operations tended to have neither the material resources nor the internal and external connections with which to counteract overbearing regulations. As a result, they turned to family members as one of their few reliable, inexpensive, and legitimate resources. However, without access to the capital to pay large bribes, these operations were often forced to pay even larger fines. The general lesson over time seemed to be that honesty does not pay.

Unlike many of the privileged operations, which made extensive use of a fairly complex division of labor, and the untouchables, in which the actual owner was often absent, the owner-operators of these family-run B&Bs were directly involved in all aspects of the business. Furthermore, many were threatened with closure and eventually forced to file futile appeals to have their suspended licenses reinstated. As a result, these family restaurants often sought to join the ranks of the "privileged operators" by increasing their links with informality and/or investing their small amount of capital back into their business. It was more likely, however, that they would sink into the ranks of the underground sector or simply go out of business since the characteristics of the privileged operators (location, space, sturdy infrastructure, and international connections) were difficult to replicate.

The Taxation of Self-Employment

In principle, it is reasonable, fair, and necessary that all types of business enterprise, small and large, private, public, and mixed in any country be taxed equitably in order to pay their share of the costs of the provision of public services. However, the tax structure and incidence of the burden of taxation must be equitable among enterprises as well as individuals. The tax regime for microenterprise established between 1993 and 1997 included a number of features that made it both unfair in terms of its incidence among different types of enterprise and counterproductive with respect to its impacts on economic behavior. The level of taxation in the microenterprise sector in Cuba escalated rapidly, from low levels in September 1993 to levels that were exceedingly high by mid-1997 and still higher by 2004, becoming lethal to the survival of many microenterprises (Ritter 2000a, b).

Cuba's tax regime during these years consisted of compulsory lump-sum licensing fees (*cuota fija mensual*, or CFM, which constitute implicit taxes) paid each month to the state revenue administration, the *Oficina Nacional de Administracion Tributaria* (ONAT) together with a self-administered annual income tax payment (*declaración jurada*) correcting for any possible under-payment (but not over-payment) through the monthly lump sum tax. Apart from the fact that the lump sum was required regardless of one's earnings, a particularly pernicious feature of the system at this stage was the 10% maximum allowable deduction from taxable income for purchased inputs.

The first element in the tax regime was the CFM, or "monthly fixed lump-sum tax payment." Rates ranged from 10 CUPs for a cleaner up to 400 pesos for *paladar* restaurants. In fact, as we describe in Chapters 5 and 8, monthly tax payments for *paladares* quickly became more severe and included additional monthly payments for hiring a maximum of two workers and for serving alcoholic beverages, as summarized in Table 4.4. If the restaurant charged in dollars (or later CUCs), taxe were also to be paid in dollars, up to a maximum up-front monthly tax payment of $520.00.

The CFM arrangement was imposed initially in 1993 when Cuba entered the first phase of microenterprise liberalization. The Ministries of Finance and Prices and of Labor and Social Security set the minimum rates, but the Administrative Councils of each Municipal government were empowered to establish rates above these minimum levels, with the approval of the relevant Ministries. Rates could be changed every six months, in January and July. The legislation permitted Councils to raise the rates if they considered the incomes of the microenterprises "excessive," although criteria for this was not defined (Decree-Law 141, 1993). The law only permitted increases, not decreases in tax rates creating an additional source of uncertainty for microenterprises. Mi-

Table 4.4: Taxation Rates for *Paladares* and Other Food Services, Monthly Lump Sum (*Cuota Fija Mensual*) Payments

	Domestic Economy, Cuban pesos (CUPs)	Tourist Sector, $US or CUCs
A. Food and Drink Vendor (*"al detalle"*)	100	—
B. Food Vendor from Home	200	$US 100
C. Private Restaurants (*"paladares"*)	400	300
+Sales of Alcoholic Beverages	100	100
+Tax for Required Minimum Two Employees	120	120

Source: Ministerio de Trabajo y Seguridad Social y de Finanzas y Precios, Resolución Conjunta No. 4/95, *Granma*, June 14, 1995.

croentrepreneurs could abandon the activity at the beginning of any month, thus immediately ceasing the monthly payments.

The initial tax rates were set at relatively low levels in September 1993, but were increased thereafter. Especially noteworthy was the distinction between those microenterprises that operated in the dollar or "convertible peso" economy vis-à-vis those in the peso economy. The former were taxed at a rate about 20 times that of the latter (at the exchange rate relevant for Cuban citizens). At the end of each year, microenterprises were required to pay a tax on their revenues on the basis of a "progressive" tax schedule, the second feature of the tax regime. However, they could deduct the total of the monthly lump-sum payments from the amount of tax owed according to the schedule.

The procedure was as follows:

1. Microenterprises add up their gross revenues;
2. They subtract 10% of the gross revenues (20% in the case of private transportation) as an allowable deduction for purchased inputs, in order to arrive at their net taxable income, regardless of the true costs of purchased inputs of materials, labor, rent, utilities, etc.;
3. They calculate the tax owed according to the scale worksheet in Table 4.5 below. The payments are cumulative with each component of income falling within each bracket being taxed at the rate for that bracket;
4. They deduct the sum of the CFM payments already made over the course of the previous year from the tax that is owed;
5. If the amount owed exceeds the amount already paid through the CFM payments, they must pay the difference. If the amount owed is less than that already pazid, they receive no refund.

Official tax rates are presented in Table 4.5. The first scale on the tax worksheet is for income and taxes in national currency (CUPs) while the second one is for income and taxes in U.S. dollars or CUPs. The tax scale applies to 90% of gross income, that is, income net of the 10% of gross revenues that was the maximum allowable deduction at the time for purchased inputs. The "progressivity" of the tax scale for *dollar incomes* is not too far out of line in the context of an international comparative perspective. It also seems reasonable from a Cuban perspective. On the other hand, for *peso incomes*, the scale increases from 5% for the first 3,000 pesos and reaches 50% for the tax bracket for income exceeding 60,000 pesos. As the peso tax rate reaches the highest tax bracket, it increases and reaches 50% on taxable income. This seems steep as the 50% marginal tax rate comes into effect at an *annual* income of 60,000 pesos, which was about US$120.00 to $140.00 *per month* throughout most of the 1996-2006 period.

Table 4.5: Tax Scale Worksheet Applied to Personal Income, 1997

Tax Bracket	Tax Rate %
PESO SCALE	
Excess of the former up to the latter:	
(a) 0– 3,000	5
(b) 3,000– 6,000	10
(c) 6,000–12,000	15
(d) 12,000–18,000	20
(e) 18,000–24,000	25
(f) 24,000–36,000	30
(g) 36,000–48,000	35
(h) 48,000–60,000	40
(i) 60,000 and over	50
U.S. DOLLAR SCALE	
Excess of the former up to the latter:	
(a) 0– 2,400	10
(b) 2,400– 6,000	12
(c) 6,000– 9,600	15
(d) 9,600–13,200	20
(e) 13,200–18,000	25
(f) 18,000–24,000	30
(g) 24,000–36,000	35
(h) 36,000–48,000	40
(h) 48,000–60,000	45
(j) 60,000 and over	50

Source: ONAT, Declaración Jurada, Impuesto sobre Ingresos Personales, Moneda Nacional, 1997: 1, and Ministerio de Finanzas y Precios, Instrucción No. 11/96, Declaracion Jurada, Divisas, 1996.

A third feature of the tax system was that a maximum deduction of just 10% from gross income was permitted for purchased inputs in the determination of taxable income. In other words, net income for tax purposes or "taxable income" was always considered 90% of gross income regardless of the real value of purchased inputs. The only exception was in transportation where the maximum deduction for purchased inputs was 20% (*Oficina Nacional de Administración Tributaria*, 1997: 6). This is referred to here as the "10% Maximum Cost Deductibility Rule." This feature of the tax regime is problematic in that microenterprises that face high costs for purchased inputs (more complex, value-added occupations) were in effect being taxed on these purchases. This means that the true tax rate on value added by the microenterprise on its actual net revenues can be much higher than those illustrated in Table 4.5, which shows the rates only for a microenterprise with actual costs of purchased inputs of 10% of gross revenues.

Perhaps a few microenterprises in fact may have had net revenues equal to or more than 90% of gross revenue, i.e. with input costs less than 10% of gross revenue. These would be microenterprises involving highly labor-intensive production processes with minimal equipment or purchased material inputs. Messenger services, bicycle guards, childcare, building attendants, masseuses, domestic servants, and possibly sports or language instruction could be of this character. On the other hand, many other activities (such as food vending, shoemakers, artisans, flower cultivators and sellers, used book or record sellers) involve the purchase and processing of substantial amounts of material inputs. Some private restaurant operators estimated their input costs as being well above 60% (interviews with *cuentapropistas*, November 1998). As argued below, this situation creates problems of equity, efficiency, and viability for the tax system.

There were a number of factors encouraging the government to adopt this tax regime. When self-employment was legalized in September 1993, prices, revenues, and net profits in much of the microenterprise sector were often very high. This was the result of the limited number of microenterprises that came into existence initially together with extreme scarcity and the excess purchasing power in the hands of citizens while prices in the state sector were fixed at low levels. The imposition of the tax regime and the escalation of tax rates were therefore designed to remove a proportion of this income for equity reasons. It should be emphasized again, however, that a large proportion of the microenterprises were involved in the provision of simple goods and services for low-income Cubans in the peso economy and generated modest incomes, though higher than the average in the state sector.

Second, the microenterprise tax regime was established at a time when there was not yet a well-established administration for this type of taxation. Prior to this, Cuba did not have a transparent tax system or an established popular culture of paying taxes, because the tax rates and payments previously had been hidden. Moreover, before the legalization of much microenterprise, many such firms had operated clandestinely, avoiding tax payments and other regulations. The tax system that was implemented was designed to enforce a high level of compliance in a context in which non-compliance in the underground economy had been the norm.

Third, there was a significant amount of theft of products from the state sector, especially in the 1990s. A proportion of these stolen goods found their way to the microenterprise sector as production inputs. One of the novel elements of the tax system—the 10% limit on the deduction from taxable income for purchased inputs—appears to have been designed to address this situation. If it were impossible to know for sure the true value of purchased inputs, it would be risky to permit microenterprises to calculate their own input costs for determining taxable income. It was administratively easier to simply declare a maximum of 10% of gross income for purchased inputs for all microenterprises regardless of their true expenses.

Vignette: Jorge, Vanguard Worker Rents Car as a Cab

Jorge, a retired doctor, began our interview by explaining that he was awarded his car, a 1985 Russian Moscovich, in 1985 after being voted a "vanguard" employee at the hospital. In fact, at the time he was abroad on an international mission in Nicaragua and did not take possession of his car until he returned to Cuba in 1987. However, when someone was awarded a car in this way, it meant he or she had the right to purchase a car from the state. In fact, he paid 4,500 pesos for the car in 1988, the current equivalent of $225. Jorge joked that the Russian Moscovitch was notorious in Cuba for its shoddy workmanship. Still, he was pleased to have the car and used it happily until the onset of the special period.

By 1994, Jorge simply could no longer to afford to use the car due to the scarcity of fuel and skyrocketing price of gasoline. At the time, his unused car attracted many offers from prospective cabbies who would show up at his home and ask to "rent" his car for use as a cab. He finally gave in and allowed a "trustworthy" man who was recommended to him by a mutual friend to use the car under the condition that he pay $5 per day ($35 per week) as a rental fee. However, the cabbie proved to be not so trustworthy after all. "He did not take care of the car, so I took it away from him," explained Jorge.

Still in need of supplementary income, Jorge attempted rent out his car on two other occasions. However, both times he came up against the same problem: The cabbies invariably ran the car into the ground. "In this way, it passed through the hands of three different people," he said exasperated. "The last guy returned it to me in the worst condition possible. It had a flat tire, the paint job had been ruined, and there were dents all over it. I decided not to rent it out again." Instead, he invested some savings in repairing the car and finally "sold" it in 1997, hoping to rid himself of the burden.

Like most other significant "private" property in Cuba (house, land, boat, etc.), at this time one could not simply sell something to the highest bidder on the open market. Jorge declared with an ironic smile, "They 'give' us these cars, but we can't sell them." He explained that while he had bought the car for $225, he managed to sell it for $1,500, a substantial profit even considering the large sum of money he invested to have it repaired. Since such a sale was not legal in Cuba, Jorge was given a semi-official IOU from the man to whom he sold it stating that he was owed 40,000 pesos. The idea behind this IOU was that Jorge had given the "buyer" the car temporarily as a kind of security deposit.

After his previous headaches, Jorge sold the car with the understanding that it not be used as a taxi. Moreover, anyone other than the legal owner of a car was prohibited from using it as a taxi at the time. However, this is exactly the use which the buyer had in mind. The original idea was that the buyer had a son who was a doctor and needed the car for work. "I found out that that was just a story he had told me to convince me to sell him the car so he could use it as a taxi," he recounted.

Since he sold the car in 1997, Jorge had been called by the police on two different occasions after the new owner was stopped, suspected of being a gypsy cabbie. Specifically, the accusation was that he was using a private car as a taxi without a license, and using a car as a taxi while not being the owner (both crimes in Cuba). Luckily, on both occasions Jorge and his buyer were able to avoid the 1,000 peso fine with the dubious explanation that the driver was actually Jorge's mechanic who used the car once in a while as he worked on it.

Reflecting on his personal scramble for a dignified retirement and on the larger state of Cuban communism in the early 2000s, Jorge declared with conviction, "As a political philosophy [communism] has been a disaster." He continued,

> Look, here in Cuba in concrete terms there is much material need. I don't mean to brag but I did more than my share [for the Revolution], but I did not do it in order to starve. The great truth is that getting enough food is still one of our biggest problems here. If you eat lunch you skip dinner, if you have dinner you may not be able to eat breakfast or lunch, etc. This is just a tragedy.

Then, referring to the government's constant marches, parades, and speeches condemning the U.S. and celebrating the great successes of Cuban socialism, Jorge argued,

> They convoke one of those "*tribunas abiertas*" (open tribunals) and all the world goes out to sing and shout. Thousands of people go to these things. But these people say the same things I'm telling you now when they're alone. It's a case of collective cowardice.

A popular view among *cuentapropistas* themselves was that the tax system was designed to punish them for ideological reasons and ultimately drive them out of business. This is a possibility and there are statements from the leadership, noted above, that seem to support this view. The heavy reliance on regulations and the severe punishment for "infractions" also suggest that this is the case. It is not likely, however, that the microenterprise tax regime was designed to kill the microenterprise sector—which would have involved it killing its own tax base and *raison d'etre*. Instead, it is more likely that it was designed to actually collect taxes in a difficult environment in which open and transparent tax-paying was not the established practice.

The initial tax regime for microenterprise instituted in the late-1990s had a variety of impacts in terms of fairness, efficiency, and viability. These impacts are summarized here for the individual microenterprise, the microenterprise sector, and Cuba's society and economy more broadly. From the standpoint of an individual microenterprise, the lump-sum payments involved a marginal tax rate of 100% of true net earnings until they are paid off at which level of income the marginal tax rate falls to zero. This zero percent rate would prevail until gross income reached the level at which the tax payments owed under the official tax scale were equal to the first imposition of the tax—at 3,000 pesos under the tax scale of Table 4.5 where the tax scale would become effective. When faced with this pattern of marginal tax rates, the microenterprise would likely try to avoid paying the higher tax rates by restricting its output and/or under-declaring income. If the firm restricted its output, society would lose the foregone goods and services, the microenterprise sector would lose income, and the government would lose tax revenues. If the microenterprise underdeclares its income, the government would lose revenue.

With the high barrier to entry created by the initial 100% marginal tax rate inherent in the CFM lump-sum payment system, some microenterprises had a strong incentive to go (or remain) underground. There can be no doubt that this occurred in Cuba, as elsewhere: tradesmen would undertake house and appliance repairs; mechanics would repair cars; estheticians would provide hairdressing and manicure services (at their homes or in the state beauty salons); private car owners like Jorge would rent their cars to others to provide gypsy taxi services despite the risks involved; and many people would provide personal services unofficially—all without a license. In these situations, the government loses a huge portion of potential tax revenues. Of course, the ONAT was fully aware of the lost revenues and used inspectors and the *Comités para la Defensa de la Revolución* (CDRs, or neighborhood watch committees) to prevent underground enterprises from operating. However, clandestine microenterprise was widespread and the members and officials of the CDRs were often involved in the underground economy so controlling it was difficult if not impossible (see the vignette about Rafael and Norma below).[10]

At the level of the microenterprise sector, the tax regime was inequitable in terms of its impacts *among* microenterprises. Because of the "10% rule," firms with higher levels of inputs paid higher marginal and average tax rates in terms of their net income than other firms with the same net incomes but lower levels of inputs. A second element of unfairness was that the tax structure discriminated against new entrants to any part of the sector, because the marginal tax rate is initially 100% due to the lump-sum CFM. Lacking savings or investment, new entrants must earn revenues immediately to have the money to pay these taxes.

From the standpoint of the microenterprise sector, the tax regime also resulted in a variety of inefficiencies. By creating a high barrier to entry because of the 100% marginal tax rate, the number of new firms entering the sector was likely reduced. High levels of uncertainty and risk for new entrants also serve as a barrier keeping out potential new participants. Therefore, there was less legal competition, higher prices, and lower volumes of production than would have been the case had these barriers to entry been lower. On the other hand, for some other types of microenterprise where entrance into the clandestine economy is easier, the result may have been increased competition from tax-evading, lower-cost suppliers of certain goods and services. The "10% rule" also has negative effects in terms of efficiency. Because of the high true taxation levels for those microenterprises that have higher levels of inputs, the volume of production of goods and services from these firms is probably unduly low.

From a societal equity perspective, taxation of the microenterprise sector is of course necessary. The sector, like all others, must pay its share of the costs for public goods and services. It is difficult to know what a fair level of taxation for the sector should have been in the period when it was established in Cuba. This is because for at least a transitional period, the incomes earned in the sector were high for the reasons mentioned above. The high taxation rates in real terms—in relation to true net incomes in the sector—reflected the desire to tap these high incomes for both revenue-raising and equity reasons. However, it is inequitable to tax microentrepreneurs with the same net incomes at different rates, but this is what the 10% rule achieves.

Perhaps one of the more disturbing inequities of the microenterprise tax regime is that it is more onerous than the tax regime facing foreign companies operating in joint venture arrangements with Cuban state firms (a situation that is likely to continue after 2014 given the very generous terms contained in the foreign investment law published in April 2014). In contrast to the regime for microenterprise, during the 1995–2010 period a normal tax regime by international standards was imposed for mixed enterprises and joint ventures involving foreign firms. These enterprises faced a reasonable tax regime, allowing the deduction of all costs of production in determining the taxable income base. In contrast, applying a tax system that is imposed on 90% of gross revenues in the microenterprise sector in effect discriminated against Cuban citizens (as illustrated by Table 4.6).

While foreign enterprises in joint venture arrangements received a fairly standard tax treatment from a comparative international perspective, their treatment was much more favorable than domestically owned and oriented microenterprise at this time. For example, foreign joint ventures were able to deduct investment costs from taxable income; domestic microenterprises

Table 4.6: Tax Regimes for Cuban Microenterprise and Foreign Enterprise Operating in Joint Ventures, 1995–2010

	Microenterprise Sector	Joint Ventures
Effective Tax Rates	May exceed 100% of net income	30% of net income (50% for mining and petroleum)
Effrective Tax Base	90% of gross income (Maximum of 10% allowable deduction for production costs)	Net income after deduction of total production costs
Deductibility of Investment	Not deductible from taxable income	Fully deductible from taxable income
Lump-Sum Taxation	Up-front *cuota fija mensual* tax payments necessary	None
Rebates for Tax Overpayment	No rebates for tax overpayment	Not applicable
Tax "Holidays"	No	Yes
Profit Expatriation	No	Yes

could not. Foreign joint ventures could deduct all of their costs of production from taxable income (gross revenues); microenterprises were allowed to deduct costs only up to a ceiling of 10% of gross income. Foreign joint ventures did not face the possibility of overpayment of taxes; microenterprises that overpaid did not (and still do not) receive a refund. Foreign joint ventures paid taxes after the revenues have been earned; microenterprises paid (and still pay) before revenues have been earned. In sum, the discrimination against Cuban citizens operating microenterprises is striking.

Again, from a societal perspective, the tax regime for microenterprises lowers living standards because it damages the rationality of resource allocation. First, the onerous levels of taxation inherent in the tax regime lead enterprises to go out of business, or in some cases to restrict their own production in order to avoid higher tax brackets. Both of these results reduce the volume of goods and services produced in the sector and raise prices. Second, the microenterprise tax regime restricts entry into the sector thereby restricting competition, reducing output, and raising prices. Third, the when microenterprises go underground, this also results in inefficiencies of resource use because they must operate on a very small scale and continuously "under cover." This lowers the quality and quantity of their products and increases their prices in comparison with those firms operating legally. Tax revenues are also reduced when enterprises go underground. By blocking the entrance of new microenterprises and promoting their exit, the tax regime reduces productive employment and the generation of incomes.[11]

One surprising result of the microenterprise tax regime is its inherent discrimination against domestically-oriented, "value added" economic activity. Microenterprises had little or no access to imported inputs except those acquired from recycled materials or purchases from the dollar stores or special state sellers of inputs—which were (and still are) prohibitively expensive. The effective exchange rate for them in 1998 was approximately 20 pesos for $US 1.00 worth of imported inputs (plus taxes of 140%). For enterprises in the state sector, on the other hand, $US 1.00 worth of imported inputs cost only 1 peso (CUC). This meant that state enterprises could access imports much more cheaply than microenterprises. The result was that microenterprises used domestically available inputs to a higher degree than did state enterprises.[12] In discriminating against private microenterprise, the tax regime therefore discriminated against domestic value added in favor of the more import-intensive state firms.

The perceived unfairness of the microenterprise tax regime has resulted in high levels of non-compliance. Indeed, the survival of some microenterprises depended on non-compliance, especially if they were unable to retreat to the underground economy due to a location or profile incompatible with clandestine operations. Moreover, it was likely that a significant proportion of microenterprises under-declared their incomes. The result of the character of the tax system and the non-compliance it engendered was that the tax system lacked credibility. Rather than leading to the gradual development of a "tax culture" in which people willingly and honestly paid their taxes, the system provoked cheating. To some extent this has been part of people's overall survival strategies in the difficult circumstances of the 1990s and 2000s—and likely long before then. The nature of the tax regime has likely led some people to think that tax evasion was not unethical even if it was illegal. In the longer term, it will be difficult to change the current "culture of tax evasion" to one of compliance. This could continue to be a problem even after a more reasonable microenterprise tax regime has been established—as has partly occurred following the 2010 microenterprise reforms (discussed in subsequent chapters).

In general, the characteristics of clandestine bed-and-breakfasts in this period were not much different from those of the family businesses described above. Underground renters—the final kind of B&B in our typology—tended to own homes with less-than-ideal conditions for renting. Their homes are small and deteriorated, offering relatively cramped quarters to their guests. Often their low-budget customers were looking for a cheap room and a little adventure outside the beaten tourist path. Furthermore, these clandestine operations tended to employ few helpers, with the owner-operator and her family (women dominated in running B&Bs) usually taking care of all cleaning and

Vignette: Rafael and Norma's Vedado Rental

Rafael and Norma are an elderly couple who occasionally rented a room in their rather spacious home in Havana's Vedado neighborhood during the late 1990s. While Rafael was a semi-retired university professor and Norma was a retired physician, they both were once quite active as students in the clandestine movement against Batista's dictatorship. Though both had become disillusioned with the Cuban political and economic system, and though Norma refused to participate any longer in what she called the government's "political hoopla," Rafael was still an active, if somewhat cynical president of their neighborhood CDR. If this couple was representative of the state of the underground economy at the time, officials, inspectors, CDR heads, and once proud revolutionary communists all seem to have had their hands deep in illegal activity.

When asked about Cuban B&Bs, Rafael explained,

> There are people in Miramar and Kohly who rent out their homes. These belong to high functionaries and retired state officials. When they were active they milked the cow for all they could and turned their homes into luxury palaces. Now, during hard-times, they rent out their homes and make a huge profit.

He added that it was exactly these people who could afford to pay high taxes, had the financial resources to pay taxes in the low season, were able to charge higher prices, and were removed from the central tourist areas and so had a substantially lower tax burden than someone like him who lived closer to the heart of the tourism economy. Beyond the obvious corruption and influence peddling that this implied, Rafael argued that this situation also discriminated against those in his position who did not have the same luxurious housing conditions to offer.

> Look at a person with a normal home. There's no air-conditioner, private entrance, refrigerator, or TV. Such a person must charge low prices and isn't able to pay even a fraction of the $250 monthly tax. How do people like that get by? They have the same necessities as anyone else. They end up renting on the sly because they're left with no other alternative. Without wanting to, they have to break the law because the law is unjust. Instead of serving to regulate, the law serves to turn the population into delinquents.

Rafael also discussed the paradox of how his breaking the laws of the state has indirectly allowed the state-sector to survive. "The money I have made here hasn't only helped us. It has also allowed me to buy the things I need for my job with the state. Ironically, I violate the state's law in order to keep serving the state. I practically spend more money to work than I receive in my monthly salary." He also pointed out that his inconspicuous location allows him to lie low and follow the golden rule of private enterprise in today's Cuba: *discretion*. "People are always interested in someone else's success, but not for good reasons. The ugly side of this is that we have to be very careful to avoid envy. To be honest, our greatest enemy isn't the state or the police." Instead, he declared emphatically, "Our greatest enemy is envy."

When asked if he thought self-employment had a future, Rafael replied: "I'm going to be honest with you. This has a future because in the real world the state cannot find a solution to all the little problems of the country. There are many areas where private enterprise can work better than the state." Rafael's basic argument was that state control of the service industry is not only not necessary, but actually detrimental to economic development.

> You have to remember the old Cuban saying, "*El que parte y reparte coge la mayor parte*" (He who divides and distributes grabs the biggest part). Of course, they probably get the "*mejor parte*" (best part) as well. But look for a moment at their salaries. The only way they can get by is stealing and after a while it becomes a matter of simple common sense. I think that the state should restrict itself to the large parts of the economy, the things that determine development.

up-keep. Though these operations did not seem to have access to much capital, it was not unknown for them to share some of their earnings with inspectors or, more commonly, with the head of the local neighborhood CDR in order to maintain good relations with the neighbors and avoid envy. Unlike the "family businesses" described above, however, clandestine operations are by definition involved in illegal activities and sometimes directly linked to the black market and other illicit activities, such as serving as private hotels where foreigners can rendezvous with their Cuban dates.

While some of these underground home-stays were previously licensed, the majority seem to have never gone public with their operation. This does not mean that they had never seriously considered getting a license. However, many did not believe they would be able to earn enough each month to pay the high mandatory tax, especially since the tax must be paid regardless of occupancy and revenue. In other words, few of these clandestine rentals were underground by choice and many claimed that they would quickly register if taxes were based on income. As one clandestine renter declared, "Of course, it's not a matter of us being delinquents, but is based on the fact that there is not another way for us to make money. We don't choose to be illegal."

Probably more so than others, clandestine renters were acutely aware of what Peruvian economist Hernando de Soto has called, the "costs of informality" (1989, 2000). Describing what he calls "legal apartheid," de Soto argues that in addition to the usual bribes and commissions, extralegal entrepreneurs must bear,

> [T]he costs of avoiding penalties, making transfers outside legal channels, and operating from dispersed locations and without credit, [showing that] the life of the extralegal entrepreneur turns out to be far more costly and full of daily hassles than that of the legal businessman. (De Soto 2000: 83)

For Cuba's extralegal renters in the 1990s and early 2000s, these costs included low earnings, little access to investment, and obviously no legal protection or ability to advertise. As such, the majority of these operations rented only occasionally and charged very low rates ($5-$15 per night), making their earnings much lower than they would otherwise have been. Furthermore, because they had no legal access to publicity, they often found themselves at the mercy of unscrupulous intermediaries who were one of their few sources of clients. Like informal entrepreneurs the world over, they found themselves in a frustrating catch-22 where they needed to publicize their operations to ensure a stable source of income, but were discouraged by fear of legal sanctions, including the possible, if rarely practiced confiscation of their homes.

Conclusion: Impact of Public Policies toward Microenterprise during the "Special Period"

Registered self-employed workers, along with other unregistered private self-employed activities, emerged during the crisis of the "Special Period" and made an important difference in the Cuban economy. They produced valuable goods and services that satisfied the essential needs of nearly all Cuban citizens, mainly using domestic inputs as opposed to the imports commonly used by state firms. They earned and saved foreign exchange for the country. They created jobs and aided Cuban families in ensuring basic survival. There are numerous instances where self-employment—even "illegal" self-employment—has acted as a supplement or subsidy to the state sector enabling workers with jobs in the "second economy" (such as the cabbies and B&B operators highlighted above) to continue to perform their socially valuable professions. Although a few types of self-employment activities have generated high incomes (especially those in the tourist sector), the great majority have provided fairly modest incomes to supplement their inadequate state sector incomes. Moreover, these activities have constituted a massive school of entrepreneurial training.

Regulations relating to health and safety, labor standards, minimum wages, and the environment, are quite reasonable. However, the main objective of the dense web of regulations concerning the purchase of inputs, marketing, size, and location within which the microenterprises functioned was to limit the size of the individual microenterprises, to limit their revenues, to eliminate intermediaries, and to contain the general expansion of the sector. Despite the contributions of the microenterprise sector, the regulatory and taxation framework within which it was forced to operate during this period has had major negative impacts upon Cuba's economic, social, and human development. It created generalized wastage of human, natural, and capital resources and blocked much needed improvements in the functioning of the economy.

It also wasted the entrepreneurial energies and talents of hundreds of thousands of Cuban citizens. It unnecessarily complicated their lives and wasted their time, energy, and resources. As mentioned in Chapter 1, *Granma*—Cuba's Communist Party national daily newspaper—would pen the most accurate and inadvertently ironic epitaph to the country's initial experiment with self-employment during the "Special Period," baldly admitting that such policies "condemned self-employment to near extinction and stigmatized those who decided to joint its ranks legally in the 1990s" (Martínez Hernández 2010).

The regulatory and taxation system has generated innumerable and ubiquitous economic irrationalities. While individually, the complex web of restrictions and regulations may seem trivial, when taken in their entirety, they result in immense wastage of resources of all types, especially human resources as people invest their time and their lives in trivial low-level inefficient survival activities with the possibilities of more rational use of their time and energies blocked by the regulatory framework and tax regime. Continuing economic irrationalities and inefficiencies and the low productivity they generate then cause the real incomes and living standards to be lower than necessary for citizens.

The dense regulatory environment made legal self-employment difficult if not impossible during this period. As a result, those microenterprises that have been able to survive more easily operating underground have done so. Moreover, each specific regulation creates a new web of subterfuges and evasions together with a need for additional inspectors, punishments, and fines. If these regulations are perceived to be arbitrary and punitive and designed to reduce the earnings of the microenterprises with little clear environmental, health, or safety rationale, the response of the microentrepreneur will be evasion. Dense and punitive restrictions therefore have the effect of promoting a generalized culture of illegality, as well as the underground economy.

The regulations also succeeded in keeping the microenterprises very small. Prohibitions on employment, access to credit, on markets, and the purchase of inputs all have had the effect of blocking the normal growth of such firms. Of course, this was long the declared intention of public policy—aiming to lower incomes, prevent the expansion of a private sector, block competition with the state, and prevent the emergence of politically independent groups of people outside state control. However, the economic consequence of the regulatory system has been that legal microenterprises are small and unable to achieve basic economies of scale. This results in a waste of Cuba's human, capital, and natural resources, as the valuable entrepreneurial skills of the microenterprise operators are expended on evasion and low level, small scale tasks.

Indeed, a central lesson of the government's policies toward self-employment during the "Special Period" is that state regulation of self-employment was accompanied by such onerous regulations that they overshadowed the benefits of legalization. What was initially hoped to be a series of reforms enabling Cuban citizens to play a proactive role in the island's economic recovery, turned out to be a mechanism of control over those engaging in self-employment. Cuba's microentrepreneurs were effectively constrained from fully and legally developing their enterprises. As a result, they made systematic use of the underground. Finally, the regulatory and tax systems promoted the underground economy and illegalities of numerous varieties. This encouraged a widespread culture of illegality and distrust of the government. While Chapter 7 focuses on Cuba's unbiquitous underground economy, Chapters 5 and 6 examine how the government of Raúl Castro has attempted to change course, moving from the "condemnation" and "stigmatization" of self-employment to its promotion as a viable, legitimate alternative and compliment to the state sector.

Notes

[1] These three occupations—private transport, private room rental, and private food service—quickly became the most popular private occupations during the "Special Period." They emerged once again as the most common activities—along with contracted workers—after the reopening and major expansion of the self-employment option after October, 2010.

[2] In this chapter we make frequent references to various self-employed individuals and enterprises in the housing (*casas particulares* or B&Bs) and transportation (*boteros* or gypsy cabbies) sectors. Chapter 8 focuses on private food service with an emphasis on Cuba's unique brand of home-based family-run restaurants, *paladares*. In these vignettes, the names of entrepreneurs have been changed. The descriptions of individual enterprises are normally composite sketches drawn from multiple interviews. All translations from the Spanish are our own. Interviews were carried out by Ted Henken between 2000 and 2011. However, those with the cabbies and B&B operators highlighted here were conducted during the general downturn in self-employment between 2000 and 2006. While it is impossible to make strictly representative generalizations from

qualitative interviews, we agree with political scientist Mark Q. Sawyer who argues in his book, *Racial Politics in Post-Revolutionary Cuba*, that "open-ended in-depth interviews allow researchers to explore how specific life experiences and information shape attitudes [...] that are complex and often contradictory" (2006: 104). Also see anthropologist Nadine Fernández's book, *Revolutionizing Romance: Interracial Couples in Contemporary Cuba* (2010), for a similar rationale for the use of ethnography and interviews as valuable research tools in Cuba, given the difficulty carrying out quantitative research there.

[3] There is a striking similarity in the survival strategies of the B&Bs described here and those of the *paladares* described in Chapter 8. As the legal requirements for running a *paladar* became more onerous between 1996 and 2005, it was common to find de facto private restaurants that were in fact legally registered as B&Bs. This way, owners could avoid *paladar* inspectors known to demand receipts for all food items and search refrigerators and garbage cans for forbidden foods. By obtaining a rental license, operators could simply pay the 30% "food service" surcharge on top of their monthly rental fee giving them a legal pretext to operate a full-scale *paladar* under the cover of their rental license. Such an arrangement also allowed these establishments to offer lodging to their dinner guests. Moreover, this legal loophole permitted them to operate two businesses at once, technically illegal at the time (but allowed after 2010).

[4] In the confiscations of 1968, small firms received no compensation. Larger enterprises were provided with bonds that were to be redeemed when the government could afford it, but which had an expiration date early in the 1970s.

[5] Another reason American cars predominated in the private sector is that their large size allowed drivers to maximize profits by filling the car up with as many as 6 or 8 passengers at a time. Also, American cars were often modified to function on diesel fuel, gasohol, or even natural gas, all cheaper than gasoline.

[6] This enterprising individual is now a successful professional in Mexico.

[7] An acquaintance of one of the authors became exceedingly thin during the difficult days of 1992–1995. However, after obtaining a position as a *paladar* inspector in 1996, he quickly packed on a significant amount of weight, perhaps as a by-product of his new post.

[8] A private ice cream vendor well known to one of the authors developed a thriving business in a main street location in Central Havana, but was soon confronted with a state vendor located immediately adjacent to him. Despite his higher prices, he continued to operate for some time because of the higher quality of his product. Ultimately, however, the operation went out of business.

[9] For example, the price of one pound of refined sugar in the state controlled sector was 0.08 pesos or $US 0.0036 at the quasi-official exchange rate of mid-1997. The black market price was 2.5 pesos or $US 0.011, while the price in the dollar stores was about $US 1.50. Obviously, if microenterprises were forced to purchase sugar, which is a major ingredient for most Cuban snacks and drinks, from the dollar stores while the state vendors purchased it at the controlled price the microenterprises could not compete with the state firms. But if the microenterprises purchased sugar on the black market they would be in technical violation of the law and vulnerable to punishment or seizure.

[10] One of the authors was familiar with a major underground enterprise operating with the full knowledge of the head of the local CDR located across the street. However the CDR official also had his own underground activities so that there was an implicit pact to remain silent.

[11] Open unemployment was stated to be 6.8% in 1996 while the open-unemployment equivalent of "underemployment" was estimated by the United Nations' ECLAC

at 27.3% in the same year (*Naciones Unidas* 1997: 378). This latter figure captures the loss to the nation arising from labor underutilization.

[12] An example of this occurred with the private restaurants where close to 100% of all of the inputs are of Cuban origin, in contrast to the state fast-food chains such as *Rápido* and *Burgui* (a Burger King look-alike), which imported almost everything: tables, potatoes, hamburger, chicken, trays, paper cups, and many of the specialized building materials.

5
Policy Reform Under Raúl Castro, 2006–2014

When Fidel Castro unexpectedly took ill and delegated governing authority to his brother Raúl in July 2006, Cuba had had considerable experience with self-employment. Its advantages and disadvantages were better understood and appreciated than during the previous decade. Despite the containment approach used under the government of the elder Castro, the benefits of small-scale and microenterprise were apparent to many citizens, observers, analysts, and—presumably—policymakers. Moreover the objective situation of the Cuban economy had become vulnerable despite ostensibly higher economic growth rates. Between July 2006 and February 2008 when Raúl Castro assumed the presidency, he seems to have become persuaded of the necessity of reforming Cuba's policy towards self-employment. Perhaps he had harbored such convictions in the past. However, during 2008 and increasingly thereafter his government began to implement a series of pilot projects responding pragmatically to specific circumstances, proceeding to cautiously liberalize policies towards entrepreneurship.

After four years of deliberation, by the late summer 2010 Raúl Castro was ready for more ambitious policy reforms. As outlined briefly in our introduction, a startling *"Pronunciamiento"* from the head of the *Central de Trabajadores de Cuba* (CTC, Cuba's official labor union) was published in *Granma* in September 2010 presenting a plan to reduce superfluous state sector workers. This was followed almost immediately by the news that policies would be introduced to facilitate the expansion of self-employment (*trabajo por cuenta propia*). While greater productivity and efficiency were targeted, the main goal behind the expansion of self-employment was to absorb "redundant" workers in the state sector. Indeed, in October 2010, new legislation was introduced aimed explicitly at promoting the expansion of microenterprise.

The new regulatory system and tax regime outlined in the legislation were dramatic and sweeping when compared to policies implemented between 1996 and 2006, which were designed to contain and to control the sector (as argued in Chapter 4). This new microenterprise-friendly approach also came in sharp contrast to the standard "official" views as expressed in the media and by the political leadership that had incessantly criticized and stigmatized those who legally worked in the sector. Further reforms and modifications to the original opening have gradually been introduced between 2011 and 2014. For example, new legislation on taxation establishing a legal framework for non-agricultural cooperatives was introduced in late 2012 and slowly implemented starting in the summer of 2013. The stage had been set for an accelerating expansion of small enterprise and a steady transformation of Cuba's economic institutions—at least as they related to small-scale private enterprise.

The potential benefits of further liberalization of self-employment had become obvious by the mid-2000s. An increase in small enterprise would intensify competition, lower prices, improve quality, and broaden the diversity of the goods and services available to citizens, thereby improving their living standards. It would generate productive employment, with the usefulness of the work and the value of people's labors proven by a hard "market test." Citizens would begin to earn real incomes. The government would collect more taxes, rather than expending ever more of its meager revenues on universal subsidies and policing lawbreakers. The massive underground economy would shrink, though not disappear. Foreign exchange earnings and savings would increase as domestic products replaced imported products and as supplies for tourist and export markets expanded. Innovation and improvement in the quality and variety of goods and services available would be promoted. In short, an urban and rural commercial revival would occur and a culture of compliance and respect for public policy, rather than regulation avoidance and illegality, would in time take effect.

If one doubted the advantages of small enterprise liberalization, consider briefly the arts and handicrafts sector. Before these areas were liberalized in 1993, the souvenirs and craft products available for purchase by tourists or Cuban citizens were of abysmal quality and without diversity, coming as they did mainly from a small number of state workshops. However, following the liberalization of self-employment in the early-1990s, this area sprang to life. Very quickly the *Plaza de la Catedral* and *Avenida "G"* (aka, *Avenida de los Presidentes*) were filled with vendors providing a wide range of arts and crafts. Very soon there were too many vendors for these locales and they were relocated to the *Malecón*, *La Rampa*, and the *Parque Luz y Caballero* between the *Malecón* and *Cuba Tacón*, near the Cathedral, the latter having again been relocated to a restored warehouse nearby.

These artisan markets constitute a major tourist attraction and earn significant amounts of foreign exchange for Cuba—quite similar to the famed French Market of New Orleans. This opening in the arts and crafts sector liberated the creative energy, innovativeness, and entrepreneurship of many Cuban citizens who quickly seized the legal opportunities available to develop new offerings. They earn a living for themselves and make a valuable contribution to society. They also relieve the state of the responsibility of providing them with employment and contribute revenue to the state for social programs through taxes. A similar opening to self-employment in other areas of the economy would make similar contributions.

Of course, there are always disadvantages as well as advantages—costs as well as benefits—in any change to existing public policy. For Cuba, there are four main concerns regarding a liberalized policy environment for small enterprise. First, greater economic freedom for Cuban entrepreneurs would allow a greater percentage of the population to free itself from universal state employment (as described in Chapter 2), with some *cuentapropistas* becoming wealthy and perhaps developing a mentality and economic interests at odds with state socialism. Such an eventuality is one of the main reasons that microenterprise has periodically been reigned in over the course of the Revolution, despite its demonstrable contribution to the efficient provision of needed goods and services and the generation of jobs.

Second, would such an opening worsen income distribution? In time, as some small enterprises increased in size, scope, and profitability, this would indeed occur. However, Cuba already has a system in place for taxing small enterprise—one that is constantly being adjusted to make it function more optimally—so that this effect could be managed. Opening self-employment and small enterprise up to all possible entrants would also increase competition in the sector, thus pushing prices down and reducing incomes towards average levels. Furthermore, socioeconomic inequality had been gradually increasing already both in the expanding black market and under the limited pro-market reforms enacted during the 1990s (as described in Chapter 4). Further legalization would at least give the government the opportunity to track and regulate the growing complexity of Cuba's class structure instead of simply denouncing it as ideologically suspect.

Third, would an opening encourage pilferage from the state sector, as has happened in the past? This is a possibility that has to be managed.[1] It could be managed by establishing a wholesale market for inputs for the small enterprise sector. If it continued to be difficult for small enterprises to obtain necessary inputs in a reasonable way, illegal purchases could well continue. A reasonable market for the provision of inputs to the sector is thus vital and has been a top concern of the *cuentapropistas* we interviewed. However, the state has so far been exceedingly reluctant or simply unable to put such a wholesale system into place.[2] However, it is important to remember that pilferage (known colloquially as "*desvio*" or "detour" in Cuba) is already a routine feature of the landscape of state employment. In fact, many workers remain in the badly remunerated state sector because such jobs provide them with access to state goods that can be stolen and resold on the black market.

Fourth, would an expansion lead to ever more "infractions" and illegalities as small enterprises tried to evade rules and taxes? This could indeed occur if regulations remained punitive and if tax burdens were unreasonable or impossible to bear. However, if an opening were accompanied by dropping vexatious regulations, and if the tax regime were made clear, reasonable, and fair, it is likely that compliance would improve. As argued in Chapter 2, a system that involves less detailed and *more narrowly focused* regulation combined with more efficient *enforcement* generally functions better than one characterized by wide-ranging and detailed regulations plus lax or corrupt enforcement. To paraphrase Centeno and Portes (2006), a state is not weakened by regulating less but by its inability to enforce the regulations it already has on the books. Building a culture of respect for regulations will take time. Due to the previous punitive approach to self-employment under Fidel Castro—along with the considerable ideological stigma long heaped upon entrepreneurs as speculators and exploiters—Cuba's entrepreneurs have come to view the government as an enemy force imposing rules aimed not at their containment but their elimination.

The Structural and Conjunctural Context for Economic Reform, 2006-2008

By 2006, when Raúl Castro became acting President, the inadequacies of the state sector in providing the basic goods and services for the population had become starkly apparent. This had been manifested for many years in the limited amount of goods and services available through the ration book. In fact, despite reasonable increases in official measures of GDP and low levels of unemployment as officially measured, the domestic economy was weak, with a collapse of sugar production, virtually no recovery of manufacturing since its 50% contraction after 1989, and an increased reliance on food imports. The increases in GDP were mainly the result of an accounting change in the estimation of the value of social services and the intensifying special relationship with Hugo Chávez's Venezuela that increased foreign exchange earnings through the export of medical services.

According to the estimates of Cuba's National Statistics Office, GDP per capita rose steadily throughout the early 2000s and began to accelerate by 2004, as can be seen in Figure 5.1. However, the increases in GDP from 2004 to 2006 are largely the result of a change in its measurement by ONE, which also renamed GDP "Sustainable Social GDP." ONE changed the measurement of the value of services from the previous cost of their provision to an estimated evaluation of their worth internationally (AEC, 2006; Mesa-Lago and Pérez-López 2006). The value of "government consumption" was thereby raised by an arbitrary 76.6 percent, mainly for health care. This increased Cuba's overall GDP per capita and led to an accelerating growth rate based on the export of health care services mainly to Venezuela.

Figure 5.1: GDP per Capita, 1989–2012 (1989 = 100)

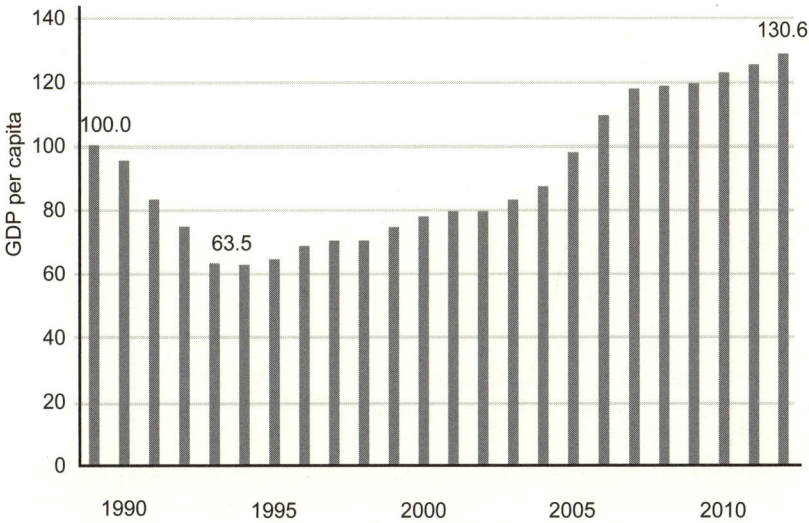

Sources: Oficina Nacional de Estadísticas (ONE). *Anuario Estadístico de Cuba* (AEC), various years.
Note: A new GDP measurement system was adopted in 2004 increasing the value of government services in health and education by 67% (Mesa-Lago and Pérez-López 2006).

Despite this apparent economic growth, the real value of wages in the peso economy remained exceedingly low at around 25 percent of the 1989 level (see Figure 5.2). This was due to the reduced availability of goods and services at the fixed—and very low—prices of goods and services available with the ration book or directly from the public sector (e.g. medical services), together with the high costs of products in the dollar stores (at the exchange rate of around 26 pesos for $1.00 of imported products plus a high sales tax of 140%), in the farmers markets, self-employment sector, and in the underground economy.

How could the economy recover so fully while real wages were still only at about 22 to 25% of the 1989 level? This is a puzzle indeed. Citizens of Cuba observed the contradiction for some years, as suggested by the oft-repeated observation: "Where's the economic recovery? We don't see it." Part of the explanation is that the value of GDP was increased arbitrarily as noted above, but this did not increase the supply of goods and services or the standard of living for citizens. A second explanation for the gap between overall economic performance levels and wage levels is that substantial portions of the goods and services produced in the state sector of the economy were pilfered and distributed through the ubiquitous underground economy

Figure 5.2: Cuba: Real Inflation-Adjusted Wages, 1989–2009 (CUPs)

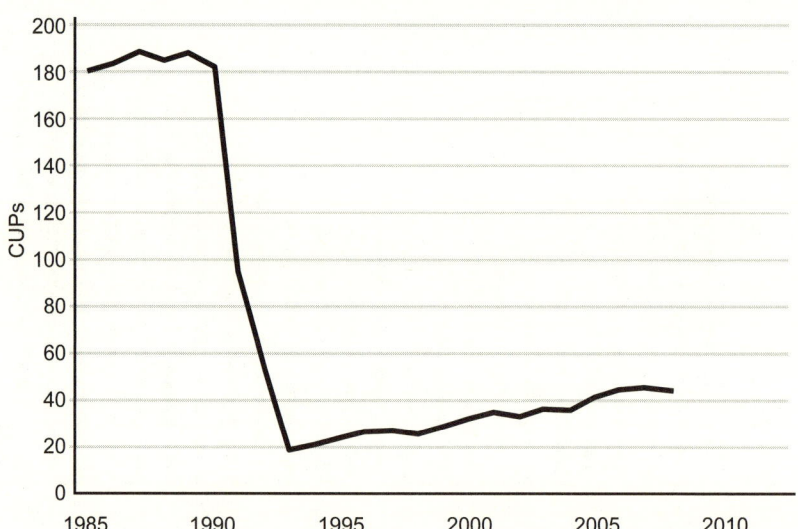

Sources: Vidal Alejandro Pavel, "Politica Monetaria y Doble Moneda," in Omar Everleny Pérez et. al., *Miradas a la Economia Cubana*, La Habana: Editorial Caminos, 2009.

so that revenues seldom seemed to permit higher wages. Probably a good deal more was actually produced in the state sector, but leaked out of official circuits (and statistics) through ubiquitous pilferage. There are undoubtedly other factors explaining this situation as well, such as remittances—both declared and undeclared.

How did Cuban citizens manage to survive in the late 2000s with real incomes still at just 22–25% of their late-1980s levels? This has been possible because many Cubans have been able to generate incomes higher than the official wages and salaries by relying on "in kind" transfers from the state, on remittances from abroad, and/or work in the second economy. The additional sources of income have included:

1. Remittance payments from overseas relatives or friends when they are visiting Cuba;
2. Work abroad in an official capacity such as serving as a doctor on an international mission, and returning with foreign exchange;
3. Tips for services rendered to foreign tourists, legal or illegal;
4. Income supplements paid "under the table" to Cubans by foreign enterprises (long technically illegal but tolerated and recently legalized and taxed by the government);

5. The per diems received during foreign travel, saved and brought home for use in Cuba;
6. Salary supplements in hard currency (CUCs) paid to workers in key sectors of the economy;
7. Legal self-employment incomes;
8. Informal economic activities;
9. "Income in kind" ranging from lunches for workers and food supplements for seniors;
10. Home produced goods and services for home consumption, for exchange with friends and neighbors or for sale;
11. Pilferage from the state sector for personal use, reciprocal exchange, or resale.

If citizens could tap such alternate income sources, as most did, then they could survive reasonably well. However, there were some who had no access to any of these additional sources of income—or perhaps only simple survival activities such as selling cigarettes, peanuts, or newspapers in the street. This group included pensioners, some agricultural workers, and workers in the state sector outside the major cities. These individuals were obviously in dire straits, because the rationed monthly food allowance was meager, covering only 10 to 14 days per month, while the rest of the food and other items needed for survival and had to be purchased in hard currency or inflated peso prices in dollar stores or the underground economy.

The volume of production of manufactured goods in 2006 was only 43.6% of the 1989 level and had not come close to recovering from the 1990–1993 melt-down. Furthermore, many lines of manufacturing production had virtually collapsed. Only tobacco products, radio and television products, beverages, and metal fabrication had recovered or were close to the 1989 levels. On the other hand, pharmaceutical production expanded quickly reaching 478% of the 1989 level. For Cuban citizens, very few products manufactured in Cuba were available in pesos (CUPs), which is the currency in which state workers are paid. Instead, what was available were various imported manufactures including clothing, footwear, and household gadgetry. However, these were available exclusively in "convertible pesos" (CUCs)—valued at approximately 24 to 26 times the CUP—in the officially named *"Tiendas de Recaudacción de Divisas"* (TRDs, "stores for the recovery of hard currency," formerly referred to simply as "dollar stores").

The collapse of the manufacturing sector was the result of a variety of factors. The economic melt-down of 1989–1993 reduced Cuba's ability to import new capital equipment, replacement parts, inputs of all varieties, raw materials, and energy. It led to a postponement of maintenance and reinvestment, so that the capital stock quickly deteriorated. The technological inheritance from the USSR hurt Cuba as well because it was relatively obsolete and immensely inefficient. A deformed public policy environment hurt manufacturing as well, notably the confusions generated by the dual monetary and exchange rate systems and a grossly overvalued exchange rate, which made competing imports artificially cheap and blocked any possibility of exportation.

It was also Cuba's bad luck that it was experiencing an economic meltdown and policy deformations just as China in particular and other newly industrializing countries such as India and Brazil were emerging as manufacturing powerhouses. China's manufactures have flooded into Cuba just as they have into much of the rest of the world. They have out-competed national industries in many areas of manufacturing everywhere. Additionally, China has some powerful advantages over Cuba regarding manufacturing. It has a new capital stock with continuous and rapid renewal. It enjoys massive economies of scale and "agglomerative economies" that help lower the costs of manufacturing. Its labor force is industrious, powerfully-motivated, still relatively low-paid, increasingly well-qualified, and abundant. Finally, China has systematically undervalued its currency making its exports artificially inexpensive—at the same time that Cuba's exchange rate for the state sector was grossly overvalued. The difficult question facing Cuba is whether its manufacturing base can ever reemerge to the prominence it had during the era of heavy Soviet subsidization.

Cuba's sugar agro-industrial complex also had virtually collapsed with the volume of production falling to around one sixth of the levels of the late 1980s as illustrated in Figure 5.3. Among the key factors in the catastrophic decline in sugar production was the lack of re-investment and maintenance going back as far as 1970, but greatly exacerbated during the special period that began in 1990. Also contributing to the decline of Cuba's once-mighty sugar industry has been the deformed structure of incentives for enterprises, their managers, and workers arising from the dual currency and exchange rate system.[3] This generated a range of problems for Cuba including reduced foreign exchange earnings (by perhaps $3.5 billion in 2010), increased idle farm land by about 32.1% (to 1.2 million hectares), and the loss of a significant proportion of productive employment.

Sugar's collapse also resulted in a major reduction in the generation of by-product electricity and all but eliminated a whole cluster of activities that produced inputs, processed outputs, and provided services to the agro-industrial complex. The collapse of the sector also destroyed the possibility of a smooth and easy switch to ethanol production, as large proportions of the former cane fields had reverted to an overgrowth of *marabú*, a sturdy and belligerent shrub that would be difficult and costly to remove when attempting cultivate the land once again. Moreover, it destroyed the economic base of many of the sugar-dependent towns, damaging rural development and increasing pressures for migration to the cities, especially Havana, or abroad.

Figure 5.3: Cuban Sugar Production, 1985–2013 (millions of tons)

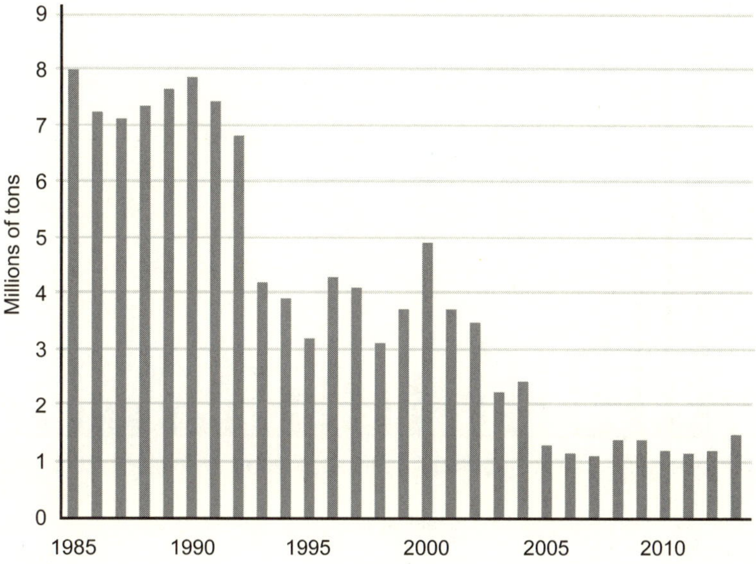

Sources: Naciones Unidas, CEPAL 2000, Table A.86; ONE 2012, Table 11.3.

The agricultural sector in general was in steadily worsening condition during much of the "Special Period." This is illustrated in Figure 5.4, which shows huge surpluses in the trade in agricultural products (excluding tobacco and alcoholic beverages) until 1992. The value of exports—mainly sugar but also coffee and citric fruit—then fell precipitously in the 1990s. Agricultural imports also fell to low levels by 1993, contributing to the food crisis of the first half of the 1990s, but then rising steadily reaching a peak in 2005, while agricultural exports continued their decline. By the second half of the 2000s, agricultural imports exceeded exports by 300% to 500% depending on the year. It was estimated that by 2005, about 58% of the calories and 62% of the proteins consumed by the Cuban people were imported, higher than the levels of 47% and 53% respectively in the 1950s and somewhat higher than in the 1980s (Nova 2012: 56). In a supreme irony, a significant proportion of these imported foodstuffs were purchased in cash from the United States.

A "perfect storm" of circumstances contributed to the decline of domestic food production. A central feature of this was the decline in cultivated land, which fell by 33% between 1998 and 2007, according to President Raúl Castro

Figure 5.4: Cuban Exports and Imports of Foodstuffs, 1989–2010 (excluding tobacco and alcoholic beverages, in billions CUP)

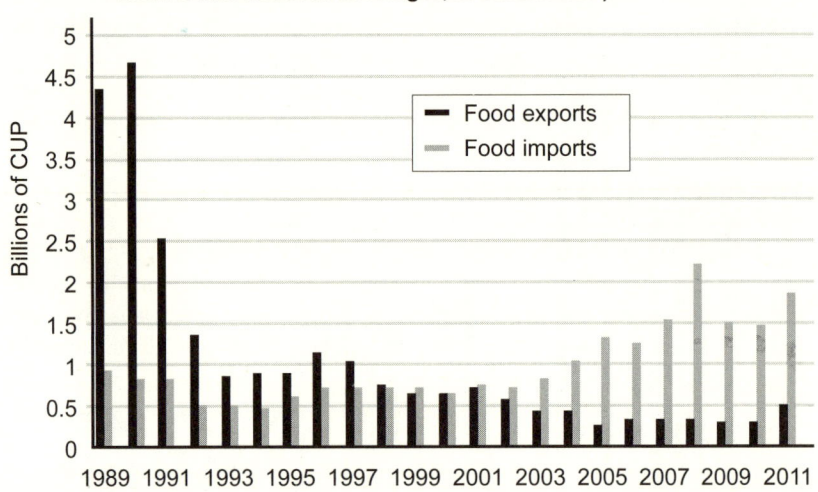

Sources: Oficina Nacional de Estadísticas (ONE). *Anuario Estadístico de Cuba* (AEC), various years.

(2008). This was generated by the myriad problems in the sugar sector, most notably the shut-down of about half the production capacity in 2002 by President Fidel Castro. Also relevant was the insufficiency of revenues and resources made available to the whole of the sector due to the general shortage of domestic and imported inputs and to the fixed low prices set by the state for the purchase of farm outputs that weakened the incentive and capacity for both state farm managers and workers and private or cooperative farmers to produce. On top of this were the usual institutional and planning problems, discussed on various occasions by Raúl Castro (ibid. 2009). Finally, the thick web of regulations constraining Cuba's private farmers and dictating what and how much they should grow and monopolizing to whom they could sell (the state, at fixed prices), acted as a powerful disincentive for greater or higher quality agricultural production.

The inadequacy of peso incomes was confirmed in April 2005 when President Fidel Castro announced major wage and pension increases for lower income citizens. Apparently, this move was in response to a report from a group of economists who were charged with examining the growing poverty in Cuba (Frank, May 3, 2005). The minimum wage was increased from 100 to 225 pesos per month, and the minimum pension from 55 pesos to 150 pesos (*Granma* 2005). However, these increases did not appear significant in convertible pesos at the exchange rate relevant for Cuban citizens (20 to 26 old pesos per convertible peso in the decade of the 2000s). This is because the increased incomes had to be spent on non-rationed products. Products from the TRD stores required convertible pesos and included tax levels of 140%. Vegetables from the *mercados agropecuarios* and the state vegetable markets are also sold at a market-determined price or close to it. Black market prices are also market determined and relatively high. The purchasing power of the income increases for pensioners and those on the minimum wage therefore does not appear to be particularly significant.

Many Cuban analysts were well aware of these trends and analyzed them openly before Raúl Castro first assumed the Presidency on a temporary basis in 2006. In the first part of the 2000s, Fidel Castro had consistently emphasized the positives and down-played short-comings of Cuba's economic conundrum. In 2005, for example, billboards appeared throughout Havana bearing a picture of the President beside the statement "*Vamos Bien*"—assuring the public that "Everything's OK." However, this did not square with perceptions of many Cuban citizens or even the analyses of many Cuban scholars. For example, researchers at the *Centro de Estudios sobre la Economia Cubana* (Center for the Study of the Cuban Economy) had continuously called attention to the difficulties of the economy.[4] Presumably analysts within the government itself have been aware of the above difficulties as well.

Over the years, some of those who spoke out critically—and courageously—were imprisoned, including the late economist Óscar Espinosa Chepe. Others lost their jobs, began to work abroad in regional or international institutions like the United Nations (such as the innovative economist Julio Carranza), or were forced into exile—where they now contribute to analyses of the Cuban economy through such organizations as the Association for the Study of the Cuban Economy (ASCE). Others suppressed their public criticisms in order to stay "in the game" and keep their jobs. Of course, many government and university-based analysts faithfully accepted the official policy line coming from the highest levels of the government of President Fidel Castro. However, the emerging realities of the excruciating "Special Period" led to an erosion of faith in the old policy approaches—and in some of the older generation policy-makers themselves.

The Policy Reform Process

On July 31, 2006, President Fidel Castro experienced a medical emergency and underwent surgery to repair gastrointestinal bleeding. He was replaced by his brother Raúl Castro, the First Vice-President, who assumed the title of Acting President. By February 2008 the elder Castro's health had not recovered sufficiently. Raúl was then declared President after being approved unanimously by the National Assembly.

President Raúl Castro's Evolving Views on Cuba's Institutional Structure

In the first years of Raúl Castro's Presidency policy changes were slow in coming. Popular expectations of new policy directions were minimalist and confused. The direction and character of possible changes in policies were ambiguous and uncertain. However, popular hopes were high relative to the last years under the Presidency on Fidel Castro. This was because Raúl Castro was widely viewed as being more pragmatic than was his older brother. Indeed, in his first major speech in July of 2007, Raúl Castro demonstrated this pragmatism, acknowledging the difficulties that the Cuban economy faced and the dimension of the effort that would be needed to overcome the problems. This was in sharp contrast to the complacency and even the misplaced triumphalism of the last years of the Fidel era. In Raúl's words:

> ... because of the extreme objective difficulties that we face, wages today are clearly insufficient to satisfy all needs and have thus ceased to play a role in ensuring the socialist principle that each should contribute according to their capacity and receive according to their work. This has bred forms of social indiscipline and tolerance which, having taken root, prove difficult to eradicate, even after the objective causes behind them are eradicated. [...]
>
> No one, no individual or country, can afford to spend more than what they have. It seems elementary, but we do not always think and act in accordance with this inescapable reality. [...]
>
> To have more, we have to begin by producing more, with a sense of rationality and efficiency, so that we may reduce imports, especially of food products—that may be grown here—whose domestic production is still a long way away from meeting the needs of the population. (Castro, R. 2007)

In this speech the younger Castro gave great emphasis to the necessity of improving the agricultural sector as well as industry and the possibility of increasing direct foreign investment. He also discussed "social indiscipline" and the expansion of the underground economy. He assured Cuban citizens that the government was studying these issues carefully and comprehensively and would bring forward appropriate policies in due course. In subsequent speeches—much shorter and less frequent than those of his elder brother—Raúl displayed increasing pragmatism and respect for reality and decreasing ideological rigidity and dogmatism. He was well aware of the difficulties of operating Cuba's central planning system, and of the ubiquitous inefficiencies and economic crime—both petty and major—that it seemed to generate:

> Harmony between planning and organization is essential in socialism. Its absence can lead to a chaos more dangerous than capitalism, where market laws establish a certain order and balance, though at the cost of the sacrifice of billions of human beings on a global scale. [...]
>
> In socialism, it is vital that the allocation of resources in the economic plans strictly reflect the available funds. We cannot expect two plus two to total five. Two plus two is four. Actually, sometimes in socialism two plus two equals three. (Castro, R. 2008)

President Raúl Castro has been equally aware of the need to break with some traditional Cuban economic institutions and policies. Such change was ultimately necessary in his view for political reasons, to ensure the long-term viability of Cuba as an independent nation, as stated below:

> We are facing unpleasant realities, but we do not close our eyes to them. We are convinced that we need to break away from dogmas and assume firmly and confidently the ongoing upgrading of our economic model in order to set the foundations of the irreversibility of Cuban socialism and its development, which we know is the guarantee of our national sovereignty and independence. [...]
>
> ...without an increase in efficiency and productivity, it is impossible to raise salaries, increase exports and substitute imports, increase food production, and to sustain definitively the enormous social expenditures characterizing our socialist system. (Castro, R. 2010b)

At times, Raúl's emphasis on productivity and efficiency as being the ultimate source of higher real incomes—a correct analysis—appears to be surprisingly reminiscent of the economic mantras and nostrums of international financial institutions such as the International Monetary Fund of the 1990s. One detail deserving of mention: Raúl praised the accounting profession in glowing terms.

> In this regard, we should emphasize the decisive contribution made by thousands and thousands of accountants to recover the place accounting deserves in economic management—and you know what I am talking about and how accounting operates in this country and in almost all enterprises—which, as we well know is an indispensable condition to ensure success and order in everything that we intend toaccomplish. (Castro, R. 2010a)

This seemingly formulaic recognition of the role of the accounting profession in the functioning of a modern economy is significant because under the Presidency of Fidel Castro both cost accounting within state enterprises and the profession itself had been effectively abolished. However, if this was a critique of Fidel, it was well countered in this speech—as in most others—by numerous laudatory references to the "Maximum Leader's" historic role and record of achievement.

President Raúl Castro's views on small enterprise were modified significantly during his first four years of bearing ultimate responsibility for the well-being of Cuba following his accession to power in 2006. By late 2010, he was stating that the government should be supporting small enterprise instead of "demonizing" the sector:

> ... we have arrived at the conclusion that self-employment is one more alternative [...], aimed at increasing the supply of goods and services to the population, which could rid the State of those tasks so that it could focus on what is truly decisive, what [we] should do is, first and foremost, facilitate their work rather than generate stigmas and prejudices against them, much less demonize them. Therefore it is fundamental that we modify the existing negative approach that quite a few of us have towards this form of private work. (Ibid.)

Furthermore, President Raúl Castro frequently stated that basic economic change is necessary for the sustainability of Cuban socialism. He did not view such changes as adoption of any sort of "capitalism," but instead, considered it an "updating" or "upgrading" ("*actualización*") of Cuban socialism. For example, in a speech on August 1, 2009, he stated,

> They did not elect me president to restore capitalism in Cuba or to surrender the Revolution. I was elected to defend, maintain, and continue perfecting socialism, not to destroy it. (Castro, R. 2009)

However, based on his repeated public statements and on the slow but consistent series of economic policy reforms enacted under his watch, Raúl Castro's current concept of socialism has changed significantly from the traditional Fidelista view. In the country that adopted common consumption standards through the allocation of equal amounts of many basic products through the rationing system, Raúl now insists that socialism means equal opportunity and rights, not a guarantee of equal outcomes.

> Socialism means social justice and equality, but equality of rights and opportunities, not salaries. Equality does not mean egalitarianism. This is, in the end, another form of exploitation, that of the exploitation of the responsible worker by the one who is not, or even worse, by the slothful. (Castro, R. 2008)

This is essentially the same approach taken in varying degrees in virtually every liberal and social democratic political system with mixed market economies, ranging from Sweden to the United States.

President Raúl Castro also emphasized that policy changes were to be introduced with deliberativeness and caution. This certainly had been the approach prior to August 1, 2010. But his August 1 speech to the National Assembly that year also included the proposal to lay off 1.5 million presumably redundant state employees with the hope that they would somehow be absorbed productively by an invigorated small enterprise sector.

> We shall proceed with a sense of responsibility, step by step, at the rate that we ourselves decide, without improvisations or haste, in order not to err and so as to definitively leave behind errors or measures that are not appropriate in current conditions. (Castro, R. 2010b)

First Steps and Pilot Programs, 2006-2010

After Raúl Castro succeeded his brother in 2006, a number of policy innovations and experiments were gradually introduced. Over the next four years, it became clearer that some major policy changes were being contemplated and tested on a pilot-project basis by the government. Below is a summary of the various policy initiatives of particular relevance to small enterprise during this period (see Appendix 1 for a more detailed small enterprise chronology under the Revolution).

In 2006, the government granted permission for Cuban citizens to enter and use hotel facilities previously reserved for foreigners—but only by using CUCs, which could be acquired at a rate of 24-26 CUPs per one convertible peso (while the average monthly wage in 2006 was 387 CUPs). The government also relaxed the rules concerning the purchase of electronic items, allowing citizens to acquire cell phones, CD and DVD players, and computer equipment more easily—again by paying in hard currency only. Permission was also granted for CUC-paying citizens to acquire personal cellular phones and contracts. Cuban citizens could also legally rent cars in their own names for the first time. Still, the fact that all these goods and services were offered exclusively in hard currency effectively kept them out of reach of the vast majority of citizens (but now based on cost not on government edict).

In 2007, the government legalized the hard-currency salary supplements often paid to Cuban employees by foreign joint ventures—an informal (and therefore officially illegal but semi-tolerated) practice that had being taking place since the early-1990s. Then, in 2008 the government eliminated the cigarette and cigar ration, expanded licenses for private taxi operators, began to allow ten-year leases of unused state land to small farmers (Decree-Law No. 259), and recognized the failure of the "emergent teacher" experiment by offering financial incentives to attract retired school teachers back to their profession (Decree Law No. 260).

In 2009, Raúl replaced Fidel Castro's economic team, an action that led to the resignation of the President of the Central Bank. A proposal was floated to reduce subsidization of rationed products through the elimination of the ration booklet, which had been a feature of the Cuban system since the early

1960s. Furthermore, worker's cafeterias were slated for elimination, replaced by an increase in wages so that workers could purchase their own lunches from private food peddlers. Additionally, small farmers were authorized to sell products directly to consumers, including the workers mentioned above.

Finally, 2010 saw a raft of policies that expanded on and deepened many of the foregoing reforms, including the privatization of state barber shops and beauty salons, many state taxi services, some small city buses, and urban parking arrangements. In all of these cases, the former state employees would now pay a rental fee (as well as income taxes and the cost of their own supplies) to the state for the right to exercise their occupation and be allowed to retain any profits. Additionally, the state set up markets that sold inputs to small private farmers, facilitated the sale of building and repair materials to house-holders, raised retirement ages from 55 to 60 for women and from 60 to 65 for men, and expanded the leasing of land to foreign tourist companies to 99 years.

Many of these policy initiatives were of minor significance. However, taken together the policies relating to small private enterprise constituted a wide range of pilot projects and added up to a major process of experimentation. They signaled a shift in the orientation of economic policy towards a greater role for the market mechanism and the entrepreneurial sector.

The Central Policy Thrust: State Sector Layoffs and Private Sector Job Creation

The intention to reduce redundant labor in the state sector was first made in a speech by President Raúl Castro to the National Assembly on August 1, 2010. Here he stated that in a series of meetings on July 16 and 17, the Council of Ministers, the Vice-Presidents of the Council of State, the members of the Party's Politburo and Central Committee, the regional Party First Secretaries, the officials of the CTC, members of the Young Communist Union, and other mass organizations had all met and agreed on a package of policies designed to reduce "inflated payrolls" or surplus workers in the state sector and to liberalize some policies affecting self-employment activities (Castro, R. 2010). At the time, no detail was provided and the changes appeared to be somewhat nebulous and of indeterminate scope and significance.

The task of spelling out the bad news, namely the redundancy of workers in the state sector, was ironically given to the official labor confederation—the CTC. A *"Pronunciamiento"* published in all national newspapers on September 13, 2010, announced that 500,000 state workers were to be declared redundant, laid off, and shifted to other areas of the economy all by March 31, 2011. Furthermore, the "pronouncement" asserted that there were an additional million workers or more in the whole of the economy who were basically redundant as well and who ultimately would be laid off and relocated. This amounted to over 20% of the total 2010 labor force (*Pronunciamiento* 2010).

Where would these workers come from and where would they go? On the basis of what criteria would workers be declared redundant? Who would make this determination? An internal report for Havana that was leaked in September 2010 spelled out in detail the downsizing that would be imposed in each of the municipalities of Havana as well as the job-creation by municipality. Interestingly, this report proposed a down-sizing of 137,000 positions for the whole of the city with job creation in the non-state sector of around one-half that magnitude, at 64,546 positions. It was expected that these new positions would be generated mainly in the small enterprise sector (84% of the total), with smaller proportions in other areas: mixed enterprises, 6.8%; cooperatives, 3.3%; foreign enterprises, 2.5%; and other private activities, 3.5% (Ciudad de la Habana 2010).

Firing 500,000 state sector workers in a period of just six months looked politically risky and socially brutal to say the least. Hoping that they would somehow be absorbed in the non-state enterprise sector looked like wishful thinking—especially after Cuba's self-employed pioneers from the 1990s had been systematically stigmatized and driven out of business or back underground under Fidel's policy leadership between 1996 and 2005. In other contexts this approach would have been labeled "neoliberal" structural adjustment of the most draconian and objectionable "shock therapy" character. Would the laid-off workers have the abilities and aptitudes necessary to start their own businesses? The biggest question, however, was whether the small-enterprise sector could create half-a-million jobs by March 30, 2011 and ultimately another million new jobs in the coming years. It appeared that Raúl had placed the "cart before the horse" in proposing that massive lay-offs from the public sector be undertaken before policy changes had been introduced to permit an expansion of the small-enterprise sector.

The massive lay-offs in the state sector together with the desired job-creation in the small-enterprise sector constituted a policy change of a truly "revolutionary" dimension. It also represented an amazing and ironic reversal of fortune for Cuba's small enterprise sector. As chronicled in Chapters 3 and 4, private small and microenterprises were almost completely eliminated from the domestic landscape between 1959 and 1968. They were then liberalized in a half-hearted pro-market reform from 1993 to 1995, but again were stigmatized and tightly contained by onerous regulations and taxation. Now they were supposed to save the economy, generating jobs, higher productivity, and higher living standards than was possible under the old system. As Pepe, a self-employed barber first interviewed in 2001, put it when he was revisited in 2011:

> I'll tell you that before, during the 1990s, we *cuentapropistas* were the most undesirable thing possible. We were opportunists, the most wealthy [...],

delinquents, that is, [portrayed as] the worst of all. Now, we *cuentapropistas* are going to save the country.⁵

Fidel Castro's almost 50-year attempt to construct his own variety of "socialism" was being repudiated and abandoned by his own brother. This appeared to be a "slap-in-the-face" for Fidel—although it was certainly not presented in this manner. Fidel remained silent on the matter and much of the verbiage on the reform measures actually paid homage to him, such as the oft-repeated (and largely meaningless) quote: "revolution means changing everything that must be changed" (*Lineamientos* 2010).

As the weeks went by, it became clear that the 500,000 lay-off target for March 31, 2011 was overly ambitious. It turned out to be difficult to identify workers who might be redundant in many cases and few people wanted to join the committees that would be given the task at each workplace to make such determinations. It also became obvious almost immediately that the small enterprise sector would not automatically expand so as to absorb this large number of displaced workers without more serious policy changes. More systematic, supportive, and ambitious measures would be vital if private sector jobs were to be created. Fortunately, the government had been working on policy modifications for the self-employment sector. These were published in October 2010 in a fairly comprehensive package of legislation, consisting of numerous Decree-Laws of the Council of State, Decrees from the Council of Ministers, and various Ministerial Resolutions (*Gaceta Oficial* 2010a and b).

The New Legal Framework

The central features of the regulatory and tax reforms were presented in a complex battery of Decree-Laws and Resolutions published in the *Gaceta Oficial* editions released on October 1 and 8, 2010. Whereas the earlier regulatory and tax regimes from 1995 to 2010 were designed to contain the growth of the sector, to stunt the size of microenterprises, and to limit the incomes of the self-employed, the intent of the new body of laws and regulations was to liberalize the framework within which small enterprises could operate and to facilitate—albeit in relative terms—the expansion of the sector. Some of the key features of this legislation are summarized here.

Resolution 32/2010 increased the activities that were permitted for microenterprise from 158 to a total of 178 (later increased to 181 in fall 2011 and again to 201 in fall 2013). Some if not most of the initial 178 occupations were of minimal economic significance, however, and included such hyper-detailed categories as "button upholsterer," "spark plug cleaner and tester," "well digger," "piñata maker/seller," "party entertainer (clowns or magicians)," "umbrella and parasol repair," and "doll and toy repair" (see Appendix 2 for the entire list). On the other hand, a small number of the categories are of considerable economic importance if licenses were to be granted freely in these areas (*Gaceta Oficial* 2010b: 119-123).

Virtually all professional activities were still prohibited. However, there were a number of exceptions such as language instructors, music and art teachers, typing instructors, computer programmers, and repairers of office equipment and electronic devices. The latter two categories could easily encompass a wide range of work relating to computers, web design, and software applications. A highly significant change was introduced regarding that the allocation of licensing. As noted in Chapter 4, previously relatively few of the applications for licenses to operate microenterprises requested were actually granted. The new legislation basically opened up the allocation of licenses to all applicants. This would permit a rapid expansion of the sector and generate a range of benefits. Increased numbers of microenterprises providing many types of goods and services would increase competition, forcing prices downwards for the benefit of all consumers, and also pushing incomes in the sector towards the national average, contributing to the objective of equitable income distribution at the same time. This would also improve quality, increase the range of choice for consumers, and increase the diversity of products.

Additionally, in an unprecedented step, the hiring of labor was liberalized, initially for 83 of the 178 categories of activities and later for all. It was also required that certain activities hire a minimum number of employees, two in the case of small *paladar* restaurants and one for street vendors of food. The tax treatment of small enterprise was relaxed in that enterprises were permitted to deduct larger and more realistic amounts for purchased inputs from their taxable incomes, as analyzed in the next section. Punishments for infractions of the regulations were also eased and their draconian character was modified.

Other encouraging changes included the legalization of renting facilities from other citizens or from the state in order to set up a small enterprise. Sales of goods and services to state entities was legalized—an important step when much of the economy was still in the state sector. Additionally, a number of vexatious regulations were eased such as the 12 seat limit on the size of restaurants which was raised to 20 (and later to 50). Also, a single person or two people in the same household were now permitted to hold more than a single license—a practice that had been illegal previously though some households were engaged in a number of self-employment activities in the underground economy.

Small enterprises continued to have some major responsibilities, codified in legislation. These included following the regulations of the superior organizations, paying taxes, purchasing inputs and equipment from legal sources, using contracted labor only, obeying labor law, and following hygienic and environmental standards (*Gaceta Oficial* 2010b: 117). Additionally, as explained in greater detail below in the section on the new tax regime, the self-employed would now also have to pay a social security tax and a labor tax over and above their income tax.

Despite this unprecedented opening, limitations on small enterprise remained. For example, most professional activities continued to be prohibited. Intermediaries were still prohibited and each producer was supposed to also be the seller of his or her output. Initially, limits on the hiring of employees in roughly half of the activities continued. Advertising continued to be prohibited. And though assurances were made, there was still no access to credit, investment, or wholesale markets, elements essential for any dynamic enterprise that could generate economic growth, provide employment, and move beyond the decidedly survival-oriented microenterprises that had existed heretofore.

In the first half of 2011, two positive signs became apparent. First, there was a significant change in the tone used in the official media when reporting on self-employment, moving from one of criticism and dismissal to encouragement and even celebration (Batista 2011; Peters 2012a: 12-13; Peters 2012b: 26-30). For example, an article published in *Juventud Rebelde* on March 22, entitled "Self-Employment Takes Off in Cuba," described self-employment "not as a temporary solution, but as a promising alternative in the new national economic strategy," and as a "new form of employment that diversifies work opportunities, boosts production, and increases the supply of goods and services" (Martínez Molina et al 2011). As such, it is a development that "has been more than welcomed by the people."[6] The article was also unprecedented coming from the official Cuban press in that it featured interviews with young *cuentapropistas* from at least five different provinces highlighting their concerns about the insufficiency self-employment reforms to date.

The most common criticisms cited by the scores of young people interviewed were the irregular availability and high cost of the variety of inputs needed by these new enterprises and the artificial limit placed on the number of self-employment options, which largely prevents "their doing something that bears more relation with their professions."[7] An additional challenge noted in the article was the fact that the vast majority of new CPs were not coming from the state sector as was hoped, but were previously "unemployed," that is, they were coming up out of the underground economy. As evidence of this development, Roberto Cruz Tamayo, an expert from Las Tunas' Labor Office, was quoted as saying, "Almost all the people registered were previously unemployed. [...] Many of them are people who used to do the same work before illegally, and have now legalized their status" (ibid.).

A second positive sign to appear in 2011 was that this time around the government was in fact listening. In fact, after a seven- to eight-month trial period, additional self-employment reforms were enacted when the government discovered that its plan to layoff of half-a-million state workers by March 31, 2011 would have to be postponed (Peters 2013a). Then Vice President Machado Ventura described this approach quite clearly in July 2011 as "systematic" and "definitive," done "with our feet on the ground and our ear to the ground," adding, "[we are] very attentive to public opinion, ready to correct ourselves as we go, to adjust our pace and to adopt new decisions" (quoted in Peters 2012b: 11). This indicated a change in government mentality from an ideological or dogmatic one of command and control—which had long characterized Fidel Castro's stewardship of economic policy—to a more pragmatic one where the new government's openness to feedback could lead to positive adjustments and deeper reforms.

As a result, between May and September 2011, CPs in all 178 self-employed occupational categories were permitted to hire employees with the number of licensable occupations increased to 181. A tax holiday to last until the end of 2011 was also declared exempting CPs from having to pay the employment tax for hiring up to five employees, indicating a significant shift in priorities that now "emphasized job creation over tax collection" (Peters 2012b: 11). In December 2011, this more permissive tax policy was extended into 2012 and accompanied by a doubling of the income tax exemption for those who made under 10,000 pesos a year (up from 5,000) (Peters 2011b; Hautrive and Rodríguez Cruz 2011). Enterprises were also now permitted to "more easily close for repairs and for longer periods, suspending their licenses and their tax obligations" (Granma 2011; Fernández Sosa 2011).

The "Lineameintos" or "Draft Guidelines for Economic and Social Reform," November, 2010

In November 2010, the Cuban government published its so-called "Draft Guidelines for Economic and Social Reform for the Party and the Revolution," which outlined a comprehensive and highly ambitions statement of future policy. It constituted a draft "plan of action" for the process of economic reform. This document was discussed and critiqued in various fora throughout Cuba and a definitive set of "Guidelines" (or in Spanish, *Lineamientos*) was then approved and published by the Sixth Congress of the Communist Party of Cuba on April 18, 2011. This document is likely to be the defining public policy initiative and the central economic legacy of Raúl Castro's Presidency.

The initial "Draft Guidelines" document of 2010 included some 291 policy initiatives and recommendations in almost every area of economic and social policy. The range of its coverage can be gauged quickly by summarizing the areas and number of recommendations in the document, which included the Economic Management Model (38 recommendations), Macroeconomic Policies (25), External Economic Policies (44), Investment Policy (13), Science, Technology, and Innovation Policy (7), Social Policy (36), Agro-Industrial Policy (31), Industrial and Energy Policy (37), Tourism Policy (13), Transport Policy (18), Construction, Housing, and Water Policy (14), and Commercial Policy (9). Indeed, the initial list of policies looked somewhat like a "wish list" or, more optimistically, a "to do" list. In either case, it represented a strong commitment to reform. While there are internal inconsistencies and opaque elements among the 291 recommendations, there are also deep-cutting proposals on many aspects of economic organization and policy. However, there were no priorities indicated among the recommendations. Nor was there a suggestion of the sequencing of policies. There was no obvious coordination regarding how the proposals were to be implemented.

The recommendations for the development of what was consistently called "non-state" sector were rather minimal in both the "Draft Guidelines" and the final version approved at the Party Congress. In the final document, there were only two recommendations focusing directly on this area together with a number of recommendations of indirect relevance. However, there were five interesting recommendations on cooperatives—examined in Chapter 6. Under the heading: "To modify the structure of employment, to reduce inflated state sector staffing, and to increase employment in the non-state sector," it was proposed that employment in the non-state sector be promoted as another alternative to state sector employment in the production of goods and services (Guideline #168). The next guideline read:

> To develop a process of labor rationalization [...] that under the principle of demonstrated suitability, contributes to the elimination of inflated staffing and paternalistic practices in order to stimulate the necessity to work and to reduce expenditures in the economy and the Budget of the State. (Guideline #169)

Under the heading of "Commercial Policy," a number of guidelines were put forward for the restructuring of the retail and wholesale system taking into account the gradual elimination of rationing and eventually—but not immediately—currency unification. This included "restructuring the selection of goods and services and revising the retail prices of products (that were previously in the ration book) towards their unrestricted sale in regular Cuban pesos without subsidy" (#310). Guideline #311 then emphasized the place of "effective consumer demand" in the determination of the goods and services to be produced and mentioned that a variety of prohibitions that limited commerce were to be reconsidered and revised. These measures implied that consumer sovereignty was now to be the main force driving and shaping the retail and hence the production systems. This suggests that consumer demand was to be the central determinant of what would be produced.

On the other hand, a previously-listed guideline (#68), states: "The centralized character of the determination of prices of products and services that are of particular economic and social interest will be maintained, while decentralizing the rest." The obvious question then is which prices are to be controlled centrally and which are to be "decentralized." This is ambiguous. The "centralized character" of price determination referred to in this guideline is contrary to the reference in #311 to effective consumer demand as the determinant of what was to be produced. This ambiguity leaves the managers of the reform process with a high degree of discretion in deciding on the balance between the central plan and the "market mechanism" for the orientation of the economy.

There are a number of other guidelines of indirect relevance to the small enterprise sector. For example, Guideline #173 envisages the "gradual and orderly" elimination of rationing and the ration book. This measure would shift a major portion of the demand for foodstuffs and everyday necessities from the controlled state sector to the market sector. Consumer choice rather than bureaucratized allotment of a range of products would dominate. Citizens could purchase most of their needed goods and services from any source including the expanding small enterprise and cooperative sectors. This implies a significant future expansion for these non-state sectors. However, larger scale state sector retailers—operating much like large retailing chains with numerous outlets—would continue to have a major role. Moreover, the objective of Guideline #9 was "to develop wholesale markets that sell at wholesale prices or rent facilities or equipment without subsidies, to the enterprise sector, the budgeted sector, and the non-state enterprise sector." This would be of major benefit to the non-state enterprises, as previously they had to acquire their inputs from the dollar stores at very high retail prices that included a 140% sales tax.

The guidelines for Industrial Policy (#s 215-239) make no reference to small-scale enterprise except for #217, which reads:

> To reorient industrial production in the short term with a view to meeting the requirements of the market for the necessary inputs for the different forms of production (in particular cooperatives and self-employed workers) as well as developing the supply of equipment for small-scale production.

Improving access to inputs of all sorts, including equipment, for the small enterprise sector would be a major improvement. In the past, there were few legal sources for equipment, machinery, spare parts, and inputs such as raw materials, intermediate inputs, chemical products, foodstuffs, construction materials, etc. This meant that small enterprises had to improvise extensively—often turning to the black market for supplies. Old machinery was reconstructed, often with great ingenuity. Leakage from the state sector was also a major source of such products. This measure could therefore improve the productivity of small scale and cooperative enterprise and reduce the widespread pilferage from the state sector that has long plagued the Cuban economy.

In the final version of the Guidelines, the section on industrial policy includes export promotion and diversification and outlines objectives for the various industrial subsectors. Unfortunately, no specific role for small enterprise is mentioned in these areas. This is unfortunate because in time and after monetary and exchange rate unification and especially normalization of relations with the United States, small enterprise could play an important role in export expansion and diversification, in cigar manufacture, clothing, publishing, furniture, web services, and some types of processed foods, for example.

Guideline #55 proposes monetary and exchange rate unification: "We will advance towards monetary unification, taking into account labor productivity and the effectiveness of mechanisms for distribution and redistribution. In view of its complexity, this will require rigorous preparation and execution on the objective and subjective levels." This will be of general national economic and social benefit—when it happens. It will also be of particular benefit to small enterprises and cooperatives, which will then have one unified market and which will thus avoid the complications of having to survive through manipulations of two currencies, two exchange rates, and two types of market.

The Tax Regime for Self-Employment

Tax Reforms

The Cuban government modified the microenterprise tax regime as part of the policy reforms designed to absorb redundant state sector workers into the private sector. Some of the modifications were positive in the sense that they reduced the heavy tax burden on small enterprise. However, the changes were modest and the tax system continues to limit job-creation and the expansion of microenterprise. The new taxation system, presented in the *Gaceta Oficial*, Nos. 11 and 12, on October 1 and 8, 2010, respectively, has four components: a sales tax, a tax on the hiring of workers, an income tax, and social security or social insurance payments. Generally, taxes are payable in CUPs. For those earning revenues in convertible pesos (CUCs), these are to be translated into CUPs at the going quasi-official rate (around 22 to 26 CUPs per convertible peso) for purposes of tax payment. There also is a special regime for bed-and-breakfast operations—a significant portion of which charge foreign clientele in CUCs—that is not considered here.

First, the sales tax is a 10% tax levied on the gross value of sales and payable by all microenterprises that do not qualify for what is called the "Simplified Tax Regime" (see below). While this tax is reasonable in principle and is used in most countries, the administrative cost of monitoring the value of sales and collecting the tax for the many of the smaller self-employed activities will be high. This indeed was recognized in the reform, which establishes a "Simplified Tax Regime" for the very small enterprises.

Second is a tax on the "Utilization of Labor." This tax on the hiring of employees was set at "25% of 150%" (that is, 37.5%) of the average national wage, which was 429 pesos per month in 2009 (ONE, AEC 2010, Table 7.4).

The tax would thus be about 161 pesos per month per employee or 1,932 pesos per year. A "minimum" requirement for the hiring of employees for tax determination purposes was set at two employees for *paladares* and one for other food vendors and a few other activities. There appears to be no exception or adjustment of the tax for part-time employees. (In this legislation, 74 self-employment activities were initially prohibited from hiring employees and another 7 could hire one employee only, a restriction that was later rescinded).

Third, there are two income tax regimes: a simplified regime for smaller self-employment activities and a more complex regime for larger activities. The "Simplified Tax Regime" applies to 91 activities. In place of the income tax and sales tax, these microenterprises instead pay a consolidated tax, constituted by the monthly licensing fee, which ranges from 40 to 150 pesos per month, payable in the first ten days of each month. (It is unclear whether overpayments would be refunded—they were not under the previous system). Other enterprises fall under the general tax regime, and pay all of the individual taxes discussed here. These activities pay the up-front monthly tax/license ranging from 40 to 700 pesos per month.

For the determination of the income tax payment, the "tax base" is defined as total revenue less a fixed amount for deductible expenses. The maximum amounts allowed for deductible expenses range from 10% for 10 activities, 20% for room rental operations, 25% for 40 activities, 30% for another ten activities, and 40% for six food and transport activities. (Bed-and-breakfast operations have their own specific tax regime based on the number of rooms rented and other spaces utilized by renters). Tax rates for small enterprise under the "General Regime" (but excluding the "Simplified Regime") rise progressively as follows (Pons Pérez, 2012):

1. 15% for the first 10,000 pesos (previously 0% for the first 5,000 pesos, through 25% for additional income between 5,000 and 10,000), plus
2. 20% for income increments from 10,000 to 20,000, plus
3. 30% for 20,000 to 30,000, plus
4. 40% for 30,000 to 50,000, and plus
5. 50% for additional income exceeding 50,000 pesos.

These rates may seem high and indeed are higher than those of many countries but they are not unprecedented in international comparison.

Fourth are social security payments destined ultimately for old age support, maternity leave, disability, and death in the family. These are determined according to a scale that may range from 25% of 350 to 2,000 pesos per month depending on the choice of the self-employed person. This is a social insurance scheme though the payments are similar to taxes.

Example: Three Taxation Cases for a Paladar

To illustrate the character of the tax regime, a case of a *paladar* is examined below, with the calculations summarized in Table 5.1. In this example, it is assumed that the total revenues or gross earnings of the *paladar* are 100,000 Cuban pesos per year (Row 1) or a modest 280 CUPs (about $US 10.50) per day. It is imagined then that there are three scenarios where the costs of production are 40% (Case A), 60% (Case B), and 80% (Case C) of total revenues. A situation where input costs for a *paladar* are 80% of total revenues is reasonable, given the required purchases of food, labor, capital expenses, rent, public utilities, etc. On the other hand, the 40% maximum is unreasonably low for many types of small enterprise—especially *paladares*.

The differing true input cost situations (Rows 2 and 3) generate different true net income (Row 6, that is, Row 1 minus Row 3). The tax base however is determined by the legal maximum allowable of 40,000 (Row 4 and 5) and is 60,000 pesos in all three cases (Row 7). The income tax payable is determined by the progressively cascading scale noted above and is 19,500 in all three cases (Row 8).[8] The tax on hiring the legal minimum two employees is 25% of 150% (that is, 37.5%) of the average national wage, which was 429 pesos per month or 161 pesos for 12 months for two employees, or 3,864 pesos per year (Row 9). The total taxes then are the sum of Rows 8 and 9, or 23,364 per year (Row 10).

The effective tax rate is then calculated as the Tax Payment as a percentage of Actual Net Income (Row 10 divided by Row 6). For Case C, where true costs of production are 80% of total revenues, the effective tax rate turns out to be an impossible 116.8% of total revenue. Again, this is because the maximum allowable for costs in determining taxable income is fixed at 40% of total revenues while the true costs of production were 80% of total revenues. This case could be relevant for enterprises such as restaurants, where food and labor inputs probably approach or exceed 80% of total revenues in some cases.

The chief result of this example is that effective tax rates can be much higher than the nominal tax rates for all the activities where true input costs exceed the defined maximum. In some cases, taxes owed could easily exceed authentic net income—assuming full tax compliance. This situation likely occurs for all activities not covered by the simplified tax regime. Such high effective rates of taxation could destroy the relevant microenterprise and block the emergence of new enterprises, which was indeed the objective of policy prior to 2006. In contrast, however, presumably the objective of the new policy approach is to foster microenterprise and to create jobs. Such unrealistically high effective taxation rates likely promote tax evasion for those enterprises with input costs that are high relative to total revenues.

Table 5.1: Taxation Calculation for a *Paladar*, Three Cases (*Moneda Nacional*, or CUP)

Assumptions: Annual Gross Revenues = 100,000 CUP (280 CUP, or about $US 10.50 per day)

Actual Costs of Inputs (labor, rental, overhead, food purchase, investment, etc.):
 Case A: 40% of total revenues = 40,000 CUP
 Case B: 60% of total revenues = 60,000 CUP
 Case C: 80% of total revenues = 80,000 CUP

	Case A	Case B	Case C
1. Gross Income	100,000	100,000	100,000
2. Actual Input Cost:			
Percent of Gross income	40%	60%	80%
3. Peso Value	40,000	60,000	80,000
4. Allowable Costs Deductable from Gross Income: %	40%	40%	40%
5. Peso Value	60,000	40,000	20,000
6. Actual Net Income before Taxes (1 – 3)	60,000	40,000	20,000
7. Tax Base: (1 – 5)	60,000	60,000	60,000
8. Income Tax Payable: Based on Gross Revenues less Value of Allowable Deductions (1 – 5)	19,500	19,500	19,500
9. Minimum Employee Hiring Tax: 2 employees at 37.5% of average national wage per year	3,864	3,864	3,864
10. Total Tax Payment (8 + 9)	23,364	23,364	23.364
11. Real Average Tax Rate: (10/6)	38.9%	58.4%	116.8%

Source: The authors, based on *Gaceta Oficial*, Nos. 11 and 12, October 1 and 8, 2010.

Evaluation of the New Tax Arrangement

This new tax regime represents an important improvement over the previous one in that it permits the deduction as costs of production of more than a maximum of 10% of total revenues as was the case previously. This is a reasonable adjustment to the tax base as most microenterprise activities generate costs that are higher than 10% of revenues. This is especially beneficial for food service, transportation, and handy-craft activities for which input costs are far beyond 10% of revenues. The progressive structuring of the income tax regime is reasonable though stiff. At the same time, there are a number of flaws in the new taxation regime, which will continue to stunt the development of small enterprise, preventing the absorption of workers displaced from the public sector. First, the tax on employment is problematic as it adds to the employer's cost of hiring workers. The obvious impact of this tax will be to limit job creation and slow the absorption of unemployment. A related result is that there is an incentive for private firms to hire employees "under the table" to avoid these taxes. Although the tax on the hiring of workers employed in a small enterprise was suspended—presumably through 2012 (*Trabajadores* 2011), its subsequent reinstatement will have the same negative effects referred to above.

The overall tax level is severe. The sum of the income tax, employee hiring tax, and public service surtax is high and can help create effective tax rates exceeding 100%, as is explained above. This will continue to promote non-compliance. It will also discourage underground enterprises from becoming legal. The establishment of new enterprises will be discouraged.

However, the most serious shortcoming of the income tax regime involves the tax base, which is not "net revenues" after the deduction of input costs, but various arbitrary proportions of total revenues, depending on the activity involved. The tax regime limits the maximum for input costs deductible from total revenues to 10% to 40% depending on the type of enterprise involved. When the actual microenterprise input costs exceed the maximum allowable, the tax rate on true net income can become very high. In the comparative example below (Table 5.2), the effective tax rate (defined as the taxes payable as a percentage of true net income) can exceed 100%. Obviously this would kill the enterprise or promote cheating. It will also discourage underground economic activities from becoming legal and block the establishment of new enterprises.

Reforms of the tax regime for small enterprise initially reduced the fiscal discrimination favoring foreign over private domestic enterprise. However, the new Foreign Investment Law,[9] which was published in April 2014 and took effect in June, granted major tax advantages to foreign investors amplifying the discrimination in favor of potential foreign investors and against Cuban-owned small business, which are denied the right to receive foreign investment. The law was passed because of the inadequacy of the previous law in promoting sufficient inflows of foreign investment and the perceived benefits that increased direct foreign investment could generate for the country. The benefits include technological, managerial, and entrepreneurial transfers within already-working enterprises, higher-productivity employment creation, access to higher income levels, to foreign markets, and to financial inflows that could supplement domestic savings and allow increased levels of investment. This last factor is of special importance in view of the very low levels of savings and investment that Cuba has achieved. Indeed, Cuba's levels of investment have been the lowest in all of Latin America for the last two decades. In 2011, this rate was 10.2% of GDP compared to 22.4% for all of Latin America (*Naciones Unidas* 2013).

There are also a number of costs to increased foreign investment, including expatriation of profits for as long as the foreign investment is profitable, the possible divergence of the interests of the foreign enterprise from those of the host country, and the possible stifling or displacement of domestic entrepreneurship. In this vein, the law has created a quite hospitable environment for foreign firms, providing greater security of tenure, greater control over the hiring and compensation of labor, and most of all, through generous tax breaks. Indeed, the tax advantages for foreign investors are now exceedingly generous. One might expect that the low level of taxes for new foreign investments will be highly successful in encouraging investment from a range of sources and especially and immediately from China and Brazil, which as of early 2014 already had various projects underway.

The tax treatment of foreign enterprise relative to small Cuban enterprise is summarized in Table 5.2, a modified version of Table 4.6, which compares the tax regime for small Cuban-owned enterprises with that now in place for foreign investors operating in "mixed enterprises" (joint ventures) or "international economic associations" for the post-June 2014 period. The most significant differences are as follows:

1. The nominal tax rates for small Cuban enterprise are 15% rising to 50% for all income in excess of US$2,000 per year, or about $167.00 per month. The profits tax rate for net corporate income is 15% in general but 50% for resource extraction.
2. Foreign investors in mixed enterprises with Cuban firms—presumably state firms—receive an eight year tax holiday. Small Cuban-owned enterprises receive no such tax break.
3. The effective tax base for foreign firms is profits or *net revenues*, that is, gross revenues minus all costs of investment and all production costs—inputs, labor utilities, rent, etc. In contrast, for small enterprises the tax base is gross revenue minus arbitrary and limited maximum allowable levels of input costs ranging from 10 to 40 percent depending on the activity, regardless of true production costs. The result of this is that the effective tax rates for foreign enterprises are reasonable. But for Cuban microenterprises the effective tax rate can be unreasonably high and could reach and exceed 100%.
4. Investment costs are deductible from future income streams for foreign firms this being the normal international convention. Again, however, for Cuban microenterprise, investment costs are deductible only within the 10 to 40 percent allowable cost deduction levels for the current year.

5. For foreign firms, all production costs—inputs, labor, interest costs, utilities, rental costs, etc.—are deductible from total revenues in calculating profits or taxable income. For Cuban-owned small enterprises, such production costs are deductible only to the maxima of 10 to 40 percent depending on the type of enterprise.
6. Moreover, under the new legislation, the profits of the foreign enterprises can all be expatriated. In contrast, the infinitely more modest after-tax incomes of Cuban citizens would virtually all be spent within the domestic economy. (It is indeed rare for Cubans—even successful entrepreneurs—to send remittances abroad rather than receive them from abroad). Indeed, if their after-tax earnings were to be taken out of the country, they would have to exchange their CUP savings for foreign currency at the rate of about CUP 26 = \$US1.00 or about CUP 34.5 = Euro 1.00.
7. Small enterprise owners also must pay a tax on the hiring of more than five employees (not a good mechanism for creating jobs). Foreign firms are exempt from such a tax, allowing them an unfair advantage in creating medium-sized firms and gaining a foothold in the nascent, non-state SME sector.
8. For small Cuban enterprises, some taxes continue to have to be paid "up-front" at the beginning of each month, in the form of the fixed monthly minimum quota (*cuota fija mensual*) tax. This certainly does not apply to foreign investors.
9. Foreign firms can import their inputs, equipment, and machinery as well as personnel directly from abroad. Cuban citizens with small enterprises must make their purchases from the state *Tiendas de Recaudación de Divisas* where markups and sales taxes are very high. (In the future, such inputs may be available at wholesale prices with sales tax rates that are not yet known—but such a promised future seems always just around the next corner.)

This differential tax treatment for Cuban citizens owning and operating small enterprises vis-à-vis foreign investors represents an astonishing type of discrimination against Cuban citizens—especially in a country with a proud nationalist/socialist tradition of supposedly prioritizing domestic rights and priorities ("Cuba for the Cubans") over those of so-called "foreign exploiters." In time, this type of discrimination will likely generate major dissatisfaction on the part of Cuban nationalists as well as Cuban entrepreneurs. One hopes that before long, political pressures and the climate of public opinion would require greater fairness in the character of taxation.

Table 5.2: Comparison of the Tax Regimes for Small Enterprise and Foreign Mixed Enterprise after the 2014 Foreign Investment Law

	Small Enterprise Sector	Foreign Investors in Mixed Enterprises or "Economic Associations"
Nominal Tax Rates	Personal Income Tax Rate: 15% rising to 50% of income above CuP 50,000 or $2,000 per year	Profits Tax: 15% of Net Corporate Income (perhaps 50% for resources); Personal Taxes Exempt for those earning profits
Effrective Tax Base	60 to 90% of Gross Revenues (Maximum of 10% to 40% allowable for input costs, depending on activity)	Net Income after deduction of all production and investment costs from Gross Revenues
Effective Tax Rates	May approach or exceed 100% of Net Income	15% of Net Income (perhaps 50% for mining and petroleum)
Tax Holiday	None	Eight years profit tax exemption
Deductibility of Investment Costs from Gross Revenues	Deductible only within the 10% to 40% allowable deduction limits	Fully deductible from Gross Revenues in determining Taxable Income
Deductibility of Input Costs from Gross Revenues	Deductible only within the 10% to 40% allowable deduction limits	Fully deductible from Gross Revenues in Income
Employee Hiring Tax	Tax exemption for first five employees: Tax required on six or more	Complete tax exemption
Social Security Payments	Yes	Yes
Lump-Sum Taxation	Up-front *Cuota Fija* Tax payments necessary	None
Input Importation Rights	Direct import purchases prohibited	Freedom to import directly
Profit Expatriation	No	Yes

Steps Forward, Steps Back, 2011-2014

A variety of measures modifying the initial regulations on small enterprise have been introduced between 2011 and 2014. The general objective of these policy changes was to further facilitate the expansion of employment in the small enterprise sector, creating new job opportunities for displaced state sector workers and to "jump-start" this process in the short run. However, some observers have interpreted these new measures as more of a smokescreen or "unloading," that is, simply a way to relieve the state from its unsustainable social and employment commitments, buy time to consolidate power during an unsure transition to a new hand-picked generation of revolutionary leaders, and prevent the total collapse of the system, while also protecting the state's monopoly control over property and import-export activities (Celaya 2013a and b). In any case, between 2011 and 2012 the government moved to correct the "cart before the horse" character of the initial proposal to lay off the state sector workers before private sector job creation could absorb them. Now job creation was to come first. In the meantime, the implementation of the lay-offs of state sector workers was delayed.

New Measures

First, loss-making state enterprises, notably state restaurants, were to be offered for rent to self-employed individuals and operated as small private enterprises (*Granma* 2011). This may be a significant measure as it provides a mechanism for employment creation to take place at the same time as state sector workers might be declared redundant. In some cases, the same employees may end up working as a small enterprise or a perhaps as a cooperative. Second, all self-employment activities, that is, all 201 rather than the initial 83 categories of microenterprise, are now permitted to hire employees. This policy change would encourage informally (and illegally) contracted assistants to be incorporated formally into many small enterprises. This also would permit many small enterprises to expand somewhat to a more optimal size thereby achieving greater economies of scale.

Third, an exemption on paying the tax on each employee was granted for small enterprises with less than six employees—a measure to promote job creation. The "minimum employment requirement" whereby for purposes of paying an employment tax, a minimum number of employees were required for tax calculation purposes, was dropped. Fourth, a variety of regulations that generally complicated and obstructed the operation of some small enterprises were relaxed further. For example, *paladar* restaurants were permitted to expand their capacity from 20 to 50 chairs—up from the infamous limit of 12 seats in place prior to October 2010. Some small enterprises, notably taxis, were permitted to cease operation during repairs of the vehicles so as not to incur taxes when the enterprise could not function.

Fifth, large-scale purchases of some inputs were permitted to be made at lower "wholesale" prices rather than the higher retail prices of the dollar stores (*Trabajadores*, July 18, 2011). Sixth, of great potential importance in the future is the opening up of credit facilities for small enterprise from the state financial institutions. Decree-Law No. 289 of the State Council November 16, 2011 legalized credit facilities for lending to the self-employed, small farmers, and persons licensed to practice other forms of non-state enterprise. The provision of micro-credits to the private sector from the banking system began in 2012. Initially, only around 10% of the credits went to small-enterprise with the rest going to home repair (Vidal Alejandro 2012). However this can change in future. Small enterprises were also given permission to buy building materials and to pay labor used in construction.

Seventh, potential markets for small enterprise were broadened further, a measure of great potential significance for the future. Small enterprises were granted permission to sell directly to the tourist sector. They were also permitted to market their goods and services directly to the hotels and restaurants as wholesalers or retailers (*Granma*, November 21, 2011) and to Agricultural Production Cooperatives (CPA), Credit and Services Cooperatives (CCS), and the Basic Units of Cooperative Production (UBPC), as well as to organic farms belonging to state entities. The goods they were authorized to provide included industrial raw materials, agricultural products, rice, and charcoal, with prices in Cuban pesos (CUPs) (Resolution No. 122 of the Ministries of Finance and Prices, and Tourism, November 14).

Eighth, it was announced in December 2011 that the "Yellow Pages" of the 2012 telephone directory produced by the *Empresa de Telecomunicaciones de Cuba* (ETECSA) would include listings of different services provided by small private enterprises (*Juventud Rebelde* 2011). This simple measure legitimizes the sector, increases the potential for competition (and lower prices and better quality) among producers, and lowers "transactions costs" for purchasers. It also provides the advantage of easier communication with buyers for legitimate enterprise vis-à-vis underground activities, and should help diminish the latter.

A number of modifications to the tax system for small enterprise were also introduced. In December 2011, the level of taxation on small entrepreneurs was reduced. The mechanism for this was to raise the initial exemption on taxable income from 5,000 to 10,000 pesos per year. The tax payment for workers employed in a small enterprise was to continue to be suspended, indefinitely (*Trabajadores* 2011), but has not been made officially permanent. In fall 2012, a further reduction of tax levels for small enterprises was included as part of the new tax law. The applicable income tax rates were lowered by 7% for lower income levels and by 3% for higher levels. The tax that must be paid for each employee will be applied only to those who employ six or more workers. The rate payable was reduced by 80% for the next five years (Peters 2012e).

These measures were intended to help provide a short-term but sharp stimulus to the creation of small enterprises. They will have a beneficial impact. The relaxation of the tax on the employment of workers in microenterprises with fewer than six employees should be particularly beneficial and facilitate the hiring of employees in microenterprises. The 80% reduction in the employment tax when six or more are hired is beneficial for job creation purposes, though only for a transitory period. Additionally, the monthly up-front payment for bed-and-breakfast operators also was reduced for the rest of 2011 from 200 to 150 pesos or convertible pesos (depending on whether they rented in CUPs or CUCs). This also was an attempt to provide a tax break in order to promote the formation of new enterprises.

One policy introduced in the late summer of 2012 could have a negative impact on small enterprise. In the absence of wholesale markets for domestic and imported goods, some small-scale entrepreneurs came to rely on periodic imports of inputs brought to Cuba by travelers returning from abroad.[10] The imposition of high rates of taxation on such imports will hurt many small enterprises. One hopes that provision will be made quickly for the establishment of wholesale markets for inputs. Additionally, the first half of 2013 saw a series of seemingly ad-hoc crackdowns on microenterprises that had set up shop in the covered walkways (*portales*) of many of Cuba's main cities, specializing in the sale of imported goods. This was followed in fall 2013 with a series of more direct and systematic legal measures and announcements aimed at achieving greater "order, discipline, and command" over the emergent microenterprise sector—described in detail below. Such operations against seemingly legal microenterprise have sent a decidedly mixed message to Cuba's struggling *cuentapropistas* (Gálvez 2013; Peters 2013c).

New Occupations

On the bright side, a major new set of self-employment regulations made pubic on September 26, 2013 (*Gaceta Oficial* 2013a, Res. 353 41 and 42) increased the overall number of legalized private occupations to 201 for the first time. Among the newly authorized activities were real estate agents (the legalization of the essential if informal occupation long known in Cuba as "*corredor de permutas*"—a "runner" or "fixer" of housing swaps), brokers for home rental (the legalization of the informal practice of all manner of hustlers who try to steer foreign tourists to private B&Bs), soap, polish, and dye making, construction services, auto-body repair ("*chapistero*"), stone-working in marble and granite ("*granitero*"), antique dealers ("*anticuarios*"), and welder/flamecutter ("*fundidor/oxicortador*").[11]

Two particularly interesting new occupations are "postal agents" who can provide retail services on behalf of the *Empresa de Correos de Cuba* and "telecommunications agents" who can provide retail services and products for the *Empresa de Telecomunicaciones de Cuba* (ETECSA) (Cancio Isla 2013; Pérez 2013). Also in early fall 2013, Cuba's Ministry of Tourism established resolution 145/2013, which began to allow state-run tourism enterprises and agencies to outsource some services directly to the self-employed and include them in tour packages offered to foreigners with payments to contracted *cuentapropistas* made in convertible pesos (CUCs). Significantly, this reform was primarily intended to begin to incorporate the unique and popular offerings of Cuba's burgeoning *paladares*, bed-and-breakfasts, and private taxis into the lucrative but often low quality state tourism sector (*El Nuevo Herald* 2013b; DDC 2013b; Carrillo Ortega 2013; Café Fuerte 2013c).[12]

Additionally, Decree-Law No. 288 of the Council of State, which had been approved two years earlier on October 30, 2011, permitted the establishment of a market for the buying and selling of private housing.[13] While not focused directly on small enterprise, this measure will have a number of collateral benefits for the self-employment sector. For example, it will permit the underground exchange of housing to come above ground. Prior to this, the market for housing was restricted to *"permutas"* or trades by which dwellings were exchanged and an under-the-table payment would be made from one party to another to equalize the deemed values of the properties. The greater fluidity of the open exchange of housing and movement of people among dwellings will be of great benefit to citizens as their housing needs evolve over the life-cycle.

As mentioned above, one of the new measures in September 2013 also permitted the *"corredores de permutas"* or "home swap runners" who acted as underground real estate agents to legalize their status and become licensed self-employed entrepreneurs. Undoubtedly, this will become an important source of income for many and an important component of the small enterprise sector—as is the case in other countries. An open market for housing will also permit some microenterprises to move more easily into premises that are more suitable for their particular activity—based on the size, location, and other amenities offered. It will also create fungible capital for property owners that could be used as investment capital in their own economic activities and home improvement. While there was not a mortgage market as of January 2014, one can imagine transactions that could free up investment funds for small entrepreneurs, such as selling a large house, buying a small one, and investing the difference in a business. This is to say nothing of the boom Cuba is experiencing in family remittances, a significant proportion of which is certainly being invested in private businesses (Morales 2013; Orozco and Hansing 2011).

There are also benefits for the state resulting from the housing reform mainly in the form of taxes. The real estate agents will pay an income tax on their earnings and the state will also levy a four percent sales tax on the assessed value of the house being transferred. This is likely to become an increasing source of revenue as the volume of houses exchanged increases and as their value rises. Similarly, the authorization of the buying and selling (or donation) of motor vehicles built after 1959, thereby establishing a legal market for automobiles, will have collateral benefits for the small enterprise sector. Like residential property, this will have the side-benefit of making transactions and investments more fluid (Decree No. 292 of the Council of Ministers, September 20, 2011).

At the same time, the move toward the establishment of a freer market in the buying and sale of automobiles in 2012 and 2013 was dealt a major blow when the initial celebratory announcements of greater imports and open sale of cars from abroad (Ravsberg 2013b) was followed by the absurd news that such cars would be sold at prices ranging between 40,000-250,000 CUCs (BBC Mundo 2014). Though not among the government's major reforms, such extreme "sticker shock" revealed what one group of civil society activists on the island described as the very essence of the entire reform process under Raúl Castro: "the formal proclamation of a right whose realization in practice turns out to be impossible" (*Grupo consultor* 2013; *Grupo consultor* 2014; Sánchez 2013).

New Limitations

By late 2013, self-employment had achieved a significant *quantitative* leap forward even as it continued to face major *qualitative* limits on its future growth, depth, and dynamism. Veteran Cuba watcher Philip Peters has perceptively called this dilemma "the hard part," writing that as the state begins the herculean task of reforming Cuba's large, unproductive, and inefficient state enterprises it will need "a strong private sector that generates jobs for excess state workers [in] larger-scale enterprises that can employ professionals and others in larger numbers, including in production of high-value-added goods and services" (Peters 2013a). He also suggests that the government seems to prefer that the newly launched non-agricultural cooperative sector (the focus of Chapter 6) play this role rather than private enterprises. Peters bases this assessment on his own analysis of the depth and sequencing of the reforms to date, but also on frank declarations from the Cuban leadership to this effect. In fact, a March 2013 speech by Cuba's First Vice President Miguel Díaz-Canel included the following statement:

> We have advanced in what was easiest, in solutions that required less depth in terms of both decision-making and implementation and now we are left with the more important aspects, more decisive for the future development of the country, and also more complex in terms of solutions. (Miguel Díaz-Canel, cited in Morales 2013a)

In fact, while the overall number of self-employed workers reached a record 455,557 by the end of February 2014 (more than triple the number from fall 2010) (*Cubadebate,* 2014b; *Mesa Redonda* 2014),[14] such unprecedented quantitative expansion belies a number of qualitative limitations as well as ideological and frankly political obstacles that continue to limit the sector's growth beyond survival-oriented microenterprises. By design or default, these restrictions prevent the transformation of self-employment into a productive and dynamic small- and medium-sized business sector that could form the basis of an emergent middle class. Specifically, in fall 2013 a set of new regulations were issued on self-employment, which—together with a series of highly unpopular official pronouncements—were aimed at reigning in "abuses" and "deformations" that had taken hold the sector. This renewed emphasis on law and order was rolled out despite, or perhaps precisely because of the increasingly evident fact that such supposed "abusers" were successfully competing against the state sector—creating employment and providing goods and services at lower prices and of better quality and wider variety than state enterprises renown for the "exorbitant prices and shoddy quality" of their products (Valdés 2013; see also Frank 2013d; Rainsford 2013; Rodríguez, A. 2013; Cuba Dice 2013; García 2013; Palacios Almarales 2013).

These law and order pronouncements included the late-September prohibition on the resale of imported goods—especially clothing brought into Cuba by "mules"—and of household items acquired in the state retail sector (Gaceta Oficial 2013a). Later, in early November—after what turned out to be a premature declaration from Fernando Rojas, the Vice Minister of Culture, favoring "regulation" over outright "prohibition" (Juventud Rebelde 2013)—*Granma* issued an outright ban explicitly prohibiting the previously tolerated and unregulated but highly popular private 3D cinemas and game rooms—ordering them closed immediately with the words: *"cesarán de inmediato en cualquier tipo de actividad por cuenta propia"* (they will immediately cease any kind of self-employment) (*Granma* 2013). The popular rejection of this top-down move toward greater "order, discipline, and command" exposed a fundamental dilemma faced by the Cuban government as it attempts to enact economic reforms that cede space to the private sector.

The outright prohibition of activities the government prefers to keep under state monopoly (such as the import-export business and most professions) allows it to exercise symbolic control over the population and impose an apparent order over Cuban citizens and society. However, this control comes at the cost of pushing all targeted economic activity (along with potential tax revenue) back into the black market—where much of it lived prior to 2010 as evidenced by the high proportion of CPs who are found in government surveys to have been *"laboralmente desvinculado"* (unconnected to the state sector) prior to becoming legally self-employed (Rodríguez, A 2013; Dámaso 2013c). On the other hand, the inclusion and regulation of the many private activities dreamed up and market-tested by Cuba's always inventive entrepreneurial sector would create more legal employment opportunities, a higher quality and variety of goods and services at lower prices, while also increasing tax revenue to target inequality and fund social programs. However, these benefits come at the political cost of allowing greater citizen autonomy, wealth and property in private hands, and open competition against long-protected state monopolies (Celaya 2013a and b).

The initial measure outlawing the resale of imported clothing was aimed at those who had been doing so under cover of the license for "seamstresses" or "tailors." Likewise, those reselling household items were accused of "speculation" since they had been licensed to sell only items that they had made themselves not to resell products originally purchased in state retail shops at a mark up.[15] According to estimates by Marc Frank and Rosa Tania Valdés of *Reuters*, these changes likely led to the closure of an estimated 20,000 microenterprises by the end of 2013 (Frank 2013c; Valdés 2013). Specifically, the law added new, more precise occupational definitions that outlawed the sale of imported products and/or those acquired in state-run retail stores by six preexisting occupational categories: agricultural street vendor, food and beverage street vendor, seamstress/tailor, seller of household items, food retailer, and maker/seller of soaps, polish, dyes, etc.

While resellers of imported clothing were eventually given until December 31 to liquidate their inventory before having to close their doors, the new restrictions surely hurt many others active in these businesses' extensive supply chains. For example, a bicycle repair shop may also sell imported replacement parts while a birthday party piñata maker and seller may also sell imported balloons and import the inputs for making the piñatas.[16] Imported products arrive through a variety of unofficial channels such as foreign sailors and Cuban workers returning from abroad, tourism by family members visiting Cuba from abroad, or Cubans travelling abroad for various purposes. However, the majority of such items surely originate with the informal supply networks of "*mulas*" (mules) developed by Cuba's microentrepreneurs due to the continued lack of a viable wholesale source of supplies and the prohibition against the private sector engaging in any import-export activity—a state monopoly (Alonso González 2013; Monzo 2013; Laffita 2013; Palacios Almarales 2013).

This measure has had a variety of impacts. It has forced many enterprises out of business—or at least out of registered and legal business. Already in early 2014, the casual visitor could observe the many abandoned "*ferias*" or market areas where some of these activities had been located (Alfonso Torna 2014).[17] Of course, as expected many of these now prohibited activities continue, but now as part of Cuba's underground economy once again. In fact, during October and November 2013, a veritable chorus of frustrated entrepreneurs and analysts began to publicly decry the government's apparently irreversible decision to chose prohibition over regulation (Rodríguez, A. 2013; Celaya 2013b; Cuba Dice 2013; García 2013; Cárdenas Lima 2013; Rainsford 2013; Palacios Almarales 2013).

For example, in early October, *Reuters* was witness to a public gathering of outraged clothing sellers led by Justo Carrillo, their representative to Cuba's official labor federation. Carrillo received applause when he pleaded loudly with the government to "reconsider" its drastic decision. "We have a lot of product and money invested in this," he reasoned. "Banning it means unemployment for these people forcing them to do whatever. They will move back into the black market, return to illegal activity" (Valdés 2013).[18] Moreover, leading Cuban economist Omar Everleny Pérez Villanueva called the ban "an error," pointing to the state's inability to compete in terms of quality, variety, and price with the private sector. "This business certainly offers serious competition to the state shops," he said. "The state should be competitive, not use these mechanisms" since they will only serve to push private operators back into the black market—precisely the reverse of the reforms' supposed aims (Rainsford 2013). Later reports from independent journalists described an October 10 public protest in front of Havana's iconic *Capitolio* building where perhaps a hundred CPs had gathered to demand the reversal of the ban (Palacios Almarales 2013).[19]

This popular pushback was even acknowledged by a pair of *Granma* editorials in November 2013 penned by Oscar Sánchez Serra, the first of which reported that the newspaper was flooded with complaints from readers arguing that the proper response to imported clothing resellers would be proper regulation and licensing, not prohibition (Sánchez Serra 2013a and b).[20] Unfortunately for both these entrepreneurs and their customers, this recognition of a "diversity of opinion" by *Granma* has not translated into any major policy modifications (Dilla Alfonso 2013; Tamayo 2013; Orsi 2013b; Xinhua 2013; Kozlowska 2013; Vega 2014) beyond the granting of a "liquidation window" of two months to clothing resellers during which time all CPs would be visited systematically by the authorities with the purpose of "gaining their understanding" (Valdés 2013).

To the extent that this measure is implemented rigorously, it will hurt many *cuentapropistas* who sell imported products as their main business, or on the side through products containing imported inputs as a supplementary activity to their main activity. It will also hurt the extensive network of citizens from all walks of life who had come to rely on the goods and services provided by these microenterprises. Indeed, writing at the proudly pro-revolutionary blog *La Joven Cuba*, Harold Cárdenas Lima openly called the measures "a step backward," specifically criticizing the government for reverting to its typical "throw the baby out with the bathwater" approach to economic problems.[21]

> A wide social network exists that depends on these stores, from the salesperson to the truck driver, even the person who rents out their home. Behind each establishment there are six people whose livelihoods depend on it and

now they are out in the street. But it's not just the supply side that is impacted. The citizens demand it as well. Their offerings are more varied and less expensive than in state stores. Whoever takes such measures should think about who is being impacted, and in this case it is a good portion of Cuban society. (Cárdenas Lima 2013)

Apart from the crackdown on clothing resellers, the newly clarified definitions of each self-employment occupation included specific restrictions on the exercise of a whole range of jobs (see Appendix 2 for a full list). For example, radio and television antennas were restricted to receiving domestic signals only; metal polishers, jewelry repairers, and art restorers were restricted to performing services only and could not sell the products they service; and event planners could not operate night clubs. Likewise, those licensed to "operate recreational equipment" were now specifically prohibited from operating any aquatic equipment.[22] Given this specification, it would seem that entrepreneurs who had been providing a wide array of recreational activities to the public (such as paintball, private cinemas, and video games) could now breathe a sigh of relief as long as they stayed away from "aquatic equipment" (*Gaceta Oficial* 2013a, Resolution No. 42, Annex: 261).

Thus, it came as quite a shock to the operators of small private movie houses, many of which featured both 3D films and video games, when the national newspaper *Juventud Rebelde* carried a lengthy story on October 27, 2013, entitled, "Life in 3D?" Perhaps most surprising and unsettling for the entrepreneurs who were then operating home-based 3D cinemas was the fact that the article stated over and over again that they operated without licenses leading to a public debate among Cuba's cultural commissars about how to deal with them. This, despite the fact that most such cinemas did in fact have licenses, usually the aforementioned "operator of recreational equipment" one, often acquired from local authorities with the expressed intent of opening 3D cinemas (Rodríguez Milán 2013; Pérez 2013).[23]

Furthermore, while Cuba's Vice Minister of Culture, Fernando Rojas, seemed to want to reassure his readers by saying, "What, then, are we to do: Prohibit or Regulate? I think that it is about regulation, starting from a fundamental premise: Compliance by all with what is established by the cultural policy." Both he and Roberto Smith, the president of Cuba's State Film Institute (ICAIC), made clear the cultural authorities' paternalistic if quixotic intention to continue to control the programming even of private entertainment venues given the supposed fact that private 3D theaters promoted "a lot of frivolity, mediocrity, pseudo-culture, and banality, which are counter to the policy that demands that cultural consumption for Cubans prioritize quality only" (*Juventud Rebelde* 2013; Cubadebate 2013c; Álvarez 2013a; Uno de Guanajay 2013; Espacio Laical 2013).

Clearing up any doubt as to the legality of such cinematic operations—and putting to rest any questions about the Revolution's cultural policy or the relative "banality" or "quality" of the 3D films shown in private spaces—Cuba's all-powerful Executive Committee of the Council of Ministers, headed by Raúl Castro himself, issued its now infamous "*Nota informativa sobre el trabajo por cuenta propia*" in *Granma* on November 2, which included the following phrases printed in bold: they "have never been authorized" and "they will cease immediately." Such a message following Rojas expressed preference for regulation over prohibition sent a decidedly mixed and disconcerting message to Cuba's *cuentapropistas* to say the least.

Clearly, the issue at hand was never the supposed banality of the programming in private theaters given that both state television and state-run theaters are filled with banal offerings—both those pirated from Hollywood as well as others produced in Cuba—to say nothing of the content of the CDs and DVDs legally hawked on Cuba's streets by thousands of other licensed *cuentapropistas* (in open violation of international copyright laws) (Pérez 2013; Palacios 2013; Álvarez 2013b; Azor Hernández 2013; Kozlowska 2013; Espacio Laical 2013). Instead, the real issue is protecting the state film production and exhibition monopoly together with its paternalistic control over private spaces lest they be used for undue enrichment or to propagate ideas at odds with the Revolution.

New Punishments

New legislation was published in January 2014 on violations and punishments of the rules under which self-employment activities are to operate. This legislation—Decree Law 315 (*Gaceta Oficial* 2014a)—replaces Decree-Law 174 of June 1997, summarized above in Table 4.3. Much of the new legislation is fairly standard, e.g. health and safety standards, environmental issues, employment of minors, prohibition of sales of protected flora and fauna, and controls on the sales of alcoholic beverages. The prohibition on the use of illegally acquired inputs certainly would be reasonable if adequate markets for their purchase were available, though this was still not the case by late 2014 (Café Fuerte 2014; Martínez Hernández 2014; Freire Santana 2014).

There also appear to be some relaxations of regulations compared to the previous situation. For example, there is no longer any restriction against using both currencies—the CUP and the CUC. Nor is there any prohibition against the use of "intermediaries" so that now a producer or artisan can have their goods sold by others legally. This is an important change because if a prohibition against intermediaries were seriously enforced, it would make a small artisanal or manufacturing enterprise difficult if not impossible to operate. There is no prohibition against selling goods or services to state enterprises or institutions. However, a number of the provisions of Decree Law 315 continue to be restrictive. For example, there is a prohibition against the formation of any type of organization—cooperatives, business associations, etc., unless specifically authorized. The objective of this is essentially political: to prevent independent organizations of small enterprises from forming and to pressure the self-employed to join the official union, the CTC.

The restriction on undertaking unauthorized activities prohibits any economic activities beyond the 201 that are now authorized. Most professional activities continue to be prohibited.[24] Furthermore, many authorized activities continue to be very narrowly defined and cannot be creatively interpreted so as to broaden the range of legal activities. Indeed some are so narrowly defined that they may apply only to four or five individuals. The best examples of this are "Musical Group '*Los Mambises*'," "Dandy," "'*Amor*' Dance Duo," "'*Benny Moré*' Dance Team," "Trained Dog Exhibitor," and "'*Los Amigos*' Musical Duo" (*Gaceta Oficial* 2013a, Resolution 42, Annex,).

The penalties for the various infractions range from "preventative notification" up to "confiscation of tools and materials." "Preventative notification"—which sounds like a warning for a first offence—applies only to the less serious offense of failure to provide current information to the relevant authorities. The fines listed apply to each infraction and are doubled at the highest rate in the case of more than one infraction. If an infraction "imposes a risk to health, life, or good habits" ("*las buenas costumbres*"—this being defined with no more detail in the legislation) the *cuentapropista* is barred from that activity but may switch to another. Prohibition from all self-employment activities is imposed when fines are not paid or if infractions continue. Confiscation of all tools and equipment is imposed when an infraction generates damages to health or if the tools and equipment have been acquired illegally (*Gaceta Oficial* 2014a).

The fines for infractions of the regulations are fixed, whereas in the earlier legislation there was a range of fines for each infraction. If a fine is paid within three days of its notification, the amount paid is 50% of the amount of the fine. Interestingly, the full 100% must be paid from day 3 to day 30 after the notification. If paid from day 30 to day 60, the fine doubles. If unpaid after 60 days, the license to operate is suspended. If the raw materials or tools and equipment have been acquired illegally, the enterprise can be shut down and the tools and equipment confiscated. Likewise, if the enterprise is operating illegally, that is in the underground economy, the tools, equipment, and inputs can be seized. If the microenterprise is generating damages to health, the tools and equipment can be seized as well. What constitutes damage to health is not defined, and presumably would not include such things as smoking cigars.

This legislation continues to grant the inspectors significant discretionary power. Their rulings on any of the infractions described above can impose great financial penalties on the microentrepreneur and may include shutting the operation down completely. Such powers can be easily abused and exercised for personal gain. Corrupt behavior on the part of the inspectors was a continuing complaint of the microentrepreneurs in the 1990s and early 2000s. The rigorous or perhaps overzealous role of inspectors combined with the closure of operations that had resold imported clothing was apparently the motivation for a protest march that occurred in Holguín in January 2014 (Tamayo 2014a; Cave 2014a).

While prohibiting the formation of independent associations of small enterprises, the government has been forming an official union for the self-employed under the aegis of the CTC (Peláez, et al 2014; Benítez 2013). By October 2013, 257,639 of the self-employed, presumably including microentrepreneurs and their employees, had joined (Peláez, et al 2014). This was around 55% of the total number of *cuentapropistas* at that time. According to a functionary of the CTC, there was some difficulty in persuading CPs to join. Some of the latter stated that "they did not want to affiliate; others argued that they did not see the CTC as a solution or the usefulness of being unionized" (ibid.). Indeed, it is difficult to know what the role such a union would be. In keeping with the character of the CTC, its central function will likely be to serve as a mechanism for top-down communication and containment of worker's grievances and demands. However, such a union might also serve as a means of protecting the self-employed from capricious behavior on the part of the powerful inspectors.

Evolution of the Small Enterprise Sector, 2006-2014

The number of people employed in the microenterprise sector reached 391,500 by the end of 2011 (ONE, AEC 2011, Table 7.2) up from 333,206 in September 2011 (Vidal Alejandro and Pérez Villanueva, 2012). By March 2014, this number had grown to 455,577 (*Cubadebate* 2014b; *Mesa Redonda* 2014; Cuba Central 2014), reaching 471,085 by the end of July 2014 (Manguela 2014; 14ymedio 2014a). This has indeed been an impressive increase relative to the 138,400 employed in the sector in 2007 and it represented a clear and significant increase over the 147,400 employed in the sector in 2010. Put another way, Cuba's once moribund entrepreneurial sector has grown more than 3-fold in almost four years (late 2010–mid-2014) (Figure 5.5).

This expansion represents a remarkable increase in comparison within the Cuban context outlined in Chapters 3 and 4. However, the 471,085 licensed *cuentapropistas* in mid-2014 are less than the 600,000 that were initially anticipated by the end of 2012. Added to this is the often underreported fact that more than 400,000 one-time CPs have decided to close their doors and hand in their licenses over this same period (Peláez, et al 2014; DDC 2014b; Cartaya 2014; Torres Hernández 2014; Tamayo Batista 2014). Still, the true expansion of employment in this sector has likely been higher than the official

Figure 5.5: Non-Agricultural Self-Employment as a Percentage of Total Employment, 2000-2014

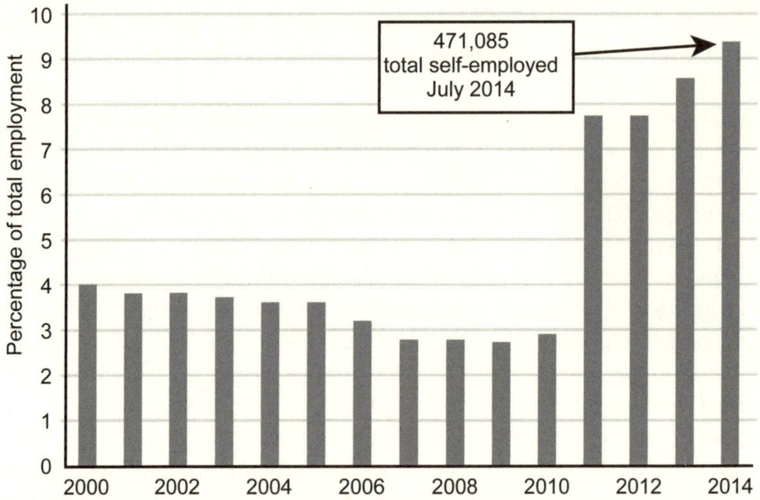

[Bar chart showing percentage of total employment from 2000 to 2014, with a callout box indicating "471,085 total self-employed July 2014" pointing to the 2014 bar.]

Sources: ONE, *Anuario Estadistico de Cuba,* Various Issues; *El Nuevo Herald,* July 2013; *Cubadebate,* March 19, 2014; Manguela 2014.

numbers would indicate due to the hiring of unregistered full-time or part-time workers—even if "contracted labor" licenses given to those who work for others are among the most common of all occupations, making up over 20% of all licenses or almost 100,000 of the 471,085 registered *cuentapropistas.* Such hiring is suggested only by anecdotal evidence as there of course are no reliable estimates or headcounts on such employment due to its clandestinity. We would estimate that up to one-half of the small enterprises employ at least one unregistered worker. The motivation for this on the part of the owners of the small enterprises is to avoid the tax on the employment of labor. For the unregistered worker, the incentive also is to avoid tax payments.[25]

If a large amount of unregistered employment exists in the legal microenterprise sector, then in 2014 the government may well be approaching or even surpassing the 600,000 employment target for the end of 2012. However, it is impossible to tell if the government's encouragement of non-state employment since late-2010 has created such jobs or only served to uncover previously existing clandestine activities. In terms of employment by economic activity in 2014, 57,776 or 12.7% of Cuba's officially registered 455,577 private workers at that time were in food service (restaurants, cafeterias, and street vendors), another 47,733 or 10.5% were in transportation, and 29,952 or 6.6% operated "bed-and-breakfasts." Another 91,978 or 20.2% were in fact employees working in the microenterprises of others rather than being the owners of microenterprises themselves (*Cubadebate* 2014b).

The major reason for the promotion of microenterprise was to generate employment for workers who were considered redundant in the state sector. Judging from the limited statistical information available, this objective has been unfulfilled. Of the 333,206 total for employment in the microenterprise sector as of mid-2011, only 17% had come from the state sector. Some 16% were retirees. And another 67% had been outside the labor force, and presumably were either housewives, working in the underground economy, students entering the job market for the first time, or perhaps out of the labor force on disability pensions (Vidal Alejandro and Perez Villanueva 2012: 47). Official statistics from March 2014 indicate that this trend has only continued, with 18% coming from the state sector, another 14% previously retired, and a whopping 68% declaring that they had been unemployed prior to registering as a *cuentapropista* (*Cubadebate* 2014b).

The microenterprise reforms have been a major success in that self-employment has grown to unprecedented levels providing a wide variety of goods, services, and employment opportunities to Cuban citizens. On the other hand, part of this growth to date seems to have been driven more by the formalization of previously clandestine operators and less by incorporation of laid-off state workers, which was the government's stated goal. Moreover, given the near prohibition on professional employment in the small enterprise sector, most of the growth in non-state employment has been in lower-technology though nonetheless important service occupations and not the higher-technology, value added professional activities that could contribute to more broadly to greater economic efficiency and productivity.

By 2013, Cuba's overall private sector had expanded considerably. An interesting estimation of the total private sector by Richard Feinberg (2013: 8) placed the total legal or officially registered private sector at 1,042,000 in 2013 out of total employment of 4,902,000 (the latest official number dating from 2012) or 21.3% of total employment. According to Feinberg's estimates, the private sector included 430,000 persons registered as being self-employed (as of late 2013), 353,000 members of agricultural service and credit cooperatives, 222,000 private and lend-lease farmers, 34,000 employees in joint state-foreign enterprises, and perhaps 3,000 members of non-agricultural cooperatives. It would be difficult to know the number of unregistered artists and artisanal workers as well as religious personnel as both activities fall across a spectrum of formality, with some officially registered practitioners and others unregistered. However, added to this would be unregistered employment both in the underground economy and in legal microenterprises. It would include full-time workers and many part-time workers as well, some perhaps operating within their state sector activity and many others operating out of their homes. As we emphasize in Chapter 7, it is most difficult to determine the magnitude of the underground economy in any country and perhaps especially in Cuba, given its unique geopolitical, ideological, and economic profile.

The relatively small number of laid-off state sector workers in the microenterprise sector suggests that absorbing large numbers of redundant state sector workers into microenterprise activities will not be easy in future. For example, when workers in former state enterprises are informed that their place of business has been selected to be part of a transfer to the non-state sector—allowing the workers to become self-employed if they wish—the other alternative is for them to become unemployed (Freire Santana 2012; Frank and Valdés 2014). State sector downsizing also has been difficult to implement in practice. This is in part because few Cubans volunteered to serve on the committees that would identify their fellow workers as "*disponible*" for layoff (Alfonso 2012; Diversent 2010; Perera 2010).

Thus, this expansion of self-employment can also be seen as a state discharge of hundreds of thousands of workers, most of whom are likely unprepared to become effective entrepreneurs. Indeed, as with the creation of non-agricultural cooperatives discussed in Chapter 6 (Frank 2013a; Frank and Valdés 2014), there is a difference between self-made entrepreneurs who create their own businesses and state workers who are bureaucratically converted into entrepreneurs when their only other option is to become "*trabajadores disponibles*" (Carrillo Ortega 2012; *Trabajadores* 2012e; *Trabajadores* 2012f; Peters 2013a).[26]

One might expect that after the rapid expansion of microenterprise in 2011 to 2013 there would be a period of consolidation and perhaps stabilization. Not all new microenterprises would be successful due to problems of location in some cases, product quality in others, or overcrowding and insufficient demand in still others. New businesses often fail (Cartaya 2014). One might also expect that the expansion of some more efficient microenterprises would squeeze some of the less efficient enterprises out of operation.[27] There was anecdotal evidence that such a growth slow-down or even reversal might have been occurring in early 2014 as some "*ferias*" or market areas were being vacated by the microenterprises that had been there earlier (Linares 2014; Alfonso Torna 2014).

However, one wonders how much of this turnover or bankruptcy in the entrepreneurial sector is the "natural" result of competition and the steep learning curve of thousands of entrepreneurs entering a new market at once (often offering the same products) and how much is due to government's still-reluctant opening to the private sector (one might say more "*pausa*" than "*prisa*"), continued desire to limit the concentration of wealth in private hands, and emphasis of order and control over facilitating growth. Moreover, following the establishment of the legal framework for non-agricultural cooperatives in December 2012 (discussed at length in Chapter 6), it is possible that larger numbers of workers will leave the state sector when a range of smaller state sector service and goods producing activities are transformed into cooperatives. In fact, a recent *Reuters* article on the state of these new urban and service cooperatives seems to indicate exactly such a development is already in its initial stages, at least for a handful of new cooperatively-run restaurants (Frank and Valdés 2014).

Summary and Conclusions

The policy changes for small enterprise introduced under the presidency of Raúl Castro have been positive and have resulted in a major expansion of the sector. Indeed, the policy initiatives have been dramatic when compared to the extremely tentative reforms of the mid-1990s. Still, employment generation by mid-2014 was still below the original targets for job creation and relatively few state employees had found positions in the microenterprise sector by this time. A major question, then, is whether these significant reforms are sufficient to achieve the government's stated goal of increasing efficiency and productivity. Perhaps a more important question is whether Raúl's reforms can keep up with the rising demands and entrepreneurial ingenuity of the Cuban people.

Among the supportive measures for entrepreneurial expansion as of mid-2014 are the following:

1. The political and media stigmatization has been reversed.
2. Licensing has opened small enterprise to most potential entrants.
3. There has been a small increase in permitted activities.
4. The legal markets for small enterprise have been broadened significantly.
5. Some regulations have been relaxed.
6. The increase in employment to a maximum of five workers will reduce the miniaturization of enterprises and permit greater economies of scale.
7. The increase in the deductibility of costs from gross revenues for taxes is beneficial as is the softening of some other tax provisions—transitory in some cases and more permanently in others.
8. Access to micro-credits, banking facilities, and the purchase of domestic and imported inputs at wholesale prices are promising, though as of mid-2014 they were still in their infancy.
9. The rental of state facilities to small entrepreneurs may stimulate the abandonment of small scale service and manufacturing activities by the state, leaving these to the private sector.
10. The relaxation of some of the harsher punishments for self-employment infractions, namely revocation of license and confiscation of equipment, is a valuable measure.

11. The legislation for non-agricultural cooperatives should stimulate the expansion of small and medium scale enterprise in the cooperative non-state sector.

At the same time, there are still some policy limitations that stunt job creation and hobble the expansion of the small enterprise sector. The more important of these are the following:

1. Despite some relaxation of taxes, the high overall level and multiple types of taxation limit enterprise creation and encourage the underground economy.
2. The tax on the hiring of (more than five) employees discourages the absorption of excess state sector labor into small enterprise and encourages the clandestine hiring of unregistered employees.
3. Small enterprises will remain stunted by the high effective tax rates that are incurred when actual costs of production exceed the minimum deductible for tax determination purposes.
4. Tax discrimination favoring foreign firms in joint ventures over domestic small enterprises continues, and is perhaps even worse than before given the generous terms of the new foreign investment law.
5. The narrow definition of legal activities continues to limit enterprise and job creation.
6. Exclusion of most high-tech and professional activities blocks the development of knowledge-intensive enterprises and wastes the training of the Cuba's highly educated population. This also blocks innovation throughout the economy.
7. Wholesale markets and access to imported inputs were still largely out of reach as of mid-2014.
8. Access to banking facilities was "en route," but not yet fully available by mid-2014.
9. There still exists a stigma to the concentration of wealth in private hands—as per the final "Lineamientos" document approved by the PCC in April 2011. Moreover, rights to ownership and private property are not protected, sending a mixed message to ambitious and innovative entrepreneurs who seek to grow beyond mere survival.
10. A number of highly publicized cases, such as that of the closure of "Ópera de la Calle" in the summer of 2012 (discussed in detail at the end of Chapter 8) indicate that Raúl Castro's reforms face internal resistance from lower-level bureaucrats who appear to look for and find excuses to impose their control as gatekeepers over entrepreneurs.

While the task of modifying the policy framework for the microenterprise sector is incomplete, major improvements have been instituted so far and more are in the process of implementation. Table 5.3 summarizes the reforms that have been made in a number of areas and the areas for which further policy steps likely would be appropriate. For some policies, notably liberalizing licensing and "de-stigmatizing" the sector in the media, major improvements have already been instituted. Cuba already has in place an effective—and formerly overzealous—institutional structure for the imposition of taxation and for the implementation of health and safety, labor, and environmental regulations. This legal framework is of course vital for the functioning of a private sector.

Progress has also been made or is in process in a number of other areas such as loosening of the tax regime, establishing micro-credit institutions, and the permitting of the expansion of microenterprises by liberalizing employment restrictions. These reforms could be pushed much further however. There has been minimal action in a few important areas, notably permitting a range of professional small enterprises, eliminating the state import monopoly, and transforming the current short and extremely detailed list of permitted occupations into one that lists only prohibited ones leaving all others open to the imagination and ingenuity of Cuba's entrepreneurs. In still other areas, reforms have been begun

Table 5.3: Major Public Policy Areas for Micro-Enterprises as of August 2014

Policy Area	Status
1. Liberalization of Licensing	Done
2. Permission for Professional and High-Tech Self-Employment	Not Yet
3. Revision of Taxation Regime	In Process
4. Increase in Ceiling on the Hiring of Employees	Not Yet
5. Establishment of Wholesale Markets for Inputs	In Process
6. Access to Imported Inputs at the exchange rate available for the state sector	Just Begun
7. Elimination of Vexatious Restrictions	In Process
8. Establishment of Micro-Credit Institutions	In Process
9. Legalization of "Intermediaries"	Just Begun
10. Permission for Advertising	Just Begun
11. Legalization of Markets for Housing, Automobiles, and Durables	Almost Complete
12. Cessation of the Media and Political Campaigns against Small Enterprise	Done
13. Establishment of a "Ministry for Small Enterprise"	Not Yet
14. Building the Credibility of Public Policy	In Process
15. Establishment of State Regulatory and Taxation Institutions	Done

Source: Ministerio de Trabajo, June 1999.

or will be implemented soon. These measures include the establishment of wholesale markets for the provision of inputs to the small enterprise sector. The legalization of advertising in the "yellow pages" of the telephone book is an interesting change as well, but other controls on advertising (such as listing paladares in brochures available to tourists) continue in place.

It will take some years before the government's public policy towards small-enterprise earns strong credibility on the part of Cuban citizens and small entrepreneurs. There have been too many capricious changes and policy reversals in the past and too much "policy hostility" towards the sector for the distrust and wariness of public policy towards the sector to vanish quickly. There have also been a number of significant retrenchments in the midst of the overall program of reform, such as the crackdown on resellers of imported clothing and private cinemas and game rooms in fall 2013 and the recent tightening of customs rules in September 2014. Thus, while a reasonable start has been made towards building trust and willing compliance on the part of the small entrepreneurs, there is certainly still a long way to go before cuentapropistas feel secure enough regarding government policy that they willingly comply with most rules, regulations, and tax measures.

Perhaps additional institutional innovations will soon become desirable. A strong micro-finance or micro-credit system is one such possibility and a start on this has already been made. Another innovation would be the establishment of a "Ministry of Small Enterprise" which would provide a higher priority and greater focus to policy making of a supportive character towards the sector. While this may not occur for some years, it is probably inevitable that new governmental organizations will be desirable and necessary when the government transfers most small-scale service, retailing, transport, construction trades, handicraft, and some manufacturing to the small enterprise and to the newly-emerging cooperative enterprise sector that is examined in the next chapter.

In conclusion, significant reforms have been instituted in the general policy environment affecting the establishment and functioning of small and microenterprise in Cuba during the Presidency of Raúl Castro. These policy changes have propelled the sector to rapid expansion—more than tripling their number between 2010 and 2014. Major benefits have been generated for the everyday material life of Cuban citizens. It is unlikely that these reforms will be reversed in future as has been the case a number of times in Cuba's economic experience since 1959. The sector should continue expansion for a number of years as the state withdraws from the provision of many types of goods and services. However, this process would be greatly facilitated by some deeper reforms. Among the most important of these would be:

• Legalizing all economic activities for small enterprise including a broad range of professional activities;

• Revising the tax system so that all costs of production and investments with legal receipts can be deducted from total revenues in determining taxable income;
• Lowering overall income tax rates for small enterprise to levels closer to those for foreign enterprises in joint ventures with Cuban state firms;
• Eliminating or reducing the tax on the hiring of workers;
• Ending the tax discrimination favoring foreign enterprise and penalizing Cuban enterprise;
• Establishing wholesale markets for imported inputs used in the small enterprise sector;
• Loosening the restrictions on advertising;
• Loosening further the limits on the hiring of labor;
• Ensuring that inspectors are neither over-zealous nor corrupt;
• Further strengthening of training for small entrepreneurs on "how to start a business," relevant laws, regulations and taxation, marketing, more formal payments systems, and at some time, relevant technical skills.

The policy reform process is likely to continue and to intensify as the benefits of the changes already instituted make themselves apparent to all. However, while Raúl's government has shown itself to be more pragmatic in terms of public policy towards entrepreneurship than that of Fidel's, it has also proven itself to be careful in ensuring that greater economic freedom does not lead to the creation of new private interest groups that could threaten its political control. Raúl's government has openly admitted that its "updated" version of a socialist Cuba needs an efficient, productive non-state sector to survive. However, the government also seems to believe that the unchecked growth of that sector may well threaten its own survival.

Notes

[1] Indeed, the initial list of 178 self-employment occupations published in fall 2010 specifically mentioned another 10 occupations that would not yet be legalized since their only source of raw materials at the time was via theft from state stores. These 10 occupations were finally legalized in fall 2013, presumably after legal sources of supplies and inputs were made available (see #s 156–165 in Appendix 2 for a complete list).

[2] In fact, the lack of such a wholesale market has been a major cause of the development of an extensive informal network of importers of all manner of goods (through the use of "mules" who hand-carry merchandise into Cuba from abroad). The government reacted to this in fall 2013 by launching a major crackdown on the resale of such imported goods—with a focus on clothing and household goods retailers—which relied almost exclusively on informal imports from abroad to supply their enterprises.

[3] The dual exchange rate system meant that for each pound of sugar exported, the enterprise earned pesos in *Moneda Nacional* at the rate of 1 peso = $US 1.00, while the

relevant rate of exchange for the citizens was usually in the area of 24 to 26 pesos = $US 1.00. This meant that the pesos in *Moneda Nacional* were insufficient for compensating sugar workers or managers appropriately and the sector was continuously starved of resources for reinvestment.

⁴ For examples, see references in our bibliography to the work of Armando Nova González, Omar Everleny Pérez Villanueva, Pavel Vidal Alejandro, Camila Piñeiro-Harnecker, Luisa Iñíguez Rojas, Ricardo Torres Pérez, Jorge Mario Sánchez, Juan Triana Cordoví, and other analysts at the CEEC who have undertaken serious analyses of Cuba's economic situation since the founding of the Center in 1992. Especially insightful is the series of annual volumes published since 2009 entitled, *Miradas a la Economia Cubana*.

⁵ "*Te digo que antes en lo años '90 nosotros los cuentapropistas éramos lo más indeseables que pudiera haber. Nosotros éramos unos oportunistas, los más adinerados, [...] un delincuente, o sea, todo lo más malo. Ahora los cuentapropistas van a salvar al país.*"

⁶ Such laudatory articles coincided with the appearance in *Granma* of a new "letter-to-the-editor" section on Fridays. However, some have noted a tendency for this new section to be used to publish letters decrying the high prices, indiscipline, and lack of proper revolutionary attitude among CPs (Diversent 2011a, b, and c; 2012).

⁷ For example, in this article, Lesvis Odanis, a previously unemployed 34-year-old owner of a food stand in Cienfuegos is described as someone held in "high regard" by his community and whose purpose is not getting rich but simply "providing for his family." Still, he said that his biggest problem was "the unavailability of ingredients. Many of the ingredients I must buy in hard currency stores, but I sell my product in Cuban pesos," he explained, adding, "the supply is very unstable and sometimes I cannot find what I need at all."

⁸

Income category	Tax Rate	Tax Payable
First 10,000	15%	1,500
Next 10,000	20%	2,000
Next 10,000	30%	3,000
Next 20,000	40%	8,000
Last 10,000	50%	5,000
Total tax payable:		19,500

⁹ Law 118/2014, "Ley de la Inversión Extranjera." *Gaceta Oficial*, April 16, 2014.

¹⁰ The authors know of one microentrepreneur who entered a marriage of convenience with a foreigner, which permitted frequent travel to that country. The main purpose of the travel—and the marriage—was to purchase inputs needed for the fabrication of the products sold in the microenterprise.

¹¹ See Appendix #2 for a complete list of all occupations including these 18-20 new ones: #39, #s 148-155, #s 156-165, and #171.

¹² In fact, according to Carrillo Ortega (2013), the new legislation also gives state tourism entities access to 28 other self-employment activities, which it can turn to for goods and services, including "masons and ironworkers, plumbers and welders, refrigeration, electrical, and electronic equipment mechanics, among others."

¹³ See Philip Peters, "Cuba's New Real Estate Market," Brookings Institution, February, 2014, for an excellent analysis of the new legislation.

¹⁴ By the end of Julty 2014 this total had reached 471,085 (Manguela 2014; 14ymedio 2014a).

¹⁵ As we describe in Chapter 8, Cuba's now ubiquitous home-based restaurants were born in the early 1990s in much the same way. While *paladares* were not included

on the original list of 117 occupations legalized in September 1993, inventive *cuentapropistas* took advantage of a vague "*et cetera*" included on the original list in order to set up Cuba's first *paladares* before they were explicitly outlawed in December of that same year. New legislation that specifically legalized them was later passed in 1995.

[16] Likewise, the small number of increasingly popular paintball arenas—some of which have partnered with moribund state-run parks and sports arenas—rely on informal import networks to obtain supplies that are simply unavailable on the island at any price (Ulloa García 2013).

[17] This shift was confirmed by observations during a March 2014 visit.

[18] Even the well-known pro-government blogger Yohandry Fontana reacted negatively to the ban Tweeting: "Bad news. Wouldn't it be easier, I ask, to approve the sale of imported clothing by the self-employed than push this activity into the black market?" (Valdés 2013).

[19] This was followed by a march and near riot of an estimated 500 people in early 2014 in Holguín after an altercation between *cuentapropistas* and police as authorities fined and attempted to close down some of the banned businesses. The *Miami Herald* quoted Eduardo Cardet, a Holguín physician and member of the opposition Christian Liberation Movement, as saying: "It's no longer the opposition protesting. Now, it's the people" (Tamayo 2014a; *Martinoticias* 2014a; Freire Santana 2014; Cave 2014a; *El Universal* 2014; *DDC* 2014c).

[20] Some of this outpouring of debate over self-employment has taken place on video. For example, the independent organization "State of Sats" (*Estado de Sats*) recently recorded an hour-long discussion entitled, "Self-Employment in Cuba: Reality or Illusion?" September 12, 2013. Likewise, a ten-minute segment of the October 9, 2013 episode of Cuban state television's weekly show "*Cuba Dice*" (Cuba Says) focused on the popular debate over the new self-employment regulations.

Other recently produced videos relating to self-employment include a two-part episode, "*Situación actual del Trabajo por Cuenta Propia*" on the official state television series *Mesa Redonda* ("Round Table"), March 19-20, 2014; A short video entitled "Cubans in the New Economy: Their Reflections and the U.S. Response" from a daylong conference hosted by The Center for Democracy in the Americas, November 13, 2103; A panel video from the conference "Cuba-U.S. Relations in the Second Obama Administration: The Cuban-American Community and Changes in Cuba," sponsored by Cuban Americans for Engagement (*CAFÉ*) and featuring Abiel San Miguel Estévez, proprietor of *Paladar Doña Eutimia* in Old Havana, March 15, 2014; and a video explaining the work of the Cuba Emprende Foundation at its website, March, 2014.

In fact, in August 2014 the pro-engagement Cuba Study Group organized the U.S. visit of five Cuban micro-entrepreneurs, some of whom had benefitted from small business training received in Havana through Cuba Emprende. During their visit they spoke at the annual conference of the Association for the Study of the Cuban Economy and Miami-Dade College, as well as engaging with some of Miami's more successfule entrepreneurs (Tamayo 2014b; Gómez 2014; Padgett 2014). For more recent reportage on "entreepreneurial Cuba," see the series of stories from summer 2014 done from Havana by *NPR*'s David Greene and his team, especially those that highlight emerging microentrepreneurs and independent media.

[21] The Cuban expression here translated as "throw the baby out with the bathwater" is actually "*botar el sofá por la ventana*." This rich expression has been used by more than one critic of the government's inflexible economic policy. It originates with the joke: What did the guy do when he returned home to find his wife having sex on the couch with another man? He got right to the bottom of the problem and immediately threw the couch out the window (*botó el sofá por la ventana*)!

[22] The exact words are: "*Instala, opera o alquila equipos para la recreación de la población. No incluye los equipos náuticos*".

[23] *On Cuba* journalist Tómas E. Pérez even interviewed a 3D cinema operator who showed him a signed, stamped official permission form from the local municipal authorities authorizing him to erect a sign advertising his business. "If the sign says '*Cine 3D El Marino*'," the man told Pérez bitterly, "what do you suppose my business is? A cafe?" Thus, despite the insinuations of both the *Juventud Rebelde* article and the later *Granma* clarification on November 2, such businesses were not something that operators sneakily "got away with" but instead activities that they "applied openly to do." Another operator explained to Pérez that she was asked for and provided photos of her operation when she applied for her license, indicating the dimensions of the theater, the size of the television, and the style and number of seats to be used (Pérez 2013).

[24] Among the few exceptions to the prohibition on professional self-employment are teacher of music and other arts (#102), teacher of languages or typing (#103), computer programmer (#104), book-keeper (#135), and translator of documents (#140). See Appendix 2 for a full list.

[25] See Richard Feinberg's fine recent report on self-employment, "Soft Landing In Cuba? Emerging Entrepreneurs and Middle Classes," published by the Latin American Initiative of the Brookings Institution, November 2013, for a detailed estimate of the true size of Cuba's current private, "non-state" sector.

[26] The standard legalese in these cases is: "*los empleados de tales unidades que no deseen incorporse al modelo, cesarán su vínculo laboral y se les aplicará el tratamiento de trabajadores disponibles*" (the employees of said units who do not want to join the new management model will lose their status as employees and will be considered as available workers) (2012). Cuban sociologist Neili Fernández Peláez captured this sentiment well when she criticized the government's new "embrace of self-employment" as more an abandonment of "the promise of full employment" than recognition of greater labor rights and economic freedoms.

[27] See Díaz Fernández et al. 2012: 21-24 for a case study of the failure of a "*cafetería*" or snack bar.

6

The Movement Toward Non-Agricultural Cooperatives

In the process of analyzing the issues and problems facing the Cuban economy following his July 2006 accession to power, Raúl Castro concluded that much of the state sector of the economy—and the planning process under which it operated—was irredeemably inefficient. Numerous attempts had been made to improve its operation, but all were without significant success. This was typified sharply by the collapse of the sugar agro-industrial sector, by the inability of the non-sugar industrial sector to be revived after its collapse in 1989-1992, by the continuing shortcomings of the consumer economy, and by the burgeoning of the underground economy. In response to this continuing predicament, Raúl Castro's government produced the "Draft Guidelines for Economic and Social Policy" (aka, "*los Lineamientos*") in November 2010 with a final, amended version approved by the Sixth Party Congress in May 2011. This guiding document for the subsequent unfolding of economic reforms notably called for the establishment of an enabling environment for small enterprise, among other things. Points #2 and #25 of the *Lineamientos* specifically called for the promotion of new non-agricultural cooperative enterprises signaling that this new form of management was the object of considerable analysis within the Cuban government between 2008 and 2011.

On December 11, 2012, a battery of new laws and regulations on these non-agricultural cooperatives was published, including two Council of State Decree-Laws, two Ministerial Resolutions, one Council of Ministers Decree, and one Ministerial "*Norma Específica de Contabilidad*" (*Gaceta Oficial*, No. 53, 2012). This legislation outlined the structuring, functioning, governance, and financial organization of the new cooperatives and provided the legal framework within which they were to operate (*Trabajadores* 2013). It permitted and defined a new type of economic institution for Cuba, one that would have been out of the question under the presidency of Fidel Castro, but that holds the potential for revolutionizing the institutional structure of the Cuban economy. In fact, in the months prior to the passage of the new cooperative law, the government made an effort to justify the expansion of this non-state form of enterprise as compatible with an "updated" version of Cuban socialism. For example, in early July 2012, Claudio Alberto Rivera, the President of the Cooperative Society of Cuba, argued that "the strengthening of cooperatives as a form of management is one of the paths of the process of updating of the Cuban economic model, and constitutes *a global alternative to the reigning neoliberal system*," (*DDC* 2012d, our emphasis).[1]

The initial 2012 legislation presented the cooperatives as "experimental," and indicated that after some 200 were initially approved and implemented, the institutional form would be reappraised and modified as necessary. There is therefore some uncertainty regarding the long-term character of the legislative framework governing the structure and functioning of the cooperatives. However, in our judgment, the reform will more likely be more "loosening" rather than restricting—assuming that Raúl and his successors do not return to the de-marketizing and centralizing orientations of the previous "*Fidelista*" era. We make this assumption based on our reading of the exceedingly cautious unfolding of self-employment since 2010 as analyzed in Chapter 5. Our analysis indicates that the government sees this new (and largely untested) form of "cooperativism" as more compatible with state socialism (and perhaps more easily controlled) than is private microenterprise. Indeed, in his most recent public comment on the sector to Cuba's National Assembly in December 2013, economic reform czar Marino Murillo said, "Cooperatives have priority over small private businesses because they are a more social form of production and distribution." He added that these new non-agricultural co-ops pay less in taxes, can deduct the full cost of expenses before paying those taxes, and benefit from access to the state system of wholesale inputs[2] unlike private microenterprises, which can make only limited deductions for inputs and must purchase their supplies at high retail prices (Frank and Valdés 2014; Nieves Cárdenas 2014), or—one might add—on the black market.[3]

In essence, the new legal regime for non-agricultural cooperatives provides for management and partial ownership of the enterprise by its employees, with mainly independent management and control over the setting of prices, the purchase of inputs, decisions regarding what to produce, labor relations and the remuneration of members. Thus, unlike the microenterprise sector (*trabajo por cuenta propia*) described in previous chapters, "cooperatives are open to professionals and there is no list of permitted lines of work." What's more, these cooperatives are envisioned as self-governing, unconnected to any state institution, though they are "free to do business with government entities, state enterprises, and private entities" (Peters 2013b).

It is notable, however, that while the enterprises themselves are "owned" collectively by members of each cooperative, the physical infrastructure (buildings, land, equipment, etc.) are rented on a ten-year basis from the state, which retains full property rights of the "means of production." Just two months after the first 124 such cooperatives were launched on July 1, 2013, an official report published by various state media outlets made this point clear. That is, while cooperatives are referred to in point #25 of the 2011 *Lineamientos* as "a socialist form of collective property," this August 2013 report makes clear that cooperatives can only be formed:

> Based on means of production *under state patrimony,* such as real estate and others, which are decided to managed cooperatively and for that purpose can cede these through rental, usufruct, or other legal forms that *do not imply the transfer of ownership of property* (*Trabajadores* 2013, our emphasis).[4]

The transformation of some state enterprises into cooperatives was announced on July 7, 2013 by the Minister responsible for the reform process, Marino Murillo (Frank 2013a). Such state enterprises were to be granted greater control over their profits—retaining 50% thereof for their own uses—as well as over wages and salaries, investment expenditures, and the purchase of imported inputs. It was still unclear at the time as to whether prices were to be controlled by the state planners or by market forces. It is still too early at the time of writing to say whether these changes for state firms will amount to a reliance on the forces of supply and demand. However, they signal a shift towards a more mixed economy, greater decentralization of economic management, and a diminished role for the central planning authority.

This type of worker enterprise ownership and management within a market environment could be regarded as a variant of "market socialism." Cuba is launched on a path towards a hybrid type of mixed economy with a still-significant state sector, an expanding small enterprise sector, a joint venture sector (foreign and domestic state enterprise), and now a state-owned and employee-managed sector. Only Yugoslavia prior to its break-up included a large part of its economy under a unique form of workers' management, though it still seems to have involved authentic workers management in theory more than in practice (Carson 1973). Most other countries have cooperative enterprises of various types that survive and thrive. However, while some cooperative enterprises are large and highly successful, no form of cooperative model has taken over a majority share of the economy in any country since Yugoslavia disintegrated in 1990-1992.

If Cuba's new legislative framework for non-agricultural cooperatives is sustained, and if they actually function with the autonomy and internal democracy outlined in the legislation, their governance and operation will be quite egalitarian in terms of the decision-making process within the enterprise and the distribution of income among members. The adoption of this cooperative model, involving workers' ownership and management of the enterprise operating under market mechanisms, could turn out to be a major institutional innovation for Cuba. Nevertheless, during their first year of experimental operation, the approval process has been painfully slow with the majority of those approved being cooperative agricultural markets, while most higher-end, value-added professional cooperative applicants were still waiting for ministerial approval as of May 2014 (Nieves Cárdenas 2014).[5] Still, in the current context of the existing economic structures in virtually all of the countries of the world, this Cuban experiment might prove to be innovative and perhaps even "revolutionary," though it is still far too early to judge.

The Cooperative Alternative

Cooperative enterprises of various sorts have an important place in the economies of most countries. Cooperatives are usually more than economic in character, however, and are widely viewed as elements of participatory democracy in the economy. In this sense, cooperatives are an attempt to combine efficiency in the economy with democracy in the workplace as well as social responsibility in the wider community. For this reason, they are often part of socio-economic and political movements.

A standard definition of a cooperative enterprise is set out by the International Cooperative Alliance (ICA) on its website:

> A cooperative is an autonomous association of persons united voluntarily to meet their common economic, social, and cultural needs and aspirations through a jointly-owned and democratically-controlled enterprise.
>
> Cooperatives are based on the values of self-help, self-responsibility, democracy, equality, equity, and solidarity. In the tradition of their founders, cooperative members believe in the ethical values of honesty, openness, social responsibility, and caring for others (ICA n.d.).

The ICA also has stated the principles by which cooperatives put their values into practice. A summary of these include:

1. Voluntary and Open Membership,
2. Democratic Member Control: Cooperatives are democratic organizations controlled by their members, who actively participate in setting their policies and making decisions,
3. Members' Economic Participation: Members contribute equitably to, and democratically control, the capital of their cooperative. At least part of that capital is usually the common property of the cooperative. Members usually receive limited compensation, if any, on capital subscribed as a condition of membership,
4. Autonomy and Independence: Cooperatives are autonomous, self-help organizations controlled by their members,

5. Education, Training, and Information: Cooperatives provide education and training for their members, elected representatives, managers, and employees,
6. Cooperation among Cooperatives: Cooperatives serve their members most effectively and strengthen the cooperative movement by working together through local, national, regional, and international structures, and
7. Concern for Community.

There are large numbers of cooperative enterprises of various sorts in many countries. For example, Chile had 2,132 co-ops in 2004 with 1.25 million members and Brazil has 6,652 co-ops with 300,000 members. Similarly, Canada has 9,000 co-ops with around 150,000 members; the United States has 30,000 co-ops employing over 2 million people; and France has 21,000 employing 3.5% of the labor force (ICA ibid.). Agricultural cooperatives are present in many countries, but credit unions, insurance services, consumer co-ops, cooperatives in retailing, mining, transportation, construction, and housing, and "second level" cooperative confederations of co-ops are all significant to varying degrees in different countries.[6] Cuba will have substantial company when it expands its non-agricultural cooperative sector.

Since the early days of the revolution, Cuba has had a cooperative and a pseudo-cooperative sector in agriculture. In 1960, Credit and Services Cooperatives (CSSs) were established for small independent farmers who continued to own their land and farm it independently. While these were not created at the initiative of the farmers and were imposed from above, they have continued to operate more or less "cooperatively" with respect to marketing, equipment and input purchases, and obtaining credit. In 1975, Agricultural Production Cooperatives (CPAs) were established by the government and small farmers were required to incorporate their farms into the larger units and become members (Mesa-Lago 2000). This process was not voluntary and it would not meet the first principle of the international cooperative movement as articulated above. In 1995, state farms were converted by the government into *Unidades Básicas de Producción Cooperativa*" (UBPCs). However, they were not voluntary either. Their managers were appointed by the state, not elected by the members. Nor did they determine the remuneration of their members. They required authorization for input purchase, decisions regarding output mix, and appropriate markets for outputs. They were also subject to the prices set by authorities. In sum, the UBPCs were far from being real cooperatives and continued to be a species of state controlled enterprise (Cruz Reyes 2014).

By 2010, there were some 579,440 members of alleged agricultural cooperatives, but the membership of the more genuine CCS cooperatives was 362,440, according to Cuba's *Oficina Nacional de Estadísticas* (see Table

Table 6.1: Cooperative Agricultural Organizations in Cuba, 2010

	Number	Members	Percentage of Total National Employment	Percentage of Arable Land
Credit and Service Cooperatives	2,949	362,440	7.2	35.3
Agricultural Production Cooperatives	1,048	30,000	0.6	8.8
Basic Units of Cooperative Production	2,256	187,000	3.7	30.9
Total	6,253	579,440	11.5	74.0

Source: Piñeiro Harnecker (2012: 81), based on *Oficina Nacional de Estadisticas*.

6.1). CCS membership constitutes a significant 7.2% of Cuba's total labor force. In view of the problems facing Cuban agriculture, the government of Raúl Castro instituted a series of reforms in the management of the UBPCs in 2012 aimed at converting them into more authentic cooperatives (*Granma* 2012a, 2012b). The directors of the UBPCs are to be elected by UBPC members rather than appointed from above. The UBPCs are to have independent control over the purchase of inputs and equipment for the production unit and for workers housing and daily necessities. Volumes of output above clearly defined amounts contracted to state sector purchasers can be sold freely in any market. Accumulated past UBPC debts will be covered by the state, with some portion to be covered by the UBPC itself paying 5% of its gross revenues over a 25-year period. Current financial losses will not be covered by the state, but UBPCs could go bankrupt if losses are unmanageable, unless the UBPC is of "special interest" to the government (a rather elastic criterion).

If the UBPCs were to become genuine producers' cooperatives, Cuba would indeed be one of the more "cooperativized" countries in the world. However, in view of the difficulties that cooperatives have faced in the past under all of the institutional variants, there is some doubt if the above reforms, useful as they may look on paper, will permit them to survive and to thrive. Moreover, it would be hard to argue that they were truly the result of free and informed decision-making on the part of their membership.

The 2012 Law on Non-agricultural Cooperatives

Some features of the new cooperatives were referred to briefly in the *Lineamientos* of November 2010 and then modified slightly in the final version that was approved at the Sixth Party Congress on April 18, 2011. For example, the original version of the *Lineamientos* included five guidelines (out of a total of 291) specifically on cooperatives. According to this document, cooperatives were to be based on the "free association" of workers, who were to be either the owners of the means of production or the leasers of state property (guideline #25). However, cooperative property could not be sold to others, be they other cooperatives or private or public enterprises (guideline #26). Cooperatives could sell directly to the public and maintain contractual relations with all other forms of enterprise (guideline #27). Moreover, cooperatives were empowered to determine the incomes of workers and the distribution of profits, while paying taxes and social security contributions (guideline #28). "Second-order cooperatives," consisting of other "first-order cooperatives," were also permitted (guideline #29). These guidelines were modified only slightly in the final version of the *Lineamientos* approved in spring 2011, the main change being to articulate in more detail what "second-order cooperatives" are—in response to nearly a thousand comments received from citizens during a nationwide discussion that took place in the first part of 2011.

Legislation published in November 2012 spelled out in detail the legal framework, governance structures, and operational modalities for the cooperatives. According to the set of laws on cooperatives, the range of activities for cooperative enterprise is not restricted (Decree-Law 305, 2012). In theory, all areas of the production of goods and services are permissible under this institutional form. This would include low-tech services of all kinds, such as retailing, transportation, construction, and manufacturing, as well as higher-level professional activities. A draft copy of a set of instructions for eliminating redundant labor for the City of Havana leaked to the international press in fall 2010 put forward some 76 possible areas in which low-tech cooperatives might operate, including 15 in agriculture, 8 in construction, 3 in construction materials, 9 in transportation, 5 in food production, and 36 in miscellaneous activities (City of Havana 2010; Peters 2010e; El Universal 2010a; *Penúltimos Días* 2010).

Higher value-added or professional services are not specifically excluded in the legislation. These services would include accounting, architecture, engineering consultants, management and environmental consultants of all kinds, as well as legal services, computer electronics and web site services, computer instruction, economic and market research, graphic design, real estate agents and travel agencies, music, dance and arts instruction, etc. All of these services would represent significant contributions to Cuban society and the economy and would permit well-educated Cubans to practice their professions within their own cooperative enterprises. One would assume, however, that the central core of educational and medical services would remain in the state sector. Yet some ancillary educational and medical services such as music lessons, educational tutoring (which is already widely practiced in the "informal" or underground economy), herbal-remedy vending and fabrication, chiropractic services, and therapeutic massage, could also be candidates for cooperative enterprise.

Any Cuban citizen or resident over 18 years of age and possessing the relevant skills can become a member of a cooperative (Decree-Law 305, 2012, Article 10.1). As noted above, professionals are not excluded, and can presumably offer services in their own profession. Members of a cooperative must in fact work within the enterprise (ibid, Article 23). The minimum size of a cooperative was set at three individuals (ibid, Article 5.1). No maximum was defined; cooperatives with over 60 members were mentioned in the legislation (ibid, Article 18.1). New prospective members must be approved by the General Assembly of the cooperative. In cases of the transfer of economic activities from the state sector to a cooperative enterprise, the original workers are to have priority in employment as founding members of the cooperative.

The approval process for the establishment of new cooperatives starts at the local level with the "Organs of Popular Power," which put forward applications to the "Permanent Commission for Implementation and Development of the Guidelines"; the latter then must obtain the approval for the new cooperative from the Council of Ministers (ibid, Articles 11.1 and 12.1). This Permanent Commission, which is headed by Marino Murillo, also bears overall responsibility for the implementation of the *Lineamientos*. Thus, Murillo is in effect Cuba's new economic czar and the main manager of its new non-agricultural cooperative sector.

The initial capital for the cooperatives is to come from the financial resources of the members plus bank credits (ibid, Article 21). For the transformation of a state enterprise into a cooperative, the latter must pay a rental fee to the state. Moreover, the prices of equipment purchased from the old state enterprise are to be negotiated between the state sellers and the cooperative buyers (Ministry of Finance and Prices, Resolution 427/2012, Paragraphs 14-15). The cooperatives are to be financially autonomous from the government. They are empowered to set their own prices, which are ultimately to be determined by the forces of "supply and demand," except in undefined cases where the relevant ministry sets fixed prices. Cooperatives are empowered to determine their own wage structure and profit distribution after paying taxes and social security contributions (Decree-Law 305, 2012, Article 25). Bankruptcy is their fate if they are unable to cover their costs (ibid. Article 30).

A cooperative can hire additional contractual workers, but only up to a maximum of 10% of the total work hours of the enterprise (ibid, Article 26.1).

A contracted worker can work only for 90 days, after which he or she becomes eligible to join the cooperative and receive equal status and voting rights with prior members. Otherwise, his or her employment must be terminated. "Second level" cooperatives can be established (ibid, Article 5.1). These would comprise smaller or lower-level cooperatives, labeled "first level" cooperatives. In effect they would be cooperative confederations of smaller cooperatives.

The ultimate authority within any single cooperative is its General Assembly, which would include all its members. This body would be empowered to elect a president, a substitute, and a secretary by secret ballot (ibid, Article 18.1). The specific managerial structure of the enterprise is to be determined by the complexity of the activity and the number of members in the co-op. Cooperatives with fewer than 20 members elect an "Administrator"; those with 20 to 60 members elect an "Administrative Council"; and those with more than 60 members elect a "Directive Committee," as well as an "Administrative Council." Thus, depending on its size and complexity, a cooperative's financial management is to be the responsibility of a single member or a financial committee. The management structures and functioning are delineated in detail in Decree 309 of the Council of Ministers.

Cooperatives are to pay a sales tax, a tax on the hiring of workers, a social security contribution, and a tax on profits, according to the Ministry of Finance and Prices, Resolution 427/2012. Sales of food products are exempted from the sales tax. The social security payments and the hiring of labor taxes are defined in other legislation. A special regimen for social security for co-op members—including pensions, disability payments, accident and sickness benefits, maternity leave, and death benefits—is delineated in Decree-Law 306. For the tax on cooperative profits, profits are defined as the residual amount after input costs are deducted (up to a maximum of 40% of revenues and for contingency reserves), after wages are paid to members (at the level of the average for that activity in the province), and finally, after payments are made for the rental of facilities (Ministry of Finance and Prices, Resolution 427/2012, Paragraph 6). Moreover, input purchases for cooperatives are given special treatment. Inputs purchased at the retail level are given a 20% discount on the going price. Inputs purchased from the wholesale market are also given a 20% discount on the going wholesale price (ibid., Paragraph 13).

The Potential of the Cooperative Component for the Cuban Economy

The 2012 legislation on non-agricultural cooperatives appears to open the door to a broad range of new entrepreneurial initiatives that had been blocked for almost half a century under the government of President Fidel Castro. The legislation allows for a wide variety of new enterprises. It may constitute a major institutional innovation that in time could promote a surge of new economic activity and productivity. The conversion of a range of state enterprises in services and light manufacturing to the cooperative format will likely be significant. As noted, under the new legal framework, it is possible that providers of professional services of various sorts could be established as cooperatives—as many providers of these types of services can operate in relatively small groupings. Whether all of this happens or not depends on how the law is applied and on what activities can be organized under the cooperative rubric. This cannot be judged yet in as much as the legislation came into effect only in November 2012.

Cuba's legislation might permit a great diversity in the types of cooperatives that could come into existence. Among the possibilities are:

1. A small corner coffee-shop, a shoe-repair shop, a beauty salon, or a barber shop consisting of three or more employees;
2. A former state restaurant converted to a cooperative, with up to 20 former employees becoming members (Frank 2013b; Frank and Valdés 2014);
3. A high-end women's clothing retailing store;
4. A manufacturing plant including some 60 plus workers;
5. A group of plumbers, electricians, or plasterers establishing a cooperative enterprise together (Recio 2013);
6. A group of citizens establishing a plant nursery and florist enterprise, growing, and selling flowers;
7. A group of computer specialists setting up a cooperative for the provision of web design, internet, computer-repair, and computer reselling activities (Nieves Cárdenas 2014);
8. A group of architects, accountants, market analysts, or consultants setting up a cooperative enterprise;
9. A combination of various building tradesmen such as carpenters, concrete construction workers, plumbers, or electricians setting up a house-building co-op;
10. A confederation of small cooperative coffee-shops or retail outlets.

Not surprisingly, the effectiveness of the cooperative form of enterprise has some major advantages as well as some disadvantages. There was a long debate within the economics profession dating back to the 1960s and 1970s concerning the relative merits of the cooperative form of enterprise. Some of this debate focused specifically on Yugoslavia, which organized its economy on the basis of state-owned worker-managed firms coordinated mainly by markets. Some analysts, among whom Jaroslav Vanek (1969) was the most prominent, argued that labor-management enterprises operating under markets were the optimal form of enterprise. Criticisms of the Yugoslav model generally were put forward by Branco Horvath (1971) and analyzed more fully by Richard Carson (1973).

Perhaps the most powerful advantage of worker-owned and managed enterprises—i.e., cooperatives—vis-à-vis state enterprises and privately-owned firms relates to incentives, motivations, and labor relations (Carson 1973: 639-641). Because cooperative members share in the benefits of the enterprise—including profit-sharing—presumably they will have a strong incentive to work hard, "pull their weight," and provide mutual monitoring, supervision, encouragement, and discipline for one another. The interests, objectives, and behavior of the workers and managers who are also the owners are in relative harmony rather than at cross-purposes.[7] In a private or state-owned enterprise where workers receive monthly wages or salaries, their incentive would be weaker because they would earn the same amount regardless of their efforts and the monitoring of their work effort and output quality from above is more difficult and costly. (On the other hand, piece-rate remuneration systems or wage bonuses for exceptional production performance would generate strong work incentives). In a workers' co-op, the members would be observing and trying to motivate their fellow cooperative members.

The widespread phenomenon of petty theft from the enterprise, as practiced by large numbers of employees in Cuba's state firms—especially after the early 1990s—would presumably not be tolerated in a cooperative firm. The foot-dragging behavior captured by the saying, "They pretend to pay us so we pretend to work," would likely be criticized and counteracted by the other members in a workers' co-op. However, if the cooperative is so large that the benefits of the efforts of one diligent worker are shared by a large number of others, there may be a tendency to "free ride" and let other workers do the "heavy lifting." This means that a smaller cooperative may generate stronger incentives for serious effort by the members than larger cooperatives. Remunerating members with an hourly wage plus a share of profits may well be optimal in order to elicit serious, sustained, and effective effort on the part of the members. In any case, the incentive to work industriously is likely stronger in a cooperative than in either a state enterprise or a private enterprise.

Second, the cooperative enterprise will likely operate with a greater degree of flexibility and responsiveness to its market than is the case with the state enterprises. Members of the co-op will observe and analyze its market directly. They will be in a position to structure its output in terms of quality, price, product diversity, and availability to more closely reflect the demands of the market and to adjust production plans accordingly. The co-op will also have some flexibility in that the income payments made to its members through the profit sharing arrangement can be directly adjusted to reflect any fluctuations and changes in the demand for the outputs of the enterprise. It is unclear whether a cooperative would have "incentive" and "flexibility" advantages over a similar-sized private enterprise, however. The continued coexistence of both cooperatives and private firms in the same type of economic activity in many other countries (e.g., credit unions, dairies, hardware retailing, etc.) suggests that neither has a huge advantage over the other in these respects. If one form of enterprise were in fact superior, it would presumably survive better and push the other forms into extinction, but this has not happened.

In the Cuban case, a third advantage for cooperatives is that they can obtain economies of scale that are unavailable to a *cuentapropista* or to a very small private enterprise. Many types of economic activity, especially in manufacturing, require larger volumes of output, a larger capital stock, and a larger cohort of workers in order to lower the costs per unit of output. This is not possible for most of Cuba's small enterprise and self-employment sector though it is possible in the state-owned and joint venture sectors of the economy. The worker-managed cooperative sector should make possible greater efficiencies associated with larger enterprises than are yet possible in the small enterprise private sector.

The cooperative form of enterprise would generate a more egalitarian distribution of income than privately-owned enterprises of similar size. This is simply due to profit sharing among the cooperative members. Control by the cooperative members' assembly over the structure of hourly or monthly wages and salaries and over the profit-sharing arrangement should also be conducive to a reasonably equitable distribution of income, notably between the workers and the elected managers. This is a major advantage of cooperatives, especially in the Cuban context where a high priority has been placed on the equity of income distribution.

The "second degree cooperatives" envisaged in the legislation are of special interest (Decree-Law 305, 2012, Article 5.1). One could envisage a "cooperative coalition of cooperatives" that might resemble a large centralized organization such as "Starbucks" or a franchise operation such as "McDonalds." Such an arrangement could permit major economies of scale for the design of facilities, the purchase of inputs, and advertising and brand-name development, etc. In contrast to large privately owned chains, the distribution of income could remain highly egalitarian among the owners of the coffee-shop co-ops who would also be the owners of the cooperative confederation. This form of cooperative might be relevant for a variety of retail outlets, personal services, or food services.

Finally, the cooperative enterprise involves democracy in the work-place, a major improvement over both state enterprise and privately-owned enterprise, in the view of many observers. Under the Cuban state enterprise system, workers have been reduced "order takers." Their labor unions have largely served as conveyor belts for orders from the top to the workers at the bottom. Rather than defending the interests of their membership, the main purpose of

Cuba's unions has been to ensure that the interests of the nation—as determined by its political leadership—are implemented through the unions. In a private enterprise in most market economies, the worker is also an "order taker," but may or may not have a strong labor union to defend his or her interests. However, with the cooperatives, the members should be in substantial control through the governing mechanisms that the cooperative legislation outlined above creates. Democratic enterprise control is an end in itself, but it also strengthens worker commitment to a shared endeavor thereby improving the intensity, dedication, and effectiveness of workers' efforts. Thus, greater democracy in the work place should result in improved productivity.

Cuba's establishment of a democratic form of workers' ownership and control is ironic since its political system is characterized by a highly centralized one-party monopoly in which genuine participation is manipulated effectively from above. Elections in Cuba's one-party system are a transparent charade and an insult to Cuban citizens. Yet the cooperative legislation envisages a system of democratic workers' control at the level of the enterprise. This is indeed an interesting paradox. Presumably the government of Raúl Castro does not feel threatened by the type of workplace democracy that is implicit in the proposed governance structures and the functioning of the cooperatives. Or, perhaps autonomy and internal democratic operation will not be permitted to develop among these new co-ops just as has long been the case with Cuba's agricultural cooperatives.

Foreseeable Difficulties and Limitations of Cuba's Cooperative Law

There are some generic weaknesses of the cooperative model and also some specific problems that one can foresee arising from Cuba's legislative framework for cooperatives. First, while convincing arguments can be made concerning the potential efficiencies of worker ownership and management, this model has not proven that it is actually more efficient. Cooperatives have certainly passed the "survival test" and indeed some of them have been highly successful (note Mondragón in Spain, and Desjardins and Home Hardware in Canada, for example). However, if they truly represented a more efficient form of enterprise, one could reasonably have expected that they would have gradually captured increasingly large shares of economic activity in many countries. This has not happened to any significant degree, though cooperatives certainly seem to be "holding their own" and maintaining their market shares.

What has held cooperative enterprises back? Cooperatives are often difficult both to establish and to sustain. Indeed, the most basic cooperative in society is marriage and the family, and this institution certainly requires continuous commitment, goodwill, compromise, hard work, and perhaps good luck in order for it to endure. Governance may be a continuing problem for cooperative enterprises. The "transactions costs" of participatory management may be significant. Personal animosities, ideological or political differences, participatory failures, and/or managerial mistakes can all serve to weaken the decision-making process and to generate dysfunction. Of course, this can also happen with private enterprises as well as state enterprises.

The conversion of state enterprises into cooperatives, with the former employees as the founding members, may be easier to establish than many other types of cooperatives. When the promotional actions and enabling environment provided by the government are strong, as presently appears to be the case in Cuba, the formation of cooperatives may well be facilitated. As cooperative enterprises get larger, the effectiveness of worker control likely diminishes, however. In complex capital-intensive manufacturing for example, management has to be delegated to higher-level enterprise managers. This is built into Cuba's new cooperative governance guidelines.

There are a number of specific features of Cuba's new cooperative law that are potentially worrisome and could cause difficulties. First, new cooperatives must go through a complex vetting process before they are certified and can come into existence. As noted above, they must be initially approved by the municipal "Organs of Popular Power," then by the "Permanent Commission for Implementation and Development of the Guidelines," and ultimately by the Council of Ministers. Will this be a reasonably automatic process or will onerous political controls be exerted to determine which cooperatives can come into existence? One can envisage efforts at the highest political levels to approve favored cooperatives or cooperatives in particular areas of the economy and thereby to shape the evolution of the sector in accordance with preconceived official ideas, as opposed to letting the sector evolve spontaneously and naturally. With such controls on the approval process, the emergence of the cooperative sector could be deformed and stunted. On the other hand, conceivably the approval process will be less controlling and permit all feasible proposals. The Chief of the Management Model Section of the "Permanent Commission" assured journalists that this process would be "open." But in the same article, he stated that some cooperatives would be established "according to the interests of the state" (*Juventud Rebelde* 2012). If this is the case, the principle of voluntary membership could be jeopardized. Cooperatives established in this manner would resemble those in agriculture that were imposed from above, with negative consequences in terms of both worker commitment and the effectiveness of the incentive system in the cooperative.

For example, an instructive article by José Jasán Nieves Cárdenas, "*Cuba y Cooperatives 'sin papeles'*" (2014) describes the problem of the proliferation of so-called "undocumented cooperatives" given the long delay in granting ministerial legal recognition as cooperatives to a growing number of informally organized groups of *cuentapropostas*. One fascinating example cited is a group of computer and electrical engineers who currently operate under the name *TISOFT* (Information Technology—SOFT).[8] They provide coordinated and cooperative services to their clients but are forced to remain individually self-employed since their application to become a co-op is still "under review" more than a year after first being submitted in early 2013. Ernesto Flores Castillo, the director of this "undocumented" co-op, highlighted the economic costs—both to the enterprise and to the government's tax revenue—of this ongoing delay, "In 2013 we paid 250,000 pesos (CUP) in state taxes (over US$12,000) and we had projected that we would have paid a million pesos in 2014 if we were a cooperative" (Nieves Cárdenas 2014).[9]

The article also highlights the significant difference in the tax regime for co-ops vs. *cuentapropisats*. Given that the self-employed can only deduct between 30-50% of their expenses before taxes, many more successful enterprises quickly reach an income threshold after which they essentially "work to pay taxes" (*trabajar solo para tributar*). The fact that cooperatives can deduct 100% of their business expenses from their taxable income is a powerful incentive for *cuentapropistas* to cooperativize. However, this bureaucratic process has proven much more time-consuming than that involved in obtaining a self-employment license.

Second, the cooperative legislation calls for the initial creation of some 230 cooperatives only, on a type of experimental basis after which they will be evaluated—perhaps in one year's time. The legal framework will then be revised in the light of this evaluation. This could be a very positive process, and is in keeping with the cautious and deliberative character of President Raúl Castro's approach to policy-making. It is also appropriate in view of the lack of experience in Cuba with non-agricultural cooperatives. However, this could also permit either a policy reversal or else an intensification of political controls on the cooperatives if their emergence displeases the Commission or the country's political leadership. For example, in his annual year-end speech during the December 2013 meetings of the National Assembly, President Raúl Castro indicated that the non-agricultural co-op experiment was moving forward well after its first six months in operation with 250 operating. While he said that it was still then too early to give an "integral evaluation" of the sector, he did stress that "permanent supervision and control is required from the guiding institutions of each activity in order to opportunely detect and correct any deviation" (Castro, R. 2013).[10]

Third, it is unclear whether or not the Commission and the Council of Ministers will permit cooperatives offering professional services to obtain certification. Such permission would represent an important a step forward in the evolution of the Cuban economy, because a wide variety of professional enterprises would likely be established quickly. These would utilize Cuba's human resources more effectively than is currently the case under the state-controlled economic system. A fourth weakness is inherent in the rules for hiring non-member workers by a cooperative. According to the legislation, a cooperative may only hire workers for a maximum of 90 days, at which time they have to be permitted to join the cooperative or else they must be dismissed (Decree-Law 305, 2012, Article 26.1). Moreover, the amount of labor that can be hired is limited to 10% of the total number of labor-hours worked in the enterprise.

These two rules will probably limit employment generation in cooperative enterprises, hardly a desirable outcome. They may impose an undue rigidity on the cooperative and do a disservice to potential short-term contract workers. If a worker provides a specialized full-time or part-time service to one or perhaps several cooperatives, the worker may prefer not to become a cooperative member and the cooperative itself may prefer this arrangement. Furthermore, a cooperative could consist of a number of professionals as principal partners who also need some different and less-skilled tasks completed. Imagine cooperatives of lawyers, architects, or web designers that need some short-term form of secretarial support or the services of a receptionist or of a computer specialist. In such cases, if the cooperative members could not hire a longer-term employee, perhaps they would have to expend their own time on such work, wasting their time, reducing the effectiveness of the operation, and also depriving someone else of a job. In these instances, a case could be made for permitting the longer-term employment of hired non-member workers by the cooperative. However, this could also lead to a two-tier arrangement in which the cooperative members—who share the profits—restrict membership in the cooperative in order to reduce the number of persons to whom profits are distributed. This is a complex issue that presumably will require future adjustment.

Fifth, egalitarian rules for membership in a cooperative (ibid, Article 21.1) may be advantageous in some sense because they seem fairer and perhaps strengthen work incentives. However, when differential contributions to a co-op are ignored by the membership rules, there may also be a harmful impact. Why would a worker who commits a major amount of personal capital into the establishment of a cooperative willingly relinquish the control over this contribution to other members who had made no such investment? This could militate against the establishment of cooperatives, and promote private sector small enterprise instead.

Sixth, will the cooperatives in fact be established on a truly voluntary basis from the standpoint of the membership? Recall that the first criterion for genuine cooperative organization according to the International Cooperative Alliance is that membership be voluntary. In practice, a central thrust for the establishment of the cooperatives is the desire of the government to shift loss-making state sector service activities such as restaurants, cafeterias, and hairdressers to the cooperative institutional form. While relatively few such cooperatives had been formed by the end of 2013, there already appeared to be a certain ambivalence on the part of the workers in some state enterprises over the decisions from government planning offices to require the transformation from state to cooperative management. Marc Frank captures this ambivalence in an article chronicling the "cooperativization" of the state restaurant sector:

> In the case of cooperatives, which are supposedly being formed on a voluntary basis, the vast majority to date have been the result of decisions made at the highest level of government and imposed on the employees, who must accept their fate or be laid off (Frank 2013b).

Governance in cooperatives can be difficult. For a very small cooperative of approximately three to seven members, perhaps it is easier and more worthwhile to have an owner-operator in charge, taking full responsibility, working seriously, and ensuring that the few employees involved also work seriously and act responsibly. Such a small-sized cooperative might not have any significant advantage over a small private enterprise of the same size. But as a co-op gets larger, perhaps its democratic governance structure and incentive environment enable it to develop a growing advantage over comparable-size private firms. Thus, it is difficult to make generalizations on the relative efficacy of cooperatives and private firms without going into the specifics of alternate governance arrangements.

The three alternative governance structures delineated in the Cuban legislation (ibid, Article 10.1) try to match the complexity of administrative structures to the size and complexity of the cooperative. However, the high level of detail in the legislation concerning the governance of the first degree cooperatives (as presented in Council of Ministers Decree No. 309) suggests that governance may be difficult, contentious, and cumbersome, and may impede more "nimble" action by the co-op. Lastly, what will be the role of the Communist Party and state controlled-unions in the new cooperatives? If the control of the general assemblies of medium and large-sized cooperatives is captured by nuclei from the Party or CTC, not only would workers' democracy be subverted, but incentives to work seriously would likely be diminished. Will the Party and CTC keep out of cooperative enterprise management?

Implementation Begins

The first sixteen non-agricultural cooperatives began operation on July 1, 2013 in the province of Artemisa (*La Nación* 2013). By August 2013, a total of 124 had been established and an additional 71 were in the process of formation (*Cubadebate* 2013b). The number of cooperatives by sector is presented in Table 6.2.

Of the sixteen cooperatives in Artemisa, thirteen were retailers of agricultural and food products, one was in transportation, one in construction, and one in recycling. The transportation cooperative had 71 members—a signifi-

Table 6.2: Non-Agricutural Cooperatives in Operation or in Process of Formation

Sector	Established	In Process of Formation	Total
Construction	12	12	24
Personal Services and Gastronomy	99	22	121
Industry	2	16	18
Transportation and Related Services	11	2	13
Other	0	19	19
Total	124	71	195

Sources: *Mesa Redonda*, August 21, 2013; *Cubadebate*, August 21, 2013; *Trajadores*, Augues 22, 2013.

cant size. For the 11 already-established transportation sector cooperatives in the whole country as of August 2013, five were for transportation directly and six were for related or auxiliary services. The former included two "*colectivo*" (fixed-route) taxis, one school bus coop, and two trucking coops. The latter included a body shop, two car repair centers, one tire repair shop, and a tow-truck operation (ibid.)

There was very limited information available on the functioning of the cooperatives as of April 2014 reflecting the novelty of this experiment. Cuban economist C. Yailenis Mulet Concepción (2013) noted a number of advantages they enjoy, namely a 20% discount on wholesale prices (apparently not always honored) and for transport cooperatives, a major discount on gasoline purchases (with an exchange rate of 10 CUPs = 1 CUC instead of 24 CUPs = 1 CUC, their revenues being in CUPs while gasoline is sold in CUCs). But there were also specific difficulties they faced, such as the hesitancy of state institutions to hire construction cooperatives, insufficient access to inputs from the wholesale markets, and difficulties in obtaining the ostensible 20% wholesale price discount. Difficulties such as these as well as many others are not surprising as the whole cooperative movement is just getting started.

Some initial reports from a number of journalists specifically invited to the island by the government in July 2013 to see the new cooperatives in action were not encouraging (Frank 2013a; Caruso-Cabrera 2013). While the economic reform czar Marino Murillo openly acknowledged that, "Life has demonstrated that the state cannot occupy itself with the entire economy, that it must cede space to other forms of administration," he also poured cold water on hopes for bolder pro-market reforms by stressing that the introduction of non-agricultural co-ops and reforms in large state companies constituted a "transfer of administration and not a 'property of the people' reform" (Frank 2013a). Additionally, during a week-long trip filled with news conferences, cocktail parties, and visits to successful self-employed enterprises, journalists were not shown a single one of the 197 new cooperatives that had presumably opened in the restaurant, construction, industry, and transportation sector on July 1, 2013. Independent efforts on the part of some of the visiting journalists to visit these cooperatives and interview their members were frustrated. In one case, a wholesale warehouse co-op on the outskirts of Havana still stood empty. In another case, a group of air-conditioning repairmen who had taken over a state-run air conditioning enterprise in the suburb of Miramar initially agreed to be interviewed, but changed their minds when the camera crew arrived (Caruso-Cabrera 2013).

In general, these cooperatives are still in an experimental, pilot project phase. They will serve as test cases for further modification of the legislative framework in order to ensure that the cooperatives can be viable (and perhaps controlled in terms of their size and generation of private wealth). This cautious approach is reasonable. Cuba is entering an area that is virtually uncharted territory for the country. Moreover, there is very limited experience in the rest of the world from which Cuba can draw insights and inspiration regarding an economic system that includes a large cooperative worker-managed and partially owned sector operating within a market framework.

Summary and Conclusion

Cuba's December 2012 initiative for the establishment of non-agricultural cooperatives may permit the emergence of larger scale non-state enterprises that could operate with greater effectiveness than state enterprises. Moreover, they may well have advantages over private sector enterprises particularly regarding the equity of their income distribution arrangements and also regarding workers' incentives and levels of commitment. If this initiative is implemented broadly in the Cuban economy, it could constitute a change and perhaps an improvement of historic dimensions. With much of the state sector of the economy converted to cooperative institutional forms, Cuba could become a country of "cooperative socialism," which is quite different from the highly centralized and state-owned system to which it has aspired for half a century.

However, authentic cooperatives are not easy to establish, manage, or operate effectively. They require independence and an environment of trust and—as the name implies—cooperation among their members. However, enterprise independence, trust, and cooperation have been sorely lacking in the

Cuban economic sphere for decades. There are also a number of uncertainties and potential problems, which are specific to the Cuban case, judging from the legislation. Perhaps the more serious of these potential difficulties include: first, the approval process which is unclear and susceptible to control from the center; second, the nebulous role of the Communist Party and CTC in the functioning of the enterprises; third, the limited possibility of hiring non-member workers; and finally, the uncertainty as to whether or not cooperatives providing professional services of various sorts will be permitted.

It is wise that the government is proceeding cautiously and that it is considering the cooperative enterprises' first phase as "experimental" and tentative in character. The legislative framework within which these cooperatives operate can then be modified on the basis of the initial experience. This pragmatic approach is pointedly different than the decision-making process under President Fidel Castro, in which substantive policy shifts and institutional changes were determined by the President and implemented rapidly such that the full foolishness of the decisions would become apparent only after it was too late to change course. If the experiment comes to fruition as envisaged in the cooperative legislation, the role of worker management and control could constitute a significant degree of "economic democracy" for Cuba. This would be a significant and, indeed, a paradoxical development in view of the near complete lack of authentic democracy in Cuba's political system. One question that this possibility raises is whether more democracy in the workplace will generate a strong pressure and impetus for the spread of genuine participation in the political sphere?

Notes

[1] The original Spanish reads: "*La potenciación del cooperativismo como forma de gestión constituye una de las vías del proceso de actualización del modelo económico en el país, y significa una alternativa mundial al sistema neoliberal imperante.*"

[2] For example, a November 29, 2013 article in the official online publication *Cubadebate*, "*Cooperativas no agropecuarias a buen ritmo*" (Non-agricultural cooperatives [moving forward] at a good pace) profiles the five-month-old Havana auto repair cooperative, "*Reconstructora de Vehículos*," indicating that its main customers are actually some of Cuba's most important state enterprises such as the telecom monopoly *Etecsa*, the tourism giant *Cubanacán*, the security firm *Seisa*, and *Cubataxi*. Moreover, the article reported that a full 90% of the co-op's inputs are purchased directly from IGT, the state transportation wholesale import company (a right not extended to the self-employed).

[3] Indeed, in their appropriately titled April 13, 2014 article, "Cuba looks to cooperatives to slow rise of capitalism," the Havana-based *Reuters* correspondents Marc Frank and Rosa Tania Valdés explicitly compare Cuba's struggling and often celebrated *cuentapropistas* with these "less well known and less common [...] cooperatives," calling them:

part of a political balancing act for the government, which needs to move hundreds of thousands of workers off the state payroll but also wants to slow the rise of capitalism. In many ways it prefers cooperatives, where each worker has a stake in the business, to private businesses where owners make profits based on the work of their employees.

[4] In Spanish: "*A partir de medios de producción del patrimonio estatal, tales como inmuebles y otros, que se decida gestionar de forma cooperativa y para ello puedan cederse estos, por medio del arrendamiento, usufructo u otras formas legales que no impliquen la transmisión de la propiedad.*"

[5] We thank Cuban economist Juan Triana for sharing this observation with us at the annual Latin American Studies Association conference in May 2014.

[6] New York City is perhaps unique among U.S. cities in that it is home to a large number and long tradition of housing co-ops. Such cooperatives elect a board of directors, which normally oversees the hiring of a management company to run the day-to-day activities of the co-op corporation. In fact, members of such co-ops do not technically own their apartments but hold corporate shares, the number of which is based on the size and value of their apartments. Ted Henken is a member of such a housing cooperative.

[7] This also presumes that co-op members have freely chosen such membership over being merely employees—not always the case with cooperatives formed when state enterprises are converted into co-ops with former employees forced to "accept their fate or be laid off" (Frank 2013b; Frank and Valdés 2014).

[8] Also see Cuban journalist Milena Recio's excellent May 1, 2013 *On Cuba* article, "Self-Employment in Cuba (Infographic)," which highlights the many imaginative ways individual CPs have banded together to create functional cooperatives out of the rigid and incomplete list of just 201 legal self-employment licenses. One quite instructive recent example of such "functional" but still "undocumented" cooperatives are the scores of private retirement homes popping up across the island to meet the growing demand for elder care. These *asilos de ancianos* are currently forced to function outside the law because while there is a license available for "elder care" it is still prohibitively expensive to combine such a license with one for "food service" and another for "room rental" (Palma 2014).

[9] The Spanish reads: "*En 2013 pagamos al fisco 250 mil pesos (más de 12 mil USD) y habíamos proyectado el 2014 contribuir con un millón, si fuéramos cooperativa).*"

[10] In Spanish: "*Ha proseguido la ampliación del experimento de las cooperativas no agropecuarias, de las cuales se encuentran funcionando más de 250, aunque el corto tiempo transcurrido no permite todavía una evaluación integral de sus resultados. En esta etapa se requiere una permanente supervisión y control de la experencia por las instituciones rectoras de cada actividad para detectar y corregir oportunamente cualquier desviación.*"

7

The Underground Economy

> How can it be that in Cuba the government recognizes that the salary is insufficient and people still live; that people who work earn salaries that are not enough even to begin to live, [but still] you see them well fed and well dressed? The answer is Cuban inventiveness. Those people invent, resolve. That characterizes Cuban life. The alternatives are infinite. There's a lot to write [in the Cuban press] about the ways that everyday life develops in Cuba and the relationship of citizens with the state, with power.[1]
> —*Cuban novelist Leonardo Padura in an interview with the Argentine cultural magazine Ñ (Martinoticias 2014)*

> "Todo está prohibido pero vale todo." (Everything is prohibited, but anything goes).
> —*Common saying on the street, Havana, 2004*

Various types of economic illegalities and underground or informal economic activities occur in all countries. In Cuba, however, public policies that enshrined state ownership of the means of production, central planning, and nearly universal state sector employment—and that periodically stigmatized all independent economic activity, as well as economic forces that provoked low productivity, inefficiency, and chronic scarcity—have promoted these phenomena in exaggerated form. During the Presidency of Fidel Castro, Cuba appeared to be awash with economic illegalities. Many Cuban citizens insisted that almost everyone was involved in economic activities that were considered illegal by the state—though many of these often did not seem unethical to the perpetrators. In fact, many would argue that they were necessary for survival. One might say that there was a pervasive "culture of illegality" in the Cuban economy and society in this era.

Another way of saying this is that Cuba's official economy—along with official Cuban economic statistics—was partly illusory and that the underground, informal, or "second" economy was an important component of Cuba's *real* economy, the one that most people relied on to make ends meet. This underground economy continued to exist after the 2010 reforms enacted under the Presidency of Raúl Castro, but probably in a somewhat reduced magnitude given the fact that the majority of the newly "self-employed" had previously been "unemployed" (*sin vínculo laboral*). That is, by becoming registered *cuentapropistas*, they were merely formalizing the status of their previously informal enterprises—not going into self-employment after having been laid-off from the state sector, as was the government's stated goal. Still, given the indeterminate nature and lack of depth of many reforms to date and the recent reemphasis of "control, legality, and discipline" described in Chapters 5 and 6, Cuba's underground economy continues to thrive. Also, given the fact—recently expressed by Cuban novelist Leonardo Padura, cited above—that state salaries are still woefully insufficient to make ends meet, "*el invento cubano*" (Cuban inventiveness) continues to characterize everyday life for the majority of the Cuban people—mediating, in Padura's words, "*la relación de los ciudadanos con el Estado, con el poder*" (the relationship of citizens with the state, with power).

There are two general types of illegal activities analyzed in this chapter. The first includes underground microenterprises that otherwise would be legitimate in that they produce legal goods and services, though outside the regulatory framework of the state. This type of economic activity, which we label "Legitimate Underground Economic Activities" or LUEAs corresponds to Category C1 in Table 7.1, a general categorization of economic activities.[2] The second group includes other "economic illegalities," including unreported economic activities operating within registered self-employment (Category C2), private activities operating within state firms or the public sector (C3); and black markets or the illegal exchange of goods and services at higher prices (C4).

Legal and officially registered self-employment or microenterprise is included in Category B.1 as it has been largely incorporated into the regulatory framework and the taxation regime of the state.[3] The "Household Economy," Category A, includes those economic activities carried out within the home in the normal process of living together with informal cooperative activities among friends, neighbors, and relatives. This is a vital part of the Cuban economy—and all others—but is not examined directly in this section, even though it has close linkages with legal self-employment as well as the LUEAs. Criminal activities of an economic character (Category D of Table 7.1) are not analyzed here either.

The causal forces at work in Cuba generating economic illegalities and the underground economy include historical roots and factors that are common to all countries. However, there are specific forces resulting from the economic policies of the government of Cuba that have produced and sustained the structural, monetary, and institutional imbalances in the economy that in turn generate many of the illegal and informal economic actions by citizens.

Table 7.1: A Categorization of Economic Activities in the Cuban Context

Type of Economic Activity	Character and Examples
A. Household Economy Non-monetized activities within the home or among neighbors	-Child rearing activities -"Do-it-yourself" activities -Cooperative work
B. Formal Economy Legal goods and services performed within the state's regulatory framework	-State enterprises -Joint ventures
1. Licensed "Self-Employment"	-Registered *cuentapropistas* -Small farmers
2. Formal Enterprises: Joint ventures, state enterprises, and formal cooperatives	-Tourism -Minerals -Sugar sector, etc.
C. Underground Economy	-Unauthorized, unregulated, untaxed, and illegal
1. "Legitimate Underground Economic Activities" (LUEAs)	-Legal goods and services outside the regulatory and tax regimes of the state
2. Within registered self-employment activities	-Unauthorized sales -Unauthorized dollar (or CUC) activities
3. Underground activities operating within state firms	-Private payments to state employees -Under-the-counter sales -Illicit private enterprises
4. Black markets	-Under-the-counter sales in state retail outlets -Sales of products outside the state system
D. Criminal Economy Unlawful activities, carried out illicitly	-Theft; sale of stolen goods; sale of jobs; personal use of public property; drugs, prostitution, etc.

Most important, many illegal actions in fact have been and are necessary for citizens as part of their personal and family survival strategies (aka, "*el invento cubano*"). Indeed, some observers view many such activities as a form of low-level but active and continuous rebellion in the context of a dysfunctional formal economy that cannot meet people's basic material needs.

The noted anarchist James C. Scott—writing initially about peasants in Southeast Asia—has perhaps done the most scholarly work in the field of political anthropology theorizing these so-called "weapons of the weak." In that work, which has spanned more than 30 years, Scott argues that subaltern groups such as workers and peasants who possess little formal power or authority are not in fact empty-handed. Instead, he argues that they typically respond to economic and political domination by formal systems of power by developing their own home-grown "moral economy," which involves myriad forms of "everyday resistance" and "hidden transcripts" that serve as alternatives to the hegemonic "official story" proffered by seemingly all-powerful government authorities (Scott 1979, 1985, 1990).

Writing about the contestation of racial ideologies, Mark Q. Sawyer (2006) has usefully applied the work of Scott and that of Robin Kelley (1994) to contemporary Cuba arguing that a sizeable gap exists between the official story and the opinions of the person on the street. This middle ground where everyday people deploy their "hidden transcripts" and counter-hegemonic survival strategies is identified as "infrapolitics." Sawyer also makes an explicit link between race, infrapolitics, and participation in the black market. "The illicit trade in gasoline, foodstuffs, consumer goods, sex, drugs, and cigars is a means of survival for many Cubans," he claims. However, he sustains that such underground economic activity in socialist Cuba has more than a merely economic meaning. "To the extent that Cubans link their economic dislocation to failures of the government," he writes, "black market participation is not only a form of survival but also a form of resistance to the new order..." (2006: 106).⁴

The economic and social consequences of such illegalities are varied. The component of the underground economy that we here label LUEAs makes a valuable contribution to the economy and society and specifically to people's survival and material well-being. With a range of policy modifications that would provide a supportive policy environment—some of which have already been undertaken under Raúl Castro –, it is likely that many enterprises in the clandestine economy would "surface" into legality. They would operate like normal small enterprises in many countries and would serve as a positive component of the foundation for future economic and social development. In contrast, some other varieties of economic illegalities can be corrosive and damaging to Cuba and its citizens, although it must be emphasized that their existence frequently helps people survive in an economy that has not functioned effectively.

To change current economic policies and structures in order to ameliorate the illegalities will be difficult. On occasion, such as the October 2005 to March 2006 campaign against "corruption," the Cuban government appeared to be aware of the phenomenon and attempted to combat it. However, prior to 2010, it confined its policy response to what we call the four "Ps": preaching, policing, prohibition, and prosecution. These actions were aimed at suppressing the phenomenon but they did not deal with its root causes.

While all countries have "underground economies" and economic illegalities, in Cuba's case, these have been comparatively larger than in other countries and have involved a major proportion of the population. The public policy framework within which Cuba's legal *cuentapropista* sector has had to operate has had the unintended consequence of promoting a generalized "underground" or "second economy." Official blockages of legal self-employment through the refusal to grant licenses, together with excruciating regulations, heavy taxation, and a negative political and press environment all served to push such legal activities "underground." A variety of forces contributed to the proliferation of other types of illegalities as well. The most powerful of these during the 1990 to 2006 "special period" has been economic necessity: people undertook various illegal economic actions in order to survive in a context where, in the words of Padura, "people who work earn salaries that are not enough even to begin to live."

Few academic analysts inside Cuba have attempted to examine the underground economy and economic illegalities in depth—at least until late 2006. Indeed, it appeared as though the government was in denial that this part of the economy even existed. A lack of information and difficulties in learning about it in a systematic way are perhaps central factors explaining the lack of focused attention that it has received. In the Cuban media, legal microenterprise was attacked relentlessly following the liberalization of 1993 until the end of 2005. However, until the October 2005 to March 2006 campaign against corruption little attention was paid to other types of illegalities.

This chapter focuses mainly on the LUEAs, or economic activities in which the goods and services produced are legal but which are not licensed and therefore are defined as illegal or criminal in the Cuban case. A secondary focus is on other varieties of economic illegalities such as the theft or the use of state property or position for personal purposes or gain. The objectives of this chapter are to analyze the character of the underground economy and economic illegalities in Cuba, the forces that produce them, their consequences, and the policies necessary to reduce them. It begins with an examination of the causal forces that produce these phenomena. Following this is a description and analysis of the character and the dimension of economic illegalities practiced in Cuba. The economic and social consequences of the culture of illegality are examined in the next section. The range of institutional changes and policy reforms that would be necessary to reverse this phenomenon is then discussed.

Historical Roots

Part of the disregard for economic authority on the part of Cuban citizens has deep colonial and pre-Revolutionary roots. From earliest colonial times, Cubans broke the enforced bilateral trade relationship with Spain. Contraband trade with the French, British, and later the United States, as well as with pirates in defiance of the Spanish Colonial authorities and the naval command at Havana, was not uncommon (see the opening section of Chapter 3 above). According to censuses of the time, the town of Bayamo in eastern Cuba was almost as populous and developed a city as Havana and Santiago, but its development was based almost entirely on contraband trade, supplying meat and leather to pirates and corsairs and obtaining goods from them (Economics Press Service 2001: 5).

By the 1950s, while Cuba had developed a diversified range of large modern corporate business, large numbers of small-scale cottage industries continued to exist in many areas of the economy. This was an authentic "informal economy"—of the sort defined by the International Labour Organisation (ILO 2002)—producing legal goods and services and tolerated by the state even though the sector stood outside the state's regulatory framework. Some of these attracted the attention of the 1951 International Bank for Reconstruction and Development ("Truslow") Mission to Cuba, described in Chapter 3. These small enterprises evaded taxes, paid lower wages than the large firms, were not unionized, avoided social benefit payments, and were generally outside the regulatory framework of the state. The large enterprises complained to the IBRD Mission of unfair competition from these small producers. However, the IBRD Report did not recommend their elimination, recognizing the economic and social benefits they generated. Instead, it urged the large-scale firms to operate more efficiently so as to be competitive with the small firms (IBRD 1951: 944, 957).

There was probably a considerable degree of continuity between the pre-Revolutionary era regarding underground economic activities and their continuing operation, as well as a culture of illegal underground enterprise after 1959. People already functioning "in the shadows" in 1958 were in a reasonable position to continue to operate underground after the Revolution. The ethnographic research carried out in 1969 on the Revolution's efforts to transform the existent "culture of poverty" in Cuba by the anthropologist Oscar Lewis (at the invitation of Fidel Castro) describes some of these still-existing informal operations in some of Havana's more "marginal" neighborhoods. Despite the fact that Lewis was eventually and unceremoniously ejected from Cuba and most of his research materials confiscated by the government, his wife and colleagues managed to publish three large volumes of their findings after his death in 1970 (Lewis, Lewis, and Rigdon 1977a, 1977b, 1978; Chomsky, Car, Smorkaloff 2003; Guillermoprieto 2004; Donate 2011).

Origins in the Revolutionary Era

Following the 1959-1961 nationalizations, a small legal "self-employment" private sector continued to exist in agriculture and in non-agricultural activities, together with the illegal "black market" networks. However, as described in Chapter 3, the nationalizations of the March 1968 "Revolutionary Offensive" and an official policy of gradual diminution of the small-scale farm sector led to large reductions of legal private sector activity. A wide range of micro- and small-scale enterprises was taken over or closed down entirely. Some were converted to state ownership, but many, including street vending, vegetable stands, bars, snack shops, and auto repair were shut down, with the entrepreneurs driven out of business or underground. An illegal but more-or-less tolerated "informal sector" continued to thrive as well as a less tolerated "black market." The impacts of these confiscations were analyzed in Chapter 3.

In the 1970-1993 period, there was a significant underground economy consisting of self-employed persons with assistance from family members and perhaps friends. There was also a legal non-agricultural sector after 1978, when Decree-Law 14 of July 1978 formally permitted some 48 categories of self-employment (Pérez-López 1995a: 95-96). A tax regime of monthly fees was enacted, ranging from 5 to 80 pesos per month (ibid.: 95). The recognized activities consisted mainly of personal services of various sorts together with some types of transport activities, tradesmen, some craft production (*artesanía*), and the three types of fabrication mentioned in Chapter 3: tailoring, shoemaking, and charcoal making. The number of officially registered non-agricultural microenterprises of this sort was placed at 28,000 in 1988, with 12,800 employees (ibid.: 112). It is impossible to know how large the underground economy was in these years. Various unrecognized activities were undoubtedly carried out, as well as unregistered but legal activities evading taxes. The existence of this microenterprise sector operating in the "underground economy" is one reason why it was able to spring to life so quickly after its legalization in 1993.

The causal forces underlying the pervasive illegal activities and the underground economy were complex but were rooted in part in the economic policies that have generated an economic environment in which citizens find it necessary for their survival to act outside the letter and spirit of the law. It is also important to bear in mind that economic illegalities of various sorts are common in most countries and there are some forces at work in Cuba that are common to most other countries as well. However, the character and functioning of the central planning system, adopted in 1961-1963 was a unique feature that promoted economic illegalities.

As indicated in Chapter 2 with reference to Centeno and Portes, "The attempt […] to suffocate any manifestation of popular entrepreneurship ends up, over time, encouraging its proliferation [resulting in] a bourgeoning 'second economy' which contradicts and undermines at every turn that subject to official rules" (2006: 31). For example, as argued in Chapter 3, the rigidity of the rationing system converted virtually everyone into an entrepreneur or mini-capitalist as it provided the virtually the same allocation of goods to everyone, regardless of need or preference. Related to the above phenomenon was the previously described and very common strategy of *amiguismo* or *socialismo*, that is, "friend-ism" or "partner-ism." The mechanics of central planning also promoted clandestine economic activities. Because a planning system cannot work perfectly, enterprise managers had to improvise solutions to problems outside the formal planning system. They had to negotiate with other enterprises, with superior officials, or with superiors or inferiors in other sectors or ministries. Solving their problems frequently required the "extra-legal" or illegal exchange of goods or favors.

There was also a "common property problem" at work. A general Cuban attitude has been that state property belongs to no one (and thus to everyone), so that if one person does not help himself to it, someone else will instead.[5] Public property therefore seems to have been treated as if it were firewood in a forest, fish in the seas, or wild blueberries in the mountains belonging to no one in particular and "up for grabs" to whoever needs it and is in a position to take it—a problem elsewhere described as "the tragedy of the commons" in reference to unchecked population growth (Hardin 1968). Similarly, public property such as vehicles accompanying an official position, are readily used for personal purposes with no qualms of conscience. In the words of Juan Clark, "The majority of people believe that stealing from the state is not a crime" (cited in Pérez-López 1995a: 99). Ironically, the standard-bearer for this type of attitude and behavior has been President Fidel Castro himself, along with the more senior members of the Party, who have been able to use state property for partisan political and often for personal purposes—essentially treating it as the private property of the Communist Party.

Another general reason for illegal economic activities has been the coexistence of the old peso economy with rationed products at very low prices, and the new economy with convertible pesos (CUCs, previously U.S. dollars) and to some extent international or market determined prices. The gap in prices between these two economies was and is enormous, creating a large opportunity for profitable arbitrage within a "black market" in which prices are determined by supply and demand.[6] The black market also includes numerous products that are pilfered from the state sector as well, connecting the dual currency and rationing systems to the previously mentioned "common property problem."

Furthermore, policy limitations on legal microenterprise have promoted economic illegalities. Restrictive licensing meant that potential legal microenterprises were pushed into the underground economy. The regulatory regime for microenterprise also made their lives difficult and led some to go underground after making an attempt to join the formal self-employed sector in the early 1990s. Tough regulations regarding the inputs that can be used and where they can be purchased push some microenterprises into illegal acquisition of inputs. Restrictions on employment have a similar effect. Basically, the more complex are the regulations governing the conduct of particular economic activities, the greater the scope for illegal actions. Heavy taxation also leads some microenterprises to try to evade taxes in various ways, as argued in Chapter 4. The result of this is that large numbers of enterprises that would otherwise operate legally above ground (LUEAs) are forced into clandestinity.

Another key restriction of the self-employment regime—that against professionals becoming self-employed in their professions still in place as of June 2014—has the effect of pushing some of Cuba's most educated and skilled citizens abroad (the classic "brain drain") or into a kind of "insile," forcing them out of their fields of expertise and into work in the much better remunerated (though perhaps not as socially beneficial) black market. This kind of "brain waste" is also true in the legal *cuentapropista* sector. "A Cuban can go into business as a party clown but not a lawyer," writes journalist Julia Cooke in a sharp *New York Times* op-ed article. "She can open a bar but not a private clinic" (Cooke 2014).

Heavy taxation and regulations such as labor laws, minimum wage legislation, and health and safety standards serve to promote underground economic activities in most other countries as well (Schneider and Enste 2002a). What is different with respect to the Cuban case is the onerousness of the taxation levels, the rigor of the regulatory regime, the long-time stigmatization and ideological illegitimacy of microenterprise, and the limited licensing of many self-employed activities. Chapter 5 describes initial efforts under Raúl Castro's Presidency to remedy some of these obstacles. Yet while the changes enacted in this area to date are certainly significant vis-à-vis the decidedly antagonistic public policy under Fidel Castro, it is doubtful that they are sufficient to lift most LUEA's out of the underground economy.

Indeed, a number of new measures enacted in fall 2013 explicitly defining and delimiting the range of activities authorized under each of the 201 legalized self-employment occupations had the direct result of pushing many licensed *cuentapropistas* back into the underground economy. For example, a recent article in the newly founded independent digital daily *14ymedio* reported that a new "screw tightening" customs regulation took effect in late May 2014. It is aimed specifically at holding the so-called "mules"—who routinely bring in foreign merchandise for illegal resale in the banned but still clandestinely active clothing boutiques—responsible for any "*bultos ajenos*" (packages not belonging to them) that they carry with them. However, the article also reports that many of the supposedly shuttered boutiques have not in fact closed but only shifted their operations underground and now reach their customers through the use of informal catalogues passed from hand-to-hand (14ymedio 2014b).[7]

Perhaps the most powerful force promoting economic illegalities of many sorts has been necessity. The general economic policy framework produced a structure of incentives facing Cuban citizens that required them to undertake ostensibly illegal economic actions in order to survive. The main reason for this is that people earned *moneda nacional* or "old pesos," but their earnings were insufficient to purchase the basic foodstuffs—not to mention everything else—that they required for survival. This means that people have had to find additional sources of income either in "old pesos" or convertible pesos (CUCs)—a "hustle" so common in Cuba that it has given birth to various popular expressions such as *resolver* (resolve), *inventar* (invent), and *luchar* (to struggle) (two of which are specifically mentioned by Padura in the epigraph cited above). Cuban citizens often expressed this situation by saying that their official monthly wage or salary would buy basic foodstuffs from the rationing system and other sources that were sufficient for only about 10 to 14 days of the month. Purchases for the rest of the month had to be made with funds "resolved" or "invented" from other sources.

Furthermore, the products actually available through the rationing system were limited. In the period 1999 to 2009, they included rice, sugar, beans occasionally, cooking oil occasionally, eggs occasionally, meat very occasionally, milk for children, pasta, bathing and washing soap, and tooth paste occasionally. Other goods and services had to be obtained from the dollar stores, from legal *cuentapropistas*, from the agricultural markets, or from the "black market" (described below). (Electricity and water—but not telephone services—were still available at the subsidized old peso prices).

People were therefore under pressure to find additional sources of income to supplement their peso incomes in order to survive. This could be done in a variety of ways. First, people could leave the peso economy for the internationalized or dollar economy where they could earn hard currency. The easiest way for many to do this was to emigrate, which large numbers, especially younger, more skilled persons, have done and continue to do. This solution allows the émigrés to continue to support their family members who remain in Cuba through remittances. Second, some Cubans could switch to the domestic internationalized economy, namely tourism, the international institutions, joint ventures, or foreign embassies, where additional incomes can be earned in dollars or convertible pesos after October 2004—for a lucky minority. For example, teachers could leave teaching for tourism, especially if they had abilities in foreign languages (Cooke 2014). Third, many Cubans received additional income supplements from other sources.

If citizens do not have access to any of these sources of supplementary income, they are in a desperate economic position and are at a below-subsistence level of income. Their very survival is in jeopardy. This constitutes the primordial force pushing citizens into the underground economy and "black market" (Martinoticias 2014b; Zurbano 2013; Sawyer 2006). This is the reason why "everyone has a scam" or some type of activity that would earn additional income. As the second epigraph that begins this chapter indicates, "Everything is prohibited, but anything goes" (*Todo está prohibido pero vale todo*). Many of these schemes involve the earning of incomes from illegal but otherwise legitimate economic activities. Some involve using state property for private purposes. Others involve buying and selling various products on the black market. Many more involve various forms of theft or pilferage from the state sector though a few also involve theft from citizens. In 2003, this was referred to as *tocando el arpa* (literally, "playing the harp"), a common expression and gesture used in Havana at the time to denote such theft, derived from the hand gesture—a guitar-like riff of the fingers.

The Range and Varieties of Economic Illegalities and Underground Enterprises

Despite the mid-1990s opening in self-employment, there were still innumerable varieties of economic illegalities that could be observed in Cuba as of the year 2005. Some of these had deep roots and a long history, while others were likely provoked by the counter-reform that began in 1996 and reached its peak in the fall of 2005 with the so-called "Battle of Ideas" and the crackdown on corruption. Below is a list, in no particular order, of some of these illegalities known to the authors. (The notation beside each example refers to the type of illegality as categorized in Table 7.1 above):

1. A bread-maker in a local bakery saves inputs for the production of buns to be sold at a market-determined price—one Cuban peso per bun—rather than at the rationed market price of twenty centavos per bun. The buns then can be sold for a profit to anyone with extra money. (D1 and C3)
2. Employees at a pizzeria reduce the size of the pizza, saving the remaining ingredients for their own use. (D1 and C3)
3. Workers and security guards at a cigar factory sell cigars to a passing tourist for convertible pesos. (D1 and C4)
4. Officials at state institutions with access to a vehicle for official purposes use it as a private vehicle. (D1)
5. A waiter or barman substitutes low-cost home-made peso-economy rum in a bar instead of official dollar-economy rum to clients. The dollar economy rum is then removed from the premises and sold elsewhere for a dollar price. (D1 and C3)
6. An inspector of private restaurants disregards discrepancies in restau-

rant owners' input purchase and receipt records in exchange for a payment or a meal. (D1)

7. A mechanic for a state sector enterprise tells a client that a replacement part is not available from official sources, but that he is able to locate and provide the part from outside the shop at a higher price. (D1 and C3)

8. A gasoline tank truck provides a larger amount of gasoline at a gas station than officially recorded. The *gasolinera* can provide the driver of the tank truck with a payment and then resell the gas unofficially at a higher price. (D1 and C4)

9. An elevator repairman requires an additional fee for repairing the elevator of a small apartment building in order to get him to come and provide the service. (C3)

10. Some state sector house and building painters dilute the paint they use on their official jobs in order to use the leftover paint on private jobs after hours. (D1 and C4)

11. An esthetician requires an additional payment from the client for services provided in the state beauty shop. (C3)

12. A security guard in a dollar store removes items from the store and sells the privately—often just outside the store. (D1 and C4)

13. A taxi driver provides a ride with the meter off and for a fixed fee, explaining that the meter is not working. (C3)

14. Following a successful treatment, a doctor accepts the provision of a gift from a patient, who knows that the doctor also needs income above his state salary in order to survive.

15. The owner of a house not licensed as a room rental facility rents a room illegally. (C1)

16. The local *Comité para la Defensa de la Revolución* (CDR) president accepts a $10 bribe in exchange for overlooking an illegal room rental in the neighborhood. (D4)

17. Toothpaste tubes in a store are missing about 25% of the paste and are filled with air instead, with the toothpaste removed for personal use or resale. (D1 and C3)

18. A citizen pays a 5 CUC bribe in order to secure an 85 CUP (3.15 CUCs) one-way bus ticket from Havana to Holguín. (D4)

19. Jobs that permit the acquisition of significant foreign exchange through tips, notably in tourism, are sold to applicants by the hiring decision-maker. (D4)

20. A citizen sets up a satellite dish, receives foreign broadcasting, hooks up his neighbors for a 10 CUC monthly fee. (C1)

21. A journalist who is allowed a certain number of hours of home-based Internet access for work sells some of the hours on the black market.

22. Tourists are overcharged in a restaurant with an additional beer or with

a "tip" included in the bill. This is also done by overstating the prices of some items, or with more planning and collusion, by having two separate menus, one for those who arrive unaccompanied and another for those brought in by a hustler—who must be paid a commission. (D1)

This list could be extended almost indefinitely. While it is difficult to know how significant these types of illegalities have been, they are pervasive. It was often stated that everything imaginable was available on the black market, ostensibly from pilferage from the state sector. The Cuban blogger Yoani Sánchez has recently reported that huge amounts of electronic data (CDs, DVDs, video games, books, "apps," computer programs, news, information, etc.) is readily available for purchase in Cuba's digital "black market." While much of it circulates via tiny thumb-drives, there is also a market for entire external hard drives of data bought and sold not in megabytes or gigabytes, but in terabytes (personal conversation March 2013; Sánchez 2014a).

Blogger and University of Havana journalism professor Elaine Díaz Rodríguez recently confirmed to us that this "package" or "combo" data sharing/selling system has become quite formalized as a key part of Cuba's underground economy by late May 2014. She explained that each Monday a new digital package appears on the black market at a price of 5 CUCs. Those who purchase it first at this price will then make extra money redistributing it to an exponential number of other customers during the rest of the week with the price for uploading it dropping gradually from 5 CUCs to just one or 2 CUCs (personal conversation, May 2014). It goes without saying that this system relies on the systematic violation of international copyright and intellectual property laws (unless it involves shareware or applications licensed through the innovative Creative Commons network).

Since the mid-2000s the very popular Cuban websites *Revolico.com*, *Cubisima.com*, *PorLaLivre.com*, and *BlosaDePermutas.com*—all of which are Cuban versions of Craig's List—have become the go-to place for a wide variety of black market services and goods—including housing swaps and a wide variety of electronics—either pilfered from the state sector or brought to the island by informal "mules" (Miroff 2009; Ravsberg 2012d; Díaz Rodríguez 2013; Nieves 2014a and b; 14ymedio 2014b). In a revelatory article entitled, "Underground Economy: From the Streets to the Web," Díaz Rodríguez describes this digital version of the black market as arising largely from the fact that many products—especially the latest electronic gadgets—are either priced far out of reach for most Cubans in state stores, in scarce supply, or not sold at all (or even banned outright). In fact, while *Revolico* remains the go-to place for many of these goods, the website has long been blocked by the Cuban government forcing users to resort to proxy servers to access the site. Ironically, Díaz Rodríguez reports that even with the site blocked and illegal due to the illicit source of most of the goods sold there, *Revolico* is still the site that provides many Cubans with their first experience of the Internet. She expertly captures the logic that has driven the emergence of this newest manifestation of the Cuban black market:

> The centralization of the state retail commercial sector and the lack of a supply of goods at quality and quantity standards capable of meeting the national consumer demand led to the consolidation and rapid growth of a buying and selling service that allowed any citizen, even if not their main job, to become a seller or buyer according to need. (Díaz Rodríguez 2013)

More recently, the small but rapidly growing number of Cubans who have joined the smart phone revolution (often purchasing their informally and illegally imported Androids or iPhones via *Revolico.com*) have benefitted from the proliferation of "apps" especially configured for Cuba's peculiar off-line smart phone environment. One "app," known as *Guía Cuba* (Cuba Guide), designed by licensed local developers who run a chain of cell phone repair stores called *La Clínica del Celular* (The Cell Phone Clinic) enables Cubans with smart phones—but without wireless access to the web via a data pan—to keep tabs on the goods and services available in the expanding non-state sector. However, they are forced to visit *La Clínica* each month to have this and their many other apps updated with new information (Benítez 2013; Nieves 2014a and b).

In a pair of posts from early 2014 on her popular blog, *Generación Y*, Yoani Sánchez describes some of the more popular and innovative apps found on Cubans' iPhones and Androids. For example, Cuban iPhones are often loaded with "OffMaps2," which provides users with digital maps of many of Cuba's provinces. Although these maps are technically "offline," the app includes a geo-localization feature that can triangulate one's location on the map using Cuba's cell phone towers. Also popular are "Minipedia" (an offline version of Wikipedia), "Messy SMS" (an encrypted instant messaging service that prevents Cuba's cell phone monopoly from eavesdropping on one's conversations), "WordLens" (a translation program that works from photos taken with one's smart phone camera), and "PhotoStudio" (an Instagram like app that allows users to easily edit and add filters and text to photos—but not share them via a social network given their limited offline functionality). Cuban smart phones that run on the Google-based Android operating system also utilize a host of apps including offline maps, encyclopedias, and translators. Some of the more inventive apps commonly found on Cuban Android phones include "EtecsaDroyd" (a pirated copy of the Cuban telephone directory, which includes the full name, ID card number, and even home address of each user), "WifiHacker" (a tool that facilitates the location and "hacking" of Cuba's limited number of wifi networks), and an unauthorized, offline version of the previously described *Revolico* classifieds site (Sánchez 2014b and c).

A glimpse of the magnitude of the illegal underground economy may be obtained from a number of examples of scandals and state crackdowns revealed in the foreign and independent press. One report indicated that in three of Havana's 15 municipalities, police and customs officials raided 150 clandestine cigar-making operations, which were then shut down. 11,935 boxes of cigars were confiscated (Cubanet 2004). If there were 150 illicit cigar operations in three of the 15 Havana Municipalities, it is likely that there were thousands across the country, because of the widely known skills, the low barriers to entry into the activity, and its profitability. A second example was the use of diesel fuel as a cooking fuel by large numbers of citizens in small towns and especially sugar mill towns. This fuel was pilfered from state supplies and sold through illegal circuits. However, because large proportions of the citizens in such towns were so dependent on it, the situation was tolerated. There also were innumerable "messengers" who made purchases from the rationed-product market for citizens willing to pay to avoid queuing. There could be at least one for every block in the more densely populated areas of Havana for most of the period from 1990 to 2012 for example.

President Fidel Castro himself provided an interesting example of an illicit economic operation, involving in the theft and resale of construction materials from a major construction project:

> I recall, we were building an important biotechnological center in Bejucal. There was a little cemetery close by. I was making my rounds, and one day I passed by the cemetery. There I saw a colossal market where the construction crew, both the foreman and many of the workers, had put up a market selling cement, steel rods, wood, paint, you name it, all kinds of construction materials. (Castro, F. 2005b)

A further example of the pervasiveness of these LUEAs was provided by Marc Frank of *Reuters* and the *Financial Times*, in describing life in the rural areas of Cuba:

> Maria's neighbor, a teacher, hitchhikes to the coast every weekend with an empty suitcase bringing it back full of fish. Another paints pictures and signs. Others sell their services as vintners, seamstresses, handymen, gardeners, bicycle repairmen, messengers, cigar venders, or make-up artists. "Just about everyone who isn't receiving money from the U.S. does something to survive," says Maria who is a Communist Party member. "Most are unlicensed but no one does anything about it because everyone is just trying to survive." (Frank 2004b)

According to anecdotal evidence, there have been a variety of illicit practices in the tourist sector as well. In the words of a manager of a five star hotel cited by Marc Frank (2004a):

This is a billion-dollar business, where millions flow daily in a poor country of people struggling to survive. Everyone finds some way to get unearned income and a few people get greedy. Just like in many other Third World countries, people often pay to work in the industry and then kickback a proportion of what they earn to their superiors. I could give you hundreds of examples. How high up these little mafias go, and if the problem is related to the *Cubanacán* scandal, is anyone's guess.

This was corroborated in early 2004 when 15 higher officials of *Cubanacán*[8] were dismissed from their jobs, as was the Tourism Minister, Ibrahim Ferradaz and some lower level employees a while later (ibid.). Partly as a result, on February 19, 2005, Resolution 10 was enacted by the Ministry of Tourism, defining a code of conduct for the workers in the sector as well as higher-level management officials.

Some Specific Cases of "Legitimate Underground Economic Activities"

Damián, owner/operator of a banco de películas, Diez de Octubre, Havana

Damián was an industrial engineer in his early 30s who began a clandestine video rental operation in the mid-1990s. He was able to get started in business due to a substantial investment of $1,000 from his mother-in-law. She had requested the money from her own parents who moved to the U.S. decades earlier. She explained to them that she needed the investment as a way to help her children survive during the economic crisis brought about by the collapse of the Soviet Union. Damián used the $1,000 to purchase two VCRs ($300 each) and 75 blank VHS video cassettes. He was also assisted in starting his operation by a friend who had her own video rental business in another part of Havana. She lent him his first 75 movies which he copied onto his blank tapes and began renting to customers in his own neighborhood.

Damián increased his stock of videos over time through contacts who would return to Cuba from destinations like the United States, Mexico, and Venezuela with new movies. Occasionally, he was also able to buy tapes from individuals who had access to satellite television within Cuba and made a business of selling tapes of popular shows and movies. Five years after starting his operation, in the summer of 2001 when our interview took place, Damián had built his inventory of video cassettes up to a total of 700. He had also recently begun the process of gradually switching his inventory over from VHS to DVDs. In fact, after hearing about his business from a mutual friend, I [Ted Henken] secured our interview by showing up at his home with a "donation" to the cause—a tower of 100 blank DVD disks, which I had purchased in the

U.S. and managed to secret into Cuba mixed in with my own extensive CD collection.

His spacious home was decorated with scores of mostly American movie posters and his master bedroom/office was equipped with a tangle of computer and electronic equipment that enabled him to transfer VHS tapes onto DVDs and to record new films, television series, and talk shows coming in via his clandestine satellite dish (hidden inside a mock water tank on his roof) onto blank DVDs. However, after his business and clientele began to grow and customer traffic to his home began to call too much attention to his clandestine activity, he decided to rent a storage space for his videos in someone else's nearby home. He also decided to divert attention from his operation by employing a small group of *"mensajeros"* (messengers), mostly college students armed with backpacks who would visit the homes of trusted customers carrying with them all the most recent titles.

On weekdays, Damián rented his videos for five pesos (CUPs) a night. On weekends, he raised the rental price to 7.50 pesos for the entire three-day period (Friday-Sunday). However, certain types of movies and shows, such as premiers and highly sought after Colombian and Mexican soap operas, were rented at a higher rate of between 7-10 pesos a night. Damián explained that as the business grew over a period of two to three years, he was able to begin to live in relative comfort, purchase most necessary household items from the more exclusive dollar stores, and build a substantial personal savings of more than $3,000 (held in a U.S. dollar savings account in a Cuban bank). He estimated that he and his wife, who was his business partner, earned an average of 20,000 pesos ($800-$1,000 US) per month in net income after expenses and payments to employees.

Despite their financial success, Damián and his wife lived in constant fear of a surprise inspection by the police and were therefore under tremendous pressure. They explained that such an inspection could lead to the confiscation of their inventory of videos and all their recording equipment, televisions, and any other material thought by the authorities to be used in the production of their product, exorbitant fines, and even the forfeiture of their home and that of the family that stores their videos as penalties for engaging in profiteering and contraband activity. In order to avoid this eventuality, Damián avoids all "pornographic" or politically controversial material—despite the great demand among their clientele for the Cuban-themed and often controversial "Show de Cristina," a popular talk show produced in Miami. In fact, despite their relatively comfortable standard of living, when I met them Damián and his wife were actively pursuing emigration in order to end their constant state of anxiety. In Damián's own words, "We want to be able to live honestly from our chosen profession, not having to hide our activities from the authorities and live a double life." By 2006, they had both emigrated to the United States and were working in professional fields.

Miguelito, Pensioner, Small Retailing

Officially Miguelito was 92 years old, but insisted that he was really 98. Each morning, at least up until early 2003 when he was interviewed, he went to a central newspaper dispensing point and acquired a number of copies of the newspapers *Granma*, *Trabajadores*, and *Juventud Rebelde*. He then went to a busy corner on Calle Monte and resold the newspapers, together with individual cigarettes and occasionally tubes of "Perla" toothpaste.

Miguelito was not alone in undertaking this modest business. There were hundreds or perhaps thousands of pensioners doing a similar thing. Why? The answer is necessity. Miguelito's pension was 90-100 pesos per month (with a purchasing power noted earlier) plus modest lunches at a senior citizens cafeteria and health service. He could purchase *Granma* for 25 centavos (about a penny), and resell it for 80 centavos or perhaps as much as one peso (roughly 5 cents). He purchased cigarettes which cost 5 pesos (or a quarter) for a 20 cigarette package (or 25 centavos each) reselling each one for 40 centavos. He resold toothpaste costing 7 pesos for 10 pesos. Some quick arithmetic will show that Miguelito could double his pension income if he sold 8 newspapers a day for a 20 work-day month or sold 13 cigarettes a day or 2 tubes of toothpaste a day. A miniature retailing operation such as this is thus well worthwhile for a pensioner.

Moncho, Peluquero (Barber)

Moncho is a former doctor who left medicine to become a hairdresser. A multi-talented individual, Moncho has appreciative clients. His income in the state hairdressing shop in 1997 was 148 pesos per month. However, knowing that he too must survive and desirous of his fine services, his clients willingly provided him with side payments or gifts for his special services. In effect, his services were provided on a private "fee-for-service" basis, but within the shell of a state enterprise. Beyond this, Moncho has a private clientele who purchase his hairdressing services outside the shop—performed either in his home (which has been equipped with a classic barber's chair) or in their homes.

It is likely that in the late-1990s and early 2000s most hairdressers, barbers, and beauticians operated at least partly in this way. How many state employed persons also operate out of their homes or elsewhere or maintain private enterprises within their state *barbería* or *peluquería* is not known. How many people provide these services unofficially but on a full time basis also is impossible to know. However, judging from the high quality of the hairdressing and manicures typical of most Cuban women, the numbers must be large and perhaps well into the thousands. Evidently, the state was well aware of the existence of such operations, which likely influenced Raúl Castro's decision to yield to reality and gradually convert most state taxi drivers, hair dressers, and barbers into private operators between 2008 and 2011 (Peters 2008; *Gaceta Oficial* 2008; Weissert 2009; Robles 2010; Peters 2010c; *CubaEncuentro* 2010a; Miroff 2010).

Pedro, Soft Drink Bottler

Pedro Caballero, an engineer, was a high ranking official in a government ministry. When he was passed over for a training mission to another country in favor of another colleague that Pedro considered to be less-qualified but politically connected, he left the ministry in exasperation—and with a disability certification and pension due to an earlier heart attack. Being technically talented and with previous experience in the underground production of rum, he decided to start a private, clandestine operation bottling soft drinks. With a small amount of capital he acquired the necessary equipment, purchased the relevant inputs, and went into business. He produced three varieties of drink and transported them by bicycle for sale in other neighborhoods. Some buyers came to his home on occasion. He employed one assistant. He earned enough to live in relative comfort and to maintain an old car but it was a tough life as all the work and transport was performed manually.

There was a surprising degree of "honor" among the clients any of whom could have turned him in to the authorities but did not. Though he lived across the street from and was friends with the local chief of the *Comité para la Defensa de la Revolución* (CDR), there was little threat of Pedro's being turned in as the CDR chief also had to survive through his own clandestine activities. Perhaps Bob Dylan was onto something when he sang, "but to live outside the law, you must be honest" (Dylan 1966, quoted in Cluster 2004).

Repair of Heritage Automobiles

For many foreign visitors, an endearing feature of Cuba is the large stock of pre-1961 American—and a few British—cars. Given their size and durability, many of these provide important services as collective taxis. Others are maintained as private vehicles. A few serve as tourist taxis in the state *Gran Caribe* line.

How are these cars maintained, repaired, revived, and rejuvenated? Much of the work is done with the skill and ingenuity of the owners. However, the more complicated and specialized work is undertaken by a large cluster of illegal specialists in body work, painting, upholstering, glass work, electricity, customized spare part fabrication and adaptation, custom fabrication of auto adornments, fabricators of rubber parts, tire repair, and innumerable skilled mechanics often with particular specializations.

This was the case at least until September 2013 when many of these activities were finally legalized either as self-employment occupations or cooperatives. When we observed them in the late 1990s and early 2000s, most if not all of these operations were apparently illegal and unlicensed. Some of the people involved also work in the state sector. It is of interest to note that even the vehicles of *Gran Caribe*, a state car-rental agency, are repaired in the underground economy. This is because maintenance and repair of these vehicles—and also some taxis—is the financial responsibility of the drivers, not the state auto rental enterprise. The drivers of course seek to minimize the cost and optimize the effectiveness of the repair and maintenance expenditures.

Social and Economic Consequences of the Underground Economy and Economic Illegalities

The economic illegalities practiced in Cuba have a range of consequences. Some of these are benign and useful, but others are socially and economically noxious, depending on the specific character of the illegality. These are summarized briefly in Table 7.2.

Costs and Benefits of "Legitimate Underground Economic Activities"

In most countries, the underground economy is viewed negatively by policy makers, analysts, and much of the broader society. The reasons for this are well-known and broadly accepted. The sector is involved in tax evasion, thereby shifting the burden of financing the state sector to legal enterprises and citizens in the legal economy. Moreover, tax evasion gives underground microenterprises an unfair advantage over the above ground enterprises that do pay taxes. The underground economy operates outside the regulatory framework of the state thereby evading minimum wages and labor laws, health and safety legislation, and environmental laws. This also gives the underground enterprises an unfair advantage over those firms that comply with these regulations and laws. The underground economy is often linked to illicit drug production and trafficking, prostitution, and the marketing of stolen property. It is associated with "sweat shops" where minimum wages are not paid and where basic labor standards are not met. Trafficking in people or illegal immigrants is also part of the general picture of the underground economy in some countries as well.

However, as we argue in Chapter 2, the Cuban case is different from the common perception of Western analysts of their own economies. In Cuba, the otherwise "legitimate underground economic activities" have consequences that are overwhelmingly positive. The first benefit that the "legitimate underground economy" generates for Cuba is the goods and services produced for the population that are not produced in sufficient number or

Table 7.2: Economic Illegalities and Their Social and Economic Impacts in Summary

Types of Illegality	Economic and Social Impacts
C. Underground Economy Legal goods and services, unregulated, untaxed, and extra-legal production	
C1. "Legitimate Underground Economic Activities"	Mainly Productive: -Produce useful goods and services; generates jobs and incomes; earns and saves foreign exchange; promotes savings and investment, develops entrepreneurship, affects income distribution in complex ways -Inefficiencies result from clandestinity
C2. Unauthorized sales or methods within registered self-employment activities	Mainly Positive: -Permits natural synergies; permits circumvention of petty regulations
C3. Underground activities operating within state enterprises	Mixed: -Permits workers to survive; may damage activities of state enterprises
C4. Black markets: Illegal exchange of goods and services at higher prices	Mixed: -Some exchanges are completely positive; some exchanges have negative dimensions (e.g., the exchange of stolen goods)
D. Criminal Economy Unlawful activities, carried out illicitly	Negative

quality and at an affordable price by the state sector. Despite some distinct advantages in terms of supportive public policy, favorable input pricing, access to foreign exchange, credit policies, etc., enterprises in the state sector are often too cumbersome, bureaucratic, and inefficient to supply many goods or services adequately. Much of the underground economy involves the production of basic products or services by low-income people and for other low income people. Some of the goods and services provided in this part of the economy are of obvious importance. For example, repair services for refrigerators and stoves are vital for meeting the basic needs of the population. Similarly, wood vendors and charcoal makers/vendors assist in feeding Cuban citizens. The sector in general adds to the diversity of products and services available to the public.

The LUEAs earn or save foreign exchange for the country. For example, authorized artisans utilize the services of many unauthorized assistants to produce the handicrafts and art that tourists buy. Many enterprises in the underground economy also use domestic and recycled materials of various sorts and substitute for imports in some cases. The small underground *cafeterías* and snack bars serve Cuban content foods in locales that are almost exclusively patronized by Cuban customers (as opposed to *paladares*—discussed in Chapter 8—which typically rely on a foreign clientele). In contrast, the state sector restaurant chains such as *Burgui*, *Rápido*, and *Di Tu* serve imported food in restaurants supplied with foreign made furniture, trays, plates, etc. The legitimate underground sector provides productive employment for large numbers of Cubans. Reasonable incomes and income supplements are earned by many permitting them to survive or survive better than would otherwise be the case.

The underground economy does evade direct taxation by the state. However, those citizens who earn US dollars or convertible pesos in their activities (or who earn enough pesos in *moneda nacional* to acquire dollars at the 24 to 26 Peso to $1.00 price in the 2000-2013 period) are taxed indirectly when they use the US dollars (or more recently CUCs) to make purchases at the hard currency stores. The sales taxes in these stores ranged from a rate of 140% on items of basic consumption, to 100% for electronic products in 2004 (a strangely regressive tax structure). Through this indirect means, parts of the sector are in fact taxed heavily—as of course are all others who spend US dollars or convertible pesos in these "*shoppings*," as they are colloquially called.

The sector also generates savings and investment. There are no sources of credit for the LUEAs except for their own savings or the savings of friends or families. Enterprises in the sector are carefully managed so that they generate surpluses for re-investment with no reliance on credits from banks or the state, but very likely some infusion of capital from foreign sources (Orozco and Hansing 2011).

Surprisingly, the underground economy often acts as an inadvertent subsidy for the official socialist economy. This is because the professionals and workers in the socialist peso economy have not received sufficient incomes to survive but rely upon their supplementary activities in the underground economy to provide the incomes that permit them to make the necessary purchases in the dollar stores, the agricultural markets, or the black market. This means that the supplementary clandestine activities and incomes often support the much touted "free and universal" health and educational system, the civil service, industry, and in effect most other parts of the socialist peso economy. Likewise, the professor who survives by being able to save the per diems from foreign travel is able to continue as a professor earning 225 pesos per month in the mid-2000s (about $US 10.00) thereby subsidizing the educational system. A teacher who survives by "moonlighting," that is, by providing after-hours tutoring to the children of better-off families, is also subsidizing the formal educational system that is unable to provide a living wage. Similarly, the doctor who periodically provides taxi services in dollars or who receives gifts from grateful patients also survives in this way. In other words, a wide variety of underground economic activities and various dollar-earning activities permit those involved to continue in their state sector jobs through a considerable personal sacrifice, and subsidize the vital sectors in which they work.

While there are major inefficiencies in the functioning of the LUEAs there are also some major sources of efficiency. The first of these is that the capital facilities of the microenterprises are usually the homes of the microentrepreneurs themselves. This means that the "overheads," in terms of especially dedicated factory capacity are avoided. This transfers some of the costs to the microentrepreneurs themselves and their families (self-exploitation) whose homes and home lives may be disrupted by such economic activities. On the other hand, apprenticeship types of learning by adolescents may also be promoted by home-based economic activities. As well, childcare and household activities may be combined with some types of economic activities in the home, especially those undertaken by women. This represents a savings for society but a special burden for those women combining child care with home based microenterprise activities (Holgado Fernández 2000; Abd'Allah-Álvarez Ramírez 2013).

Finally, the legitimate underground enterprises are valuable "schools of entrepreneurship" for Cuba. Paradoxically, during the years in which the exercise of entrepreneurship in a market-oriented setting was effectively prohibited (from 1968 to 1993) or tightly restricted (from 1993-2010), Cuba created a nation of entrepreneurs. Unfortunately, much of the entrepreneurial talent and energies of those working in the legitimate underground economy has been wasted or not used effectively due to the small scale of the operations and the constrictions imposed upon them because of their clandestinity.

In the Cuban case, the underground economy also has negative consequences similar to those in mixed market economies. Underground enterprises in Cuba evade some taxes. They may evade health and safety standards. Some criminal activities are also included in Cuba's underground economy such as drug production and sales, prostitution, and the sale of stolen property. Some of the negative aspects of the functioning of the LUEAs have resulted from the policy environment that either places artificial limits on "above-ground" small enterprise—such as outlawing its ability to import inputs or banning professionals from joining its ranks—or eliminates it outright. This creates inefficiencies at the level of the underground enterprise, some unfairness in income distribution and taxation between legal and illegal enterprise sectors, and a number of societal losses.

At the level of the individual underground microenterprise, clandestinity means that enterprises must remain excessively small to avoid detection forgoing economies of larger scale production. They must engage in many sorts of "attention avoidance" activities in order to remain clandestine, thereby creating additional costs, for example in the transportation of the outputs or the inputs in small batches so as to avoid detection. Clandestinity probably affects the quality of the goods and services produced on some occasions. While the close contact between buyer and seller of the goods and services may focus more attention on quality, the lack of necessary inputs may adversely affect quality. Illegality plus the various restrictions that apply to self employment, prevent or impede the employment of additional workers, deny access to credit, deny access to foreign exchange, and prevent active advertising and marketing. For all of these reasons, entrepreneurs in legitimate but underground enterprises often waste their energies on low level and relatively unproductive but necessary activities. They are also under pressure to spend precious resources on "rent seeking" behaviors—such as paying bribes or currying special favors from officials. All this adds up to a major loss for Cuba in general.

At a broader "sectoral" level, the avoidance of direct taxation by enterprises in the underground economy is unfair for above-ground microenterprises which do pay taxes. This constitutes a significant comparative advantage for the underground enterprises. The advantage is significant enough to persuade some entrepreneurs to prefer to remain clandestine than becoming authorized. For them, the costs of formality are greater than those of continued informality (De Soto 2000). From the standpoint of the microenterprise sector, official policy towards self-employment results in a variety of inefficiencies. Clandestinity may limit the numbers of enterprises in some areas, especially those with higher visibility that cannot operate easily within the home. High levels of uncertainty and risk serve as a barrier keeping out potential participants. Therefore, there may be less legal competition, higher prices, and lower volumes of production than if these barriers to entry were lower.

There are also disadvantages at a societal level. Over and above the tax losses, already noted, a major societal loss is the wastage of human energies and entrepreneurship arising from all the implications of clandestinity and small size. The impairment of the quality of the goods and services produced is a also disadvantage for society. If the future is uncertain due to clandestinity, then there is a reduced incentive to undertake longer-term planning. Instead, the microentrepreneur has an incentive to make as much money as possible in the very short run. As a consequence, prices may be higher than necessary. Savings, investment, and enterprise development may be sacrificed and impaired, with the microentrepreneurs themselves losing out in the longer term. Also, Cuban consumers lose in the short and longer term and Cuba as a nation loses through the waste of its entrepreneurial, human, and material resources.

Finally, the result of the character of the tax and regulatory systems and the non-compliance they engender is that these systems lack credibility and respect. The government seems to be viewed by many microentrepreneurs as a hostile force whose actions are arbitrary and whose long-term vision for Cuba excludes them. Rather than leading to the gradual development of a "tax culture" in which people willingly and honestly pay their taxes, the system has provoked the habit of cheating. To some extent this is part of people's survival strategies in the difficult circumstances of the "special period." The nature of the tax and regulatory regimes leads some people to think that tax evasion and clandestinity are not unethical even if they are illegal. In the longer term, it may be difficult to change this "culture of tax evasion" to one of compliance. This could continue to be a problem even after a reasonable microenterprise tax regime has been established. This bodes ill for the government and public policy, for the microenterprise sector, and ultimately for the Cuban people as well. To build a relationship of trust will be a slow and difficult process.

Costs and Benefits of Other Varieties of Illegalities

At the other end of the spectrum of illegal activities is theft from state enterprises and institutions and the use of public property for personal purposes. While pilferage may help some people survive, it is noxious for society. First, it damages the enterprises and institutions in which it occurs, as their capacity to provide goods and services to the general public is impaired. Second, it worsens income distribution in that those who are not in a position to pilfer have lower incomes than those who do. The income distribution effect of the use of state property for personal purposes may be less visibly noxious. However, it damages income distribution because those with privileged access gain at the ultimate expense of the broader society.

Corrupt practices, such as the taking of bribes or the selling of employment positions, are particularly odious. In this case, strategically placed individuals are able to use their roles or positions of privilege and trust. Those who are able to pay bribes or purchase their jobs also gain privileged access to scarce goods and services, again damaging other people's access and thus harming the broader society. Likewise, black markets may be either welfare enhancing or welfare diminishing. If the black market exchange between a willing buyer and seller does not involve stolen property but only the re-circulation of rationed goods, for example, then it is of benefit to both seller and buyer. On the other hand, a good deal of black market merchandise is stolen from the state sector. Obviously, this is a negative phenomenon. Even if both buyer and seller gain, they are doing so at someone else's expense.

Finally, stealing from the state breeds attitudes and cultures of lawlessness that damage trust and the ethical foundations of the economy and society. The practice of economic illegalities could escalate and become a sort of undeclared civil war among citizens for spoils from the system. The practice of illegalities could accelerate and become a set of interacting vicious circles that ultimately could deform and paralyze the economy and society. Various Cuban "public intellectuals" have recently voiced their growing concerns about the damage to the nation (or revolution) that the ubiquity of corruption and lawlessness leaves in its wake.

For example, longtime editor and lay Catholic leader Dagoberto Valdés has repeatedly described the rampant cynicism, economic crime, and the double-dealing known as "*la doble moral*" (all played out on an individual level) as the "*daño antropológico*" (anthropological damage) that is the legacy of "the deepest and gravest wound that the totalitarian Marxist-Leninist system has inflicted on controlled and depersonalized societies" (Valdés Hernández 2013: 3; Valdés Hernández and Echániz 2004). At the same time, a blistering series of articles about the mortal threat corruption poses to the Revolution has come from within the ranks of the Communist Party itself. Written by Esteban Morales, a noted Afro-Cuban scholar of Cuban race relations, the most forceful of these articles boldly called corruption "the true counterrevolution," much more dangerous than the internal opposition since it involves state officials at all levels "girding themselves financially [...] ready to transfer state-owned assets to private hands, as happened in the old USSR" (Morales 2010a).[9] In fact, below we describe one of Raúl Castro's own recent remarkable fulminations where he gave listeners a good scolding for everything from rampant corruption and the theft and resale of public goods, to public urination and the raising of pigs in cities (Orsi 2013a; Burnett 2013).

Public Policy and Other Economic Illegalities

In view of their corrosive and perverse effects, widespread illegalities and the culture of petty corruption in time should be reduced. What measures might be effective in this regard? The government periodically has campaigns of a punitive and exhortatory character. However, these are seldom effective for more than a short period of time. To deal with the culture of petty corruption will require deeper policy measures that get at the root causes of economic illegalities. While the government of Raúl Castro has continued and even increased punishments for corruption, it seems to have shifted its focus more toward prosecuting high-level "cadre entrepreneurs" (corrupt officials) and away from pursuing petty economic crime as had been the case under Fidel Castro. Also, while Raúl continues to preach to Cuban citizens about the need for order and discipline and against a supposed loss of civic values, he has also repeatedly called on low-level bureaucrats to rid themselves of their prejudices against entrepreneurs (Castro, R. 2010a) warning them that "all bureaucratic resistance will be useless" (Mesa-Lago 2013). Are the bureaucrats falling in line?[10]

Recent Approaches by the Cuban Government

As mentioned above, the main methods used by the government of Cuba to deal with the phenomenon of economic illegalities have been preaching, policing, prohibition, and prosecution. The effects of this approach in the past have been transient and the illegalities have surfaced as soon as the pressure and the campaigning subsided. If the underlying forces that generate the economic illegalities are not addressed, it is unlikely that the latter will disappear with this type of approach. The government often asserts that the principal source of pervasive illegalities is the existence of the licensed and therefore legal microenterprise sector and the private farmers markets. Invariably, it then moves to further restrict their operation. But limiting legal microenterprise numbers and tightening the regulations on them merely pushes them into the underground economy. Those formerly self-employed legally would also have an incentive to engage in a variety of other illegal activities as well, in order to make ends meet. For this reason, actions such as the elimination of 40 categories of self-employment for the issue of new licenses in October 2004 and the removal of some 2,000 licenses from existing microenterprises in mid-June 2005 (Frank 2005a) were unlikely to lead to net reductions in illegal activities and instead probably provoked an expansion of economic illegalities of many varieties.

A frequently used approach to dealing with the more odious economic illegalities is to monitor and police them more vigorously. A major role for the police has been to stop and question anyone traveling by foot, bicycle, or car on the street with large packages or backpacks, in order to apprehend anyone engaged in the transport of black market products (call it "stop-and-frisk," Cuban style). They are charged with watching out for any types of illegalities. However, the police themselves may overlook possible or actual infractions out of friendship with the perpetrator, empathy for his or her situation, or perhaps because they have received a pay-off of some sort.

Infractions may be punished by prohibitions of the relevant activities, but this may only push the activities underground. To prevent infractions, monitors or inspectors are required to police the legal self-employment activities. The role of the inspectors for the *paladares* and bed-and-breakfast operations is well known. However, it is also reported that in some cases, the inspectors have become avaricious, and require pay-offs for infractions that may be real, imagined, or fabricated. In other cases, the inspectors seem to be somewhat less officious in enforcing the letter of the innumerable regulations relevant for the microenterprises.

Part of the task of monitoring people's activities in order to prevent illegalities is passed on to the previously mentioned CDRs or the neighborhood "watch" committees. In some areas, CDRs may carry out this task effectively. However, the local officials of each CDR also need additional income to survive. They are likely to be involved in illegal activities themselves, and therefore may not be diligent in exposing and prosecuting their neighbors. Or they may acquire a small share of the benefits of such illegal activities. In other contexts, security guards are used to try to prevent theft or other illegal activities. However, these individuals also would like to survive, so that they may look the other way when an infraction or theft is occurring in order to obtain a payment. They may also pilfer articles from their place of work or obtain a payment from others who may be doing the pilfering.

In other situations, the government uses a pretext to undertake house-to-house searches for illegal activities. In January 2003, for example, a campaign against drugs was used to search numerous homes and to penalize any illegal and underground economic activities encountered. This led to a cessation of some underground activities, but only until the pressure was off, at which time they resumed. Another method used to reduce economic illegalities is exhortation through speeches—notably under the Presidency of Fidel Castro—and statements or articles in the media. However, it is not clear how much heed people paid to the marathon protestations of the former President Castro. The attention paid to Fidel's words probably met diminishing returns long ago. Raúl Castro seems to have largely eschewed this "preaching" approach (notwithstanding his own exhortations in July 2013), or at least he has made his fulminations much more brief and to the point than those of his elder brother.

The October 2005 to March 2006 Campaign

Numerous attempts to reduce illegalities in the microenterprise sector and corruption in the official economy have been undertaken in the past in Cuba. As far back as September 1970, a campaign was waged against "privilege-taking by officials" (*Granma* 1970). From 1995 to 2005, there was a low-intensity but unrelenting campaign in the press and through the enforcers of the regulatory system and to prosecute non-compliance and tax evasion by microentrepreneurs. In January and February of 2003 a major campaign against drugs was undertaken, but this was also used as a means of searching homes and prosecuting other types of illegalities. All of these had limited long-term impact on the scale and scope of economic illegalities given that they focused on their effects while ignoring their causes. For example, the campaign of early 2003 led to some underground microenterprises ceasing operation for a while. However, four or five months later many recommenced their operations.

Then, in October 2005, President Fidel Castro announced a major campaign against economic illegalities. This was perhaps the most vigorous anti-corruption drive to date at the time. The campaign began with a high profile operation on October 17 by some 28,000 young "social workers"[11] who took over all of Havana's gas stations in an effort to counteract the systematic pilfering and black market resale of fully half of the city's gas (*BBC Mundo*

2005). This was followed by a revealing speech given on November 17, 2005, where then President Fidel Castro announced an all-out crackdown on corruption, theft, pilfering, and the "new rich." In this 6-hour speech, delivered to students at the University of Havana, Castro called for a return to egalitarianism as part of a "total renewal" of Cuban society aimed at eliminating the rising differences between Cuba's haves and have-nots (Castro, F. 2005a; Ritter 2006).

Included in this series of actions were the following:

1. October 17, 2005: A multi-pronged government "Death to Corruption Operation," was launched, authorizing military intervention in the Port of Havana, where the embezzlement of merchandise from arriving container shipments had become pervasive. The Military assumed the management of the Port to replace corrupt officials (*Nuevo Herald* 2005);
2. October: There were fulminations in the press about those who had become the "new rich" from microenterprise activities and corrupt practices (not-so-subtly linking the two);
3. November 7 to 9: Official raids took place in the "*mercados agropecuarios*" aimed at farmers selling their produce in the private markets prior to fulfilling their state quotas (Cubasource 2005);
4. November 17: Castro's University of Havana speech emphasized an anti-corruption theme mainly aimed at legal microenterprise, and singling out *paladares* and private taxis, but also alluding to deficient ministers and other officials[12] (Castro, F. 2005a);
5. Late November: "*Operación Araña*" (Operation Spider) was undertaken against illegal satellite TV access (Cubasource 2005);
6. November 22: The minimum pension was raised from 150 to 164 pesos and wages were also increased 43 pesos on average per month (Ibid.; *Granma* 2005);
7. November 29: An operation was commenced against unlicensed bicycle taxis in Havana. Unlicensed *bicitaxistas* (pedicab drivers) had their pedicabs confiscated while drivers without the right to live in Havana were sent home (*Cubanet* 2005);
8. December 5: According to President Castro, the "social workers" also began working in the Havana food distribution system, as well as state farms, cooperatives, and state enterprises, in order to detect illegalities and corruption there.

These measures seem to have had a transitory impact on the underground economy and various illegalities. In time, slippages of control intensified and the illegal activities returned to their previous level of normalcy. The increases in pensions and social assistance may have lowered the intensity of illegal activities slightly, but the necessity of using such income increases in the high priced *"shoppings"* or the farmers' markets reduced their purchasing power and incentive effects. As long as the basic conditions of people's lives required them to acquire additional income to survive, the various layers of inspectors, monitors, security guards, and CDR officials constituted merely additional corruptible layers in the system. Their true effectiveness in enforcing the regulations and preventing illegalities of various sorts was limited.

"The Big Old Swindle"

On Ted Henken's first trip to Cuba in the summer of 1997, he ventured into the maze of streets in the *Cayo Hueso* section of Central Havana to find some dinner rolls. With a pocket full of pesos and completely ignorant of the proper etiquette of making food purchases in socialist Cuba, he spotted a small bakery and in the most Cuban Spanish he could then muster, blurted out in a loud voice, "*Oye compañero, dame ocho panes por favor*" (Hey comrade, give me eight rolls please). While his Spanish was passable, the attendant responded as if he had been speaking Chinese. Quickly noting that he was indeed an ignorant foreigner, but also realizing that the foreigner had money to spend, the baker motioned for him to move down the street out of sight. Within minutes, however, he sent a young "messenger" offering a plastic bag filled with eight freshly baked rolls. The author happily handed over the eight pesos the boy demanded and, a bit confused by the whole odyssey, made his way back to the private apartment where he was renting a room. It wasn't until he recounted the whole episode to his hosts, however, that he realized what had actually gone down.

First, he learned that he had unknowingly made his purchase at a state bakery, which is legally restricted to selling just a single roll per day to each Cuban citizen and must do so strictly "*por la libreta*" (from the ration card). So, his demanding in a loud voice that he, a foreigner, wanted not one but eight rolls was tantamount to asking the baker to violate the law (in at least two ways). However, he also learned from his hosts that the baker reacted in the way he did because, while wary of getting caught breaking the law, he also responded to a "higher" law, that of supply and demand. In short, the author's hosts explained that his baker accomplice, like most other workers in the food service sector and indeed throughout the state-run retail sector, routinely set aside a portion of their state allocations that are meant to be sold exclusively *por la libreta* in order to have products to sell "*por la izquierda*" ("out the back door"), thus augmenting their meager incomes with a bit of private enterprise.

Of course, the problem with this scenario, repeated systematically throughout the state enterprise system, is that this spontaneous, grassroots privatization scheme has the result of reducing the size and quality of the rationed food stuffs, raising the prices on the black market, and socializing an unending chain of producers, vendors, and customers in everyday illegal, yet ostensibly necessary activity. At the same time, though the author paid five times the established price of 20 cents (CUP) for each of his eight rolls, he also received what he wanted at what he considered a fair price (of course, not many Cubans are able to purchase foods at such prices). For his part, the baker was able to continue to perform a socially necessary service to the public while finding a material incentive to keep coming to work.

This short vignette illustrates in a most vivid and elemental way the dilemma facing the efficient functioning of state socialism in an environment of chronic scarcity. While the ostensible aim of state ownership and fixed prices is to provide a needed good or service to all at a "fair" price, in practice such a system often has the effect of diminishing personal incentive, provoking frustrating inefficiencies, and socializing the entire country in systematic illegalities. As a result, many if not most workers in Cuba's state enterprise sector see their jobs not as a means to earn an honest living or perform a necessary or useful social function, but as an access point for the theft and resale of state property. In fact, state jobs in Cuba are often evaluated not for their pay or benefits, but based on whether they provide prospective workers with access to state goods that they can "resolve" (i.e., take home with them). However, as one of these "criminals" pointed out to the authors in an interview, it would be wrong to simply attribute such behavior solely to insufficient control or the lack of proper revolutionary consciousness. "If indeed we are criminals," said this anonymous Cuban, "*somos criminales de necesidad*" (we are criminals of necessity).

While relatively rare, journalistic exposés of petty corruption and even large scale scandals involving communist cadres and strategically-placed officials have periodically appeared in the Cuban press (Díaz-Briquets and Pérez-López 2006).[13] Indeed, the entire history of the Revolution can be characterized as a back-and-forth struggle between periods of relative openness toward the role of the market (and the law of supply and demand) and periods where strict socialist ideology seeks to reign in market "abuses" leading to highly public crack-downs on black marketers, middlemen, and "profiteers" (often disparaged in the Cuban press as *macetas*) (Mesa-Lago 2000; Mesa-Lago and Pérez-López 2005; Mesa-Lago 2013; Mesa-Lago and Pérez-López 2013). The most recent anti-market thrust in this recurring cycle began in the early 2000s and was christened "the Battle of Ideas" by Castro (Anderson 2006). Reaching its peak in 2005, this ideological battle manifest itself in the previously described fight against the deepening corruption at all levels of the Cuban economy and the rising levels of economic inequality in Cuban society (Castro, F. 2005a).

Given the Cuban press' timidity in airing the revolution's "dirty laundry" in public or in addressing any contentious economic policy issues, perhaps more surprising than the 2005 crackdown was the three-part series that appeared a year later in the fall of 2006 in the newspaper *Juventud Rebelde* under the provocative title, "*La vieja gran estafa*" (The Big Old Swindle) (Orta Rivera 2006a-b; Orta Rivera, Montero, and Rodríguez 2006; Orta Rivera, Montero, and Suárez 2006; Peters 2006a). Essentially, the series of articles consisted of descriptions of what happened when a number of undercover journalists (often in the company of state inspectors) visited a series of state-run stores (including small, neighborhood bars and cafeterias) and sought out a number of basic services (such as buying a beer, having a pair of shoes resoled, or catching a cab).

What they found is instructive and only reinforces the point made above in reference to the "eight rolls." However, in these cases consumers were not given more than the limit but often less and at inflated prices (with the excess product resold for a profit and the extra money shared among those in on the swindle). For example, in one bar the reporters found that the workers routinely shortchanged customers by serving beer in glasses smaller than the stipulated size. As a result, each day they managed to pocket as much as 222 pesos, the then equivalent of the average worker's salary for an entire month (Orta Rivera et al 2006a; Peters 2006a).

However, what made this exposé unique from many others like it to have appeared in the past was the fact that the article often quoted the "delinquent" workers when they defended themselves. Most often they made the convincing argument that they were often forced to provide their own supplies in an effort to keep their state-run businesses open due to the government's chronic inability to provide them with raw materials. Thus, in charging more than the established price, they argued that they were only doing what was "just" and "natural": recouping their original investment and having something "extra" to show after a hard day's work. In one shoemaker's words:

> This bottle of glue cost me 150 pesos. The roll of string 50 more. The work implements that you see here on the table are also mine. I bought them all with my own money. The enterprise gives me nothing to work with. That is why I have to charge you 25 pesos to repair your shoes. If you don't like it, you can go to the corner where you will find a private shoemaker and you can see how much he will charge you. (Orta Rivera et al 2006c)[14]

The extraordinary thing here is that we are witnessing what amounts to an internal, grassroots privatization of many ostensibly state-owned enterprises. The state cannot provide the necessary materials, so the workers gradually take control and run a private business (or a series of semi-private businesses) within the shell of an official, state socialist enterprise (Peters 2006a). However, when questioned about these practices at the time, Jorge Almaguer, the general director of Havana's Trade and Food Service Administration, argued that such claims are only "a justification used by some in order to continue cheating and swindling the customers" (Orta Rivera et al 2006c).[15] Nevertheless, many of the economic adjustments instituted in Cuba since 2010—especially those that have transformed many such state service enterprises (taxis, barbers, hairdressers, and now many food service providers) into private microenterprises or non-agricultural, worker-run cooperatives—have been based not on Almaguer's arguments but on the shoemaker's economic logic quoted above.

Even though these *Juventud Rebelde* reporters gave frequent lip service to the idea that these "crimes" are the result of a rampant "lack of control, organization, and general demoralization in state enterprises [...] against the moral principles that the Revolution has always defended," to their credit they also raised a number of important questions about what they call the "socioeconomic implications" of such widespread petty corruption in state enterprises (ibid.). Specifically, the final article in their series went beyond mere description and condemnation of delinquency and preaching of proper revolutionary morality, to include a discussion, however coded and tentative, of the chronic problems of overbearing economic centralization and bureaucracy, a lack of enterprise autonomy, little relationship between efficient performance of state jobs and proper material incentives, and the theory of socialist property itself (Orta Rivera et al 2006d; Peters 2006a).

The Underground Economy during the Presidency of Raúl Castro, 2006-2014

By the late 2000s it was clear that preaching, policing, prohibition, and prosecution alone were earning diminishing returns and that a pragmatic approach towards the regularization of the legitimate underground economic activities would be of significant benefit to Cuba and its citizens. In sum, a pragmatic approach would help improve standards of living and economic development generally. It could also strengthen the public sector by providing increased tax revenues.

However, enacting a more pragmatic approach would require some basic regulatory changes to tackle the roots of the illegalities. As argued earlier, the dual monetary and exchange rate system that generates the primordial economic forces that motivate people to undertake various types of illegalities must be unified in time. This is easier said than done and it is an important element in the government's agenda. The regulatory, fiscal, and policy environment within which legal microenterprises operate in order to permit them to thrive need further revision. An appropriate approach would be to permit licensing for all microenterprises that want to establish themselves, and that paid taxes and that respected reasonable regulations (as opposed to the current, albeit expanded list of 201 permitted occupations).

Additionally, the government could simplify its regulations and establish a taxation system so that there would be less incentive to remain underground—effectively making the costs of formality lower (and the benefits greater) than those associated with informality. One key incentive for formalization of underground enterprises (one likely more effective than the past "4Ps" approach) would be to establish a normal wholesale source of inputs for legal, licensed microenterprises—simultaneously undercutting the lure of the black market (where many microenterprises currently turn for inputs) and the high, monopolistic prices of the hard currency *"shopping"* stores. Of course, doing this would require a commitment of both financial and political capital from the government as cutting into the state's own retail monopoly would surely meet with fierce resistance from affected parties.

State property poses a difficult problem. As argued earlier, the pervasiveness of state property in itself helps to promote a culture of pilferage and other illegalities, through the "common property problem." Dealing with this deeply rooted behavior will not be easy. Reducing the role of the state in running many of the smaller economic enterprises may reduce the scope for the pilfering of public property. Changing behavior at the highest political level so that there is a strong demonstration effect regarding public use of public property would help as well. In the longer term, the task of reducing economic illegalities will be one of changing the economic culture that has evolved together with central planning and state ownership. The deeply ingrained behavior of pilferage, extraction of personal benefits from positions of power and responsibility, and use of public property for personal gain will be changed only with changes in the conditions that generate such behavior (Díaz-Briquets and Pérez-López 2006). Tougher regulations and reduced licensing of microenterprise in the past had the contrary effect of pushing some economic activities underground. Intensified exhortation has also shown itself to be of dubious benefit.

Still, old habits die hard and while Raúl Castro has acted with far more economic pragmatism when it comes to economic illegalities than was characteristic of his elder brother, he occasionally slips into an "old scold" mode, blaming Cuban citizens for the country's lack of order, discipline, decency, and proper decorum as if he were a grandfather presiding over a huge family home or better yet a general giving orders to cadets at a military barracks. For example, in a July 2013 speech he excoriated listeners for their "decaying morals," "loss of civic responsibility," and general "social indiscipline" (Orsi 2013a), enumerating with embarrassing detail his long list of complaints: Unauthorized home construction, illicit logging, fishing, and slaughter of livestock, the taking of bribes, hoarding goods and reselling them at inflated prices, shouting and swear in the street, public drinking and drunk driving, dumping trash and urinating in public parks, routinely showing up late for work, graffiti and vandalism, playing loud music, evading fares on public transportation, violating dress codes at work and school, teachers taking bribes for grades, throwing rocks at passing cars and trains, and a general lack of deference to the elderly, pregnant women, the disabled, and mothers with small children (Orsi 2013a; Burnett 2013).

However, though he put his finger on very real social problems, many of his listeners pushed back arguing that such behaviors are only the everyday cultural consequences of a centralized, authoritarian, and paternalistic system of politics and economics characterized by thick layers of bureaucracy that in turn lead to chronic inefficiencies and scarcities. Without his also recognizing and attempting to rectify the root economic and political causes of these admittedly noxious behaviors, the President may come across to Cuban citizens—especially the young—as a crotchety old man totally out of touch with their lives and everyday struggle for basic survival. Asked by *The New York Times* to comment on the speech, Anthropologist and specialist on Cuban youth culture Katrin Hansing reasoned that scolding young people without also inviting them to join an open discussion about the problems facing Cuban society only serves to alienate them further, exposing the "very visual discrepancy between who is running the show and who's living it" (Burnett 2013).

Ultimately, economic recovery, increased real wages in the old peso economy, and an authentic improvement of living standards should reduce the incentive of people to pilfer state property or use it for their personal purposes and undertake other types of illegality. While living standards have improved somewhat since the dark days of 1992-1994, relative material hardship continues for many—probably the majority. It is unlikely that many people could survive on their peso incomes alone without additional sources of income even in 2014. Until this situation changes, the economic illegalities will continue as a routine part of life; what Padura referred to as *"el invento cubano,"* or the Cuban inventiveness that characterizes life on the island and mediates most citizens' relationship with the state to a greater or lesser degree.

How far has the government of Raúl Castro gone in dealing with the forces that have produced such a large underground economy? To begin with, it may be useful to state again that the underground economy will never be extirpated from the Cuban or other economies, but will always exist for tax avoidance or evasion purposes and for dodging regulations of various sorts. However, it can and should be reduced considerably in size for the reasons noted above.

A number of the policy changes during the Presidency or Raúl Castro affecting the legal microenterprise sector will also have important impacts on the underground economy. The granting of licenses to virtually all applicants is of obvious importance as it will lead some underground microenterprises to become legalized quickly, if the viability and profitability of their activity is enhanced by legal above-ground operation. This is especially true of the imported clothing boutiques, private 3D cinemas, and game rooms that were once legal and licensed but are now either out of business or underground following the fall 2013 crackdown.

The easing of the tax burden and the removal of some of the previous regulations that made legality difficult if not impossible for legal microenterprises have been modified significantly. These include the lifting of the 10% maximum for allowable deductions for costs of production from gross income, the relaxation of the draconian penalties (confiscation and shut-down) for some regulatory infractions, and raising the legally permissible number of employees to five (or more) for all microenterprises. The easing of various petty regulations designed to stunt microenterprises and to contain the growth of the sector are also important in cultivating a respect for the regulations as well as the regulators, that is a culture of compliance rather than evasion.

A reduced role of the state and public ownership in small enterprise will also help to eliminate pilferage and reduce illegalities generally and the underground economy. As the Cuban government shifts ownership and operation of small business activities from within the state sector to the private and cooperative sectors, pilferage will diminish. This is because the microenterprise owners or the cooperative owners themselves will monitor and police more carefully the administration of resources in their enterprises because their incomes and livelihoods depend on it—which is less the case with the managers of the state enterprises. As the old Spanish saying goes: "*el ojo del amo engorda el caballo*" (the eye of the owner fattens the horse). It will also be more difficult (but not impossible) for employees to operate what are in effect their own private enterprises within the operations of their private employer's microenterprise in contrast to the common practice of operating privately within the shells of state enterprises.

So far, as of August 2014, the government of Raúl Castro has not unified the two currencies and two exchange rates though it continues to study how to proceed with this difficult task. The *Lineamientos* did not indicate how or when this would be done, though it did emphasize the importance of the issue. When this is achieved, it will remove a major incentive for people to undertake arbitrage of various sorts between the two sectors, and engage in numerous illicit activities in order to acquire some of the convertible pesos that provide a crucial income supplement to the old-peso wage and salary that is necessary for survival.

Unfortunately there is little hard information on the recent evolution and changing magnitude of the underground economy. However, the almost immediate doubling in the number of legal microenterprises as soon as the liberalization measures came in to effect between late-2010 and early-2011 indicates that many microenterprises were ready to go into legal operation—probably because they were in fact already operating underground at some level. Many of the approximately 300,000 new legal microenterprises to emerge by early-2014 likely surfaced from the underground economy. We have little hard information on how many would fall into this category relative to newly established microenterprises. One still sees illegal vendors of products on the streets. Some observers judge that the numbers of illegal enterprises has not fallen that much. In fact, the continued lack of a wholesale market for Cuba's new micro-enterprises may actually feed the growth of the black market as it remains the standard "go to" source of inputs for many legal *cuentapropistas*.[16]

The response to the September 2013 prohibition against *cuentapropista* retailing of imported goods has undoubtedly had the result of moving a large proportion of such sales to "under the table." Some of the retailers of contraband clothing also went underground—what proportion we do not know. But it is likely that some of the demand for these lower priced imported goods shifted to the higher priced state retailers as well, effectively becoming "formalized." Most of the basic forces generating the conditions under which the underground economy thrives are still in place. Thus a preliminary estimate would be that indeed the underground economy and especially the LUEAs have diminished in number but that the sector is still a significant one.

One telling statistic—reported by *Granma* in early 2014—is that a total of 407,608 licensed *cuentapropistas* handed in their licenses between 2010 (when the self-employment reform was first enacted) and November 2013 (Peláez et al 2013; DDC 2014c; Cartaya 2014). This is nearly the same number as the just over 450,000 self-employment license holders as of March 2014 (only 300,000 of which are "new" *cuentapropistas* who joined the ranks of the private sector after 2010) (*Cubadebate* 2014b). Such a high "turn-in" rate gives us an indirect measure of the difficulty many entrepreneurs are having making a go of it in the legal self-employed sector, forcing them to turn in their licenses and perhaps shift operations (back?) into the underground economy.

Summary and Conclusions

A Cuban joke popular in the 1980s mocked that the revolution had eradicated capitalism's three classes (upper, middle, and lower) only to replace them with three new socialist ones: the *dirigentes* (the few communist officials at the top), the *diplogente* (the fewer diplomats and foreigners in the middle), and the *indigentes* (the indigent masses at the bottom). The egalitarianism of socialism had made everyone equal by making them equally poor. Except, of course, that some were more equal than others. This joke changed with the advent of the special period and its concomitant dislocations and piecemeal reforms. A fourth group was added to the hierarchy, the *delincuentes* (delinquents, people who survived by breaking the law) (Cluster 2004). However, given the low salaries of most Cubans and the many tangible benefits to breaking the law, the joke concluded by wondering whether these *delincuentes* should be placed at the bottom or the top of Cuba's new socialist class hierarchy.

All joking aside, as this chapter has illustrated how people who live by breaking the law are nothing new to socialist Cuba. Given the chronic scarcities and structural constraints inherent to state socialism, such systems have always provoked thriving black markets and second economies. However, the economic crisis that began in the late 1980s, worsening precipitously after 1990, transformed a low-level, if chronic characteristic of the Cuban economy into a daily reality not just for Cuba's *delincuentes*, but also for most of its *indigentes*, *diplogente*, and *dirigentes* as well. In short, Cuba's second economy had gone "from behind the scenes to center stage," often replacing the first or official economy in the daily lives of many Cubans (Pérez-López 1995a).

Despite some negative consequences, these clandestine economic activities produced important benefits for Cuba and its citizens, including low-cost goods and services, productive employment and incomes, domestic savings and investment, foreign exchange earnings and savings, and training in "entrepreneurship." Clandestine operation of these activities also generated losses for Cuba. Among these were the waste of human, capital and natural resources due to small size of operation, losses due to clandestinity and "attention avoidance," reduced numbers of enterprises and volumes of output so that prices are unnecessarily high, waste of the entrepreneurial talents of Cuban citizens in low level activities and the generation of a "culture of illegality."

The social and economic benefits of the legitimate underground economic activities would be greater if they were authorized and operated formally "above ground." This could be achieved by liberalizing the licensing and authorizing any and all applicants (including professionals), establishing a more reasonable and progressive tax regime for microenterprise that allowed for the deduction of actual expenses, reducing the still dense regulatory burden, providing reasonable and affordable sources for inputs, and providing long term security for their very existence. Perhaps a more important but less tangible change is the necessary shift in mentality among Cuban citizens of all stripes from one that associates self-employment with illicit enrichment and the black market (seeing it as "more of a danger than an opportunity") to one that embraces it as a legitimate alternative to the state sector (Torres Hernández 2014). In fact, the traditionally moribund Cuban press has begun to encourage this change in mentality by adding nuance to its previously rigid, dogmatic, and dismissive portrayal of all private economic activity as "undue enrichment." For example, a January op-ed published in the state-run *Radio Coco* website entitled, "Myths and Realities of Self-Employment in Cuba," sought to dispel unfounded negative myths about private entrepreneurs with these words:

> Among the most common myths that surround self-employment is that those who engage in it are lazy. It is true that many "*vivos*" (hustlers, rascals) have seen it as an easy way to avoid work and make money without sweating.

However, we should separate very clearly those who don't work and engage in illegalities from those who are self-employed. (Torres Hernández 2014)[17]

The government of Raúl Castro has made some important policy changes that provide a more supportive and "friendly" environment for legal microenterprise. These changes produced a three-fold increase in the numbers of microenterprises and their employees to over 450,000 by March 2014, and most likely a major reduction in underground microenterprise. Future policy changes such as a unification of the dual currency and exchange rate systems, further regulatory and tax reforms, plus sustained improvement in incomes per capita should lead to further reduction in the various components of the underground economy and further expansion of the legal microenterprise sector. However, the question remains whether Raúl Castro's government is prepared to make these more fundamental changes that would strike at the roots that nourish Cuba's still ubiquitous underground economy (Ravsberg 2014).

Notes

[1] In Spanish: *"Como puede ser que en Cuba el gobierno reconozca que el salario no alcanza y las personas viven, que a personas que ganan salarios que no les alcanzan para empezar a vivir tú las ves bien alimentadas y se viste bien? La respuesta es el invento cubano. Esas personas inventan, resuelven. Eso caracteriza la vida cubana. Son infinitas las alternativas. Sobre esas formas en que se desarrolla la vida cotidiana cubana y la relación de los ciudadanos con el Estado, con el poder, habría mucho que escribir en Cuba."*

[2] These LUEAs could also be called LIEAs, that is "Legitimate Informal Economic Activities." In fact, Table 7.1 is an expanded version with reference to Cuba of Table 2.2, "Characterization of the Components of an Economy," introduced in Chapter 2.

[3] Based on the definition of the "second economy" introduced in Chapter 2, "those economic activities in socialist economies neither regulated by the state nor included in its central plan" as well as "all private profit-driven activities (legal or not) which contradict the socialist ideals of egalitarianism, the plan, state ownership of the means of production, and universal state employment," Cuba's own second economy would include the LUEA's discussed here (C1), as well as most if not all of the activities described in cells C2, C3, and C4. However, given both its legal and *ideological* components (predicated on private gain in a context of state socialism), the Cuban second economy would also include a good portion of the newly expended self-employed sector (B1), parts of the cooperative sector (B2), and a good portion of the household (A) and criminal economies (D) as well.

[4] In a much-discussed op-ed article published in *The New York Times* (the publication of which seems to have gotten him fired from his job as the editor-in-chief of the renown *Casa de las Américas* publishing house), Cuban writer Roberto Zurbano (2013) reiterated Sawyer's point, lamenting the fact that Afro-Cubans are often unable to tap into many of the major growth areas of Cuba's new economy.

Most remittances from abroad—mainly the Miami area, the nerve center of the mostly white exile community—go to white Cubans. They tend to live in more upscale houses, which can easily be converted into restaurants or bed-and-breakfasts—the most common kind of private business in Cuba. Black Cubans have less property and money, and also have to contend with pervasive racism.

As the economic liberalization progresses, Zurbano argues, Afro-Cubans are being excluded by default or design. However, when they turn to the black market as often their only means to benefit from greater economic opportunities, this is often used by their white counterparts as "proof" of their natural proclivity toward crime. "Now in the 21st century," Zurbano laments, "it has become all too apparent that the black population is underrepresented at universities and in spheres of economic and political power, and overrepresented in the underground economy, in the criminal sphere and in marginal neighborhoods." For a more recent report from *Reuters* on how Cuba's economic opening is widening the racial divide on the island, see Valdés and Trotta (2014).

[5] In fact, summarizing the internal debate in today's Cuba over the need for non-state forms of property, the eminent Cuban-American economist Carmelo Mesa-Lago has indicated that Cuban economists are well aware of this "common property problem." The problem with state property, for example, is "that which belongs to all doesn't really belong to anyone, and therefore, no one takes responsibility for it" (*lo que es de todos no es de nadie y, por lo tanto, nadie responde por ella*). There is even an effort to expand the traditional understanding of "socialist property" beyond simply the equivalent of "state property," and include self-employment and cooperatives as legitimate and indeed efficient and productive forms of property as well. At the same time, there continues to be a general aversion to even using the term "private property" among institutional economists on the island (Mesa-Lago 2013: 79).

[6] An example of the price gap between the two economies will illustrate the scope for arbitrage. The "dollar stores" in particular have been expensive, charging prices that are literally hundreds of times higher the prices for the rationed products. For example, the price of sugar with the ration book was 0.15 old pesos per pound in 2000. In comparison, in the "dollar stores" a pound of sugar was 1.50 convertible pesos or 39.00 old pesos (at the exchange rate relevant for Cuban citizens, that is 1.00 convertible peso = 26 old pesos). This was 260 times higher that the ration system price. Every product available at an "old peso" price through the rationing system can be resold in the black market at a higher price.

[7] At the same time, the *14ymedio* article reports that an "warning" video posed on the *Gaceta Oficial*'s website focuses not on the illegal import of clothing but dramatizes the arrival of a traveler hand carrying over 150 USB flash drives into the country instead. The message is clear: the standard excuse, "I didn't realize what it was since I'm just carrying it in for someone else who asked me to deliver it to their family," will no longer be accepted. Also see the recent August 2014 *AP* story "Cuba Cracks Down on Goods in Flyers' Luggage," which reports on the new much stricter Cuban customs rules set to take effect on September 1 (Weissenstein 2014).

[8] Cubanacán is a state conglomerate enterprise that includes 51 hotels, 52 restaurants and cafeterias, a chain store with about 300 outlets, two marinas, a travel agency, a car rental and taxi service, a convention center, and 15 entertainment centers.

[9] This and his subsequent article, "The Mystery of the Holy Trinity: Corruption, Bureaucracy and Counterrevolution," touched so close to home that they were immediately erased from the Writers' Union website where they had first appeared, with Morales briefly kicked out of the Party for washing the Revolution's dirty laundry in public. See also his follow up article, "How Far Will We Allow Corruption to Spread in Cuba?" *Havana Times*, December 16, 2013.

[10] The conclusion of Chapter 8 on *paladares* chronicles the recent experience of the Cuban tenor Ulises Aquino who had his very successful and fully legal dinner theater known as *Ópera de la Calle* unceremoniously shuttered. There we dig deeper into the question of bureaucratic resistance to Raúl's reforms and ask whether the closing was an anomaly or an omen?

[11] The "social workers" were young people, not otherwise gainfully employed, who were hired to undertake various tasks for the government such as visiting every household to remove incandescent light bulbs and replace them with energy efficient florescent bulbs, to remove energy-inefficient appliances such as refrigerators, stoves, washing machines, and fans to be replaced with energy-efficient variants.

[12] In Fidel Castro's words, "In this battle against vice, nobody will be spared. [...] Either we defeat all these deviations and make our revolution strong, or we die." Castro also criticized Cuba's "new rich" focusing particularly on the owners of small restaurants, private taxis who drive gas-guzzling vintage 1950s American cars, and gas pump attendants. "I'm not theorizing. We are acting. We are marching toward a total renewal of our society. [...] The work of these young people will put an end to a lot of vices, pilfering and sources of dishonest money for the new rich," he said.

[13] A better place to find a rich and deeply observed, if fictional description of Cuba's myriad economic illegalities is in the novels of Cuban writer Leonardo Padura, whose words were cited in this chapter's opening epigraph. Instead of focusing on small-scale illegalities, Padura's books tend to highlight the "cadre corruption" at the top of the state enterprise food chain. Since this kind of malfeasance is much more embarrassing to the power structure, it is almost never reported on in the official press. In describing his intent in choosing the crime novel as his genre, Padura has said that one of his goals was to reinvent the simplistic socialist crime novel by shifting the focus away from the counter-revolutionary crooks, spies, and black marketers—that were the common villains most previous "revolutionary" crime novels—onto normally untouchable and supposedly "incorruptible" communist cadres turned opportunistic peddlers of influence (Padura Fuentes 2000; Padura 2005; de la Soledad 2006; Ferman 2006; Wilkinson 2006).

[14] "*Este pomo de pegamento me costó 150 pesos. El cono de hilo 50 más. Los implementos de trabajo que usted ve en esta mesa, también son míos. Todos los compré con mi dinero. La empresa no me da nada para trabajar. Por eso es que tengo que cobrarle 25 pesos por coserle sus zapatos. Si no le conviene vaya a la esquina, allí trabaja un particular, verá cuánto le cobra.*"

[15] "*Eso es más bien una justificación utilizada por algunos para seguir inventando y estafando al pueblo.*"

[16] See Fernando Ravsberg's perceptive article at *Havana Times* for a rich analysis of what he calls "The Causes and Consequences of Cuba's Black Market," still a fundamental feature of the Cuban economy now four years after the start of the expansion of self-employment (Ravsberg 2014).

[17] The Spanish reads: "*Entre los mitos más comunes en torno al trabajo por cuenta propia se encuentra el de que quienes lo ejercen son vagos. Es cierto que muchos vivos han visto en esto un filón para no trabajar y dedicarse a ganar dinero sin sudar. Pero hay que separar bien a quienes no trabajan y a los ilegales de los trabajadores por cuenta propia.*"

8

The Rise, Fall, and Rebirth of the *Paladar*, 1993–2014

> Today, the political, military, and ideological problem of this country is looking for food... We must be clear about one thing: if there is food for the people, the risks do not matter.
> —*Raúl Castro, September 28, 1994* (Castro, R. 1997: 466)

> It's good that these markets and self-employment have taught people a little bit of capitalism... But we have to think of how to do things correctly... Some *paladares* and other self-employed workers earn more in a day than our honored teachers earn in a month.
> —*Fidel Castro, December 27, 1995* (Castro, F. 1995a; Peters 1997: 5)

The following brief vignette acts as our point of departure, allowing us to draw various lessons from Cuba's past experience with private *paladar* restaurants—the history and development of which over the past 20 years is the main focus of this chapter. These lessons can be applied to the overall situation in which Cuban microentrepreneurs found themselves in early 2013, after more than two years of major economic reforms and at the start of Raúl Castro's second and final five-year term as president.

First, the initial policy of "legalization" of parts of the island's private sector inaugurated in 1993 under former President Fidel Castro was accompanied over time by such a thick web of legal restrictions that, by design or default, the original aim of legalization was lost. Original restrictions both on these *paladares* and on self-employment in general were so great and taxes so high that they often overshadowed the benefits of legal status itself. Government policies effectively prohibited the full development of these legal microenterprises and forced them to utilize informal strategies or to go into outright clandestine existence to make a living.

Second, legal restrictions put in place to control and limit the growth of these private enterprises often gave rise to corresponding (and often illegal) survival strategies. For example, restrictions against intermediaries and advertising provoked an extensive underground network of *jineteros* like Gregorio.

Vignette: "*Las Doce Sillas*"

As I [Ted Henken] went through the makeshift front door of Central Havana's *Paladar Las Doce Sillas* ("The Twelve-Chair Restaurant"),[1] an irreverently named private *paladar* restaurant in *Centro Habana*, Orestes, the owner, expressed his pleasant surprise at receiving another customer for lunch at the late hour of 3:00 p.m. He also seemed astonished at the resourcefulness of Gregorio, my *jinetero* (hustler)[2] guide who had brought in a group of four Spaniards not ten minutes earlier. However, Orestes was also a bit exasperated at now having to pay another US$5 on top of the $20 commission he already owed Gregorio for services rendered. Confirming these suspicions, I spied Orestes deliberately count out the full $25 commission to Gregorio, who, clearly content with himself after his few hours of work, quietly folded the cash into his shirt pocket and walked out into the afternoon heat.

Playing the fool, I inquired of Magalis, my waitress, how it was that I did not see lobster on my menu, yet found a large shell lying empty on a plate nearby. She lowered her head and whispered, "You know we can't put that on the menu!" However, she then turned toward a small, improvised service door to the kitchen and asked in a loud, confident voice, "Hey, is there any more 'L' back there?" Returning with a plate of *langosta enchilada* (lobster in red sauce), she explained, "If they catch us with lobster, they can confiscate all our equipment, charge us with 'illicit sales,' and close us down."

As I happily dug into my "L," I noted that there were just four tables in the cramped dining room with exactly twelve chairs divided among them. When I inquired about the peculiar name of the restaurant as I finished my meal, Magalis explained that while it ostensibly originated from a well-known 1962 film by famed Cuban director Tomás Gutiérrez Alea, it was really the owner's mocking, indirect way of poking fun at the government's ridiculous restriction against having more than 12 chairs in any private restaurant. But Magalis then blurted out, "Let me show you something," and proceeded to proudly lead me back through the double doors past the kitchen to a hidden second dining room where excess customers dined when business was booming.

Before leaving, I spoke briefly with Orestes, who claimed, "Through this experience, I realized I was born an entrepreneur." However, with typical Cuban *choteo* mockery, he added, "The only problem is I was born in the wrong country!" As a born entrepreneur, Orestes said he liked the challenge of creating his own business. However, he expressed frustration at the regulations that forced him to constantly cheat

> and improvise. "I see you met Magalis, my 'cousin'," he joked. "Everyone knows we're not related, but the rule against non-family employees forced us to invent that fiction." Orestes also hinted at the bleak future of microenterprise in Cuba by declaring, "I wouldn't buy stock in any *paladar*. It's all part of a game and you have to know how to play it. The government can benefit from the positive image that the token existence of private enterprises creates, but it will remain little more than that, an image."

Likewise, the prohibition against contracting any salaried employees outside of cohabitants and family members often led to the practice of employing fictitious "distant cousins" like Magalis. Menu and size restrictions led to the proliferation of forbidden foods and hidden dining rooms. In short, with reference to Table 2.1 in Chapter 2, the Cuban government's total regulatory *intent* was increasingly at odds with its diminishing regulatory *capacity*, not to mention clashing with the deepening material need for scarce goods and services among the Cuban population during the worst years of the "special period." As a result, Cuba's emerging class of entrepreneurs began to develop a host of innovative business strategies to stay afloat during the economic crisis. We chronicle some of these strategies below.

Third, while often understood as the Cuban equivalent of the informal economies found throughout the rest of Latin American and the Caribbean, Cuba's own underground economy—including the myriad "legitimate underground economic activities" (LUEAs) described in Chapter 7—as well as its emergent legal self-employed sector are more comparable to the "second economies" that existed in the various countries of the former Soviet Union. Like similar private economic activities that took place within those centrally planned systems (as described in Chapter 2), even while parts of Cuba's own second economy were legalized and regulated after 1993, it remained ideologically illegitimate and was actively stigmatized and repressed (Miroff 2012c). Indeed, the 13-year period between 1993 and 2006 indicates that the legalization and regulation of self-employment did not lead to significant or sustained job creation or economic productivity. Instead, public policy toward microenterprise was used in practice as a temporary, stop-gap measure aimed at halting the economic hemorrhaging of the mid-1990s, eventually becoming but another mechanism of state control over the economy.

A final lesson is that Cuban microenterprise faced a bleak future by the end of Fidel Castro's 47-year rule in August 2006. While most still surviving operators doubted that they would be closed down outright by the state (especially if they learned "how to play the game," as Orestes would say), few believed that they would ever be able to grow beyond their subsistence level and become a native small- and medium-sized enterprise (SME) sector. The aura of illegitimacy that accompanied any independent economic activity under Fidel, the government's fear that such activities presented a long-term political threat to the centralized command and control structure, and the government's antagonistic, paternalistic attitude toward self-employment, effectively condemned Cuba's *cuentapropistas* to an informal, provisional existence, reducing the economic benefits they generated.

However, before we write the epitaph to Cuba's experiments with self-employment—and write off the Cuban *paladar* along with it—we must consider the extent to which Raúl Castro's own policies toward microenterprise have differed from those of his brother. In other words, just how far as Raúl's policy apple fallen from the tree of his older brother Fidel during his more than eight years as Cuba's president and especially in the four crucial years since 2010, when he inaugurated major economic reforms that included a new and much more pragmatic approach toward self-employment? In Chapter 5, we described Raúl's microenterprise reforms as *significantly* different than those instituted during the 1990s under Fidel, especially in terms of the relaxation of certain key regulations, the less onerous tax structure, and the liberalized licensing environment that has been in place since 2010. At the same time, we have argued that these reforms are not yet *sufficiently* different from previous policy in order to meet the declared goals of Raúl's own government: a shift of as many as 1.8 million state workers to the non-state sector by 2015, a concomitant increase in the efficiency and productivity of the state sector, and the creation of a vibrant self-employed sector together with an independent and productive non-agricultural cooperative sector.

In this chapter, we focus specifically on public policy toward private *paladar* restaurants (along with other non-state food service operations, and to a lesser extent on the private transportation and room rental sectors), as an illustrative case study[3] in evaluating these still unfolding and to our mind incomplete reforms. Despite the fact that full scale private *paladar* restaurants currently make up only a tiny fraction of the currently existing 471,085 self-employed enterprises (as of July 2014), overall food service licensees (13%) and hired workers (20%—the majority of whom work in either food service or bed-and-breakfast enterprises) make up the largest two groups of *cuentapropistas* today, together accounting for 33% of all private employment outside of agriculture, followed in third and fourth places by private transport and room rentals, which make up roughly 11% and 7% of the self-employed, respectively (Martínez Molina et al 2011; Opciones 2012; DDC 2012c; *Trabajadores* 2012a, b, and c; Manguela Dáiaz 2012; Lotti 2012; Fernández Sosa 2012; Café Fuerte 2013b; Rodríguez, J. A. 2013). That is, these four occupations alone account for just over 50% of all licensed self-employed people in Cuba today (*Cubadebate* 2014b; Manguela 2014; 14ymedio 2014a).

Private restaurants and other food service operations rely heavily on inputs and credit, have a significant income tax burden (as outlined in Table 5.2), need to hire labor (for which they also must pay a tax if they hire more than 5 workers), and are quite conspicuous along the major streets and sidewalks of Cuba's main cities. Furthermore, the government has recently begun a push to close many state restaurants and cafeterias, allowing their former workers to run them now as *cuentapropistas* (*Trabajadores* 2012d; Café Fuerte 2012), or transform them into independent, worker-run cooperatives (Frank 2013b). For all these reasons, singling *paladares* out as a "test case" of the depth, breadth, and boldness of Raúl's self-employment reforms to date—that is, his taste for "a little bit of capitalism," in the words of his elder brother—is particularly instructive.

In our focus on the rise, fall, and recent rebirth of the Cuban *paladar* over the past two decades—a particularly instructive example of the ambivalent economic reform typical under state socialism –, we review the evolution of self-employment regulations as they apply to *paladares*. We also augment our analysis with brief illustrative vignettes where selected *paladar* operators describe how they have balanced the demands of state regulation with their need for innovation and survival.[4] Because our research focus emerged out of such grounded observations of the day-to-day reality of what we initially thought of as the island's "informal tourism economy," the methods used in collecting data were qualitative in nature (participant observation and in-depth interviews with both licensed and informal entrepreneurs).[5]

Also, because of efforts by the Cuban government over the last two decades to incorporate clandestine self-employment into the official economy, many once informal CPs now serve their customers legally with government licenses and must pay a monthly licensing fee and year-end income taxes. Thus, our study included both those CPs who hold licenses and pay taxes, as well as those who work informally. In fact, although we specifically wanted to compare licensed CPs with their clandestine counterparts, taking a random, scientific sample representative of both components of self-employed workers was impossible. While even legal, licensed independent workers have little reason to open up to outsiders, the "hidden" character of unlicensed operators made it necessary to employ a targeted, "purposive" sampling strategy (a non-random sampling technique often called "snowball" or "theoretical" sampling) where potential interviewees are identified through observation and future subjects are added through referrals from initial contacts.[6]

Finally, given that *paladares* have been among the most lucrative, dynamic, and sizeable examples of private enterprise (in terms of both income and employment) both during the antagonistic 1993-2006 policy period and during the more encouraging post-2010 period,[7] understanding the interaction between a shifting public policy and the sector is important as it holds the greatest potential among the currently allowed group of 201 self-employment occupations of avoiding the curse of informality and transforming itself into a network of small- and medium-sized enterprises (SMEs) in a more flexible future regulatory environment that may now be at hand under Raúl.

The Rise and Fall of the Cuban *Paladar*

Birth and Premature Death, 1993-1995

Perhaps because it is one of the most visible manifestations of private enterprise and pro-market reform to foreign visitors in Cuba, much media attention has been given to the emergence of the so-called Cuban *paladar*.[8] Literally meaning "palate" in both Spanish and Portuguese, the name's curious origin hints at Cubans' initial high hopes for the potential of these private, homegrown eateries during the worst stage of the "Special Period." The name *paladar* comes from the Brazilian soap opera, *Vale Todo* (Anything Goes),[9] which was popular in Cuba in the early 1990s. Raquel, the enterprising protagonist of the *telenovela*, was a poor woman who moved from the Brazilian provinces to Rio de Janeiro, where she worked as an itinerant food vendor on the famous beaches of Copacabana. Raquel eventually made it big after setting up her own chain of small restaurants, which she christened *Paladar* (Baker 2000: 153; Sosín Martínez 2013). Journalist Howard LaFranchi captured the implications for Cuba of the spark ignited by this example of entrepreneurial success:

> Night after night the show recounted how a poor Brazilian woman traded her rags for riches as she astutely turned a modest street food stand into a chain of restaurants named *Paladar*. Not immaterial was the fact that "Raquel," the Brazilian success story, told her tale just as Cuba was experiencing a steep economic decline and widespread food shortages. *Paladar* left Cuban mouths watering. (LaFranchi 1996)

Another ironic implication of this peculiar origin of the *paladar* is the fact that Cuba's restrictions on internal migration together with prohibitions against engaging in more than a single self-employed operation made a duplication of such success impossible in Cuba at the time despite the liberalizations of the early 1990s. In fact, at the time *Vale Todo* was making Cubans' mouths water, the size of the legal self-employed sector was negligible and private restaurants were forbidden by law. However, *paladar*-like "speakeasy" eateries began to pop up throughout the island in the early 1990s in response to the growing scarcity of food. Because these informal food service networks were providing an essential service primarily to the Cuban population, they were initially tolerated. This would change later when *paladares* began to compete with the state for the tourist dollar. Their eventual legalization was an administrative response to a multitude of homegrown survival strategies (most of which were illegal) developed by the Cuban people (Whitefield 1993).

In September 1993 the government issued an initial list of 117 legal self-employment activities. Included among the occupations were four food service activities, including what became known as the infamous "et cetera"—"producer of light snacks (refreshments, sweets, fritters, et cetera)" (Decree-Law #141 1993: 4-5; Alonso 1993; CEPAL 1997). Essentially, the Cuban government decided to legalize large sectors of the expanding informal economy because it realized that these clandestine activities were filling the gaps left behind by dwindling and insufficient state sector. These informal and often illegal practices allowed Cubans, and ironically the socialist system itself, to survive (Domínguez 2001; Fernández 2000).

In the months following the September 1993 announcement, scores of Cubans who were already active in the food service sector took out licenses to begin doing legally what they had previously done clandestinely. However, in early December the government reversed its initial decision, because many Cubans who had obtained licenses were, in fact, running full-fledged restaurants under the broadest possible interpretation of "et cetera." Debates in the National Assembly in December 1993 over the offending "et cetera" concluded that legalization had been a mistake due to the suspicion that these fledging restaurants encouraged competition with the state sector, depended on pilfered supplies, and unlawfully contracted employees (Whitefield 1994a). Soon thereafter, legislators noted that the suspension of the law had largely been ignored by many of the operators necessitating stepped-up enforcement and inspections (Ricardo Luis 1993).

The refusal of many of Cuba's fledging restaurateurs to close up shop led to the first of many crackdowns against purported "illegalities, indiscipline, and abuses" in the self-employed sector in January and February 1994 (Scarpaci 1995; Segre et al 1997; Whitefield 1994a, 1994b). Police raided and closed down over 100 *paladares* in Havana, charging their owners with "illicit enrichment" despite the fact that many did possess "producer of light foods" licenses (Segre et al 1997: 233). Having learned the lesson of discretion (continue to operate but avoid growing too large or flaunting your profits),[10] many operators were back in business soon thereafter, finding various ways to stay in business such as serving only take-out meals to a select clientele or having customers place orders over the phone. In fact, despite the crackdown, the number of *paladares* was estimated to be as high as 4,000 nationwide in early 1994, with between 1,000 and 2,000 of these located in Havana alone (Whitefield 1994a; Farah 1994; Segre et al 1997).[11]

Despite the crackdown against *paladares*, however, overall self-employment was judged by most National Assembly delegates to be very popular with the Cuban people because it provided them with needed employment and constituted a key source of goods and services during the harshest period of the economic crisis. Furthermore, delegates reasoned that by legalizing underground activities, the state could control them and reign in abuses and "undue enrichment" (Ricardo Luis 1993). As described in Chapter 3, this same tension between the economic success and the political-ideological threat of pro-market reforms characterized Cuba's previous experiments with self-employment and farmer's markets in the early 1980s. Such tension would continue to be an enduring feature of the government's ambivalent approach to self-employment throughout the special period and into the significantly reformed post 2010-era.

Resurrection and Regulation, 1995-1996

The second stage in the life-cycle of the Cuban *paladar* began with the approval in June 1995 of Joint Resolution #4 ("Ampliación de actividades: Paladares" 1997). This new law specifically addressed the previously suspended self-employment category of "producer of light snacks (et cetera)"[12] and laid out three specific types of food service operations that would be allowed in the future. The first category, known as "maker-seller of food and non-alcoholic beverages *al detalle*," was intended for those who wanted to sell foods on the street, either as roving vendors or from a fixed point in front of their homes and required a monthly 100-peso tax.[13] The second category, known as "*a domicilio*," was aimed at caterers and required a 200 peso monthly tax ($100 if business was done in dollars).

Finally, true home-based restaurants, or *paladares*, were given the legal moniker, "*servicios gastronómicos*." Monthly taxes for full-service peso-charging *paladares* were initially set at 500 pesos, while operations that charged in dollars were required to pay a tax of $400 per month, rates that in-

---

Vignette: "*El Rinconcito*"

The genesis of *Paladar "El Rinconcito"* (The Little Corner Café), illustrates how some entrepreneurs creatively navigated the rapidly changing legal environment during the early years of the special period. Patricia, the affable, sharp-witted, and university educated middle-aged Afro-Cuban woman who ran the operation, explained that she originally registered *"El Rinconcito"* under her mother's name in 1995 since she herself was not retired (as was then required). She also admitted that she had operated the *paladar* clandestinely in 1993 and 1994 prior to getting a license when they became available in 1995. She justified her clandestine activity by saying she needed to generate sufficient capital before taking the costly and risky step of formalizing her business.

cluded the right to serve alcohol ("Ampliación" 1997: 485-487). Additionally, while no other self-employed activity was permitted to hire salaried employees, the state recognized that *paladares* had always operated with the help of a service and kitchen staff. Therefore, the law established a peculiar regulation prohibiting "salaried employees" on the one hand, while mandating the hiring of at least two "family helpers" on the other.

At this stage, the state placed limitations on the size and scope of *paladares* in order to limit competition and reduce what it saw as profiteering. The most well-known restriction was the previously mentioned seating limit of just "*doce sillas*" (12 chairs). Specific prohibitions were made against the sale of seafood and horsemeat, and though later banned altogether, beef, milk, and milk derivatives were only allowed if obtained in dollar stores (Dirmoser and Estay 1997: 485-487). The law also indicated that each household was restricted to a single self-employment license. While prices could be freely set, operators were required to purchase inputs from the expensive state-run dollar stores and private farmer's markets and retain receipts for all such purchases. No foods or ingredients from the state-subsidized bodegas could be resold in *paladares*. However, because dollar stores were not yet prepared to provide customers with receipts, many entrepreneurs understood the requirement that they purchase supplies in dollar stores as the legal loophole that could be used to close them down at a future date (Segre, Coyula, and Scarpaci 1997). Along with the other legalized food service activities, *paladares* would be subject to unannounced visits from a number of different inspector corps.

Just a month after *paladares* were legalized, new regulations were issued covering self-employment activities in Havana's 15 municipalities. Accord #84 (1997), as the new law was known, established detailed regulations over the use of Havana's public spaces, specifying where self-employment would be prohibited (Dirmoser and Estay 1997: 490-495). The law itself, as well as subsequent official press reports explaining it, claimed that its intent was to "neutralize and combat any and all actions against the positive development of the self-employed individual, avoiding the impunity of those who violate existing legislation" (Martínez 1995: 2). However, such an exhaustive list of prohibitions likely struck private entrepreneurs as a sign that their activities remained essentially illegitimate even if now legal and licensed. It is also likely that such a conclusion led many of them to begin to develop elaborate survival strategies and turn more frequently to the black market to obtain expensive and scarce supplies.

Statistics made public at the end of 1995 indicate that these three types of food service operation (*al detalle, a domicilio*, and *paladares*) were already among the most common self-employed activities. For example, *Granma* reported that in Havana the five most common licenses were street vending and porch-front cafeterias (*al detalle*), messenger, artisan, hair stylist, and private taxis drivers. Furthermore, Havana authorities had granted 278 *paladar* licenses out of 984 applications only in the first two months that licenses were available (Martínez 1995: 2). However, the overall number of registered self-employed workers in Havana dropped to 58,000 by the end of 1995, from a peak of almost 64,000 in August. Havana's number of registered self-employed workers would never again exceed 60,000 during the 1993-2010 period, and by April 1997 it had fallen to just 35,171 (Avendaño 1997; *DPPFA* 1997).

Still, the relative weight of the self-employed occupations of food service, transportation, and private lodging is clear when we look at the most common occupations for 1999 across the entire country. The three occupations of "*al detalle*" (street vendors), "Family helper" (in which family members obtain self-employment licenses to aid in the preparation of foods), and "preparer-seller of food products and beverages '*en puntos fijos de venta*'" (retail sales from small, porch-front cafeterias) made up nearly 37% of all self-employed workers.[14]

When we include private transportation services and private lodging (along with the already described private food services) in our analysis, the predominance of these three occupations within the self-employed sector becomes pronounced. For example, the distribution of self-employment licenses by occupation in the single Havana municipality of "Plaza de la Revolución" (Table 8.1) highlights this trend. Grouped into nine different categories, the 3,572 self-employment licenses active in "Plaza" in June 1999 reveal the overwhelming concentration of licenses in food service, transportation, and room rentals. Individually, each of these three occupations easily outranks each of the other six categories, and, in the case of rentals and food service, stretch

Table 8.1: Distribution of Self-Employment Licenses by Economic Activity, Plaza Municipality, 1999

Economic Activity	Number of Licenses
Transportation	320
Food Services	1132
Bed-and-breakfast (Room Rental)	1113
Housing Repair	98
Personal Care	123
Domestic Personnel	221
Small-Scale Manufacturing	123
Assorted Services	196
Others	246

Source: Fernández Peláez 2000

well beyond the others. Moreover, taken together, licenses for self-employment in private home rental (1,113), food service (1,132), and transportation (320) accounted for nearly 72% of all self-employment licenses in the "Plaza" municipality in June 1999.[15] Partly for these reasons, these three self-employed occupations were chosen as our case studies.

Increased Regulation, Stigmatization, and Decline, 1996-2000

Unfortunately for the operators of Cuba's *paladares*, the next few years of their existence as legal, licensed microenterprises coincided with a major shift in government policy. Whereas prior to December 1995 the government expanded the number of occupational categories of self-employment from 117 to nearly 160, permitting a concomitant rise in the total number of licensed self-employed operators (peaking at 208,786 in December 1995), the government legalized few new occupations after that date and discontinued the issuance of new licenses for many occupations thereafter.

Indications of a growing antagonism toward self-employment were evident in the repeated declarations in the official Cuban press reminding operators of their legal, fiscal, and moral responsibilities.[16] It also became increasingly common for articles in *Granma* and *Trabajadores* to reiterate the state's rejection of self-employment as anything more than a decidedly small-scale, complementary, and temporary development option, with National Assembly President Ricardo Alarcón even labeling it at one point "the lowest socio-employment level in any part of the planet" (*la última escala social laboral en cualquier parte del planeta*) (Lee 1997d). The best gauge of the policy change is the reduction in the numbers of registered self-employed workers, and the near elimination of the *paladar*.

Legal and fiscal changes during these years included, (1) the announcement in February 1996 of an increase in the monthly tax rates for many occupations, including the doubling of peso *paladar* rates to 1,000 pesos and raising dollar operations to $600, (2) an end to the granting of any new *paladar* licenses in Havana in April 1996, (3) a nationwide re-inscription of all self-employed workers begun in June 1996, and (4) a new comprehensive law aimed at strengthening the sanctions against the violators of self-employment regulations (Decree-Law #174, 1997).

Though the February 1996 tax increase affected 144 of the 162 self-employed occupations, *paladares* were hit hardest. Peso-charging *paladares* had their taxes doubled from 400 to 800 per month, reaching 1,000 pesos for those serving alcoholic beverages. Though the change was less drastic for dollar operations, these *paladares* also saw their taxes jump from $400 to $600 per month (Avendaño 1997; Ritter 1998, 2000a, b; Segre et al 1997). Coming on the heels of these tax increases was a new declaration (Joint Resolution #1)

Vignette: Patricia's Survival Strategies

Patricia, the proprietor of "*El Rinconcito*," introduced above, explained that her monthly taxes rose drastically over the six years she had been in business at the time of our original interview. Upon obtaining her license in 1995 she was required to pay just 500 pesos ($23) a month. Six years later, in January of 2001 when our interview took place, she was paying a total of $775 dollars a month to keep her license (almost 34 times her previous monthly rate of $23). She also employed five people. However, only three of them were legally registered so as to avoid paying extra taxes. Furthermore, none of her employees actually lived with her, nor were any of them her relatives, as required.

Patricia explained that part of the monthly $775 tax was paid for the right to hire three legal employees at $97 per employee. She also paid each employee separately, but argued that this job was by far their best earning possibility. She voiced deep frustration at having to pay a tax to employ another person and then not being free to choose whom she actually employed. "How dare they tell me who I can and cannot hire in my own business. I pay a tax, I should have the right to hire who I decide." She also called the taxes plainly "abusive," aimed at "choking *paladares* to death, along with constant fines, inspections, and restrictions. Some call it pressure, but I call it harassment (*hostigamiento*)."

When asked about how much she normally owed in taxes on top of her fixed monthly tax of $775, Patricia laughed, saying that she paid just $15 on her 2000 tax return. Seeing my surprise, she explained, "Given the fact that the state has built so much aggressiveness into the laws for private enterprise, we have no alternative but to respond with the same aggressiveness when 'complying with' the law." She went on to justify her routine dissimulation, cheating, and misrepresentation as her only options.

For example, when asked if she would characterize her *paladar* as a "family business," she said simply, "No way. That's false and absurd. The rule about not having more than 12 chairs is also absurd." According to her, "the system is set up such that it obliges us to lie in order to survive." Furthermore, she explained that the fact that there seems to be a law against everything has produced a climate where law-breaking and cheating is commonplace and seen as part and parcel of doing business. "In order to survive, everyone is forced to become a 'criminal' leading to a generalized disrespect for law itself. As you can see, there are things that have no logic at all. Everyone is so accustomed to breaking the law that the law itself has become meaningless."

> When asked about obstacles, she went right to the heart of the matter, saying, "There are many details, but we have to start with the essence of the problem: the government doesn't want *paladares* to exist. It clashes with the basic political orientation of the country. It is opposed to the economic model." However, Patricia maintained that "you cannot understand any of this from an economic point of view. That's because everything in this country is political. They set up a political goal – an ideological frame – and the economy must fit into that." She joked, "It's ironic because this is just the opposite of what Marx taught – that everything has a material base. This is how the entire rest of the world functions, but here in Cuba it is just the reverse."

that mandated a nationwide re-registration of all self-employed workers. At the same time, re-registration was accompanied by a host of new regulations for self-employed workers (*Trabajadores* 1996).

First, porch-front cafeterias ("*puntos fijos*") were legally separated from roving street vendors ("*al detalle*"), the former being issued the detailed stipulation: "These *puntos fijos* (cafeterias) cannot be equipped with tables, chairs, benches, or the like; and should be performed through direct dispensation of products without any mediating type of gastronomic service" (*Trabajadores* 1996: 4; Rodríguez Cruz 1996: 5). Therefore, it bears pointing out that not only were *paladares* prohibited from having *more than* 12 chairs, but these smaller food stalls were forbidden from having *any* chairs or tables, or engaging in any kind of customer service beyond direct sales.

Second, new regulations for full-fledged *paladares* included a prohibition against having televisions, live music, or even a bar area where customers could have a drink while they wait for one of the 12 chairs to become vacant. The law reads, "When alcoholic beverages are offered, they cannot be consumed in an isolated space specifically built for that purpose" *Trabajadores* 1996: 4; Rodríguez Cruz 1996: 5). The wording here was important since the law did not prohibit bars per se. As a result, nearly all *paladares* visited by the authors did have a bar and operators were simply careful about openly serving drinks to waiting customers there.

Third, the 1996 resolution stipulated that all "family helpers" in the private food service sector would henceforth have to take out their own self-employment license and pay a monthly personal income tax equal to 20% of the tax paid by the *paladar* itself. In practice, this tax was usually paid by *paladar* operators, thus increasing their monthly tax from 1,000 to 1,400 CUP in the case of peso operations, and from $600 to $840 for dollar operations (see Table 8.1).[17] Finally, the Resolution prohibited all advertising by *paladares* apart from the hanging of a sign outside their home, for which they were required

Vignette: Magda's "*La Azotea*"

Magda, the matron of "*La Azotea*," a rooftop *paladar* located just a few blocks from the University of Havana, has been forced to change her business strategy in a number of ways. When I arrived for lunch at her elegant, vine covered, but surprisingly well-hidden home, she immediately inquired how I had found her place. She was relieved to find that a friend in the U.S. had given me the address, explaining that if it had been a *jinetero*, she would be forced to add another $5 to the standard $8 price, in order to cover his commission.

Magda openly expressed frustration at this system whereby *jinetero* middle-men do little work compared to the restaurateurs, yet according to her can make upwards of a hundred dollars a day. She had even begun to refuse to pay commissions to the hustlers and, as a result, they had begun to spread rumors that her food was bad and expensive. She reacted by removing her sign from the front of the house and began to publicize her operation exclusively by word of mouth. She seemed to appreciate the government's efforts to stamp out speculative activity. She believed these young people were mostly high school dropouts who made her business less profitable and added to her mounting frustrations of restrictions, fines, and taxes.

At the same time, Magda pointed out that most *paladares* are dependent on *jineteros* as their only means of attracting customers since advertising is prohibited. Like many other self-employed workers, Magda is caught in a situation where she needs to advertise to bring in as much business as possible and avoid relying on costly *jineteros*. However, she can only advertise the legal services for which she is licensed, since whatever she publicizes to potential customers will also be seen by government inspectors and police. Though she has space for far more than 12 diners, serves lobster and beef, and rents rooms in her home, she cannot publicize these services since doing so would subject her to sanction.

As I sat waiting for my meal, the phone rang. When Magda returned to serve my food, she explained that the call was in fact a long-distance reservation from Spain. Feigning surprise that someone would call all the way from Spain just to make a reservation for dinner, I joked that the food must be extremely good. She laughed and explained that the reservation was in fact for a room in her home, which she also rented out occasionally. Magda jumped at the opportunity to suggest that I consider staying there on my next trip to Cuba since meals for guests are discounted to just $5 a plate.

> In fact, when I returned to dine at "*La Azotea*" six months later, I found that Magda had made an innovative change in her business strategy, deciding to turn in her *paladar* license and reopen as a bed-and-breakfast. This strategy was immediately clear as I approached her home, which now featured a new sign that boldly and bilingually declared, "Room for Rent with Gourmet Meals—*Renta de Habitación con Servicio Gastronómico*." In the past, Magda solved her *jinetero* problem by removing her sign, but struggled to attract customers and navigate onerous *paladar* restrictions. Now, realizing that operating under a *paladar* license was much too onerous, she has discovered that operating as a bed-and-breakfast allows her to reduce her dependence on *jineteros*, advertise her services openly, and rent rooms in her expansive home without fear of being caught, while legally serving meals to her house guests (and to others under the cover of her bed-and-breakfast license).

to pay another tax equal to 20% of their base monthly tax (Whitefield 1996a, b; Mayoral 1996: 2; Lee 1996b: 2).

Added to the fiscal and legal changes outlined above was a concerted government effort starting in May of 1996 to improve the state food service sector and compete directly against private *paladares* and cafeterias. Scores of new state-run cafeterias were opened in Havana and as many as 600 new state food vendors were put on the street offering light snacks in direct competition with private cafeterias (Whitefield 1996a; Ferreira 2000). As a result of changes in the tax structure and increased competition, many *paladar* operators attempted to shift into operating exclusively in pesos to avoid the increased tax (Whitefield 1996b). However, due to their inability to survive without relying on the dollar/tourism market, most operations were forced back to operating in dollars and paying the higher dollar tax rates. Many also found that restrictions on what they could serve and rules against advertising forced them to become dependent on the illegal services of sometimes unscrupulous *jineteros*. Furthermore, as Magda's vignette shows, by the late 1990s many had developed the resourceful strategy of turning in their *paladar* licenses and reopening their restaurants under the much less onerous legal cover of a bed-and-breakfast license. Under such bed-and-breakfast licenses, operators could simply continue to serve food to their traditional clientele, while seeming to offer an additional food service exclusively to their house guests (as stipulated by law). In response to the increasingly onerous *paladar* regulations, many entrepreneurs began to complain bitterly in letters sent to *Granma*'s column "For the Taxpayer" (*Para el Contribuyente*).[18] Others have aired criticisms to foreign journalists, including to

Vignette: "*La Guarida*"

Easily Cuba's most famous private restaurant, "*La Guarida*," has served its international cuisine to a host of visiting dignitaries, including the King and Queen of Spain, movie star Jack Nicholson, and the late Nobel laureate Gabriel García Márquez. The reason for its great success and popularity begins with the fact that it is located in the very same apartment where the breakthrough Cuban film *Fresa y Chocolate* (Strawberry and Chocolate) was filmed in 1993. Directed by Cuba's late master filmmaker, Tomás Gutiérrez Alea, the film treated the taboo subject of homosexuality in socialist Cuba head on. Roughly translated as "The Hideout," the restaurant's name originates with the nickname Diego, the homosexual lead character in the film (expertly played by Cuban actor Jorge Perugorría), gave to his own third-floor apartment in the building (González 2012).

The founder, owner, and operator of *La Guarida*, the affable entrepreneur Enrique Núñez, explained in our interview that after the international release and eventual world-wide popularity of the film, a series of foreigners began to show up at the third floor apartment of their truly impressive ruin of a building to get a glimpse of where the film had been staged. "No one can even calculate the amount of tourist dollars that have been brought to Cuba as a result of *Fresa y Chocolate*, declared Enrique. "I have witnessed it first hand through this place." Unexpectedly finding himself out of work in 1995, these never-ending visits gave Enrique the "crazy idea" of transforming his parents' small apartment into a *paladar*.

Enrique spent the next eight months pouring his savings and a number of loans into the apartment, turning this "crazy idea" into a reality. While he was making constant renovations to the apartment, most of his friends told him he was indeed crazy, pointing out a number of major flaws in his business plan. The apartment is on the third floor with no elevator; it sits in the middle of a neglected and intimidating Cuban tenement; and was located in the middle of drab and overcrowded Central Havana, far from the usual tourist haunts. However, Enrique thought that it would be just these factors mixed with the apartment's celluloid allure that would assure the restaurants success. "Besides," he concluded, "I have nothing else to do."

Enrique kept setting a date to open, but had to continually push the date back due to construction delays. Providentially, he decided to go ahead and get his license in April of 1996, since he had expected to open at the end of that month. By ironic coincidence, less than two weeks after his license was issued on April 20, the government suddenly suspended the issuance of any new *paladar* licenses, likely making La Guarida one of the last *paladares* to be legally licensed in Cuba in the initial 1990 period under Fidel. One unforeseen problem with which Enrique was presented by getting his license early was being forced to pay a steep monthly tax starting in April, three months before he began to operate and generate revenue. Finally, after much delay and anticipation, he inaugurated *La Guarida* on July 14, 1996, inviting the entire cast of *Fresa y Chocolate* to the *paladar*'s grand opening.

In our interview, Enrique explained that among his biggest obstacles were the constant threat of fines from inspectors and the continual search for hard-to-find supplies. Many times the items he needed were simply not available in Cuba. He joked, "You should see my baggage whenever I return from a trip abroad. I pay a fortune in overweight charges!" For example, much of the kitchen equipment was obtained during trips abroad. He also argued that he had so far successfully avoided any hefty fines since he knows which laws are best complied with and which ones can be successfully winked at.

When asked for suggestions that would make the laws more rational, Enrique left hardly a stone unturned claiming that nearly every restriction was not only unjust but simply illogical. First, he would get rid of the "completely absurd" restriction that all employees be members of one's family. He would also end the "absolutely and totally illogical" 12-chair size limit for *paladares*. Finally, he admitted that these changes would allow *paladares* to increase their profits and so he would support an increase in taxes to mirror increased profits. He stressed that changing the current legal framework would have to be accompanied by a reliable system of tracking earnings since no such system currently exists in Cuba. "In Cuba," he explained, "the government has little trust that the individual will report income accurately, and so has created an authoritarian, patronizing tax system." The Cuban tax system expects dishonesty and so demands an abusive quota payment, leading to even more dishonesty in a vicious cycle of self-fulfilling prophecy, implying that the entire tax system would have to be overhauled if more space were given to small businesses.

Mimi Whitefield of the *Miami Herald*, who was confronted by an exasperated waiter with the dilemma of the "so-called cousin." "Why must we continue with the ridiculous myth of the family business?" he asked. "These rules have turned us into liars and hypocrites" (Whitefield 1996a). While

Cuban entrepreneurs are forced into becoming "liars and hypocrites" out of frustration with unworkable restrictions, the state maintains the fiction that splits the self-employed into "honest and honorable" workers on one side and "abusive speculators and delinquents" on the other. For the government, it is not the taxes and regulations that are abusive and provoke lawbreaking, but a handful of abusive and unscrupulous "*macetas*" (black marketers) who encircle and live off otherwise hardworking, law-abiding citizens.

Indeed, in interviews with private restaurateurs who admitted to engaging in some violations in order to survive, the authors were often told how things would improve if only the government would deal more harshly with the delinquents, hangers-on, and *jineteros* who gave them a bad name. Furthermore, knowing that no registered operator wants to be grouped together with "*los macetas del cuentapropismo*" (the "big shots" or "crooks" of self-employment), journalists in the official media have encouraged this practice within the private sector by reminding readers of their revolutionary duty to report economic crimes to the proper authorities (Lee 1997c: 2).[19] The irony here is that while most self-employed workers are forced to bend the rules in order to survive, they seem to readily buy into the government line that portrays lawbreakers as exceptional individuals who are getting rich by exploiting others.

The final major law passed during this period to regulate the self-employed sector was (Decree-Law 174, 1997), "On the Personal Violations of Self-employment Regulations," outlined briefly in Chapter 5. Harsher laws, stepped-up enforcement, and calls for vigilance against crime have paid off if measured by the precipitous drop in the number of registered *paladares*. Of the 1,562 *paladares* that had successfully become registered by 1996, there were just 416 by August 1998 (half in Havana) (Lee 1998: 2). Of these, only 253 were still left in 2000, two-thirds of them located in Havana (Latin American, Caribbean, and Central American Report 2000: 4). Articles in the international and independent Cuban press confirmed this downward trend reporting that over 200 *paladares* were closed down in the year 2000 alone (Viño Zimerman 2001; Vicent 2000; Newman 2001; Duany 2001: 48). By 2003, various researchers and journalists put the number of legally operating *paladares* at less than 200 in the entire country (Escobal Rabeiro 2001; Jackiewicz and Dolster 2003). Our own observations and interviews with *paladar* operators in Havana and Santiago between 2003 and 2006 confirm this. In fact, during a 2006 visit to Havana *Reuters* correspondent Marc Frank informed us that a government source had told him that there were then just 98 remaining licensed *paladares* in Havana.

Economic Recentralization and Offensive Against Self-Employment, 2001-2006

As described in Chapter 4, after 2001 Cuban economic policy gradually shifted away from the market reforms of the early 1990s toward more centralized control of the economy. The granting of new self-employment licenses in many occupations was discontinued and many licensed microenterprises were forced out of business or underground by a predatory tax structure and stepped up public attacks on entrepreneurs as corrupt "new rich." The three areas of self-employment most directly affected by this new offensive and most commonly criticized in the official Cuban press are precisely private transport (taxis, cargo trucks, and pedicabs), bed-and-breakfasts, and food service operations (especially *paladares*). The message could not have been clearer: You may still be legal, but you are no longer legitimate (Jatar-Hausmann 1999).

In fact, since Cuba's economy reached a relative stability by the late 1990s and even began to show signs of incipient growth, the government was able to gradually scale back the opening in the domestic economy by limiting or wholly eliminating many internal economic reforms. The fate of self-employment is the clearest example of this retrenchment. Many of Cuba's entrepreneurs came to understand that self-employment was but a stop-gap measure grudgingly instituted by the government and "tied directly to the Special Period." Thus, their implicit interpretation of their reversal of fortune since 2001 was that the government's strategic, if contradictory gamble of using entrepreneurial capitalism to save state socialism had paid off, with the unavoidable conclusion, "when [...] things stabilize, this sector would be eliminated" (Jackiewicz and Bolster 2003: 375).

In the summer of 2003, new regulations were announced for bed-and-breakfast operators that included raising overall tax rates, requiring all operators to pay an additional 30% tax for providing meals to their guests, charging an additional tax on common areas of the home used by renters, limiting renting to a maximum of two rooms with just two guests per room, prohibiting the hiring of anyone from outside the family, revoking the right to rent out an entire apartment, and requiring that a family member always be present in the home. This laundry list of new regulations against a type of self-employment only first legalized in 1997 (Henken 2002a), was justified based on the conviction that "negative tendencies and behaviors have emerged in the exercise of this activity that distort the very essence of renting" (*Resolución* No. 270, 2003). At the same time, by 2003 the overall number of registered self-employment operators had dropped to a new low of 100,000 from 208,500 in 1995 and 153,800 in 2001 (Grogg 2003).

Starting in the fall of 2004, the U.S. dollar was officially removed from domestic circulation, replaced universally by the convertible Cuban peso

Vignette: *"El Hurón Azul"*

"*El Hurón Azul*" is an elegantly decorated two-room *paladar* that sits inconspicuously on a dirty, commercial street just off of 23rd in the *La Rampa* district of *El Vedado*, near the *Cayo Hueso* neighborhood of *Centro Habana*. It is actually the first restaurant that I, Ted Henken, ever visited in Havana in August of 1997, brought there by a *jinetero* who noticed me searching for a place to eat lunch nearby on Calle "O". When I returned again four years later in 2001, I was surprised to find the same no-nonsense, extremely professional and efficient waiter answering the door. Talking to him after lunch, I learned that his name was Fran and that the owner was named Juan Carlos Fernández. Fran told me that he had been working there for the past four years after leaving another *paladar*. At the time, I wondered how he could change jobs since a *paladar* is supposed to be a "family run" operation. However, he laughed saying that all *cuentapropistas* have to "*hacer su propia trampa*" (play their little tricks) and confirmed that he is not related to Juan Carlos.

Though my first visit to this *paladar* was through a middleman, it seemed on my subsequent visits that they were trying to discourage this practice since just outside the front door, just below the blue and white sign declaring, "*El Hurón Azul—Paladar,*" is another sign, permanently fixed in tile to the wall reading: "*No Pagamos Comisión*" (We don't pay commissions). In my interview later with Juan Carlos, he argued that they did not need to rely on touts to drum up business since they had a fairly constant clientele, the majority of whom are Cuban artists and intellectuals. Furthermore, he said that he would have to pass any commissions on to his customers by raising his prices, and preferred not to do that. He also seemed to reject the practice of giving bribes, even if he understood that it is likely a common practice for other *paladares*. "It depends on the type of business you run and on the kind of relationship that you have with the inspector," he argued. "If you are clean, you have nothing to fear, but if you do much that is illegal I imagine that you need to have a 'special relationship' with the inspector."

Though he would not share the amount of his exact earnings with me, he did say that he makes a profit and that being self-employed pays much more than the 400 Cuban pesos he earned each month in his previous job as a university professor. He also said that he worked 2 or 3 times more hours as an entrepreneur than he did as a professor. Whereas he worked six days a week five hours a day in his previous job (30 hours a week total), he estimated that he now worked all the time: "*todo el día, todos los días.*" In terms of his somewhat unique, and clearly pragmatic

> approach to the government restrictions, he explained that if you decide to open a restaurant or any kind of business (in whatever country), you must be willing to play by the given rules of that society. While not denying that Cuba had many "absurd," ridiculous, and senseless regulations, he argued that complaining and decrying the injustice of those rules is simply a waste of time. *"Hay que vivir en el mundo real"* (you have to live in the real world), he argued, not in some future world that may never exist.
>
> Though Juan Carlos was generally not openly critical of the tax system or of the strict restrictions and regulations on *paladares*, he was under no illusions about the conflictive relationship private enterprise like his has with the socialist government of Cuba. "The Cuban state is not interested in private property. For them, we are a unwanted evil, but a necessary one at present." Furthermore, he argued that, "The socialist system sees private enterprise as an anachronism." Still, he does not worry too much about it. For example, when asked if there was a future for self-employment in Cuba, he responded in a typical way given his other responses. "I don't lose any sleep over it but I'd have to bet on it. I don't waste time worrying about it, but I do worry about my business and make sure I comply with all the laws such as they are." Given that the Cuban authorities ultimately decided to throw the proverbial book at Juan Carlos (as we describe below), it is a supreme irony that he ended our interview with these words: "You must conform to the laws in the country in which you find yourself or pay the consequences."

(CUC), giving the government more control over expenditures and forcibly channeling foreign economic exchanges through the central government (Mesa-Lago and Pérez-López 2005: 22-25). Havana also responded to the Bush administration's new measures limiting remittances and family visits by beginning to exact a 20% surcharge on exchanges of U.S. dollars. This measure was tantamount to reducing the value of family remittances by 20%, redirecting that portion directly into government coffers. At the same time, a new set of self-employment restrictions was enacted that included the suspension of new licenses in 40 occupations, including licenses for such specific and seemingly innocuous occupations as magicians, children's party clowns, used book sellers, makers of flower wreaths, masseuses, and newspaper vendors (*Resolución* 11, 2004).

Also included in this list of jobs were all four food service occupations: street vendors, cafeterias, caterers, and *paladares*. This change reduced from 158 to 118 the number of licensable occupations. Additionally, non-*paladar* food service operators were now prohibited from using potatoes in their products and required to hire (and pay taxes on) at least one family helper. *Paladar* operators were instructed that their required three (up from two) family helpers must have been members of the family or co-residents in the home for at least the three preceding years. Finally, in reaction to the fact that most operators had indeed been skirting the rule against serving drinks to waiting guests at a bar, the government now stipulated explicitly that "alcoholic drinks will only be served with the meal" (*Resolución* 11, 2004).

Finally, in 2005, responding to growing concern over increasing inequality in socialist Cuba, the government increased the minimum wage, raised pensions, began to charge for electricity based on consumption. Towards the end of the year, it kicked off an ideological mobilization that included a crackdown on corruption, theft, pilfering, and the "new rich." In a six-hour speech, delivered on November 17 to students at the University of Havana (described in previous chapters), an aged but energized Fidel Castro called for nothing short of a cultural revolution (Ritter 2006). In his speech, Castro focused specifically and repeatedly on the self-employed, attacking them as the backbone of the rising class of "new rich" and singling out taxi drivers, bed-and-breakfast operators, and especially *paladar* owners as the most egregious flouters of socialist morality. Finally, referring to U.S. promotion of private enterprise in Cuba, he reminded his listeners that self-employment has no real future in a socialist Cuba. "The empire was hoping that Cuba would have many more '*paladares*' but it appears that there will be no more of them," roared the aged revolutionary in what would prove to be one of his final marathon speeches as Cuba's "maximum leader." "What do they think that we have become neo-liberals? No one here has become a neo-liberal" (Castro 2005b).

At the time, the government explained the drop in self-employment as the result of the economic upturn. As the economy improved (with help from China and especially Venezuela), the self-employed supposedly returned to their state jobs. However, such an explanation ignores the fact that most Cubans continued to need to supplement their meager state salaries and insufficient rationed provisions. Furthermore, the earnings of even the most humble self-employed entrepreneurs were still well above the average state salary. The government's facile explanation for the drop in the numbers of licensed self-employed workers also disregarded the possibility that many did not willingly abandon their microenterprises, but did so only after being fined into bankruptcy or closed down outright by state inspectors. Finally, as indicated in Chapter 7, former licensed operators did not necessarily shift back into state jobs, but often simply took their enterprises underground.

In the case of *paladares*, it is ironic that enterprises that have survived to date have been forced by legal limitations and high taxes to raise their prices, charging an increasingly exclusive (and thus almost solely foreign) clientele in dollars (Holgado Fernández 2000). This is a significant change compared with the initial relatively low peso prices and decidedly domestic function of most *paladares* in the first half of the decade (Scarpaci 1995; Segre et al 1997). Such a shift is even more unfortunate given the great difficulty most Cubans already have in procuring enough food. It seems that Raúl Castro's surprisingly bold declaration of 1994 cited above as an epigraph, "if there is food for the people, the risks do not matter" (1997: 466), no longer applied to the risks presented by *paladares*. Indeed, the fact that *paladares* no longer mainly served the consumption needs of the Cuban population may have been the perfect pretext for the government to deepen its repressive policies against them. However, the fact that many foreigners, especially influential ones like the Spanish Royal Family, were frequent patrons of these restaurants may have helped to preclude their total elimination.

Living Underground: Survival Strategies of Cuba's Self-Employed

As the above vignettes indicate, for every unreasonable legal restriction placed on *paladares*, entrepreneurs have developed specific strategies to circumvent those restrictions. Quite literally, Cuba's *paladar* operators have taken inspiration from the Brazilian soap opera *"Vale Todo"* (Anything Goes), despite (or perhaps precisely because of) the many legal restrictions (Henken 2008a). Until the relaxation that began in late 2010, restrictions on *paladares* included limitations on menu offerings, the physical size (12 place-settings) and location of the operation (restricted to one's own home), supply sources, modalities of advertising, and the hiring of non-family employees. These limitations are exacerbated by the fact that existing legal supply sources for foods and other necessary materials are quite expensive. All items must be purchased at retail prices, either in state-run dollar stores with often exorbitant prices or in the farmer's markets where prices are set by forces of supply and demand. No legal wholesale sources of supplies exist for *paladar* operators, or for any other self-employed activity. Finally, taxes are set administratively and not based on earnings, forcing many operators to underreport their income to reduce their unmanageable tax burden.

As illustrated in the opening vignette from *Paladar "Las Doce Sillas*," as well as in the snapshots of *"El Rinconcito," "La Azotea*," and *"La Guarida"* (and *"El Hurón Azul"* as we will see later), the most common strategies that microentrepreneurs developed during the 1993-2006 period in the face of these onerous legal and fiscal requirements include the serving of forbidden foods, the use of hidden rooms with additional place-settings, and (after 2005) the increasingly common presence of *paladar* sites on the Internet (with Trip Advisor becoming the dominant Internet site to find, evaluate, and promote such operations after 2010). Also, as indicated above, *paladares* make common use of intermediaries (*jineteros* and *boteros*—gypsy cabbies—to whom they pay illegal commissions) to bring in customers, rely on black market goods, and purchase bogus receipts to account for those illegally obtained supplies. Due to the high commissions charged by intermediaries (usually $5 per person per meal) and to the prohibition against many foods, some *paladares* have designed two or three different menus. Diners in these establishments are offered a distinct menu based on intermediary costs, "special" menu selections, and, sometimes, their nationality.

Because of the high retail prices and limited supplies in the dollar stores and farmer's markets, *paladar* proprietors often turn to the "wholesale" prices of the black market. Cuban sociologist Fernández Peláez pinpoints the economic logic behind this strategy.

> In general, the strategy employed to guarantee profitability can be summed up as the lowering of costs through opting for the generally cheaper supplies

Vignette: "*Paladar del Mar*"

In a 2006 interview with Arturo, the operator of a veritable gastronomic showplace provocatively named, "*Paladar del Mar*," located in Havana's exclusive Siboney diplomatic district, I was told, "Here we serve typical Cuban cuisine (*comida criolla*), but we try to distinguish ourselves by offering fresh seafood to our customers." Expressing little fear of sanction for such a bald violation of the restriction against seafood, Arturo only became more effusive about the wide range of offerings when he thought I might publicize what he told me abroad. In fact, he explicitly asked me to report a litany of catch-phrases that captured the *paladar*'s unique offerings as he gave me a guided tour of the extensive grounds of his culinary compound.

> Tell them that we offer an "ample presence of seafood," have a classic Cuban "*bohío*" (thatched hut) dining area, have a second "in-door air-conditioned" dining area, feature the "artwork of some of Cuba's most distinguished painters," have a full bar with a range of "tropical drinks," cook our food on "an open grill right in front of the customer," and even have a "wine cellar stocked with an international selection of wines from France, Spain, Chile, South Africa, and the United States" ranging from $12 to $45 a bottle.

of the black market. These producers can only make a profit by making purchases in this market since they cannot count on wholesale state supplies of raw materials. [This is] one of the greatest current problems of the institutional platform that obliges [paladar] operators to make purchases at retail prices, which of course are higher. (2000: 30)

In the case of the few large-scale operations, more egregious violations are common. For example, while some *paladares* employ non-family workers, large scale operations are often staffed by numerous employees, including cooks, private security personnel, taxi drivers, and troupes of musicians who entertain guests with live music.

The availability of rooms for lodging, drastic underreporting of earnings, and special "arrangements" with the inspector corps, are salient features of some of these high-end operations. Again, Fernández Peláez indicates the economic logic behind the common practice of bribery:

One of the principal strategies is that of bribing the authorities charged with the responsibility of carrying out inspections and levying fines. For example, faced with the impossibility of diversifying the products one can offer due to current regulations, the self-employed pay for the "silence" of inspectors [to avoid] fines. (2000:30)

One negative effect of the use of bribes is that it tends to push smaller operations that are unable to afford them out of business, resulting in the survival of a small number of lucrative and/or well-connected large-scale operations.[20] For example, in our interview with Magalis, the waitress at "*Las Doce Sillas*," she explained that the government is especially rigorous in enforcing regulations when an operation is successful. According to her, the government singles out these so-called "new rich" for vigilance and eventual closure. "Their objective is to restrict us and force us to close down," she explained. "If it looks like you are making some money, they come running and look for an excuse to close you down. You know what they say, 'He who sticks out his neck...' Here, you can only be successful until they catch you in something." Maglis' extensive knowledge of the workings of the entrepreneurial underworld come from the fact that she was a waitress in another *paladar*, which was closed down two years earlier in 1999. Then, before getting her current job at "*Las Doce Sillas*," she worked as a maid in a bed-and-breakfast for 16 months.

When asked about the existence of bribery, Magalis claimed that in her experience nearly all entrepreneurs resort to bribing inspectors and police at least occasionally. As for inspectors, she claimed, "A minority refuse, but the majority go along with the bribes. Let's face it, these guys only get paid about 180 pesos ($8) a month and the temptation is too great for them especially when they exercise bureaucratic power over people with a lot of money." She added, "You can even bribe them with as little as a plate of food." Laughing, she described how inspectors tended to complain about how hungry they were during their periodic "visits." Alternately, whenever they uncovered a violation, they might ask about their "*aguinaldo*," a pre-revolutionary practice whereby workers would be given a year-end bonus. Indeed, Magalis confirmed that "inspections" tended to increase as the Christmas holidays approached.

Finally, prior to 2010 a pair of "last-resort" survival strategies seem to have become increasingly common in the food service sector. First, a number of entrepreneurs who have felt pressure to close their doors due to the impossibility of surviving under the maze of legal requirements put in place for *paladares* have decided to turn in their food service licenses and apply for the much less onerous license to rent rooms, as did Magda. However, having invested much time and capital in equipping their homes with the infrastructure necessary to provide quality meals, these clever operators continue to operate unofficial *paladares* behind the legal façade of a bed-and-breakfast.[21] The second "last resort" strategy is that of turning in one's license, but continuing to operate the *paladar* clandestinely.

This final strategy of operating completely "in the dark" is necessary in places like Varadero where self-employment in tourism-related activities is severely restricted. Likewise, interviews with the operators of a number of Havana *paladares* that had been forced to close down, and with others that continue to operate clandestinely, confirm both the stepped up repression of the mid-2000s as well as the systematic use of informal strategies to stay in business. For example, when the previously described *paladar* "*El Hurón Azul*" was closed down in early 2009 after a dramatic, months-long, undercover police sting operation that began the previous December, the restaurant's proprietor Juan Carlos was shown to have engaged in all the most basic strategies described above to cut corners (a fact which he had denied in our interview). This included hiring unauthorized employees, using more than the obligatory 12 chairs, and serving illicit foods such as beef and seafood (which were hidden in a water tank on the roof). However, until the December 2008 tip that put authorities on his trail, no violations had ever been detected despite the fact that *Hurón Azul* had been inspected three times each month, indicating that Juan Carlos had indeed made "special arrangements" with officials.

However, a truly disturbing 192-slide Power Point presentation leaked from Havana's Prosecutors Office of Drugs and Corruption and published in a post entitled, "Feast Envy," on Yoani Sánchez's *Generation Y* blog (2009), revealed that Juan Carlos had in fact developed a far more intricate and multifaceted *paladar* operation than most. The slideshow begins:

On December 1, 2008 the DTI received information in reference to citizen Juan Carlos Fernández García, age 47, residing at 153 Humboldt, between O and P, Vedado, who, while engaged in illegal activities as the proprietor of the private restaurant "*Hurón Azul*," had obtained great sums of money which allowed him to maintain an extravagant lifestyle characterized by the acquisition of several houses, hundreds of works of art, appliances, and frequent trips abroad, among other manifestations of undeserved enrichment.

In fact, the sting uncovered the fact that Juan Carlos ran not one but three different restaurants simultaneously (the second and third of which were registered under others' names). The scores of photos featured in the Power Point document his car and motorcycle, seven homes, seven safes filled with cash in the amounts of 22,000 convertible pesos (CUCs) and 29,000 pesos (MN), six cell phones, an extensive art collection, and a storage unit fully stocked with hundreds of bottles of wine and liquor and cases of beer.

Juan Carlos was also accused of other supposedly nefarious dealings such as "involving himself in activities not associated with the social objective of the eatery" such as "sponsoring cultural activities like an art gallery and other cultural projects" with "documented evidence of donations and contributions to different cultural entities." One particular art show he supposedly conceived of, directed, and financed took place at the Spanish-American Cultural Center and had an estimated budget of 50,000 CUCs. As part of a large shipment of industrial equipment and foodstuffs he obtained from Panama, Juan Carlos was actually found to have imported two photocopiers as well, which he donated to Cuba's National Museum of Fine Art. It seems that he was so successful that he was also in the process of opening up a fourth restaurant in Milan.

In fact, Enrique Núñez, the previously described owner of *La Guarida*, was a close friend of Juan Carlos' and watched with increasing horror as the extent of the police surveillance of *Hurón* was revealed. Núñez was particularly worried since, while he and Juan Carlos had achieved similar success, they had also engaged in similar extra-legal strategies to do so. Juan Carlos had perhaps crossed the line by secretly running more than one restaurant, accumulating multiple homes, and becoming a quite conspicuous patron of the arts, but his arrest in the spring of 2009 and subsequent imprisonment were quite sobering for Núñez. As a result, Núñez decided to take a trip to Madrid in the summer of 2009 in order to think things over. When he returned to Cuba in August he decided it was over for him as well. As he later explained to his crestfallen employees, it was no longer worth it for him to constantly "live with the strain of state inspectors coming to the restaurant all the time and haggling and negotiating to avoid facing the fate of his then imprisoned friend" (Usborne 2011). "*La Guarida* survived almost everything," the leading exile blog *Penúltimos Días* reported, "but in the end the government's axe came down on it and cut it to pieces, giving the owner the chance to close it today to avoid jail time" of his own (*Penúltimos Días* 2009).

Vignette: "*Paladar Maravillas de Alicia*"

Less dramatic than "*El Hurón Azul*" but equally instructive is the case of the *paladar* "*Maravillas de Alicia*" (Alice's Wonderland), an elegant, spacious, but now defunct *paladar* where Magalis (the waitress from *Las Doce Sillas*) used to work in Miramar. Alicia, the restaurant's former operator, explained that *Maravillas* was given a substantial fine and closed down in October 1998 after a surprise inspection late one night uncovered a single unregistered employee "scrubbing a plate." Alicia was especially frustrated since she had been in business for four and a half years, had invested a substantial amount of money and time in the business, and had never had a previous violation. However, she finally came to accept her fate since she was unable to have her license reinstated after two full years of bureaucratic efforts.

Though she maintained that she was normally scrupulous about following the rules, Alicia did argue that the government's size and seating restrictions placed an artificial limit on her growth potential. "A restaurant is different from a bar," she explained. "A bar has customers all day and all night long. A restaurant, on the other hand, does its most important business between 12:00 and 3:00 p.m. and then comes the dead time. Later, at around 7:30 or 8:00 p.m. it takes off again and lasts until around 10:00 p.m. The biggest problem with the seating restrictions," she argued, "is that if all my customers arrive at the same time, I can't attend to them and they won't wait forever. Nor can I ask those already here to hurry up and finish." Such restrictions forced her to choose between losing business or being flexible with the seating rules when necessary. She chose the latter.

During our interview, she showed me one of the two guest rooms she rents to foreigners to compensate for the loss of her business. Each of the two rooms was well equipped with two beds, a bathroom, and an air-conditioner. However, when I questioned her about the legality of this new activity, she smiled and said simply, "I rent, but I don't rent. Understand? So don't put anything about it down there," pointing to my notebook. As she told me this, however, I recalled the words that a uniformed sentry posted in front of a nearby embassy compound shouted to me as I neared Alicia's home. "If you're looking for the lady who rents rooms," he said warmly, "her house is the one on the corner." As the Cuban saying goes, "*Todo está prohibido, pero vale todo*" (Everything is prohibited, but anything goes) (Henken 2008a).

Taken together, the common use of most of the above survival strategies by licensed *paladar* operators contradicts the assumption that illegality is the result of a lack of adequate top-down control, a deficiency in revolutionary consciousness, or the delinquency of a few individuals out to exploit the masses and "live off the work of others." Undoubtedly, there are those who abuse the system for personal gain, but the vast majority of entrepreneurs bear the burden of Cuba's extensive economic uncertainty, combine a variety of inputs while navigating complex regulations, engage in constant innovation, and make a notoriously inefficient system work effectively, all while providing jobs and licit goods and services to a population in need. Instead of recognizing and encouraging the positive contribution that entrepreneurship could make to the country's economic recovery, the state's antagonistic legal framework as it developed between 1993 and 2006 created an ideological environment where entrepreneurship, even when legal, was still not considered legitimate. As a result, *paladar* operators found it necessary to rely on a host of informal strategies, including bribery, illicit networks of black market supplies, multiple income streams, and a flexible interpretation of self-employment laws to survive.

Paladares in Relation to Other Self-Employment Activities

As mentioned above, self-employment legislation defines four distinct types of licenses allowable for food service occupations: street vending, catering, porch-front cafeterias, and home-based restaurants or *paladares*. Academic studies produced in Cuba (Núñez Moreno 1997; Fernández Peláez 2000) as well as numerous reports in the official Cuban press (Lee 1997c; Lee 1998) have established food service as the most common area of self-employment. For example, Núñez Moreno reported that in April 1996 the food service occupations street vendor and porch-front cafeteria, along with their "family helpers," together made up for over 30% of all licensed self-employed workers (1997: 46).

Following from this kind of characterization, it is often assumed that *paladar* operators also constitute a large proportion of self-employed workers. However, not only do private restaurants not constitute a large portion of all licensed *cuentapropistas*, but neither do they make up large percentage of the licenses issued in the area of food service. The total number of licensed *paladares* never reached beyond 2,000 nationwide, and fell to less than 200 by 2001. In fact, a provincial study of self-employment in Havana published in July 1997 made exactly this point. While there were a total of 8,891 licensed food service operators active in the city at that time, *paladares* accounted for just 5% of this total (445) while porch-front cafeterias made up the majority at 68% (6,046) (DPPFA 1997: 5). Therefore, while the economic impact of these relatively few *paladares* is considerable since they operate and pay taxes in dollars, they are much less important numerically when compared with their much more abundant fellow food service operators.

What characteristics distinguish *paladares* from other self-employment occupations? First of all, on average they are more lucrative than other self-employed activities (recall Mesa-Lago's scale of income inequalities by occupation cited above). This difference is partly due to the fact that *paladares* have become directly connected to the international tourism market and as such operate almost exclusively in dollars or CUCs. For many visitors, these restaurants are both their premier dining experience while on the island and, "above all a 'sociological' experience, a different and authentic way to get to know Cuba," as a journalist from the Spanish daily *El País* once described them (Vicent 2000).

Furthermore, because of the very nature of food service, these operations generate more (private) employment and income than any other self-employment activity (save perhaps their porch-front cafeteria counterparts, which are also authorized to hire "family helpers"). Finally, due to their relative large size and high sales volume, the private restaurants are the closest thing Cuba currently has to a small private business sector. Along with private bed-and-breakfast operations (with which they are sometimes informally linked), *paladares* function based on a fairly complex organization and employment of labor, render multiple services to clients, engage in the intricate preparation of products, and often utilize expensive, high-tech equipment (Fernández Peláez 2000). They also generate strong backward linkages to other areas of the economy, creating employment through their constant demand for goods and services.

These characteristics also help explain why *paladares* have been the target of more state scrutiny and repression when compared to other, more humble and less lucrative areas of self-employment. For example, Cuban sociologist Núñez Moreno placed food service operations atop a four tiered hierarchy of *cuentapropistas* that includes small-scale owners/employers, independent workers, private salaried workers, and unpaid family helpers (1997: 45).

> At the national level, the subgroup of restaurants—the so-called *"paladares"*—and cafeterias have the greatest concentration of registered [self-employed] workers. One can infer that a high-income, high-consumption, and high-lifestyle segment is becoming consolidated within the self-employed sector, with relatively great economic means and possibilities for accumulation. This subgroup would be in the process of configuring itself as a stable and relatively numerous small bourgeoisie, which employees an additional workforce, grouping together around 22% of the officially registered self-employed workers. (Núñez Moreno 1997: 47)

Given this tendency within the food service sector, the government's repressive treatment of *paladares* becomes more understandable. In other words, the transformation of clandestine *paladar* operators into what Núñez Moreno refers to as a "small bourgeoisie" was clearly not the government's intent when it legalized private restaurants in 1995. Apparently, during the 1993-2006 period, the employment opportunities and goods and services provided by *paladares* proved to be less important than the threat they came to represent in terms of a loss of state control.

Ideologically, the existence of an independently wealthy business class flies in the face of the Revolution's traditional commitment to egalitarianism (now explicitly abandoned under Raúl Castro's presidency). As a result, the government has continually raised taxes for *paladares* and publicly reiterated the central principle of the tax system: "whoever earns more pays more" (Lee 1998: 2). While one might think that the economic competition posed by *paladares* to the state food service sector (especially in the tourism sector) could be obviated through increased tax revenue, the fact is that all personal income taxes (of which *paladares* contribute only a fraction) together made up less than two percent of the annual state budget in the late-1990s as self-employment was being phased out (Lee 1997b: 2). Therefore, the economic threat presented by the *paladar* is more a function of the liberating character of non-state employment and income. In other words, the growth of private employment and income represents a latent political threat to state power since it erodes the ideals of state ownership of the means of production, the central plan, and especially universal state employment (as discussed in Chapter 2).

Economic freedom leads to greater political freedom, since it allows normally dependent workers to disconnect from the state. Thus, though Fidel's government was said to have considered for a time allowing for the existence of a legally constituted private business sector (Mesa-Lago 2000: 619), in the end it rejected this possibility and declared that the only small business sector in Cuba would be a "perfected" sector of small state enterprises. Raúl's re-ignition of self-employment described in Chapter 5 and his concomitant efforts to reinvent the Cuban cooperative described in Chapter 6 to may indicate that this calculus has changed.[22] We now turn to how the Cuban *paladar* has fared since 2010.

The 2010 Rebirth of the *Paladar*: Is the Third Time the Charm?

> Self-employment in Cuba: The sum of a Haitian bazaar, a Swedish tax rate, and North Korean political representation. Quite a model for the 21st century.
> —*Twitter feed of Manuel Cuesta Morúa* (@Cubaprogresista), April 13, 2013

In our interviews with Cuba's microentrepreneurs over the past 15 years, we occasionally heard them intone one of the two following old Cuban/Spanish sayings: "*El ojo del amo engorda el caballo*" (roughly translated as, "The eye of the owner fattens the horse") and "*El que tenga tienda que la atienda (o si no que la venda)*" (Whoever has a store should tend to it, and if not then sell it). The first of these adages seeks to convey the wisdom that the quality and efficiency of a good or service naturally improve when the person performing the job enjoys a degree of autonomy and has a personal stake in the outcome. The second saying warns the Cuban government that if it is unwilling or unable to "tend to its own store," that is, provide quality goods and services to the population, then it has no right to punish Cubans for bettering their lives through their own efforts. In essence, these pieces of popular wisdom demand that the government turn over to the people those economic activities it cannot run well—many of which are already widely practiced in what we have called the "legitimate underground"—because doing so would increase production, efficiency, and general welfare—not to mention the bottom line for Cuban entrepreneurs themselves.

However, the recentralization and retrenchment that took place in the Cuban economy between 1996 and 2006 indicated that Fidel Castro continued to prefer a skinny socialist horse to a fat capitalist one.[23] More aware of the political risks that popular entrepreneurship would pose to his centralized control than of the economic benefits it could provide to the population, he was neither ideologically disposed nor politically willing to cede more than a token portion of the state "store" to the ingenuity of the Cuban people. In sum, although the socialist horse may be a skinny one, it is easy to control and we all know who gets to ride in the saddle.

The underlying goal of economic reforms in socialist states has everywhere been the same: To perfect and preserve socialism. Indeed, these are the very goals expressed in the "*Lineamientos*" document approved at the Sixth Congress of the Cuban Communist Party in April 2011, under the direction not of Fidel but now Raúl who has himself consistently reminded any doubters, "I was not elected president to restore capitalism in Cuba or to surrender the Revolution. I was elected to defend, maintain, and continue perfecting socialism, not to destroy it" (Castro 2010, quoted in Corrales 2012). In fact, Eastern European economic reforms failed to "perfect and preserve socialism" and the role of the second economy in eroding and undermining key state economic institutions (state ownership, the central plan, and universal state employment) was clearly subversive there. Given this history, Fidel Castro's open rejection of the reform path taken in Eastern Europe is understandable. Reforms accomplished few of their stated goals, destroyed leadership's control over labor, and deprived leaders of a social base. They also created new, increasingly powerful and wealthy interest groups who pushed back against efforts to reign in initial reforms (Róna-Tas 1997).

Learning from these lessons, up until 2006 the Cuban government was able to squeeze enough benefits from its initial economic reforms in the 1990s to survive the worst years of the special period (Corrales 2004). However, a change in leadership combined with recent conjunctural economic developments in both the domestic and international spheres (outlined in Chapter 5) have increased the urgency and perhaps the inevitability of undertaking deeper and more irreversible economic reforms. Moreover, unlike his elder brother Fidel, Raúl Castro seems convinced of the wisdom of the above pair of popular sayings and has begun to slowly but deliberately shrink the state "store," allowing Cuban workers to take some of it over or open and tend their own (Frank 2013b). He has also shown a curiosity about the alternate path of economic reform undertaken in China and Vietnam, which has so far proven uniquely successful in achieving economic growth while maintaining political stability and one-party rule.

Although to date, Raúl's reforms are still far less ambitious or successful than what has taken place in these Asian cases of "market socialism," his changes have directly resulted in a significant increase in the *quantity* of legal entrepreneurship, as his policies no longer force the bulk of entrepreneurs into the underground (LUEAs) as described in Chapter 7. This is reflected in a dramatic three-fold growth in the overall numbers of registered *cuentapropistas* (from roughly 150,000 in 2010 to over 470,000 by July 2014) and—as we will see below—in an almost fifteen-fold growth in the numbers of *paladares* (from just 113 in October 2010 to 1,651 by May of 2012, to perhaps more than 2,000 by 2013). However, as we also indicate below, much more remains to be done in reforming public policy toward microenterprise to sufficiently alter the *quality* of self-employment so that it is truly transformed from a marginal, survival-oriented activity into one that contributes to enterprise innovation, productive employment, and economic growth (Whitefield 2013).

Initial Reforms and Subsequent Adjustments, October 2010-December 2011

Imbedded in the initial self-employment legislation published in October 2010 were a group of small but symbolically significant changes that had a direct impact on *paladares*, other similar food service occupations, and bed-and-breakfasts. These changes included the issuing of licenses for new private restaurants, something not seen for more than a decade. Additionally, the requirement that all workers be "family helpers" was lifted, as were the infamous policies that had limited *paladares* to just 12 chairs and severely restricted the foods that they could serve. Additionally, Cuba's B&B operators could now rent out their entire homes (eliminating the previous limit of just two rooms), rent by the hour, and those who possessed legal "permission to reside abroad"—known as "*el PRE*"—would now be allowed to rent out their residences while out of the country and designate a representative to handle the rental for them in their absence (DDC 2010; Peters 2012a). Initially, however, the seating limit for *paladares* was only raised to 20—indicating the continuance of a mentality of bureaucratic control and arbitrary limits on private enterprise and wealth generation. Likewise, the planning and sequencing of the initial reforms seemed wrongheaded since no credit or wholesale markets were made available to support these new enterprises and it seemed that mass layoffs in the state sector would begin *before* the self-employed sector was up and running (Gálvez Chiú 2010; Ritter 2010). The marginal improvements in the tax structure as it relates to *paladares* were described in Chapter 5.

Despite the problems with these initial adjustments, the new self-employment regulations did in fact "distance [Raúl's policies] from those [of Fidel] that condemned self-employment to near extinction" in the 1990s, as *Granma* so succinctly put it in fall 2010 (Martínez Hernández 2010). Perhaps the most revolutionary change in regulations directly impacting *paladares* was the allowance of the hiring of contracted labor in 83 of the 178 originally legalized occupations (later expanded to all), something not seen since 1968 (*Gaceta Oficial* 2010a,b; Martínez Molina et al 2011). Moreover, while the previous incarnation of self-employment allowed only retirees and those holding down a state job to become self-employed, this time anyone could do so—opening the floodgates to applicants from the informal sector (who have in fact dominated self-employment making up perhaps two-thirds of all new licensees). Furthermore, for the first time a single individual or household could obtain a license in more than one occupation—a change that would theoretically allow *paladar* operators to legalize many of the informal, auxiliary economic activities they had commonly engaged in under the cover of their food service license as described in multiple cases above (Magda's "*La Azotea*," Juan Carlos' "*El Hurón Azul*," Arturo's "*Paladar del Mar*," and Alicia's "*Maravillas*"). *Paladares* could also expand beyond the owner's own home as other spaces—even government spaces—could now be rented out to enterprising CPs so they could run private businesses out of them (*Gaceta Oficial* 2010a; Martínez Hernández 2010; Peters 2010a).

For example, the long-time state sector chef Justo Pérez jumped at the chance to realize the dream of opening his own restaurant, which he inaugurated in early December 2010 with the very appropriate name "*La Comercial Cubana*"[24] in an elegantly restored home in Centro Habana. "There are many people waiting to do this," explained Pérez to a foreign journalist. "This is only the beginning. I'm sure that there will be many good proposals [since] the rules of the game seem very clear, much more so than before." However, Pérez was wise to temper his enthusiasm with a dose of well-earned realism given what happened to *paladares* the last time around. "Still," he insisted, "until this [experiment] is fully implemented no one knows how it will end" (*Cubaencuentro* 2010c).

Around the same time, the previously described Centro Habana *paladar* "*La Guarida*"—one of Cuba's most famous and long lasting private restaurants—made the decision to reopen its doors after being "closed for repairs" for more than a year, also motivated by the apparent change in government mentality behind the new self-employment regulations. Its founder and proprietor Enrique Núñez explained his decision to the international press saying, "Now *La Guarida* reopens in an optimistic context; one in which we will be able to work. I never thought that the opening would be so rapid," he added. "Conditions are very favorable now [and] I can say that right now I am running the place completely by the book," he explained, noting that he now employed (and paid taxes for) ten workers under the new "contracted labor" policy, four of whom were chefs (*Cubaencuentro* 2010b; Usborne 2011).[25]

The *Lineamientos* also made clear Cuban authorities' intent to avoid "the concentration of ownership" (Miroff 2012c), so as to "prevent citizens from achieving greater economic freedom with which they could advocate for more political freedom" (Espinosa Chepe and Henken 2013: 167). This intention is evident in the introduction of a steep system of taxation for the emerging self-employed sector; one more severe and restrictive than that which applies to joint ventures (as indicated in Chapter 5). On the positive side, the new tax regime significantly increases tax deductions—especially important for *paladares*—allowing the self-employed to deduct up to 40 percent from income for the cost of inputs (but still well below the true input costs for most *paladars*), compared to just 10 percent under the old tax regime. However, the new system also includes five different, and at times overlapping kinds of tax on *cuentapropistas*, making it potentially much more cumbersome, confusing, and costly than the old one (Frank 2010; Peters 2010b).

A pair of continuing problems keenly felt by larger-scale, input-dependent operations like *paladares*, is the fact that the reformed self-employed sector was launched without first creating wholesale markets or assuring access to credit. Therefore, "business owners have no place to turn where they can purchase inputs or obtain loans under reasonable conditions. Instead, they are forced by the circumstances to rely on expensive hard currency stores [...] or the black market for inputs, and on relatives or loan sharks for credit" (Espinosa Chepe and Henken 2013: 168). The late independent economist Óscar Espinosa Chepe anticipated that the lack of sources for legal credit and supplies wiould likely lead to an expansion in the black market as a way to meet this new demand for investment and inputs—thus counteracting the expected shrinkage of the underground that should normally result from operations becoming formally licensed.

Perhaps most interestingly for the future growth of the *paladar* and larger food service sector, underperforming state enterprises—mainly in food service—were to be identified, closed, and transferred or transformed into private or cooperative businesses allowing "the premises to be better utilized by renting to the self-employed" (*Cubaencuentro* 2011a; Peters 2011a)—the same strategy previously implemented with success with taxis in 2008 and beauticians and barber shops in 2010 (Morales 2011). In late December 2011, this same strategy was expanded once again to include a number of personal, technical, and household services previously performed by state employees—such as carpenters, photographers, locksmiths, and a wide array of repairmen (Peters 2011c; Café Fuerte 2011). Finally, a handful of other small changes were enacted, including expanding the seating limit for *paladares* from 20 up to 50 along with a 25% reduction in the fixed minimum monthly fee required of Cuba's bed-and-breakfast operations (Espinosa Chepe and Henken 2013: 173).

Recent Paladar Growth amid Continuing Ambivalence, 2012-2014

Despite evidence of a significant change in mentality toward self-employment, government announcements from the first half of 2012 that had confidently projected as many as 600,000 CPs by the end of the year (*Opciones* 2012) had to be scaled back when statistics revealed that there were in fact still less than 400,000 by October 2012 (Peters 2013a). This development also forced the government to concede that the necessary 1.5-1.8 million state sector layoffs would have to be postponed with the half-million layoffs originally slated for April 2011 now targeted for 2015 (Peters 2013a). This slower than expected shift from state employment to self-employment over the next two years indicated that the leadership's mental shift was a necessary but still insufficient element in achieving the goals set out by Raúl Castro himself between 2010 and 2011.

For these goals to be achieved, a number of other key elements are still lacking. For example, despite further reforms during 2012 and 2013 and the continued growth of the non-state, self-employed sector, a fundamental obstacle continues to be the leadership's ambivalence toward any reform that recognizes full property rights and the creation of wealth in private hands, not to mention greater civil liberties or political rights (Corrales 2012: 178). Additionally, investment capital and disposable income in the pockets of Cuban consumers is still lacking. Cuban activist Eliécer Ávila has argued that this is necessary "so that investors are willing to take risks, search for credit, and seek out alternatives. No one," he reasons, "will risk anything in order to sell to skinny ghosts and neutral onlookers" (*fantasmas flacos y mirones neutros*) (2012). A final necessary element in pushing the reform agenda forward is an equal mental shift on the part of the thousands of anonymous—and self-interested—bureaucrats upon whom Raúl relies to implement his reforms (Domínguez 2012).

Statistics reported in *Trabjadores* between May and July 2012 revealed

Vignette: "*El Rinconcito*" and "*Buen Provecho*" in 2011

In April 2011, upon returning to revisit Patricia, the proprietor of "*El Rinconcito*," she informed us that as the political climate for *paladares* worsened in the early 2000s, she decided to turn in her license and continue to operate her *paladar* underground. However, given her estimation that the changes announced in September 2010 amounted to a significant shift in mentality, she eventually applied for and quickly received a new license in January 2011. When asked specifically what kind of food service license she had obtained, she replied "for a *paladar*, you know what they like to call here: '*elaborador—vendedor de alimentos y bebidas con servicio gastronómico*' (maker and seller of food and beverages with gastronomic service). No, no, medieval. It's a medieval name for someone's occupation!" Still, she argued that she reentered licensed self-employment because:

> this time around the government seems to have the full intention of supporting us private entrepreneurs. Instead of doing what they did before, which was always get in our way and make the process arduous, now there is support. But we wouldn't be in the sorry state we are in if they would have set up this same frame of possibilities years ago. Not physical possibilities but legal ones.

And though she said that she fully intends to succeed given the new more favorable domestic context, she lamented the fact that the government had to wait until a global recession to realize the error of its ways and change course. "Perhaps it's too late," she added wistfully.

When asked to identify specific changes in the law that had been beneficial to her since reopening, Patricia listed the most common and obvious changes including permitting larger sized operations (more than 12 chairs), the hiring of non-family employees, and allowing all foods to be served. "Luckily, we don't have to lie so much any more," she added. "We are approaching a more logical situation, more normal state of affairs. In fact," she emphasized, "we are approaching a normalcy that people were loudly demanding." Still, she explained that the country now finds itself in the middle of a momentous transformation, while not knowing exactly where it is headed.

> We entrepreneurs are still caught in a strange situation where we are forced to exist in a very narrow legal framework where our ability to do business with other enterprises is very limited, very poor. I'm not sure up to what point a country can be half socialist and half capitalist. Who knows? But what I do know is that what's most important is not one system or the other, but simply letting people be free. Letting them make decisions for themselves and respecting the legal framework.

Continues

Located further west of *El Rinconcito* in the tony district of Miramar, the *paladar "Buen Provecho"* was originally inaugurated in June of 1993—when it was not yet fully legal to do so—and has remained in operation continuously ever since. Its uniqueness lies in its effort to create a fusion between Italian and Cuban Creole cuisines. The founder of the *paladar* is named Miriam Infante but by April 2011, when the interview took place, Miriam had begun to spend the majority of her time in Spain (where she has dual citizenship) and taken a back seat to her nephew Alfredo who worked as one of the principal chefs and managed the restaurant on a day-to-day basis. Alfredo said that their specialization in Italian food did not take shape until after they had been in business for a few years and noticed that pastas and pizzas appealed to a wide array of international tourists—who still make up as much as 90% of their clientele—and especially to Italian visitors who were quite common (even "too common" according to Alfredo) in the late-1990s.

He claimed that the operation was run for many years with "family help," as was required by law. But now that the new regulations allow for contracted, non-family employees, they have tried to bring in more workers with experience and specialized training. There are now a total of 15 employees in all. In fact, Alfredo is a highly trained gastronome himself, having graduated from Eusebio Leal's Advanced School in *Habana Vieja* as a chef. As manager of the restaurant, Alfredo has also instituted innovations in advertising by systematically canvassing the areas near foreign embassies and large hard currency shops with flyers and business cards. He has also set up a website that allows foreigners to make reservations on-line. Those who do so receive a complimentary cocktail and a 10% discount when they arrive for dinner. "People like those small details and want to feel welcome," he said.

When questioned about his biggest challenges in running the *paladar*, Alfredo claimed that they have always avoided paying commissions but he immediately cited the ongoing difficulty he has in obtaining a stable supply of the foods and special ingredients he needs. "We are somewhat lucky in that the owner, my aunt Miriam, has Spanish citizenship and lives a good part of the time there." He explained that she often purchases things on credit in Spain and ships or brings them back to Cuba when she travels. Alfredo added that many successful *paladar* owners have used this strategy, some even becoming Spanish citizens for the expressed purpose of accessing goods so as to supply their restaurants from abroad. The alternative, he explained were "the scarce and excessively expensive products available at Cuban hard currency stores. This leads to our inability to always serve what we have on the

> menu. It's quite a catastrophic situation." However, Alfredo also claimed that this reality has forced him to be more creative, always making changes to the menu and making suggestions of daily specials for customers. Still, Alfredo pointed out another "supply side" problem:
>
>> The excessive prices we find in the stores are what force us to drive up our own prices as well, because we have to make all our purchases of inputs at state-run retail stores, unlike the state owned restaurants, which enjoy access to wholesale goods at incredible prices in turn allowing them to keep their prices very low.
>
> On the bright side, Alfredo said that he had seen a marked change for the good in the behavior and professionalism of the inspectors. "This has significantly stabilized since the new measures came out last year," he explained. "In the past the kind of people who typically worked as inspectors were not well trained and had low culture. They came looking for things and creating problems, if you know what I mean." However, Alfredo stressed that with the new measures for *paladares* and self-employment under Raúl has also come a new, more supportive mentality.
>
>> Even the minister came on television and spoke in support of CPs. I think that that will send a helpful message to the new inspectors. Just let us work. We want to work. It's fine for them to put someone there to control us, but not to come looking for or creating problems. They should just let us work, especially since in the end we are the ones who keep the government running with our taxes.

for the first time the rapid expansion in the numbers of *paladares* since 2010. For example, while Havana could count just 74 *paladares* in October 2010 (down from hundreds in the late-1990s), there were a total of 376 by May 2012 (*Trabajadores* 2012b), with only four reported cases of licenses being revoked (Yhanes 2012). Expansion was even more impressive nationwide with the 113 total number of *paladares* of October 2010 growing more than 15-fold to 1,651 by May 2012 (*Trabajadores* 2012c). To this could be added the 5,207 B&Bs, many of which were new given the more flexible regulations and lower tax rates (DDC 2012c). Looking more closely at the popular private food service sector we find that street vendors have become the most numerous by far (with 46,200 registered as *cuentapropistas*). This is followed by cafeterias (also known as "*puntos fijos*," with 9,060), which is followed in turn by *paladares* (1,651) and caterers (*a domicilio*, 713) (*Trabajadores* 2012c; Beaton Ruiz et al 2012; Perdomo 2012).

Aimed at spurring this demonstrated growth of the non-state sector further, the 2012–2014 period witnessed the introduction of a number of quite unprecedented food service projects that—as we say above with reference to the *caballo* and the *tienda*—essentially concede to the popular wisdom that demands that the government transfer to the people economic activities it cannot run well (Orsi 2012; Havana Times 2012; González Mirabal 2012; Frank 2013b; Frank and Valdés 2014). However, this concession is a mixed one in practice since as with the transfer of taxis, barber shops and beauty salons, and certain kinds of services, the workers who become self-employed in these areas do not do so with any concomitant property rights over their businesses, the physical real estate, or the equipment used in the performance of their jobs (*Trabajadores* 2012d; *Cubaencuentro* 2012; *Cubadebate* 2012). They also must pay taxes and rent to the state landlord and cover the costs of all supplies, electricity, and other utilities out of pocket—though there are some tax exemptions and rent reductions built into the programs in special cases (Café Fuerte 2012).

For example, in fall 2013 more than 20 state restaurants began to transition into employee-run cooperatives as part of a pilot program that—if successful—would be expanded throughout the island essentially doing away with state-run restaurants (Cuba Central Blog 2013). This is indeed good news for Cuban entrepreneurs and customers alike as it hints that the government is indeed ready to begin to turn the "state store"—at least in this small area of the retail sector—over to co-op workers themselves. "The government is hoping that cooperative owners," reasons Brookings Institution fellow Richard Feinberg, "with pride in their establishments and motivated by profits, will offer much better service and higher quality goods to customers, both tourists and fellow Cubans" (Frank 2013b). However, this shift is also motivated by the state's desire to—in Raúl Castro's own words—"relieve itself" of non-strategic economic activities (a decision imposed from on high), without also extending full ownership and property rights to the new "owners" of these cooperatives (Frank and Valdés 2014). Still, at least one perceptive Cuban observer has embraced this shift on purely pragmatic grounds as it means more autonomy for Cuba's entrepreneurs and more choice for customers:

> Some will consider these projects to be examples of small capitalist enterprise, others will label them cooperatives. I dare say that at this point Cubans are more interested in prosperity than terminology. In the end, as the late Deng Xiaoping would say, "It matters not the color of the cat, what is important is whether it can catch mice." (Rodríguez López 2013)[26]

Conclusion: *La Opera de la Calle's "El Cabildo"*—Omen or Anomaly?

While President Raúl Castro has shown himself to be more serious and pragmatic in his reform agenda than was Fidel, he is also ruling over a weakened state relative to the "command and obey" government apparatus created by his elder brother. (Fidel was known as *"El Comandante"* for a reason). Moreover, this weakened governing structure inherited by Raúl is itself facing what has been described by the eminent Cuban-American political scientist Jorge Domínguez as a "bureaucratic insurgency" (2012: 273). This epidemic of self-interested foot-dragging on the part of some public officials has been cited by Cuban economist Ricardo Torres as one of the main internal factors hindering the economic reforms. "People's minds are the hardest thing to change," he argues. "If they have done something a certain way for 50 years, it is not easy for them to agree to do it differently [...]. In fact, in some cases, that learning process will be impossible."

At the same time, Torres recognized a more intentional and perhaps intractable aim on the part of some bureaucrats to derail or at least delay the full implementation of reforms that ultimately threaten their interests since they undercut their power as gatekeepers over entrepreneurs—who are often cash rich but bureaucratically poor.

> The changes are affecting certain groups and segments of the population, which, therefore, are going to oppose them, using whatever resources they have within their reach to prevent or at least hinder their progress. It is a natural reaction by people to protect themselves against whatever may affect them. (Torres, cited in Grogg 2012)

Likewise, Domínguez has pointed out the "extraordinary frustration" evident in many of Raúl Castro's speeches confronted as he is with routine procrastination or even scheming defiance from many lower level officials who resist implementing his policies (2012: 273). This was the main focus of his brief remarks that closed the August 2011 National Assembly meetings where he forcefully argued that the greatest threat to the revolution was not imperialism but "our own errors," adding that the greatest obstacle standing in the way of change were in fact "archaic mentalities" and "the psychological barrier formed by inertia, immobility, simulation or *la doble moral* [two-facedness], indifference, and insensitivity." Then, making a direct reference to bureaucratic foot-dragging at implementing the *Lineamientos* approved just four months earlier at that April's Sixth Party Congress, he assured his listeners: "We will be patient and persevere in the face of all resistance to change, conscious or not. [But] I warn you that all bureaucratic resistance to the strict implementation of the accords [...] will be futile" (quoted in Peters 2011c; *Cubaencuentro* 2011b).

The striking irony here is that while public policy toward microenterprise under Fidel was often very bad, officials and bureaucrats treated those policies as orders to be obeyed and implemented. After all, one of the most common phrases used to celebrate Fidel's leadership style has long been the militaristic: "*¡Comandante en Jefe, ordene!*" (Commander-in-Chief, at your order). In contrast, Raúl's much more pragmatic, rational, and potentially productive policies are often received by lower level bureaucrats as threatening reforms to be resisted and undermined. Again, Domínguez notes the unprecedented nature of this bureaucratic insurgency:

> Cuba's government has weakened. It has weakened because its own officials resist the implementation of new policies. The government has weakened because its own bureaucracy engages in petty acts of insurgency. Raúl Castro's government has weakened because communist party officials, for the first time in a half-century, are beginning to assert their authority in policy setting over government agents and decision makers. (Domínguez 2012: 274)

Thus, although Raúl's public policies toward microenterprise since 2006 have been much more encouraging than were his brother's between 1993 and 2006, it is unclear whether he possesses the ability (or authority) to have his policies fully and consistently implemented on the ground. Put differently, while the "updated" policies toward self-employment so far devised by Raúl Castro may be a welcome, even unprecedented improvement over the past ones "that condemned self-employment to near extinction and stigmatized those who decided to joint its ranks legally" (Martínez Hernández 2010), devising a new system—and new policies—is only half the battle. Other equally fearful dangers lurk in the challenge of making the new system work, a task entrusted to Cuba's all important bureaucrats who actually implement (or not) the decisions made on high.

Having already described the impressive growth of self-employment between 2010 and 2014—along with the record number of new *paladares* and other private food service operations—we conclude here by briefly chronicling the ominous (or perhaps anomalous) case of the unique if now sadly defunct *paladar*-cum-dinner theater known as "*El Cabildo*," run for a time by the Cuban Opera virtuoso Maestro Ulises Aquino together with his troupe, "*La Ópera de la Calle*." As with the cases of "*La Guarida*" and "*El Hurón Azul*" described above, the fate of "*El Cabildo*" is instructive since it reveals both the promise and the peril of mounting a successful private enterprise in Raúl's Cuba. The case of *El Cabildo* also highlights the limits of tolerance (or perhaps the limits of power) of Raúl's government, as well as the fundamental ambivalence it continues to harbor toward self-employment and private "enrichment."

During the summer of 2012, four Havana-based foreign journalists—Marc Frank of *Reuters*, the *BBC*'s Fernando Ravsberg, Nick Miroff of *NPR* and *Global Post*, and *CNN*'s Patrick Oppmann—each published installments in the ongoing and as yet unresolved case of the *paladar* restaurant and cabaret *El Cabildo* and it's in-house theater company, *La Ópera de la Calle*. The innovative entrepreneurial genius of *El Cabildo* and its mastermind proprietor and emcee Ulises Aquino was to combine a project that celebrated and showcased the richness and diversity of Cuban culture with a tourist-friendly *paladar* (McAuliff 2012; Opera de la Calle 2012a). In order to do this, Aquino took advantage of the newfound flexibility in the self-employment legislation by taking out not one but three *paladar* licenses (legally allowing him to host 150 patrons at once), along with a fourth license as an "organizer of events and other activities" (Frank 2012a).

Already quite well known in Cuba for his success at bringing the often elitist fine art of classical opera to the people by repackaging it in a style that was both uplifting and accessible (thus the name, *Ópera de la Calle*, or Street Opera), Aquino's signature show was also very Cuban (Ópera 2012a). It was a creative fusion of the powerful vocals of traditional opera, the flash and fun of a Broadway musical, and the gritty, home-grown characters and rhythms of the Cuban "street," with equal parts Spanish *zarzuela* (musical comedy) and Afro-Cuban folklore—in other words, a true representation of Cuban Creole culture (McAuliff 2012; Ravsberg 2012a).

While the full *Ópera de la Calle* company performed at *El Cabildo* on Friday and Saturday nights filling the stage with as many as 40 performers at once and bringing in the lion's share of the revenue based on the $25 cover charge for hard currency paying foreign tourists, on weekday evenings individual members of the company had the run of the piano bar where they were able to develop their skills and share their personal projects in a more intimate setting (León 2013). On Sunday nights the whole affair became a discotheque (McAuliff 2012). This innovative strategy allowed Aquino to pay the quite generous salaries of his almost 130 employees and cover his extensive overhead costs (including monthly taxes of 20,000 pesos [$833] and supplies purchased at retail prices from the state), while at the same time providing affordable access to Cuban patrons, who in fact made up the vast majority of the clientele and paid a cover charge of just $2 (50 pesos) to see the show (Frank 2012a).

Though the theater troupe itself was founded in 2006, it had been operating out of its newly refurbished home—the *paladar El Cabildo*—for just over a year when *Reuters* correspondent and long-time Havana resident Marc Frank paid a visit. Quite taken with the uniquely large scale and dramatic back story of the operation as a kind of sign of Cuba's changing economic times, on July 11 Frank published the provocatively entitled article, "In Cuba, an Opera Singer Builds an Empire," breathlessly qualifying the establishment as Havana's "largest private business and perhaps a harbinger of things to come" under Raúl (2012a).

What was particularly striking about the operation in Frank's estimation was that it was born out of a felicitous combination of Aquino's individual entrepreneurial initiative and his clear commitment to community uplift and revolutionary activism at a time of economic opening. In fact, the article made a point of emphasizing *El Cabildo*'s sponsorship of free cultural and educational activities on weekend mornings for area children, the low peso cover charge for the weekend *Ópera de la Calle* show, and the sharing of the revenues among the performers and support staff on the theatrical side of the operation, as well as among the waiters and chefs on the *paladar* side—each of whom earned between 1,800 and 2,000 pesos a month (roughly four times Cuba's average monthly salary of 450 pesos, or $20) (ibid.).

"It is not enough to have an ugly socialism," Frank quoted Aquino as insisting. "It has to be more beautiful than the other systems so everyone will embrace the idea" (Frank 2012a). To that end, in the nine months leading up the April 28, 2011 grand opening Aquino invested his considerable savings from years of international touring and with the help of the members of his theater company transformed a vacant lot filled with the remnants of one of Havana's many ruined buildings into a showplace (Monzó 2012; Yhanes 2012; Ópera 2012a, b). His patriotic confidence in Raúl's new, more encouraging policy toward citizen-led, do-it-yourself initiatives came across powerfully when he argued, "The country has moved on from a tendency to degrade things," noting to Frank that, "the government's policy is to support this type of phenomena [where] an artist, or a worker, or a farmer can put his own means of production to work to help meet the goals of the nation" (ibid.). Frank's article closed with an inadvertently ironic quote from the Cuban economist Rafael Betancourt, a specialist on local development at the National Association of Cuban Economists, who said that Aquino's successful enterprise was only one of many other similar projects in the works that would help spread Cuban culture by harnessing the power of individual initiative. "*El Cabildo* is just the beginning," he insisted (ibid.).

While Frank's article served as a great introduction to *El Cabildo* and its resourceful and revolutionary founder and director—providing free global advertising syndicated through *Reuters* in a country sorely lacking in any internal PR industry apart from the Party controlled mass media—perhaps the journalist should have left the word "empire" to government (or Madison avenue) propagandists. Even though journalists rarely write the headlines for their copy, soon after the article was published the provocative headline caught the attention of none other than the Ideological Department of the Provincial Communist Party of Havana who called Aquino in for questioning. Apparently unimpressed with his business plan that included multiple *paladar* licenses and a cover charge, authorities carried out a surprise raid on *El Cabildo* on Saturday evening, July 21, interrupting his show and pulling him off the stage as the shocked audience looked on (Frank 2012b). They then proceeded to carry out a 4-hour "commando" inspection that Aquino himself later qualified as "fascist," despite the fact "only three days before Raúl had argued for the need for a change in people's mentality" (Ravsberg 2012a; *DDC* 2012b).

As was later reported by *BBC* correspondent Fernando Ravsberg, in the end, Aquino was stripped of his various business licenses for a two year period and accused of a number of economic crimes including having too many chairs (150) for a private restaurant, serving products whose origins could not be determined, having unauthorized employees, and, most galling of all for the proud revolutionary opera singer, of "undue enrichment" since he charged his patrons a $2 cover without authorization and paid his employees what were considered exorbitant salaries (Ravsberg 2012a). All this took Aquino quite by surprise, given the fact that both Rafael Bernal, Cuba's Vice Minister of Culture, and Edel Rodríguez, the President of the Municipality of Playa where *El Cabildo* is located, had attended the grand opening of the dinner theater in April 2011, roundly praising Aquino and his troupe for having successfully transformed an abandoned lot into a cultural oasis. In the case of Rodríguez, Aquino was also singled out for "not having lost his connection with his Cuban roots" despite his international stardom and for consistently "working together with the authorities of People's Power and the local municipality" (Ópera 2012a).

Not one to endure challenges to his honor in silence, Aquino began to protest what he considered an arbitrary, destructive, and disproportionate punishment both in comments to the international press and in a series of open letters circulated among Cuban artists and intellectuals via e-mail and posted on the Internet. For example, he told *CNN* correspondent Patrick Oppmann that the faceless bureaucrats who dared accuse him of illicit enrichment had made a high profile mistake that shouldn't be hushed up in order to prevent it from happening again. He also said that he considered the whole ordeal a "tremendous test" of the will and strength of the government in the face of an opportunistic and destructive bureaucratic class (Oppmann 2012; Ópera 2012b). In many ways, it was a case of the artist armed with poetry, proverbs, and righteous indignation against the bureaucratic insurgency going on within a divided and weakened state under a new leader attempting to enact far reaching and much needed reforms.

For Aquino, the clear if shrouded impetus behind the shut-down of his successful operation came from "a hidden fifth column" within the government bureaucracy "that is attempting to stop the unstoppable movement that's being promoted by President Raúl Castro. They are a bureaucratic class trying to preserve their power from a position of obscurantism," he railed. Turning the tables on the bureaucrats, Aquino attempted to take the revolutionary high ground, claiming to *BBC* reporter Fernando Ravsberg, "It hurts most because I'm a revolutionary and I believe deeply in the humanistic work of the revolution" (2012a). In the first of his three open letters, he alleged that the closure of *El Cabildo* had nothing to do with any supposed illegalities, but sprang from the opportunism and jealousy of conservative elements within the state bureaucracy.

> Those who started this fight are afraid that the worker, the intellectual, and the artist might find their own productive path. They are not revolutionaries but conservatives who enjoy the comforts of power that give them the ability, as in this case, to make decisions about the destiny of other people's creations, not to help them flourish but to destroy them. (Ópera 2012b; Frank 2012b)

NPR correspondent Nick Miroff followed up with an insightful report that indicated that the case had sent shock waves through Cuba's fledging community of private entrepreneurs since Aquino seems to have been punished for doing exactly what the government of Raúl Castro had been energetically promoting for nearly two years: creating well-paying jobs in the non-state sector, producing higher quality goods and services, and reducing the economic burden on the government. However, it seems that not everyone—especially those Aquino called "mid-level bureaucrats endangered by all these new opportunities [who] see Cuba changing and know that they're going to lose their power"—was on board with tolerating, much less promoting, Cuba's new entrepreneurial sector (Miroff 2012a).

In a follow up story at *Global Post*, Miroff noted that *El Cabildo* had quickly become a test case whose outcome would show just how serious Raúl Castro's government is about the depth and permanence of its economic reforms. "If they intervene to help re-open *El Cabildo*," wrote Miroff, "they will send a clear signal that Cuba's new small businesses deserve encouragement, not strangulation" (2012b). However, if the operation which employed as many as 120 workers (having quickly become perhaps the largest private business on the island) is left to die a bureaucratic death, it will show "that the skeptics are right, and Cuba hasn't changed much after all" (2012a). Miroff also noted the lesson other entrepreneurs will inevitably draw if this cautionary tale is not openly, forcefully addressed from on high:

> [I]f *El Cabildo* stays closed, it can send a different message about Cuba's incipient capitalism: that new entrepreneurs here should not be too ambitious with their plans or too proud of their success. And any business, no matter how big, can be shut down on a whim, if a local official orders it so. (2012b)

If that happens, Miroff notes that Aquino will have lost, but quotes him as saying: "The [real] loser here won't be me. It'll be our country" (Miroff 2012b).

Epilogue

In the more than two years since *El Cabildo* was shuttered, Aquino has made no headway in getting approval to reopen. The *BBC*'s Ravsberg noted that soon after the closure, Aquino received encouraging public support from the Ministry of Culture's National Council of the Performing Arts (NCPA), which advised him in a July 28, 2012 communiqué that *La Ópera de La Calle* would be able to "maintain their activities as a funded community cultural project" (2012b). However, the NCPA was silent about the issue of the loss of independent funding, which had come from the *paladar* side of the *El Cabildo* operation, an economic activity controlled not at the national, ministerial level but by bureaucrats in the provincial and municipal governments (*DDC* 2012a; CubaNet 2012; López Corzo 2012; Nieves Cárdenas 2012). In April 2013 Aquino was given a brief glimmer of hope when the Ministry of Culture informed him that none other than U.S. entertainer Beyoncé Knowles would be visiting Cuba and had specifically requested to see his show. However, after rousing his troupe and rushing to reopen *El Cabildo*, Aquino was intercepted once again by functionaries from Havana's provincial government and the capital city's Communist Party who overruled the Ministry and forced the troupe to perform elsewhere—and without the presence of the American star (*DDC* 2013a; Ravsberg 2013a).

Likewise, while a review posted in the summer of 2013 on Trip Advisor excitedly claimed that "*La Ópera de la Calle* returns," in fact the post reported that the show reemerged in March 2013 now as a free, state-sponsored public concert under the aegis of the Ministry of Culture. Furthermore, given the state's meager resources and the fact that the show no longer earns any revenue of its own, it has been moved to Playa's *Teatro Arenal*, "a very rundown facility that lacks the charming ambience, as well as the food and cocktail service of it's former location" (Trip Advisor 2013). Worse still, Aquino's former success at providing affordable access to a Cuban clientele (and spreading earnings liberally among his Cuban employees) has been lost. Now admission is tightly controlled by the Ministry of Culture, which charges foreign tour groups a $15 CUC per person cover, but presumably retains the bulk of this income and pays the performers in Cuban pesos.

To his credit, Aquino has not taken his reversal of fortune lying down. Instead, he has repeatedly sounded off both to the foreign press and by continuing to issue "open letters" via e-mail to his colleagues in the world of Cuban arts and letters (tilting at what he considers to be a moribund and totally ineffective UNEAC, the Cuban Union of Writers and Artists (DDC 2014d)). For example, in a November 2013 interview with the Miami-based newspaper *Diario Las Américas*, Aquino was nothing short of devastating in his assessment of Cuba's self-employment reforms, arguing that a real desire for change is sorely lacking among Cuba's economic policymakers. Based on his own bitter experience and his sober assessment of existing regulations, he has concluded that the kinds of occupations given over to Cuba's *cuentapropistas* are those that "no one wants to do for the state given the low pay or others where the state hasn't achieved success for more than 50 years" (León 2013). He also complained that college educated professionals remain trapped in the poorly paid state sector and—worst of all—that no one seems to know to where exactly Raúl's road of reforms is taking the nation.

The only thing that is clear to him is the state's selfishness and lack of imagination in its design of the legal framework for Cuba's entrepreneurial sector:

> Only thinking in lightening its load, [the state] turns to 200 authorized lines of self-employment, which represent very little, or nothing at all, since these are *"timbirichis"* [little holes-in-the-wall] and semi-enterprises with tax rates and obligations, whose incomes and benefits do not allow them to develop nor improve the quality of their services, forcing them to turn to the black market or other unorthodox sources to get results. (ibid.)[27]

Despite such an exasperating endgame, Aquino's unique enterprise took strategic advantage of a number of the key changes in the regulations for Cuba's *paladares*, especially those having to do with hiring private employees and running more than a single business at once. He also came up with an ingenious way of financing his operation and sharing the wealth it generated among his nearly 130 employees and their families. Successfully combining the forces and talents of as many as 60 performers, 26 support staff (including a musical director, a chorus coach, and a choreographer), along with 43 employees divided between the bar and three *paladares* (McAuliff 2012), Aquino showed what could be unleashed in terms of quality goods and services and productive, well-paid employment when some of what Raúl himself has termed "ridiculous prohibitions" are removed.

In other words, nearly all of the restrictions that hobbled development of the Cuban *paladar* in prior to 2010—as vividly highlighted in the various vignettes presented above—have been recognized and remedied. However, what could have been "just the beginning" of a new wave of many such innovate and prosperous non-state establishments as was anticipated by Cuban economist Rafael Betancourt, has turned out to be an ominous cautionary tale on the limits of entrepreneurial reform. Ultimately, this outcome is due to Cuba's as yet unchecked bureaucratic insurgency, the leadership's continued allergy to private wealth generation (even if that wealth is shared cooperatively), an ongoing fear of private individuals establishing an independent economic base (as opposed to their remaining dependent on—and controlled by—state sponsorship), and a staunch refusal to recognize citizens' inalienable rights to private property.

Notes

[1] The ethnographic details related in this chapter were recorded by Ted Henken on various trips to Cuba between 1999 and 2011. While there was no so-named *paladar* that we know of in Cuba in the summer of 2001 when this visit took place, the caustic humor of naming a private restaurant after such a satirical movie reflects Cubans' well-developed sense of "gallows" humor, known as *choteo*. As we did in Chapter 4 with

reference to private cabbies and bed and breakfast operations and occasionally in Chapter 7 with various "legitimate underground economic activities," throughout this chapter we make frequent references to various self-employed individuals and enterprises. Except in the three cases where we discuss *paladares* whose travails have been covered in detail in the international media—"*La Guarida*," "*El Hurón Azul*," and *La Ópera de la Calle*'s "*El Cabildo*"—all *paladar* names have been changed to protect informant anonymity and descriptions of individual enterprises are normally composite sketches drawn from the more than two-dozen *paladar* proprietors Ted Henken interviewed between 2000 and 2011. All translations from the Spanish are our own.

[2] Though we translate *jinetero* as "hustler," readers should be aware that the term has multiple meanings in Cuba based on context and gender. While *jinetero* denotes a male hustler who offers a variety of (often illegal) products and services to foreign tourists, *jinetera* (in the feminine) is normally used to describe the peculiar kind of female prostitution that emerged on the island during the 1990s.

[3] Hakim likens the case study to the spotlight or microscope in that "its value depends crucially on how well the study is focused." She adds that "at the minimum a case study can provide a richly detailed 'portrait' of a particular social phenomenon." Furthermore, she distinguishes *descriptive case studies* as exploratory exercises that are particularly useful when relatively little is known about a topic. Such descriptive case studies can also be "illustrative 'portraits' of social entities or patterns thought to be typical, representative, or average" (1987: 61). It is this understanding of the case study that we employ in our study of Cuban *paladares*.

[4] These case studies are based on an extensive, original series of interviews and ethnographic work done with Cuban entrepreneurs between July 2000 and April 2011. Specifically, ethnographic interviews were carried out with 22 different *paladar* proprietors on five separate visits to Cuba between July 2000 and December 2001 (along with parallel interviews with 15 private cabbies and 27 bed and breakfast operators—many of whom came to operate pseudo-*paladares* under the cover of their room-rental licenses). These initial interviews were later augmented by follow-up interviews with the same proprietors and supplemented with observations of more than 40 other *paladares* conducted on four subsequent research visits to Cuba between 2002 and 2006.

These original interviews were also supplemented with notes collected by Neili Fernández Peláez (2000) from her own sample of 15 food service, 20 transportation, and 18 renter interviews. Included in this data set graciously provided to the authors by Fernández Peláez are also two interviews with Popular Council presidents in Havana and one interview with the Ministry of Transportation official in charge of granting licenses (LOT) for the operation of private taxis in Havana.

Following the implementation of major reforms in self-employment regulations instituted under Raúl Castro, many of the same *paladar* operators were revisited and interviewed once again in April 2011—along with a number of newly opened ones. These ethnographic interviews allow us to understand the experiences, opinions, and evaluations of these two most recent rounds of reform (1993-2006 and 2006-present) from the perspective of these entrepreneurs themselves as respondents compare and contrast past microenterprise reforms to current ones.

[5] Schwandt defines "qualitative methods" as "procedures including unstructured, open-ended interviews and participant observation that generate qualitative data" (2001: 213). He also indicates that most scholars would include ethnography, case study research, naturalistic inquiry, ethno-methodology, life-history methodology, and narrative inquiry under the rubric of "qualitative inquiry." Schwandt has also defined "participant observation" as "a procedure for generating understanding of the ways of

life of others. It requires that the researcher commit to some relatively prolonged period of engagement in a setting [...], take some part in the daily activities of the people among whom he or she is studying, and reconstruct their activities through the process of *inscription, transcription*, and *description* in *fieldnotes* made on the spot or soon thereafter" (2001: 185-186).

[6] Schwandt distinguishes between two general sampling strategies commonly employed in qualitative studies: empirical/statistical and theoretical/purposive strategies. *Statistical sampling* is used when units are chosen based on their representativeness of a wider, known population. Then, a "sample is chosen from within that population using a procedure that ensures that all samples have an equal or known probability of being selected." On the other hand, in *purposive sampling* "units are chosen not for their representativeness but for their relevance to the research question, [...] because there may be good reason to believe that 'what goes on there' is critical to understanding some process or concept or to testing or elaborating some established theory" (2001: 232). This study uses purposive sampling for these reasons.

[7] For example, Mesa-Lago (2001: 139) has compiled a useful scale of income inequalities by occupation in Cuba for the year 1995. Of the 16 different wage rates he lists (pensioner, teacher, surgeon, bartender in tourist hotel, cabbie, self-employed worker, prostitute, etc.), owners of small private restaurants and those who rent rooms in their private homes are the top two occupational categories, making between $2,500 and $5,000, and $467 and $654 per month, respectively (many times the average worker's wage of the equivalent of $6 a month at the time). Moreover, private taxi drivers who serve tourists were estimated to make between $100 and $467 per month, ranking sixth on Mesa-Lago's occupational listing (see also Lee 1997c: 2). Mesa-Lago uses the annual average exchange rate for 1995, which was 32.1 pesos per one US dollar.

[8] In addition to the many newspaper reports on the rise of these speak-easy eateries (Whitefield 1994a; 1994b; Farah 1994; Fletcher 1995; Lee 1997a; Vicent 2000; LaFranchi 1996), scholarly studies include, Scarpaci 1995; Segre, Coyula, and Scarpaci 1997; Núñez Moreno 1997; Togores González and Pérez Villanueva 1996; Peters and Scarpaci 1998; Rivera 1998; Jatar-Hausmann 1999; Ritter 1998; 2000a, b; Fernández Peláez 2000; Duany 2001; and Jackiewicz and Bolster 2003.

[9] For a more detailed analysis see Henken (2008a).

[10] For an excellent reflection on this unwritten but very powerful Cuban rule of "not standing out" (*no te destaques*) so as to "not look for problems" (*para no buscarte problemas*), see Yoani Sánchez's recent blog post, "*Y tú, hijo, no te destaques*" (2104d).

[11] As we chronicle in Chapters 5 and 7, this creative reaction by Cuba's *cuentapropistas* to the island's self-employment laws—seizing on vague language and legal loopholes so as to make ends meet and stay afloat financially—continues to characterize the relationship (by turns antagonistic and accommodating) between Cuban entrepreneurs and the state. For example, in the post 2010-era, many CPs took out licenses as seamstresses and tailors when in practice they were resellers of imported clothing in private retail boutiques across the island. After the government moved to protect its import and retail monopoly by issuing a new September 2013 law that explicitly delimited such practices, operators responded by shifting their activities into the black market relying now on catalogues to reach their customers (14ymedio 2014b).

[12] In fact, the new law officially cancelled the occupations producer of light snacks, maker of dairy products, producer of agricultural preserves, and cook from the self-employment list. Those who had been exercising one of these occupations were allowed to re-register under the new food service law.

[13] During this period, the exchange rate between the Cuban peso and the US dollar was 26:1.

[14] Note that *paladares* do not account for a significant percentage of self-employment licenses and are thus not included among these most common occupations. See Núñez Moreno (1997: 46) for a similar numeric breakdown showing the predominance of food service activities among self-employment occupations as early as April 1996. She also indicates that 74% of all registered CPs were concentrated in just 16 of the then allowable 157 occupations. *Granma* journalist, Lee (1997c) gives similar numbers on the concentration of self-employed workers in these occupations.

[15] It should be noted that the 1,132 licensed food service operators shown for Plaza Municipality groups together four distinct self-employment activities (caterers, street vendors, porch-front cafeterias, and *paladares* proper), of which *paladares* make up a distinct minority. Though detailed information is not included, it is likely that this number also includes the self-employment occupation "family helper," the official designation given to those licensed to assist their family members in the preparation and sale of foods.

[16] In her insightful essay, "The Political Economy of Caudillismo," Mary Katherine Crabb argues that this "campaign against indiscipline and inefficiency" intensified in the spring of 1997, aiming to increase penalties for economic crimes and enlist the island's Committees for the Defense of the Revolution (CDRs) to "aggressively police their neighborhoods" (Crabb 2001: 170).

[17] Given the rapidly changing legal environment during the 1993-2004 period, it should be noted that monthly tax rates for Cuba's dollar-*paladares* reported elsewhere vary between $520 (Ritter 2000a, b), $710 (Ritter 1998), $750 (Stanley 2000: 122), $800 (Newman 2001), $850 (Smith 2001), $895 (Whitefield 1996b), and $1,250 (Reyes 1998).

[18] See two articles by Susana Lee published in *Granma* in 1996: "Self-employment: A Necessary Reflection," September 13, p. 4 (1996b), and "Self-employment: We Must Combat Disorder" September 19, p. 4 (1996c).

[19] A *Granma* article announcing that self-employment would be a major subject of the upcoming National Assembly of the Committees for the Defense of the Revolution reminded lawbreakers that the revolution had eyes in every neighborhood:

> We know about those who have become "sympathetic" and their populism leads them to be protected by their neighbors when severe tax evasion and "*mercachifleo*" [black market sales] with products are discovered. We know who complies and who does not comply. Who is loyal and who is disloyal. You will not enjoy impunity in our neighborhoods. (Lee 1997e: 2)

Of course, apart from the image of the Orwellian big brother that this kind of double-speak brings to mind, the irresistible comparison here is to the paternalism of ever-watchful Father Christmas, Santa Claus, who "sees you when you're sleeping, knows when you're awake; knows if you've been bad or good, so be good for goodness sake."

[20] Though it is common for the official Cuban media to publish reports of state inspectors being offered bribes by unscrupulous *cuentapropistas* (Lee 1996d: 4), a variety of sources, including at least one state publication, have indicated growing levels of abuse of authority among inspectors. For example, in the spring of 1999, the Cuban newspaper *Juventud Rebelde* reported that a group of inspectors along with their direct superior had been accused of taking advantage of food vendors by levying unjustified fines and confiscating goods for personal use ("Corruption Revealed," 1999: 7). As a response to growing levels of corruption, the state has begun to periodically rotate inspectors through Havana's different municipalities to avoid their becoming too familiar with the self-employed operators under their jurisdiction (Zúñiga 1999; Fernández

Peláez 2000). The authors' own interviews generally confirm these reports (also see Rodríguez Aguila and Rodríguez Causa n.d.; "Indicaciones a los inspectores laborales para el trabajo por cuenta propia" (1995) and "Código de Ética y Conducta" (1995)).

[21] Such operations can legally offer "gastronomic service" to their houseguests after the payment of a fee equal to 30% of their monthly tax (*Granma* 1997b: 4-5). Though this payment allows for the right to serve meals only to one's houseguests, in practice many operations with an already well-established reputation and clientele function as de facto private restaurants.

[22] The following are all examples of useful research done by Cuban analysts on self-employment: Hernández and González 1993; Carranza Valdés et al 1995; Gutiérrez Urdaneta et al 1996; Pavón González 1996; Pérez Villanueva and Togores González 1996; Quintana Mendoza 1997; González Gutiérrez 1997; Togores González n.d.; Espina Prieto 1997; Espina Prieto et al 1998; Fernández Peláez 2000; López Levy 2002; Leiva 2003; Vidal Alejandro and Pérez Villanueva 2010; Gálvez Chiú 2010, 2013; Díaz Fernández et al 2012; Triana Cordoví 2012, 2013; Antúnez Sánchez et al 2013; Carthy Correa and Núñez Valerino 2013.

[23] Or, to paraphrase Mao Tse-tung, he would rather have the people eat socialist grass than capitalist wheat.

[24] In this final section of the chapter, we again refer to the qualitative experiences of various self-employed *paladar* operators. However, this time in most cases we use the actual names of operators and their restaurants. We do this either because the descriptions are drawn from published articles in the Cuban or international press (which is the case here with Pérez and Núñez) or because nearly all the *paladar* proprietors we interviewed in April 2011 agreed to go "on the record" giving their names and allowing the interviews to be recorded. This in itself is indicative of a gradual shift away from the aura of illegitimacy that had dominated self-employment between 1993 and 2006.

[25] Journalist and blogger Tracey Eaton (formerly the Havana-based foreign correspondent of the *Dallas Morning News*) has indicated that *El Hurón Azul* also reopened in the summer of 2010. When he inquired, a restaurant employee informed him that the same owner as before, Juan Carlos Fernández, was running the place once again but this information has not been independently confirmed.

[26] In Spanish: "*Algunos podrán considerar estos proyectos como ejemplos de pequeña empresa capitalista, otros los denominarían cooperativas. Yo me atrevo a afirmar que a estas alturas, los cubanos están más interesados en prosperar que en denominaciones. A fin de cuentas, como dijera el finado Deng Xiaoping, no importa de qué color sea el gato, lo importante es que cace ratones.*"

[27] In Spanish: "*Solo pensando en aligerar su carga acude a 200 formas autorizadas del trabajo por cuenta propia, que representan muy poco, o nada, pues se trata de "timbirichis" y semiempresas con niveles de impuestos y de obligaciones, cuyos ingresos y beneficios no alcanzan para desarrollarse ni incrementar la calidad de sus servicios, por lo que para lograr resultados están obligadas a transitar por el mercado negro u otras vías nada ortodoxas.*"

9

The Future of Small Enterprise in Cuba

> The steps we have been taking and shall take towards broadening and relaxing self-employment are the result of profound meditations and analysis and we can assure you this time there will be no going back.
> —*President Raúl Castro* (Castro, R. 2011b)

The objective of this study has been to analyze Cuba's changing policies towards "self-employment" and small enterprise including both licensed, legal enterprises and underground or "extra-legal" enterprises during the Revolutionary period. While the whole of this era is examined, this study has focused especially on the extent to which the policy reforms towards small enterprise under the Presidency of Raúl Castro after 2006 have contrasted with the policies of the government of President Fidel Castro during the so-called "Special Period" after 1990. We have also sought to evaluate the effects of these policy changes in terms of the generation of productive employment in the non-state sector, the efficient provision of goods and services by this emergent sector, and the reduction in the size and scope of the underground economy.

As we have chronicled, the shifting approaches of the Cuban government toward micro- and small- private enterprise in the guise of "self-employment" has been a central defining policy area since 1959. With the nationalizations of 1961 to 1963 and especially with the "Revolutionary Offensive" of 1968, legal small-scale private enterprise was virtually eliminated, except for about 30,000 very small self-employment activities, which were allowed to reemerge after 1978. Then, as a result of the unprecedented economic crisis of 1989-1994, President Fidel Castro was forced by circumstances to liberalize state policy towards the sector somewhat leading to the brief flowering of a range of nearly 160 private occupations. However, after 1996 the government proceeded to contain it with tight, even asphyxiating regulatory, taxation, and licensing regimens (which were chronicled in Chapter 4). Fidel Castro's approach was driven more by ideology and less by a pragmatic concern for the day-to-day well-being of Cuban citizens.

Since his accession to power as Acting President in July 2006 and President after February 2008, Raúl Castro has focused on addressing Cuba's continuing, chronic economic challenges and has sought to design pragmatic policies to deal with them. A central focus of these policies after late-2010 has been the liberalization of policy towards the small enterprise sector and the strengthening of the role of the "market mechanism." In effect, self-employment in the non-state sector was seen as the primary means to reabsorb state sector workers considered redundant (referred to as "*no idoneo*" or "*disponible*" but never simply "*desempleado*," or unemployed) and thereby to achieve improved productivity and ultimately higher incomes for the remaining workers.

A range of other reforms of relevance to the expansion of the small enterprise sector were also enacted between 2011 and 2014. The result of all these reforms has been a rapid expansion of "entrepreneurial Cuba" as a wide range of new small enterprises were established while others surfaced from the underground economy. A further reform of potential significance was the enactment in December 2012 of legislation permitting the establishment of non-agricultural cooperative enterprises (the focus of Chapter 6), the first of which were established on July 1, 2013.

The central argument of this study is that the policy approach of President Fidel Castro towards small enterprise from 1960 to 2006 (and especially between 1993 and 2006), was counterproductive for the economy and damaging to the Cuban people in terms of their access to well-paid employment and quality goods and services at affordable prices. It worsened their material well-being and inadvertently promoted the expansion of the underground economy as well as pervasive economic illegalities in both the state enterprise sector and the tiny legal *cuentapropista* sector. The minor policy liberalizations in 1978 and the major liberalizations in 1993-1994 were promising. Unfortunately, both were reversed after only a few years.

In contrast, the reform measures so far enacted under the Presidency of Raúl Castro have been more ambitious, deeper-cutting, and are likely irreversible. As Raúl himself makes clear in the epigraph quoted above, "we can assure you this time there will be no going back" (Castro, R. 2011b). By mid-2014, Raúl's reforms were still in the early stages of implementation but have already had positive consequences for the material well-being of Cuba's citizens. However, while our analysis applauds Raúl's reforms as far as they go, we also argue that the reforms must go much further if the demonstrated entrepreneurial talents of Cuban citizens are to be fully activated for the benefit of the Cuban people.

In Chapter 2, we place our analysis of small enterprise and the underground economy in Revolutionary Cuba in a broader, comparative Latin American and Eastern European context. Like almost all countries and especially those of Latin America and the Caribbean, Cuba had an "extra-legal," informal sector before 1959. It also had a long and deeply rooted tradition of illegal "contraband" economic activities going back to the early colonial era, which was provoked both by the isolation and neglect of much of the eastern part of the island and more directly by the monopolistic mercantilist economic policies of the Spanish crown during much of Cuba's nearly 400-year colonial era (1511-1898). The small enterprise sector and the "underground economy" of the Revolutionary era are thus rooted in the island's historical heritage from Spanish colonialism and the uneven economic development that characterized its nearly 60 years as an independent republic (1902-1958). Thus, its initial character at the start of the revolutionary period was similar to that commonly found in the other countries of Latin America and the Caribbean.

However, Cuba's informal economy together with its legal "self-employment" sector was also shaped by the unique features of state socialism rapidly put into place following 1959, that is near-universal state employment, the central planning system, and state ownership of the economy (both its "commanding heights" as well as its micro-, small-, and medium-sized enterprises). This model was essentially copied from the countries of Eastern Europe in the early 1960s and consolidated beginning in the mid-1970s after an interlude of radical but ultimately unsuccessful economic experimentation from 1964 to 1970. As was the case with the command economies of the countries of Eastern Europe, a substantial underground or "second" economy grew up to produce the goods and services that the state sector was unable to provide efficiently in sufficient quantity, quality, and diversity (Pérez-López 1995a). For example, excessive and eventually almost exclusive employment in the state sector as the government sought to achieve universal state employment was gradually accompanied by "moonlighting" on the part of many state sector workers in the second economy. The "second economy" eventually became a chronic structural feature of Cuba's labor system during the revolutionary period (Los 1990). Cuba's economic structures thus have had a hybrid character, sharing some similarities with the rest of Latin America and the Caribbean and others with the former state socialist systems of Central and Eastern Europe.

The evolution of public policy towards small, private enterprise and the consequences thereof are analyzed in Chapter 3. The chapter begins with a brief commentary on the nature of the small enterprise sector and the informal economy on the eve of the Revolution. The nationalizations of mainly larger economic enterprises occurred in the first years of the Revolution, from 1960 to 1963, while most remaining micro- and small enterprises were not nationalized until the "Revolutionary Offensive" of 1968 at the peak of the most radical, anti-market phase of the revolutionary trajectory. After the failed effort to harvest a record 10 million tons of sugar cane in 1970, Cuba changed course and began to adopt the economic orthodoxy of the Soviets in both institutional and policy terms. However, the policy approach towards the small enterprise sector underwent only minor modification over the next twenty years—until the termination of the special relationship with the former Soviet Union between 1989 and 1991. The most important such change occurred in 1978 when 48 types of self-employment were legalized, leading to a brief legal expansion of such activities.

However, with the "Rectification Process" adopted in 1986 following the Third Congress of the Communist Party, policy towards small enterprise was reversed once again and returned to one of tight containment and vilification. The driving force behind this hostility towards small enterprise was ideological. In the view of President Fidel Castro, such activities were basically capitalistic—leading inevitably to greater economic inequalities and the loss of state control over society—and were therefore deemed to be incompatible with the type of state socialist economic model towards which he aspired. However, his periodic anti-market offensives resulted in economic stagnation or worse on a national scale. On the other hand, the previous (and subsequent) policy moves to loosen the controls and limitations on self-employment were driven by pragmatic considerations, namely the economic benefits in terms of employment, productivity, and efficiency that a less restrictive policy approach to the sector would generate (Mesa-Lago and Pérez-López 2006; 2013).

Chapter 4 focuses on the policy changes and their implementation in the 1990 to 2006 period. With the ending of the generous Soviet subsidization of the Cuban economy after 1989, Cuba underwent a disastrous economic meltdown. Thus began the "Special Period," as the new era was euphemistically labeled in 1990 by President Fidel Castro. When the economy shrank by almost 35% from 1990 to 1993 and the state sector no longer provided citizens with wages and salaries sufficient to buy the necessities of life, many people desperately sought to generate their own employment and livelihoods with economic activities outside the state sector, expanding the ranks of Cuba's "second economy" to record levels.

Many were forced into self-employment activities during these years in order to survive. With the failure of the state sector of the economy to provide the necessities of life for citizens during the 1990s, the underground economy expanded rapidly and became a major source of livelihood for many citizens as well as a source of the goods and services necessary for sustenance. In effect, for many Cubans the "second economy" became the *real* economy producing goods and services in unlicensed economic activities that were technically "illegal" in Cuba—but legal everywhere else in the world at the time (including Russia, China, and Vietnam) with the sole exception of North Korea. Thus, our oft-quoted quip that *"todo está prohibido, pero vale todo"*— everything is prohibited, but anything goes. At the same time, the underground economy was dependent to a considerable degree on the pervasive pilferage of needed inputs from the state sector, while the state sector relied on the underground economy to generate citizens' real incomes necessary for survival, thereby subsidizing state sector employees and the government itself—an interesting type of symbiosis.

By 1993 the government was pushed by circumstances to ratify what many people were already doing, that is to legalize a range of self-employment activities and to increase the number of licenses that it granted to Cuba's so-called *cuentapropistas*. In response, the sector expanded quickly. Though the liberalization worked to improve citizens' material well-being significantly, it continued to be viewed with distaste by President Fidel Castro. This was echoed in the state-owned official media. By 1995-1996, the government again began to limit and contain the sector by curtailing licensing, imposing punitive taxation, punishing infractions of the numerous regulations severely, and criticizing the sector continuously in the media.

This policy approach was in place and then intensified by the so-called "Battle of Ideas" until President Fidel Castro unexpectedly left the presidency due to a life-threatening intestinal illness in July 2006. In fact, for many key self-employed occupations such as private *paladar* restaurants and bed-and-breakfast rentals, this antagonistic policy continued with only minor softening until late-2010, when President Raúl Castro changed the policy approach definitively. Fidel Castro's policy approach successfully halted the expansion of the sector and indeed reduced its size precipitously between 1996 and 2006. The negative consequences of this containment policy, outlined in Chapter 4, were obvious to the *cuentapropistas* themselves (some of whom are profiled in that chapter), to Cuban citizens generally, and analysts both on the island and abroad.

The more pragmatic policy approach of President Raúl Castro since 2006 is analyzed in Chapter 5. Continuing and intractable economic difficulties led to a rethinking of economic policy generally and a reconsideration of what were the appropriate roles for the private sector and market mechanism on the one hand and public sector and planning on the other. Major policy reforms designed to promote small enterprise were then announced in late-2010 and instituted with mixed results thereafter. In response to the liberalized licensing, taxation, and regulatory framework, small enterprise expanded quickly growing more than three-fold by 2014 and generating major benefits for Cuban citizens.

A major additional policy change was announced in late-2012 with new legislation permitting non-agricultural service and retail cooperatives mainly in urban areas. This reform is explored in Chapter 6. Unlike Cuba's prior discouraging experience with agricultural cooperatives, these new cooperatives are meant to be self-governing, independent from the state, and theoretically allow professional activities. However, it seems that outright ownership of these cooperative enterprises (and of the land and physical infrastructure upon which they are developed) will remain in state hands. Moreover, the required co-op approval process has so far been discouragingly limited in terms of the scope of the types of enterprises allowed and needlessly bureaucratic, putting a break on their economic impact. Still, this policy innovation has the potential to be of great material benefit to Cuban citizens and may introduce an interesting form of workplace democracy—which could have implications for democratization in Cuban society and polity more generally.

However, at the time of this writing in summer 2014, it is too early to judge how such a new cooperative sector might evolve and how well it might perform. The liberalization of self-employment, microenterprise, and small enterprise and the legalization of non-agricultural cooperative enterprises will likely lead to a contraction of the underground economy as well as a reduction the innumerable "illegalities" that have permeated the Cuban economy since 1959 but especially during the "Special Period" from 1990 until about 2010 (the focus of Chapter 7). In this context, there is a strong potential for new market-oriented, small- and medium-sized cooperative enterprises (SMEs) to emerge and to thrive in many sectors of the economy. This would be of special interest for Cuba, as it could be in the process of developing an innovative institutional structure of a character that is not out of step with cooperative enterprises that exist in virtually all other mixed economies in the world. The key difference is that while non-agricultural cooperatives occupy a minority position in other economies, they could emerge as a much larger component of the Cuban economy because medium- and large-scale private enterprise is still blocked through the severe limitations that continue to constrict the growth and evolution of the small enterprise sector. Of course, these same limitations do not exist for mixed or joint ventures between foreign-owned and state enterprises—a disappointing feature of Cuba's new foreign investment law published in 2014.

Cuba's ubiquitous underground economy and economic illegalities were analyzed in Chapter 7. The attempt to eliminate virtually all private economic enterprises and the inadequacy of the state sector in generating incomes and volumes of goods and services adequate for survival, especially after the economic crisis of 1989-1994, led to a major expansion of the underground economy and a proliferation of illegal economic practices—all necessary for people's survival. The vast majority of these illegal or unlicensed enterprises produced valuable goods and services and created productive employment and incomes for citizens. They generated domestic savings and investment, foreign exchange savings and earnings, and training in entrepreneurship. They have made a valuable contribution to the economy. For these reasons, we have labeled them "Legitimate Underground Economic activities" (LUEAs). On the other hand, their clandestinity and very small size, plus the ubiquitous pilfering of state property or use of public property for private purposes have had a deleterious effect on the economy and society.

Open licensing, "de-stigmatization" in the media, fairer taxation, and a liberalized regulatory framework for legal enterprise all should contribute to an expansion of legal small private and cooperative enterprise and a contraction of underground economic activities. However, until there is an effective credit system and wholesale supply network, these self-employed and cooperative enterprises will likely have no alternative but to turn other black market or foreign sources for loans and necessary inputs. The shift to "above-ground" enterprise would be of great benefit to Cuba in terms of tax revenues, and the fulfillment of health, safety, environmental, and labor regulations. Moreover, legalized and licensed enterprises will be able to avoid the costs of clandestinity and "attention avoidance." They will be able to advertise, operate at a larger scale, and to legally hire employees. This will be of benefit for Cuba as the wastage of human, natural, and capital resources produced by the underground operation of such enterprises will be reduced. Moreover, shifting small enterprise from the public sector to the private and cooperative sectors should help to diminish the ubiquitous pilfering and petty corruption that has long characterized the Cuban economy, as monitoring of employees and cooperative members should be stronger and more effective in the latter vis-à-vis the former sectors (Ravsberg 2014).

As a way to more vividly illustrate the interaction between public policy and the various survival strategies of actual Cuban microentrepreneurs, Chapters 4, 7, and 8 provided illustrative case studies of various Cuban microenterprises (both licensed and clandestine). Chapter 8 focuses specifically on what is perhaps the single best known, lucrative, and economically dynamic sector within the world of private self-employment: food service and particularly the Cuban *paladar*. Our focus on the evolution of the *paladar* over the past two decades allowed us to provide a comparative analysis of self-employment (both licensed and clandestine) using grounded, qualitative research techniques such as ethnography, participant-observation, and in-depth interviews. Furthermore, these occupational categories were highlighted here in part because, though now largely licensed and legal, they have tended to straddle the state's strict regulatory line in the past by obtaining licenses for a single activity while systematically resorting to informal methods of operation (like hiring unauthorized employees or selling unauthorized products) and to the black market to obtain necessary supplies.

Illustrative vignettes presented in Chapter 8, like those of Patricia's "*El Rinconcito,*" Magda's "*La Azotea,*" Enrique's "*La Guarida,*" Juan Carlos' "*El Hurón Azul,*" Alicia's "*Maravillas,*" or Alfredo's "*Buen Provecho,*" portray both the peril of the previous state antagonism toward entrepreneurship and the promise of new, more supportive policies enacted under Raúl. At the same time, the conclusion of chapter 8 highlighted the case of Ulises' *paladar*-cum-dinner theater "*El Cabildo,*" indicating that there is still much insecurity facing Cuba's *paladares* given that they are often subject to the whims of a shifting government policy and the ambitions of self-interested bureaucratic turf protection on the part of lower-level local officials. Additionally, the closure of *El*

Cabildo indicates that too much success and private wealth generation, too much independence from state institutions, and too high a profile in the international media may all spell doom for private entrepreneurial projects in Raúl's Cuba—even for ones as communitarian and proudly revolutionary as was *El Cabildo* (DDC 2012a, b).

An Evaluation of Raúl's Reforms: Significant but Insufficient

If we evaluate the success of President Raúl Castro's economic reforms to date based on the goal of moving the bulk of informal workers performing "legitimate underground economic activities" (LUEAs) out of the underground, then the reforms have been reasonably successful. The roughly 150,000 registered *cuentapropistas* as of October 2010 have grown more than three-fold to over 470,000 by mid-2014. Seventy percent of these claimed to have been previously unemployed so it is likely that the origins of a good proportion of them were in the underground economy. Thus, the new regulations have allowed many, perhaps even the majority of Cuba's previously clandestine entrepreneurs to exit the underground, obtain a license, and operate within the law. They are no longer "condemned to informality and clandestinity" as they were under the Presidency of Fidel Castro. Moreover, as described in Chapters 5, 7, and 8 their entrepreneurial activities are now generally portrayed as legitimate and promoted by the state media instead of being vilified and stigmatized as in the past.[1]

However, the declared goal of the employment reforms was to create a microenterprise sector that could absorb the large-scale layoffs planned in the state sector. Because only 18% of the registered microenterprise personnel report having previously worked in the state sector it is evident that this goal is *not* being met. Moreover, only seven percent of *cuentapropistas* are university graduates and very few of these are likely to be employed in their professional areas but instead in one of the many low tech, survival-oriented, so-called *"timbiriche"* activities. This underscores the continuing blockage of the effective use of Cuba's well-qualified labor force in the small enterprise sector with the resultant blockage innovation, productivity, and growth.

Even more important than the goal of absorbing former state workers, however, is the issue of creating a small- and medium-sized enterprise (SME) sector that can contribute to sustained improvements in material standards of living. In other words, can Raúl's initial efforts at improving economic productivity through the creation of a non-state sector be deepened and expanded so as to begin to "put some meat on the bone" of the economic reforms (Peters in Frank 2012c; Peters 2013b)? In our opinion, this would be promoted if Raúl's first wave of microenterprise reforms were followed by a second, deeper and broader wave that does away with "the list" of 201 occupations, grants private entrepreneurs the ability to import goods (and export their products), supports the creation of wholesale supply markets and bank credits, and permits university graduates to become self-employed in their professions. However, it remains to be seen whether Raúl's government has the political will and technical capacity to fully implement existing reforms and to further intensify the reform process in order to yield greater levels of economic freedom and material well-being for Cuban people (Miroff 2012c; Miroff 2013).

President Raúl Castro's initial efforts in 2010 at reforming the past antagonistic policies toward self-employment amounted to "two steps forward and one step back" or perhaps to "two half-steps forward." That is, the unprecedented economic reforms announced in September 2010 put the "cart" of the necessary 500,000 to 1.8 million state sector layoffs before the "horse" of the necessary creation of jobs in the private sector (Ritter 2010). Furthermore, the details of the new self-employment legislation analyzed in Chapters 5 and 8 were initially worrisome. For example, while the limit of just 12 chairs in any *paladar* was indeed lifted (together with prohibitions on foods like seafood and beef and on non-family employees), the new law did not leave it up to the business owner and the market to determine the optimal size of an operation. Instead, it initially set a new, arbitrary seating limit of 20. Similarly, instead of allowing entrepreneurs to innovatively respond to consumer demand by establishing any kind of business they saw fit (save a short list of specifically prohibited occupations), the government did the opposite. In a mocking inversion of Deng Xiao Peng's famous declaration to "let a hundred flowers bloom, a hundred schools of thought contend" (i.e. trust the creativity and ingenuity of the people), Raúl's initial self-employment legislation sought to micro-manage and control Cuban entrepreneurs instead by "letting exactly 178 (and eventually 201) flowers bloom," but no more.

However, as described in Chapters 5–8, Raúl's government pragmatically amplified some of the initial reforms announced in September 2010 after initial results did not meet expectations. Taxes judged as too heavy and harsh for fledging entrepreneurs were waived though only for a temporary "jump-start" period. Contracted employees were permitted in all 201 private occupations, instead of just half as originally stipulated. The arbitrary and "20-chair rule" for *paladares* then was increased to 50. The "cart" of massive layoffs in the state sector was postponed, and placed decidedly behind the "horse" of first expanding microenterprise and—for the first time ever under the Revolution—the new, non-agricultural cooperative sector. These kinds of second and third wave follow-up adjustments to the first wave of reforms indicate a major change in mentality on the part of the Cuban leadership, one that, as President Raúl Castro indicates above, appear to be the "result of profound meditations and analysis" instead of President Fidel Castro's ideological and often ad-hoc economic mobilizations and offensives. This pragmatic and market-oriented approach contrasts sharply with the previous cycles of reform and retrenchment under the Presidency of Fidel Castro, described in Chapters 3 and 4.

A Cautionary Insight from Eastern Europe: Modernity or Duality?

In his incisive essay, "Modernity or a New Kind of Duality? Second Thoughts about the 'Second Economy'" (1994), the Hungarian sociologist Istaván Gabor described the post-transition trend in Eastern Europe as the effective "Third-Worldization" of the socialist second economy. In other words, he argued that the second economies of former-socialist countries have come to resemble the informal sector of the weak, "frustrated" capitalist states of Latin America described in Table 2.1 of Chapter 2. The dualistic character that the second economy begins to take on during the transition from state socialism to market socialism stems both from the insecurity private operators feel under a tenuous and changing legal system and from the informal survival habits they acquired while operating underground as chronicled in Chapters 7 and 8. In short, many of the strategies they developed to survive under socialism did *not* prepare them to function within a fledging mixed market system.

There is a tendency for private operators to become "myopic profit maximizers" (Kornai 1989: 56), instead of investing in a long-term future for their enterprises. In order to mitigate the many uncertainties in the new legal framework, private entrepreneurs tend to build up bribed connections leading to the corrosion of business morality (Gabor 1989). There is also a tendency for entrepreneurs to hedge their bets, so to speak, by participating in both the first and second economies, making their full-time investment in private enterprise less than it would be otherwise. All these contingencies lead to the stratified, bimodal, or "dualistic" character of the private sector. "While restrictions on the second economy are often imposed to counter excessive inequalities in income," writes Gabor, "it is mostly those with exceptionally high incomes who have the financial reserves and personal connections necessary to weather restrictions" (1989: 602).[2] Thus, as socialist reforms and the growth of the second economy give way to an outright transition to a new economic order, we find that "[w]hat was instrumental in undermining the old communist regimes may not always contribute to the integration of new democratic ones" (Kovács 1994: xiv-xv). In other words, what worked to bring down communism may not work to build up capitalism. Of course, this may be good or bad news depending on what Cubans have in mind when they argue that "another, better world is possible."[3]

Stark (1989) warns of the same dilemma when he argues that while a post-socialist system will likely have fewer outright restrictions on economic activity, there may very well be a need for more, and more explicitly defined (and focused) regulations. This is the case because after generations of mutual mistrust, fear, and confusion, as well as the development of extra-legal survival strategies (bribery, theft, corruption, influence peddling, etc.), there exists a very real potential for both bureaucrats and fledging entrepreneurs to revert to their tried and true habits, preferring informal *socio-lismo* (the reliance on one's friends or "associates") over the transparent and impersonal rule of law. All of these lessons are applicable to Cuba today as it begins deeper and more deliberate economic reforms that cede space to private microenterprise and small- and medium-sized cooperatives (Kubalkova 1994).

Because it operates outside the realm of government control, the growth of Cuba's second economy (often euphemistically labeled the "non-state sector" in today's Cuba) may pose a long-term threat to the state monopoly of central economic planning on the island—even while it helps hold a flawed system together in the short-term. In light of this history, Raúl Castro's method of moving forward with his reforms "*sin prisa pero sin pausa*" (without haste but without pause)—as he has said on many occasions—is quite understandable. However, the question remains whether Raúl's reforms can keep up with the rising demands and entrepreneurial innovations of the Cuban people (Economist 2012). Now that Raúl Castro has placed "updating" Cuban socialism at the very center of his agenda—though he is loathe to ever use the words "reforms," "entrepreneur," or "private sector,"—accompanied by a major shift away from past policies that "condemned self-employment to near extinction" (in the words of *Granma*), the reform experiences of Eastern Europe and the related theories of new institutionalism (described in Chapter 2) become especially pertinent to Cuba.

Of course, Cuba could follow the "other path" blazed by China and Vietnam: major expansion of the private sector together with economic growth and political stability—all under the watchful eye of the state and party. While Fidel has been accused of "coveting Beijing, but imitating Moscow" (Pérez-López 1995b: 15) when it came to the dilemma of economic reform under state socialism, Raúl may eventually decide to both covet and imitate China. However, it remains to be seen whether the triple-threat of growing inequality, official corruption, and ubiquitous economic crime (significant problems in all failed state socialist regimes), can be remedied by the Castro brothers' age-old cocktail of preaching, policing, prohibition, and prosecution (Ritter 2005), without resorting to even deeper and perhaps more irreversible economic reforms than those so far contemplated by President Raúl Castro.

The Future of Small Enterprise in Cuba and The Role of U.S. Policy

Our analysis leads to the conclusion that if an important objective of the Cuban government is to stimulate the expansion of micro- and small-enterprise activities in order to produce needed goods and services efficiently and to generate productive employment for those that are to be displaced from the public sector, a variety of additional policy measures or modifications are necessary. Perhaps most important in a future round of policy reforms towards small enterprise would be the legalization of virtually all types of economic activity including professional services which are now illegal. It makes little economic sense to permit professionals to operate "low-technology" microenterprises outside their fields of expertise and prohibit them from doing so in their own areas of expertise—though this is very likely seen as a political and ideological question for the current government, not an economic one.

Opening up any and all areas for microenterprise rather than limiting them to the 201 narrowly defined areas also would be useful. Moreover, assurance of automatic licensing for anyone wanting to open a small enterprise would be beneficial. Open licensing would harness the forces of competition among all participants in a particular activity, thereby stimulating innovation and quality improvement. It would also push prices down and ensure that incomes in much of the sector (aside from the privileged tourist-oriented activities of some *paladares* and bed-and-breakfasts) were also pushed downward towards the national average.

The taxation regime for small enterprise has been improved, but the 40 percent ceiling on deductions for all costs of production (including labor, purchased inputs of goods and services, investment and maintenance) from total revenue in the determination of net revenue (or taxable income) is counterproductive as well as inequitable. It means that the real or "effective" tax rates can approach or even exceed 100 percent of net revenues for larger, more input-dependent heavy enterprises. This does not help promote job-creation or the efficient operation of enterprises. The five person ceiling placed on the number of employees that can be hired in a small enterprise without incurring higher taxes, while better than before, will continue to stunt enterprises and prevent them from reaching an efficient size. Perhaps that is exactly the intent of such a rule. Still, a higher limit, perhaps 20, 40, or even 50 employees would permit a more natural evolution of enterprises—allowing them to grow from "small" to "medium" in scale based on their needs as a business and on consumer demand, not on official fiat. The tax regime that is in place—with a 50 percent marginal tax rate—for such enterprises would help contain income inequalities.

A variety of additional reform measures have been proposed and are in process of implementation. The establishment of wholesale markets for inputs, access to foreign exchange and imported inputs under reasonable terms, the establishment of micro-credit and credit facilities, full legalization of "intermediaries" and permission for advertising are all areas where further policy development would be appropriate. The challenge will be to ensure that policies and institutions in these areas are implemented optimally. Policy measures in these areas should be instrumental in permitting the further flowering of small enterprise so as to absorb the labor from the state sector and in providing for the needs of citizens in the future. They should also encourage enterprises still in the underground economy to legalize their situations, thereby generating tax revenues and coming under the influence of the regulatory framework on the environment, health and safety, and labor legislation.

In what direction will public policy towards small enterprise move in the future? Predictions are obviously difficult if not impossible. However, there are a number of possibilities assuming no further political evolution under Raúl Castro or a similar successor, such that there would be no movement in the areas of fundamental freedoms, civil liberties, and political rights. Of course, with major political change that takes on these issues—either from within the government itself or coming up from Cuba's emergent civil society—it is likely that there would be a policy change towards small enterprise specifically and towards the private and public sectors in general as part of a larger plan to recognize and guarantee Cuban citizen's full property rights.

A first possibility would be a movement towards the approach of President Fidel Castro to small enterprise. At this time, this is very improbable. The old approach has been publicly discredited by its failures over the last 50 years. It has been discredited in multiple speeches by President Raúl Castro who has made a compelling case for reform—especially in the epigraph quoted above. It has been discredited in the Cuban state media. Raúl Castro has been successful in maintaining the broad support for his reforms on the part of the citizenry, the politicians, and the media—even if consistent and timely implementation of his reform agenda has been a frustratingly slow process due in part to the "bureaucratic insurgency" described in Chapter 8. There has been an almost complete change of personnel in the highest levels of government, notably the Cabinet, as *"Raúlistas"* and military figures loyal to Raúl Castro have replaced the *"Fidelistas."*

There are undoubtedly officials in government who dislike the reforms and prefer the earlier policy orthodoxy of the Fidel era. Perhaps they could try to slow down or even to block the implementation of some of Raúl's policy changes. However, they have thus far been unwilling or unable to organize politically to obstruct the reforms. It is not surprising, in view of the nature of Cuba's political system, that so far there has been no overt opposition or even criticism in the media or the universities to Raúl's policy reforms on small enterprise, even though these are contrary to the conventional wisdom and policy towards small enterprise during the almost half-century of the Presidency of his Fidel Castro.

A second approach that one could imagine would be for a stabilization of the current state of public policy towards small enterprise. This would involve acceptance of the current objectives and policy measures which are themselves designed to promote change. It will likely require a period of time to implement the current policies, especially those towards the non-agricultural cooperatives. It makes sense to see how the current institutional framework and policy measures will function before changing them further. In view of Raúl Castro's age (he was born on June 13, 1931), it is unlikely that he will be interested in instituting another ambitious set of policy reforms at this stage in his life. He has also indicated that he will not stand for a third term as President, making his current term set to end in February 2018 his last. It is therefore reasonable to conclude that the current reform package towards small enterprise will remain in place for the rest of Raúl's Presidency and that the current cautious approach towards establishing cooperatives will be carried out as planned. For these reasons, we would expect a high degree of policy stability towards small enterprise, implying a systematic implementation of the policies already proposed perhaps with minor adjustments at the margins to make them work better as we have already seen between 2011 and 2014.

The current approach also includes the conversion of some state enterprises to cooperatives and the establishment of new cooperatives operating under the market mechanism. If this initiative were implemented to the maximum, it would include a large proportion of the production of goods and services. The Cuban economy would then include a relatively small private sector of micro- and small enterprises, a sector of medium-sized worker managed cooperative enterprises, a joint state/foreign owned enterprise sector, and a reformed state enterprise sector. This is an interesting and indeed radical possibility as there are no economies at this time that have functioned with such a large cooperative sector, though most economies do have small cooperative sectors acting as a complement or an alternative to the dominant private sector. Some observers have christened Cuba's new economic structure as "market socialism" or perhaps "state capitalism." However, both of these labels may be too simple to capture the internal complexity of the Cuban economy as it transitions from a classic form of state socialism to an unclear future. With a large cooperative sector as well as the other components outlined above, perhaps such a hybrid economic system might better be labeled a "mixed cooperative market economy."

Under this second scenario and given the reforms that have already been introduced, the small enterprise and cooperative sector would expand significantly. However, there are a number of major shortcomings that seriously constrain the optimal development of the small enterprise sector and reduce the benefits that it could generate for Cuban society. For example, as noted in Chapter 5, the current tax regime and the prohibition of professional services small enterprises limit the development of the sector, thereby fueling the underground economy and impairing the revitalization of the Cuban economy. Furthermore, while there has been a quantitative leap in the numbers of *cuentapropistas* from 2010 to 2014, there continue to be limits on the self-employed sector's economic dynamism, on its ability to absorb laid off state workers, and on its contribution to innovation, productivity, and economic growth. These limits are due more than anything else to the leadership's political resistance to private wealth generation and full property rights, not to mention the recognition of and respect for full civil liberties and political rights (Corrales 2012).

There also has been significant though lower-level bureaucratic "foot-dragging" and hostility on the part of some of the officials relied upon to implement the reforms. As President Raúl Castro put it: "It is worthwhile reiterating that our cadres must get used to working with the guiding documents issued by the institutions empowered to do so and abandon the irresponsible habit of putting them on ice" (2011a). In the extreme, if bureaucratic inertia were to become "bureaucratic insurgency" the capacity of the state to implement policy initiatives could be damaged. As Jorge Domínguez succinctly put it: "Can Cuban Rulers Rule Cuba?" (2012). In our estimation the "foot-dragging" undoubtedly will continue but likely will be contained.

A third approach would be an acceleration of reforms towards small enterprise, medium and large enterprise, and an institutional rebalancing among public, private, and cooperative sectors. This would ultimately include a somewhat different mix of enterprises than the second approach. Presumably, medium and large private enterprises could evolve at the expense of cooperative and smaller private enterprises. This path would be more likely if Cuba's new pilot programs in non-agricultural cooperatives fail to take hold and provide employment and produce goods and services in sufficient quantity and quality.

The viability of this third approach would also depend somewhat on changes in United States policy toward Cuba and on Cuba's own policy toward its large and wealthy diaspora, which already plays a significant, though largely silent role in the Cuban economy as suppliers of credit and start-up capital via the billions of dollars they collectively send to the island annually in remittances and in kind. As argued above, however, this third approach will not be promoted under the Presidency of Raúl Castro—to the extent that he is able to maintain control over the pace and depth of economic changes on the island. One wild card that has become increasingly prominent during 2014 is the rising chorus of voices from a surprisingly diverse set of stakeholders in the United States calling for a serious relaxation of U.S. policy toward Cuba, especially as calibrated changes in that policy can encourage the Cuban governments pro-market openings and provide both material and technical support to Cuba's fledging entrepreneurs. We believe that such principled engagement with Cuba's emergent civil society—and particularly of the island's increasingly robust and independent small enterprise sector—can and indeed should be allowed to play a role in the consolidation and expansion of Cuba's economic reforms.[4]

However, in time a successor will continue the rethinking that has occurred under Raúl's Presidency and will likely further liberalize public policy towards small enterprise, legalize medium and perhaps larger enterprise in the private sector, and permit an expansion of the private sector generally in the production of goods and services while continuing the predominant role of the state in the provision of public goods. Under this approach, we could expect that ultimately the Cuban economy would present a mixture of private, cooperative, and state enterprise that would not be too different from those in much of the rest of the world. Of course, this type of mixed economic structure has advantages and disadvantages. The citizens of no nation are fully satisfied with its particular mix of economic institutions.

At some point, important decisions regarding the role of large-scale privately owned enterprises—domestic or foreign—will have to be made. Will Cuban policy makers of the future permit the type of concentration of private ownership—a "Walmartization" of the economy that would generate significant income and wealth, but also intensely concentrate it and exacerbate already rising inequalities as well? This seems unlikely unless there were a dramatic change in government. However, it might be noted that Cuba already has an intense concentration of control within the state sector with conglomerate state enterprises such as Grupo Cimex S.A., Cubanacán S.A., and Gaviota S.A. (owned by the Cuban Armed Forces). Any full or partial privatization of these could lead to a Walmart-like concentration of wealth and income—as occurs in other countries.

Given the Scylla of private corporatization and increased income and wealth inequality and the Charybdis of monolithic and undemocratic state capitalism, we sincerely hope that Cuba, in the more distant future and like most other countries, will strive continuously to adjust its mixture of small, medium, and large private enterprises, cooperatives, joint enterprises, foreign enterprises, and public enterprises in order to best provide the jobs, goods, and services needed by its citizens in the context of maintaining an equitable distribution of income.

Notes

[1] This is notwithstanding the recent reemphasis of "law and order" in the private sector (described in Chapter 7) along with a highly public crackdown against the operators of clothing boutiques that relied on informal imports and private 3D movie theaters and game rooms, which had taken creative advantage of the limited list of self-employment activities (described in Chapter 5).

[2] For more on this, see *Associated Press* correspondent Peter Orsi's provocative story, "Cubans with money revel in booming social circuit," March 24, 2014, and photographer Michael Dweck's surprising peak into the emerging world of the *farándula cubana* (Cuban highlife), *Habana Libre: The Other Side of the Story* (2011).

[3] For example, the kind and direction of economic reforms enacted to date have been harshly criticized as the introduction of a non-democratic form of "state capitalism" (as opposed to a better version of "participatory and democratic socialism"—

socialismo participativo y democrático) by at least one group of mostly young Cuban self-described "libertarian" socialists associated with the independent Cuban group *Observatorio Crítico*. For examples of this kind of criticism, see the writings of Isbel Díaz Torres and Dmitri Prieto Samsonov posted at the *Havana Times* and *Observatorio Crítico* websites.

[4] Easily the most surprising of these calls came in the form of an "open letter" to President Obama from a bipartisan group of former U.S. government officials and Cuban-American business leaders and philanthropists. The four point letter requested that the President: "(1) Expand and safeguard travel to Cuba for all Americans, (2) Increase support for Cuban civil society, (3) Prioritize principled engagement in areas of mutual interest, and (4) Take steps to assure financial institutions that they are authorized to process all financial transactions necessary and incident to all licensed activities" (Open Letter 2014; Adams 2014). Other, similar calls and initiatives have been launched by the Americas Society/Council on the Americas Cuba Working Group (AC/COA 2014), the Cuba Emprende Foundation (Cuba Emprende 2014), and the new pro-engagement lobbying group #CubaNow (Herrero 2014). Also see a fascinating pair of *New York Times* articles in early March by Damien Cave, which provoked a sustained criticism from the Cuban-American congressional caucus (Cave 2014b, c, and d).

In addition to the U.S.-based and Cuban-American supported Cuba Emprende Foundation mentioned above, it should be noted that there are already a number of university-level programs in existence aimed at providing business administrative courses to Cuba's *cuentapropistas* (and presumably members of these new non-agricultural cooperatives). One such course is offered by the *Centro Cultural Padre Félix Varela* of the Archdiocese of Havana, in cooperation with the *Universidad Católica San Antonio*, Murcia, Spain. Other such courses are being offered by the University of Havana and the University of Las Tunas (Batista Valdés 2014; AIN 2014).

Appendix 1
Timeline of Small Enterprise Under the Revolution*

Economic Nationalizations, Confrontation with the United States, and Consolidation of the Revolution, 1959–1962

1959–1962: Nationalization of U.S., German, British, and other foreign corporate holdings. Agrarian reform limits size of farmlands and breaks-up sugar and tobacco lands into smaller private or state holdings. Urban reform slashes rents and allows for renters to become owners. State takes control of housing market, especially property "forfeited" by émigrés. Most SMEs owned by Cubans are gradually nationalized.

1959: April: Castro visits United States, but refuses aid; **June**: Castro's originally moderate cabinet breaks apart.

1960: February: First Deputy Soviet Premier Anastas Mikoyan visits Havana as part of a science exhibition; **March**: President Eisenhower secretly authorizes the CIA to begin planning Castro's overthrow; **May**: Cuba and the USSR re-establish diplomatic relations; **June**: Cuba nationalizes U.S. petroleum refineries after their refusal to process Soviet crude; **July**: The United States eliminates Cuban sugar quota and the USSR immediately offers to purchase the rest; **August–October**: All remaining U.S. businesses nationalized. The first elements of the U.S. trade embargo is imposed on Cuba.

1961: January: The United States cuts off diplomatic relations with Cuba; **April**: The Bay of Pigs invasion fails; **May**: Castro establishes revolutionary cultural policy with his "words to the intellectuals" speech that includes the declaration: "Within the Revolution, everything; against it, nothing."

---

*We thank our colleague Phil Peters for permission to use parts of his reform chronology here for the period 2006-2013 (2013a). It is available at: "A Chronology of Cuba's Economic Reform," *Cuban Research Center*, August 19, 2013. http://www.us-crc.org/a-chronology-of-cubas-economic-reform/.

1962: Additional elements of the U.S. trade embargo are imposed making it complete. Goods from the Soviet Union and Eastern European members of the Council of Mutual Economic Assistance (CMEA) replace American consumer goods. The ration book is introduced; **October**: The Cuban Missile Crisis brings world to brink of nuclear war. Fidel Castro is not consulted during negotiations; **December**: Law #1076 nationalizes 4,600 large- and medium-sized commercial enterprises, leaving only family and microenterprises in private hands.

Socialist Economic Experimentation, 1962–1970

1965: UMAP camps established to "re-educate anti-social elements," including homosexuals. Last significant guerrilla fighters are eliminated in Escambray mountains. Emigration through "freedom flights" begins, more than 250,000 leave by 1973.

1967: October: Che Guevara captured and executed in Bolivia.

1968: Castro approves of the Soviet invasion of Czechoslovakia in response to the "Prague Spring"; **March–April**: In the "Revolutionary Offensive," the Cuban government eliminates or confiscates over 55,000 small private businesses.

1970: Failure to harvest Castro's goal of 10 million tons of sugarcane leads to a Soviet-style "institutionalization" of the revolution over the next decade, accompanied by a gradual turn toward new "market-socialist" economic policies.

Communist Institutionalization, 1971–1986

1971: Show-trial and coerced confession of prize-winning poet Heberto Padilla causes an international scandal. First National Conference of Education and Culture outlines policies for "true creative freedom," beginning the *quinquenio gris*—a long "gray" period of rigid parameters for art and culture and repression of critical-minded artists and writers.

1972: Cuba joins the Eastern Bloc trade organization CMEA.

1974: Grass-roots governance organization, *Poder Popular* (People's Power), is established.

1975: First Communist Party Congress takes place followed by the passage of Cuba's first socialist Constitution in 1976.

1977: The Carter administration oversees a brief thaw in bilateral relations between the United States and Cuba, including the opening of "interest sections" in one another's capitals, the release of Cuban political prisoners, and the first ever family visits of exiles back to Cuba.

1978: Summer: The Cuban government approves Decree-Law #14 on self-employment, legalizing parts of the underground economy. The law is aimed at absorbing unemployment, improving the supply and quality of goods and services, and shrinking the size of the black market.

1979: Castro is elected the president of the Non-Aligned Movement. He also comes out in support of the Soviet invasion of Afghanistan.

1980: April: Decree-Law #66 permits the opening of *mercados libres campesinos* (MLCs or farmers' markets) where private farmers can sell their produce; **May–October**: Massive boatlift out of port of Mariel sends 125,000 refugees to the U.S., most of whom are transported aboard small ships captained by Cuban exiles.

1982: September: Decree-Law #106 is passed explicitly excluding intermediaries from MLCs, revoking the right of workers on state farms to grow food privately, and restricting participation in MLCs to private farmers associated with National Association of Small Farmers (ANAP).

Mid-1980s: The unraveling of the Soviet and CMEA economies impacts foreign trade and consumption. Some market liberalizations allow MLCs, craftsmen, and artists to sell their wares but this ends in 1986-1987 through the "Rectification of Errors and Negative Tendencies" campaign, the official name given to the set of policies aimed at snuffing out timid privatizations.

The Rectification Campaign, 1986–1990

1986: The "Rectification Campaign" begins. It is Cuba's answer to the Soviet Union's glasnost (openness/transparency) and perestroika (reform/restructuring).

1988: Cuban troops are withdrawn from Angola after helping to secure victory for the MPLA against the South African-backed UNITA.

1989: Decorated Cuban general Arnaldo Ochoa is executed for high treason, along with other military officers in the wake of a corruption scandal, followed by a major restructuring of the Cuban Military and Interior Ministry. Collapse of the Berlin Wall symbolizes the denouement of the Soviet-inspired global communist movement. Rationing tightens in Cuba.

The Special Period, 1990–2006

1990: The USSR switches to hard-currency deals with Cuba. Castro declares the beginning of a "special period in times of peace" to confront the looming economic crisis.

1991: The Soviet Union collapses and the CMEA is dissolved with the end of their special political and economic relationship with Cuba. Trade deficits mount in Cuba. Rationing of consumer goods and services deepens. The Fourth Party Congress approves self-employment yet enacts no legislation to allow for its implementation for two years.

1992: The U.S. Congress passes the "Cuban Democracy Act," hardening the U.S. embargo as a way to spur the collapse of the Cuban government during the post-Soviet "special period" crisis.

1993: July: Fidel Castro includes self-employment among the new internal economic reforms that he announces in his public speech marking the 40th anniversary of his attack on the Moncada Barracks; **September**: Decree-Law #141, "On the Exercise of Self-Employment," is published in *Granma* along with a list of 117 newly allowed private occupations; **October**: *Granma* article indicates that over 40,000 Cubans already legally engaged in self-employment prior to the declaration of Decree-Law #141. The total number of legally registered self-employed reported to be 46,505. New occupations are added to list of self-employed jobs, including *bicitaxis* (bicycle-taxis); **December**: Five occupations initially included in the self-employment list are suspended, including chauffer service, the sale of flowers, and "producer of light snacks (refreshments, sweets, fritters, etc.)," which had been used by many Cuban entrepreneurs to set up small, home-based restaurants, Cuba's first *paladares*. During a discussion of self-employment at the National Assembly it is described as "necessary and popular" and a decision is made to slowly advance its development "based on a sense of social justice with strong measures against *macetas*" (intermediaries and exploiters).

1993 to present: Foreign remittances from the Cuban diaspora gradually increase as hard currency can now be used to purchase goods in non-peso stores.

By 2000, remittances account for the single-largest source of hard currency, surpassing tourism. Trained professionals start to abandon state jobs to work in tourism, joint-venture operations, or self-employment.

1994: The Cuban Convertible Currency (CUC) is implemented as a way to capture other hard currencies. CUCs can be purchased in national pesos (*moneda nacional* or Cuban pesos, CUPs), Euros, sterling pounds, and even dollars, but can only be used on the island. CUCs become one of the most over-valued currencies in the world because their exchange rate is set arbitrarily without corresponding gold reserves or Central Bank guarantees. The Cuban government legalizes use of the U.S. dollar and allows for the return of private farmers' markets (now called "*agros*" or *mercados agropecuarios*). A first ever riot occurs in the *Centro Habana* section of the capital in the midst of a massive rafter emigration from Cuba to the United States. This emigration crisis leads the U.S. to change its policy of automatic acceptance of all Cuban émigrés. A February article in the Cuban magazine *Bohemia* puts the number of registered self-employed workers at 142,585 in a total of 135 occupations among which artisan and taxi/coach driver are by far the most common. Havana is home to nearly one-fourth (35,646) of all *cuentapropistas*.

1995: A new law allowing for direct foreign investment is approved; **February**: An inspector corps to provide vigilance of the self-employed is created. Havana reaches legally registered 48,353 *cuentapropistas*; **June**: New resolutions expand self-employment into 19 new activities, including the three food service categories: "*al detalle*" (street vending and take-out service), "*a domicilio*" (catering), and "*servicios gastronómicos*" ("*paladar*" home restaurants); **July**: Initially prohibited from self-employment, professionals are now allowed to become self-employed in areas outside their training and expertise; **August**: Accord #84 dictates a series of restrictions on the exercise of self-employment in the City of Havana, including spatial limits. An article in *Granma* on indicates that the Havana municipality of *Centro Habana* is home to the greatest concentration of self-employed workers and that just two months after being legally allowed, food service "*al detalle*" has become the most common occupation along with 278 *paladares* licensed so far.

1996: February: A peso tax increase is announced in many areas of self-employment, including "driver of rented car" (from 100 to 400 CUPs), "*al detalle*" (100 to 200), "*paladares*" (400 to 800), and the sale of alcoholic drinks in *paladares* (100 to 200). If customers in *paladares* are charged in dollars, the enterprise must pay an additional monthly fee in dollars ($300 for food and $100 for alcohol). The number of registered self-employed workers peaks at 208,786. Cuba shoots down a Brothers to the Rescue plane over international waters resulting in the passage of the Helms-Burton law by U.S. Congress.

Clinton signs it, yet suspends its implementation; **April**: The issuance of new *paladar* licenses is suspended for Havana; **June**: New self-employment regulations require that those who wish to sell in dollars, must pay 75% of their monthly tax in dollars. A six-month re-inscription of all self-employed workers begins, mandating that all workers (including "family helpers" in food service operations) now pay a monthly tax; **November**: Decree-Law #168, "On Licensing Transportation Operations," is issued moving all private transportation services under the jurisdiction of the Ministry of Transportation. This is followed by Resolution #97 (March 24, 1997), which regulates the issuance of licenses for private transportation.

1997: Cuban Dissidence Working Group issues the statement *La Patria es de Todos* ("The Homeland Belongs to Us All"); **May**: Decree-Law #171, "On the rental of houses, rooms, and spaces," is approved and set to go into effect on July 15, 1997; **June**: Decree-Law #174, "On the Personal Violations of Self-Employment Regulations," outlines specific punishments for self-employed workers, including fines, revocations of licenses, and confiscation of materials and equipment; **November**: Cuban official Raúl Valdés Vivo compares domestic "self-employed" capitalists to "piranhas [...] capable of rapidly devouring a horse down to the bones" and declaring that letting Cubans invest in private businesses "would introduce a social force that sooner or later would serve the counterrevolution."

1998: January: Pope John Paul II makes an extended visit to Cuba, holding a public Mass in Revolutionary Plaza; **July**: The newspaper *Trabajadores* announces an increase in the tax rates for many private occupations and declares that any self-employed worker charging in dollars will now have to pay their entire tax in dollars.

1999: Fidel Castro launches law-and-order crackdown against economic crime carried out by new specialized police force; **May**: At the Second Meeting of the National Secretariat of the Committees for the Defense of the Revolution, leaders call on committee heads and citizens to "confront the noxious tendencies and illegalities that have shown themselves [...] in neighborhoods" and to "prevent antisocial and criminal conduct hide beneath the legal façade [of private rental]."

1999–2000: Migration problems erupt when the Elián González case creates and international incident (November–December 1999). Massive rallies are organized in Havana demanding Elián's return. Miami rallies demand that the child remain in the United States. After a dramatic pre-dawn raid and subsequent legal custody battle, the child is returned to Cuba (summer 2000).

Cuba in the Twenty-first Century

Early 2000s: Venezuela sells Cuba oil at greatly discounted prices. In exchange, Cuban professionals, especially health-care workers and physicians, opt for foreign service in Venezuela as part of Fidel Castro and Hugo Chávez's bilateral relations to strengthen socialism in Cuba and build it in Venezuela.

2001: Castro faints during a speech, causing a frenzy in Miami. First major purchases of U.S. foodstuffs by Cuban government follow destruction of Hurricane Michelle. Between 2001 and 2005 the U.S. becomes a leading exporter of food goods to Cuba as a result.

2002: Former U.S. president Jimmy Carter leads a delegation to Cuba. He reads a nationally televised speech (in Spanish) condemning the U.S. embargo, recognizing Proyecto Varela, and criticizing human rights abuses in Cuba. The full text of Carter's speech is published in *Granma*, the Communist Party newspaper. About half of the 152 sugar mills across the island are shut down due to inefficiency. Government policies further encourage private agricultural producers to sell surplus crops in local agricultural markets. Monthly taxes for bed-and-breakfast operators in certain central Havana locations are raised from $100 to $200.

2002–2003: Chief of U.S. Interest Section, James Cason, meets repeatedly with Cuban dissidents, 75 of whom are arrested, charged with sedition, and sentenced to long prison terms (spring 2003). After two successful air hijackings to the United States, the Cuban Coast Guard apprehends a group of boat hijackers. The three ringleaders are quickly executed after secret trials.

2003: New regulations are announced for bed-and-breakfast operators, including a raise in their overall tax rates, a requirement that they pay an additional 30% tax for providing meals to their guests, an additional tax on common areas of the home used by renters, a limit of renting a maximum of two rooms with just two guests per room, a prohibition against hiring anyone from outside the family, the revocation of the right to rent out one's entire apartment, and a requirement that a family member always be present in a rented home.

2004: May: New self-employment restrictions suspend the granting of new licenses in 40 occupations, including for children's party clowns, used book sellers, makers of flower wreaths, masseuses, newspaper vendors, and each of the four food service occupations legalized in 1995: street vendors, cafeterias, caterers, and *paladares*. This change reduced to 118 from 158 the number of self-employment occupations for which licenses were still available. Additionally, non-*paladar* food service operators are prohibited from using potatoes in their products and required to hire (and pay taxes on) at least one family helper. *Paladar* operators are instructed that their required three (up from two) family helpers must have been members of the family or co-residents in the home for at least the three preceding years. Finally, the government now stipulated explicitly that "alcoholic drinks will only be served with the meal" (and not at a bar) (Resolution No. 11, 2004); **Fall**: The Bush administration sets a new hard-line policy under the Commission for Assistance to a Free Cuba, designed to deny funds to the Cuban government. The policy names a "transition coordinator," restricts educational exchange, and limits remittances and family visits. In response, Fidel Castro eliminates domestic use of the U.S. dollar, replaces it with the convertible Cuban peso (CUC), and adopts the Euro as the preferred foreign currency. Cubans using dollars are charged a 10% penalty and a 10% processing fee in an attempt to encourage the use of CUCs over dollars.

2005: The Cuban government scales back economic reforms and recentralizes control over the economy, raises minimum and retirement wages, and begins a new offensive against economic crime and corruption as part of Fidel Castro's "Battle of Ideas." Self-employment and *paladar* operators are singled out by Castro for criticism.

Cuba Under Raúl Castro, 2006–2014

2006: The Commission for Assistance to a Free Cuba issues a second report on Cuba under the motto "Transition, not succession." On July 26, the Cuban government celebrates its 47th anniversary, which is quickly followed by the unanticipated July 31 announcement that Fidel Castro has taken gravely ill and must undergo a serious intestinal operation. Prior to the procedure, Castro issues a written statement temporarily transferring his presidential duties to his younger brother, Raúl, for the first time. General calm prevails in Cuba as Castro turns 80 on August 13.

2007: Soon after taking over from Fidel, Raúl Castro creates commissions to diagnose economic and social problems including pricing policies, growing inequalities, and the deterioration of social services; **May**: Private taxi drivers notice that police are no longer stopping them to check to see if they are licensed; **July**: Raúl Castro's first major speech delivered a year after taking over as acting President gives a glimpse of his reform ideas, calling for "structural and conceptual changes" and placing a priority on agriculture with an eye to the need to increase efficiency and productivity as a way to replace costly food imports; **August**: Raúl Castro signs a law ordering all state companies to adopt a system of "perfecting management" (*perfecionamiento empresarial*), which was initially developed by the military using capitalist-style management techniques; **December**: The under-the-table pay supplements that foreign companies had long provided in hard currency to Cuban workers are legalized.

2008: February: Raúl Castro is elected as Cuba's chief executive, President of the Council of State, a post he held provisionally since 2006; **March**: Following Raúl Castro's promise to remove "unnecessary prohibitions" that affect citizens' lives, a series of consumer restrictions are lifted allowing access to computers, DVD players, cell phone accounts, tourist hotels, and rental cars for those with hard currency. A sweeping reform also begins in agriculture that decentralizes decision-making, increases state prices paid to farmers, leases unused state land to private farmers, and allows farmers to sell produce directly to consumers; **July**: A program of agricultural land grants that had been under way for months was formalized in Decree-Law 259, providing for the distribution of idle state lands to individual farmers and cooperatives. The transportation ministry announces that it will soon begin granting new licenses for private taxis; **August**: A new labor policy removes ceilings on individual earnings in the state sector and directs state sector employers to develop sliding pay scales that reward productive workers with higher pay. Hurricanes Gustav and Ike cause severe infrastructural, economic, and agricultural damage to the island, exacerbating the impact of the global financial crisis.

2009: January: Regulations are published to enable licensing of new private taxis, and their numbers double within six months; **March**: Castro purges his brother's economic cabinet and places trusted military men and reform-minded technocrats in key posts; **April**: The state begins turning over barber and beauty salons to their workers, who pay rent and utilities and run the shops as their own business; **June**: *Granma* begins to publish letters to the editor from readers each Friday weighing in on economic reforms; **August**: The National Assembly establishes the office of the Comptroller General of the Republic, to be headed by Gladys Bejerano, with the aim of strengthen auditing inside state entities, improving "economic discipline," and cracking down on corruption; **September**: *Granma* reports that as part of efforts to achieve "economic rationality," the government will begin the process of closing 24,700 workplace cafeterias. Licenses are issued to food vendors in various cities, making them legal so that they can provide food to Cuban workers on a private basis.

2010: January: Municipal governments are ordered to draw up economic development plans that may include cooperatives and small private business. A pilot project where taxi drivers lease cabs instead of receiving a state wage begins in Havana; **April**: Small barbershops and beauty salons with up to three chairs are privatized under a new leasing system that requires private workers to pay business expenses and taxes but pocket profits; **May**: A meeting between Raúl Castro and Cardinal Jaime Ortega begins a process, also involving the government of Spain, whereby 166 political prisoners would be released from jail, including the 52 remaining from the 75 arrested in the spring of 2003; **June**: The sale of construction materials to the population is liberalized; **August**: New rules authorize Cubans with small garden plots and small farmers to sell produce directly to consumers in kiosks situated along Cuban highways. In his speech to delegates of the National Assembly, Raúl Castro emphasizes his pragmatic approach to economic reform, saying: "We have to erase forever the notion that Cuba is the only country in the world where one can live without working"; **September**: Responding to American journalist Jeffrey Goldberg's question about whether the Cuban model was still something worth exporting, Fidel Castro states: "The Cuban model doesn't even work for us anymore." A statement by the Cuban labor union federation published in *Granma* announces that half a million state sector workers will be laid off by April 2011, with a "parallel increase in the non-state sector." This measure is coupled with an anticipated 250,000 new licenses for family businesses over six months (but both the layoffs and the growth in self-employment will be much slower). Self-employment regulations are loosened and taxes tightened (allowing greater deductions of expenses before taxes), with 178 private occupations legalized. Family businesses are authorized for the first time to hire labor, do business with the state, and rent space from both the state and private entities; **October**: In the first month, 29,000 new entrepreneurs are licensed; **November**: Publication, distribution, and wide-ranging debate of draft version of Cuba's *Lineamientos*, or "Guidelines for Social and Economic Policy of the Party and the Revolution" begins; **December**: Addressing the National Assembly, Finance Minister Lina Pedraza announces that she anticipates that 1.8 million workers will join the "non-state" sector by 2015. Raúl Castro calls on bureaucrats and party cadres at all levels to "facilitate the work [of *cuentapropistas*] rather than generate stigmas and prejudices against them, much less demonize them."

2011: March: Castro announces the original timetable to layoff 500,000 state workers by April has been scrapped and there is no fixed date to complete the process as workers resist losing their jobs and balk at the high cost of proposed leasing arrangements; **April**: The Communist Party Congress elects Raúl Castro to its top position, First Secretary, a post he held provisionally since 2006. Celebration of Sixth Congress of the Cuban Communist Party and commemoration of the 50th anniversary of failed Bay of Pigs invasion takes place. Following the congress a final, amended version of the *Lineamientos* is published, which will guide economic decision-making in the coming years. Included in the new version of the guidelines is the announcement of the coming approval of the sale of private homes and automobiles, potentially providing new sources of capital for budding entrepreneurs. Authorities announce 180,000 people have taken out licenses to work for themselves and rent space to new entrepreneurs since October 2010. State banks are authorized to issue microcredits to new entrepreneurs and state bodies to do business with them; **May**: To help entrepreneurs get on their feet and to spur job creation, certain taxes and regulations affecting entrepreneurs are eased including now allowing all licensed self-employed enterprises to hire employees; **September**: Three new occupations (insurance agent, event planner, and mason) are added to the original September 2010 list of 178, bringing the total to 181; **October**: Car sales are legalized; **November**: A new decree permits Cubans and foreigners legally residing in Cuba to buy and sell residential real estate; **December**: Cuban banks begin to offer loans to entrepreneurs, small farm producers, and persons needing funds to fix up their homes.

2012: March: Cuban media report on a Council of Ministers meeting that approved pilot projects for the creation of private cooperatives in three provinces in sectors other than agriculture; **April**: Cuban labor federation official Raymundo Navarro says that state payrolls have been reduced by 140,000 in 2011 and will be reduced by a further 110,000 in 2012, with the goal of reducing state employment by 500,000 by 2015 (a figure originally targeted for April 2011). The number of licensed Cuban *cuentapropistas* including both entrepreneurs and their employees, reaches 371,200, an increase of 230,000 since October 2010; **October**: The *Gaceta Oficial* also issues new tax rules that stipulate that the per-employee tax that *cuentapropistas* must pay will now apply only to those who hire six or more employees, with an 80 percent rate reduction in this labor tax over the next five years. Official statistics report that 397,167 licensed entrepreneurs are in operation, including 5,500 who rent their premises from the government; **December**: New laws take effect permitting creation of private cooperatives outside the farm sector through conversion of state enterprises and by citizens who apply for permits to create new cooperatives. Unlike the *cuentapropista* sector, cooperatives are open to professionals and there is no list of permitted occupations.

2013: January: Major migration reform law takes effect eliminating the "exit visa" requirement. Travelers are now allowed to remain abroad for 24 months, instead of the previous 11 month-limit, now without losing their property or right to residency on the island; **July**: The labor ministry announces that 429,458 licensed entrepreneurs are operating in Cuba. In late 2010, the figure was 143,000. The pilot project phase for non-farm private cooperatives moves forward slowly with 197 approved to run farmers markets, take over bus transportation, provide construction services, etc. Most are converted state enterprises, but 12 were formed by self-employed workers. Remittances are estimated to reach $2.5 billion with another $2.6 billion in goods sent to Cuba by members of the diaspora; **September**: Resolutions 41 and 42 are published in the *Gaceta Oficial* expanding the total number of legal self-employment occupations to 201. The new regulations amount to both a step forward and a step back in the eyes of many *cuentapropistas* since the law gives the specific definition and reach of each legal self-employed occupation, emphasizing restrictions on use/resale of imported products and others acquired in state retail stores; **November**: *Granma* publishes a special note clarifying that the private occupation of 3D cinema and game room operator was never legalized. All those who have set up such businesses are informed that they must "immediately cease all such self-employed activity"; **December**: The market-based sale of used and new imported automobiles commences in Cuba with initial prices ranging between 21,000 and 51,000 CUCs for used Geely, Hyundai, Kia, and Volkswagen models to between 91,000 and 262,000 CUCs for various models of Peugeots.

2014: January: *Gaceta Oficial* publishes a new list of penalties for the violation of self-employment regulations; **March**: The Cuban television program "*Mesa Redonda*" airs a two-part series on self-employment reporting that there were 455,577 licensed *cuentapropistas* as of the end of February 2014. The report also confirmed earlier trends, noting that 68% of all *cuentapropistas* claimed to have previously been unemployed, another 18% continue to work in the state sector, while the remaining 14% were previously retired. These numbers confirm the likelihood that the vast majority of Cuba's self-employed workers have come out of the informal economy, not from the increasing numbers of laid-off state employees; **April**: New foreign investment law approved; **May**: Officials from Google, including co-founder Eric Schmidt, visit Cuba meeting with students, touring computer science campus, and confering with independent cyber-activitist Yoani Sánchez. Upon his return to the U.S., Schmidt criticizes Cuban government control of the Internet and says the U.S. embárgo "makes no sense"; **August**: Number of self-employed reaches 471,085; **September**: Cuban government imposes strict new customs controls that severely restrict the value of goods travelers can bring into the island.

Sources: Cruz and Villamil 2000; *El Universal* 2010b; Frank 2011; Henken 2002b; Henken 2008b; Morales and Scarpaci 2012; Pérez López 1995a; Peters 2013a; Peters and Scarpaci 1998; Cuba Central Blog 2014; CubaDebate 2014b; Mesa Redonda 2014; Manguela 2014; Weissenstein 2014.

Appendix 2
201 Legalized Self-Employment Occupations (as of June 2014)

As described in Chapters 3, 4, 5, and 8, the total number of legally permitted self-employed occupations has fluctuated significantly over time. After 1968, the "Revolutionary Offensive" wiped out virtually the entire remaining nonagricultural private sector (then made up of some 58,000 small and microenterprises). Then, in 1978 the government allowed a very limited experiment in self-employment legalizing 48 private occupations along with *mercados libres campesinos* (farmers' markets) through Decree-Law #14, enacted on July 3, 1978. Most of these were run out of business during the "Rectification Campaign" that began in 1986.

In 1993, as a response to the economic crisis of the "special period," the government changed course once again and reinstituted self-employment, this time legalizing 117 occupations (Decree-Law #141, September 9, 1993; Alonso 1993), which grew to 157 by 1997, including the famed *paladares* (legalized in 1995) by Joint Resolutions #3 and #4, enacted on June 8, 1995, private taxis and other forms of transportation (legalized in 1996) by Decree-Law #168, enacted on December 6, 1996, and bed-and-breakfasts (or *casas particulares*), legalized by Decree-Law #171, enacted on May 16, 1997, but already quite common in the informal economy by then.

By the early 2000s, however, the government had instituted policies that ran many of these small enterprises out of business or back underground and officially ceased to issue new licenses in 40 of the total 157 legal self-employed occupations based on Resolución # 11 of *Gaceta Oficial* #32, enacted on May 11, 2004. Thus, the total numbers of licensed *cuentapropistas* dropped from a peak of 209,606 in January 1996 to 149,000 by January 2004 (Peters 2006) and would dip below that level in the six years before Raúl Castro changed policy once again in September 2010 with a new round of legislation that legalized 178 occupations (*Gaceta Oficial* #12, October 8, 2010), which grew to 181 by fall 2011 (*Gaceta Oficial* #29, September 7, 2011) and again to 201 in September 2013 (*Gaceta Oficial* #27, September 26, 2013).

Authorized by the Municipal Labor Authority (Occupations #1–#165)

1. Musical Instrument Tuning and Repair—90 CUPs
2. Water Delivery—70 CUPs
3. Construction Laborer—80 CUPs (see related #155)
4. Animal Rental—80 CUPs
5. Formal Wear Rental—250 CUPs
6. Knife and Scissors Sharpener—40 CUPs
7. Party Entertainer (clowns or magicians)—100 CUPs
8. Mule Driver—30 CUPs
9. Artisan, Maker of Arts and Crafts (professional artists not allowed)[1]—300 CUPs
10. Mechanical Saw Operator (as in a sawmill)—60 CUPs
11. Babysitter/Nanny (sanitary licenses required)—80 CUPs
12. Barber (see related #187)—varies by region, 80-220 CUPs in urban areas, 60-130 CUPs in rural areas, and 15-70 CUPs in mountainous areas
13. Embroiderer/Knitter—40 CUPs
14. Wagon or Pushcart Operator (for transportation and/or as a plow with oxen)—50 CUPs
15. Stone Mason ("*cantero*") (requires special authorization from the Ministry of Energy and Mines; see related #147)—60 CUPs
16. Carpenter—200 CUPs
17. Agricultural Street Vendor from Mobile Hand Cart (not permitted to sell imported products; must adhere to all itinerary, traffic, and sidewalk regulations)—70 CUPs; (see related #39)[2]
18. Locksmith—80 CUPs
19. Furniture Repairman—100 CUPs
20. Collector/Payer of Bills (fines, taxes, services rendered, utilities, etc.)—100 CUPs
21. Operator of Children's Fun Wagon Pulled by Horse, Pony, or Goat—80 CUPs
22. Buyer, Seller, and Renter of Records/CDs (must follow copyright regulations)[3]—60 CUPs
23. Buyer, Seller, and Renter of Used Books—60 CUPs
24. Builder, Seller, and Installer of Radio and TV Antennas (restricted to domestic signals)[3]—80 CUPs
25. Builder, Seller, and Repair of Wicker Furniture—70 CUPs
26. Breeder/Seller of Pets—60 CUPs
27. Window Glass Installation and Repair (does not include the production of arts and crafts made of glass)—70 CUPs

28. Animal Caretaker—120 CUPs
29. Public Bathroom and Box Office Attendant—70 CUPs
30. Caretaker of Sick/Elderly/Handicapped Persons—20 CUPs
31. Caretaker of Public Parks—50 CUPs
32. Leather Tanner (except cows and horses)—60 CUPs
33. Decorator—150 CUPs
34. Palm Tree Trimmer—20 CUPs

Five Primary Food Service Occupations (#35–#39)

35. Restaurant ("*paladar*") Owner/Operator (in one's home or a rented locale; maximum capacity of 50 seats; allowed to sell alcoholic beverages, cigars, and cigarettes; allowed to offer take-out/catering; must obtain sanitary license; see related #168)—700 CUPs
36. Cafeteria ("*punto fijo*") Owner/Operator (in one's home or a rented locale; maximum capacity of 50 seats; not allowed to serve alcoholic beverages without specific authorization; allowed to sell cigars and cigarettes; allowed to offer take-out/catering; must obtain sanitary license)—400 CUPs
37. Caterer ("*a domicilio*") (not allowed to sell alcoholic beverages and must obtain sanitary license)—250 CUPs
38. Cafeteria Specializing in Light Snacks (in one's home or a rented locale; without the use of any tables or chairs; not allowed to sell alcoholic beverages, cigars, or cigarettes without specific authorization; must obtain sanitary license)—200 CUPs
39. Food and Beverage Street Vendor (can sell from cycles, food carts, etc. but not from fixed kiosks or the like; must adhere to all itinerary, traffic, and sidewalk regulations; must obtain sanitary license; not allowed to sell alcoholic beverages, imported products, or those obtained in retail stores)—150 CUPs; (see related #17)[2, 4]
40. Charcoal Manufacturer/Seller (must adhere to forestry regulations)—30 CUPs
41. Wine Maker/Seller (must obtain sanitary license)—120 CUPs
42. Maker/Seller/Repairer of Yokes, Harnesses, and Rope for Oxen—40 CUPs
43. Electrician—100 CUPs
44. Automobile Electrician—150 CUPs
45. Building Superintendent—30 CUPs
46. Book Binding and Repair—30 CUPs
47. Electric Motor Rewiring—100 CUPs
48. Animal Trainer—80 CUPs
49. Flower Wreath Arranger and Seller—80 CUPs

50. Button Upholsterer (wraps buttons in cloth, for upholstery and cocktail dresses popular in the 50s and 60s)—30 CUPs
51. Photographer/Videographer—200 CUPs
52. Car washer/Oil Changer—40 CUPs
53. Bus/Train/Taxi Stop Barker (calls out instructions to waiting passengers; see related #191-#193)—80 CUPs
54. Engraver of Numbers—40 CUPs
55. Maker/Fitter/Seller of Horseshoes and Nails—30 CUPs
56. Buyer/Seller of Tin, Scrap, or Sheet Metal—40 CUPs
57. Driving Instructor—100 CUPs
58. Coach/Sports Trainer (does not include martial arts, scuba diving, or windsurfing)[3]—150 CUPs
59. Gardener—60 CUPs
60. Clothes Washing/Ironing—30 CUPs
61. Woodsmen/Logger (must adhere to forestry regulations)—30 CUPs
62. Shoe-Shiner—20 CUPs
63. Spark Plug Cleaner and Tester—40 CUPs
64. Septic Tank Repair and Cleaning—20 CUPs
65. Manicurist—varies by region, 70-200 CUPs in urban areas, 40-100 CUPs in rural areas, and 20 CUPs in mountainous areas
66. Make-Up Artist—45 CUPs
67. Masseuse—80 CUPs
68. Plasterer—50 CUPs
69. Refrigerator Mechanic—100 CUPs
70. Typist and Copier—30 CUPs
71. Messenger (does not include postal or remittance services)—40 CUPs
72. Seamstress or Tailor (does not include the sale of industrial or imported clothing)[2]—80 CUPs
73. Miller of Grains—60 CUPs
74. Audio System Installer/Operator (must adhere to established noise level norms)—100 CUPs
75. Tire Repair and Operator of Air Compressor—100 CUPs
76. Installer/Operator/Renter of Children's Recreational Equipment (does not include aquatic equipment; subsequent announcement ruled out private cinemas –3D and otherwise– and video game rooms)[3]—100 CUPs
77. Parking Attendant for Cars, Bicycles, and Tricycles—80 CUPs
78. Hairdresser—varies by region, 100-400 CUPs in urban areas, 70-200 CUPs in rural areas, and 20-80 CUPs in mountainous areas
79. Animal Groomer—60 CUPs
80. Cleaning/Household Help—30 CUPs
81. Car Painter—300 CUPs
82. Furniture Painter and Varnisher—80 CUPs

83. House Painter—100 CUPs
84. Sign Painter (does not include applying paint to people's skin)[3]—60 CUPs
85. Ornamental/Pet Fish Farmer (includes the sale of feed and other accessories)—45 CUPs
86. ID/Photo Laminator—30 CUPs
87. Plumber—80 CUPs
88. Well Digger—30 CUPs
89. Producer/Seller of Household Items (self-made or made by other self-employed individuals, but not imported or acquired in retail stores; see related #118)[2]—70 CUPs
90. Producer/Seller of Rubber Accessories (relates to shoe soles, pressure cooker seals, blender O-rings, etc.)—80 CUPs
91. Producer/Seller of Clay Goods (pots, planters, and cookware)—80 CUPs
92. Producer/Seller/Collector of Bricks and Tiles—100 CUPs
93. Producer/Seller of Religious Articles (except those deemed National Patrimony by the Ministry of Culture) and Seller of Animals for Use in Religious Rituals—100 CUPs
94. Producer/Seller of Harnesses, Blankets, and Saddles—40 CUPs
95. Producer/Seller of Costume Jewelry—300 CUPs
96. Shoemaker/Shoe Sales (professional artists not allowed; see related #144)[1]—400 CUPs
97. Producer/Seller of Brooms and Brushes—60 CUPs
98. Producer/Seller of Plaster Figurines—40 CUPs
99. Grower/Seller of Ornamental Flowers and Plants—100 CUPs
100. Piñata Maker/Seller (including other birthday party items)—80 CUPs
101. Grower/Collector/Seller of Plants for Animal Feed and Medicinal Purposes—80 CUPs
102. Music/Art Instructor—100 CUPs
103. Shorthand, Typing, and Language Instructor—100 CUPs
104. Computer Programmer—80 CUPs
105. Metal Polisher (does not include the sale of any products)[3]—40 CUPs
106. Collector/Seller of Natural Resources (i.e., sell shells; adheres to regulations of the Ministry of Science, Technology, and Environment)—20 CUPs
107. Collector/Seller of Recyclables (adheres to regulations of the Ministry of Science, Technology, and Environment)—30 CUPs
108. Watch Repair—50 CUPs
109. Leather Repair—40 CUPs
110. Jewelry Repair (does not include the sale of gold, silver, bronze, plat-

inum, etc.)³—200 CUPs
111. Bed frame repair (see related #117)—40 CUPs
112. Automobile Battery Repair—60 CUPs
113. Bicycle Repair—60 CUPs
114. Costume Jewelry Repair—60 CUPs
115. Fence and Walkway Repair—20 CUPs
116. Stove/Range Repair—50 CUPs
117. Mattress Repair (see related #111)—100 CUPs
118. Small Household Goods Repair (see related #89)—60 CUPs
119. Office Equipment Repair—45 CUPs
120. Electronic Equipment Repair—90 CUPs
121. Mechanical and Combustion Equipment Repair (automobiles, trucks, motorcycles, etc.)—100 CUPs
122. Eyeglass Repair—30 CUPs
123. Sewing Machine Repair—35 CUPs
124. Saddle and Harness Repair—50 CUPs
125. Umbrella and Parasol Repair—30 CUPs
126. Disposable Lighter Repair and Refill—40 CUPs
127. Tutor (currently active state sector teachers not eligible)[5]—60 CUPs
128. Doll and Toy Repair—30 CUPs
129. Art Restorer (cannot sell artwork)[3]—250 CUPs
130. Night Watchman or Doorman—20 CUPs
131. Welder ("*soldador*"; see related #159)—60 CUPs
132. Leather Craftsman (professional artists not allowed)[1]—50 CUPs
133. Upholsterer—100 CUPs
134. Roofer—30 CUPs
135. Accountant/Tax Preparation/Bookkeeper (currently active state sector accountants not eligible)[5]—120 CUPs
136. Textile Dyer—30 CUPs
137. Machinist—60 CUPs
138. Roaster (i.e. of peanuts, coffee)—40 CUPs
139. Part-Time/Seasonal Farm Laborer—50 CUPs
140. Document Translator—60 CUPs
141. Shearer (as in sheep)—40 CUPs
142. Thresher/Plow Operator—50 CUPs
143. Highway Vendor of Agricultural Produce (from fixed venues or kiosks)—50 CUPs
144. Shoe Repair (see related #96)—50 CUPs
145. Contracted Employee of Another Self-Employed Person's Business (open to all self-employed occupations but most employees are concentrated in the food service sector, see occupations #35–#39 and #168)—Monthly tax varies

146. Event Planner (weddings, etc.) (does not include the creation and operation of night clubs, cabarets, etc.)[3, 6]—300 CUPs
147. Mason ("*granitero*") (work in Old Havana requires license from the Office of the Historian; see related #15)[6]—150 CUPs

New occupations added on September 26, 2013

148. Real Estate Broker[4]—500 CUPs
149. Repair of Measurement Instruments (scales, etc.)[4]—90 CUPs
150. Food Wholesaler (not allowed to sell imported products)[4]—500 CUPs
151. Food Retailer (in kiosks and farmers' markets) (not allowed to sell imported products)[2, 4]—300 CUPs
152. Runner/Arranger of Private Room/Home Rentals (someone hired to scout out renters for private bed-and-breakfasts; cannot work in airports or hotels; see related #166)[4]—100 CUPs
153. Postal Agent (must obtain a special "Designated Operator" license from the Cuban Postal Service)[4]—20 CUPs
154. Telecommunications Agent (retail services and sales for ETECSA; must first contract with ETCSA)[4]—20 CUPs
155. Building Construction Services (see related #3 and #169)[4]—400 CUPs

Previously discontinued occupations reactivated on September 26, 2013

156. Car Body Remolding[7]—300 CUPs
157. Maker/Seller of Marble Objects[7]—250 CUPs
158. Maker/Seller of Soaps, Polish, Dyes, Etc. (does not include the sale of products acquired in retail stores)[2, 7]—80 CUPs
159. Welder ("*fundidor*"; see related #131)[7]—50 CUPs
160. Iron Worker (makes, sells, and installs grating for doors, windows)[7]—50 CUPs
161. Welder/Flamecutter (cutting with gas)[7]—45 CUPs
162. Maker/Seller of Aluminum Products[7]—100 CUPs
163. Maker/Seller of Non-Ferrous Metals[7]—80 CUPs
164. Floor Polisher[7]—40 CUPs
165. Repairer of Water Pumps[7]—60 CUPs

Authorized by the Municipal Housing Authority

166. Private Room/Home Rental (B&Bs or "*casas particulares*") (allows license holder to rent out room(s) or entire home to houseguests or to rent space to other self-employed individuals who wish to operate their own business there; see related #152)—varies based on the size, number, and kind of space rented; range is typically between 150-200 per room and can be in CUCs or CUPs based on currency in which customers are charged.

Authorized by the National/International Insurance Authority

167. Insurance Agent[6]—20 CUPs

Authorized by Havana's Provincial People's Power Authority

168. Maker/Seller of Food and Beverages in "Chinatown" (operated out of locales rented from the state; maximum capacity of 50 seats or more with previous authorization; can designate a contracted manager to run the business; allowed to sell alcoholic beverages and, cigars, and cigarettes; see related #35)—set by Office of the City Historian

Authorized by the Office of the City Historian of Havana and the PALCO Business Group

169. Private Construction Contractor (working under contractual arrangement with the Office of the City Historian or the PALCO Business Group; see related #155)—set by Office of the City Historian

Authorized by the Office of the Historian of the City of Havana (special self-employment occupations restricted to Old Havana)

170. Horse and Carriage Rides—600 CUPs
171. Antique Dealer[4]—400 CUPs
172. "*Habaneras*" (women who pose for tourists wearing colorful colonial attire)—150 CUPs
173. Fortune Tellers—150 CUPs
174. Folkloric Dancers—150 CUPs

175. The Musical Group *"Los Mambises"*—150 CUPs
176. Caricaturists—150 CUPs
177. Artificial Flower Seller—150 CUPs
178. Street Painters (who sell renderings of scenes that feature colonial architecture)—150 CUPs
179. *"Dandy"* (man dressed in colonial era garb)—50 CUPs
180. Hair Braider—100 CUPs
181. Fresh Fruit Peeler—70 CUPs
182. *"Amor"* Dance Duo—150 CUPs
183. *"Benny Moré"* Dance Team—150 CUPs
184. Trained Dog Exhibitor—100 CUPs
185. *"Los Amigos"* Musical Duo—150 CUPs
186. Extras (people paid to pose for photos in colonial period dress)—70 CUPs
187. Traditional Barber (see related #12)—200 CUPs

Authorized by the State Traffic Unity of the Ministry of Transportation

188. Truck driver—varies based on the size (tonnage) of the truck, ranges between 75 and 450 CUPs
189. Station Wagon Driver—same as above
190. Small-Truck Driver—same as above
191. Bus Driver (see related #53)—varies based on the size (number of passengers) of the bus, ranges between 350 and 575 CUPs
192. Mini-Bus Driver (see related #53)—same as above

Cargo and passenger transport

193. Taxi Driver (see related #53)—for licensed private taxis the tax varies based on the size (number of passengers) of the taxi, ranges between 350 and 575 CUPs; for those self-employed who contract out their services to the state sector, tax is based on the kind of vehicle used (modern, old, or one's own vehicle) with a tax range between 300 and 4,000 CUPs
194. Handcar Operator (on rails)—between 40-60 CUPs
195. Jeep Driver—Same as taxi above
196. Passenger Boat Operator—30 CUPs
197. Motorcycle Driver—250 CUPs
198. Three-Wheeled Pedal Taxi Driver—between 40-60 CUPs

Animal and Human Traction

199. Cart Operator—30 CUPs
200. Horse-Drawn Carriage Operator—30 CUPs
201. Pedal Taxi Driver—60 CUPs

Sources: *Gaceta Oficial*, No. 32, May 11, 2004; No. 12, October 8, 2010; No. 29, September 7, 2011; No. 27, September 26, 2013; Associated Press, January 30, 2011; Peters 2006; D'Cubanos, n.d.; Feinberg 2013.

Notes

[1] Occupations #9 (artisan), #96 (shoemaker), and #132 (leather craftsman) do not permit the licensing of professional artists.

[2] Occupations #17 (agricultural street vendor), #39 (food and beverage street vendor), #72 (seamstress/tailor), #89 (seller of household items), #151 (food retailer), and #158 (maker/seller of soaps, polish, dyes, etc.) do not allow licensees to sell imported products and/or those acquired in state-run retail stores. These restrictions have caused quite a furor among those holding seamstress/tailor licenses (#72) since they had been reselling imported clothing as a significant part of their businesses until licensed activities were narrowly redefined in September 2013. They were given until December 31, 2013 to liquidate their inventory of imported clothing after which all sales of such items became illegal.

[3] Occupations #22 (record/CD sales), #24 (installer of radio and TV antennas), #58 (coach/trainer), #76 (children's ride operator), #84 (sign painter), #105 (metal polisher), #110 (jewelry repair), #129 (art restorer), and #146 (event planner) all include caveats with specific restrictions on their exercise. Likewise, holders of license #76 (operator of children's recreational equipment) were restricted by Resolutions 41/2013 and 42/2013 from operating any aquatic equipment. However, the fact that many had been operating 3D cinemas and/or video game arcades between 2011 and 2013 led to a further clarification published in *Granma* on November 2, 2013, explicitly outlawing such activities as well. This crackdown has been very unpopular (see "En torno al cierre de los cines 3D," *Espacio Laical*, 4/2013, pp. 128-142 and "Un paso atrás," *La Joven Cuba*, October 24, 2013).

[4] An additional ten new occupations (#s 39, 148–155, and 171) were added on September 26, 2013 in Resolutions 41/2013 and 42/2013 by the Ministry of Labor and Social Security, bringing the total to 191.

[5] Occupations #127 (tutor) and #135 (accountant) do not allow private employment for those currently working in that profession for the state.

[6] An additional three new self-employment occupations (#s 146, 147, and 167) were added between 2011 and 2012, increasing the total from 178 to 181.

[7] These ten additional self-employed occupations (#s 156–165) were first authorized during the late-1990s and early-2000s as part of the then 157 licensable occupations. However, they were not reauthorized in October 2010 due to lack of licit sources of inputs. They were reactivated on September 26, 2013 in Resolutions 41/2013 and 42/2013 by the Ministry of Labor and Social Security, bringing the new total to 201.

Glossary

Acopio: The portion of a private farmer's crop that must be sold to the state.
Amiguismo: Connections between friends or family that allow for economic survival, as in *socio-lismo* (see below) or "friend-ism."
Bicitaxi: Pedicab.
Bisnear: Literally meaning "to do business." In Cuba, the word means negotiating on the black market.
Botero: A private taxi driver (often unlicensed).
Casa particular: Private residence used as a bed-and-breakfast.
Casa de Contratación: Contracting house.
Centro de Estudios sobre la Economia Cubana (CEEC): Center for the Study of the Cuban Economy.
Chinchalitos: Pejorative term referring to small businesses.
Colero: A person who queues for goods or services; a professional "*colero*" queues to purchase products for other people, for a fee.
Consejos Populares: Popular councils.
Cuentapropista (CP): In literal terms, "own-account worker" or someone who works for him or herself, or is "self-employed."
Cuota fija mensual (CFM): Fixed minimum tax paid monthly by licensed self-employed workers.
Conciencia: Revolutionary consciousness and commitment.
Corredor: A real estate "runner" who informally acts as an agent bringing real estate buyers and sellers together for a fee (as in *corredor de permutas*, or attanger of housing swaps).
Declaración jurada: A self-administered annual tax payment (literally, a "sworn declaration" of one's tax liability).
Desvio: Literally, a detour or diversion, popularly used to mean "pilferage" or petty theft, usually from the state.
Forrajear: In literal terms, "to forage," or to continuously search for products that are in limited supply.
Inventar: To figure out a way to solve a problem arising from a shortage of goods.
Jefe de Servicios: Chief of Services.
Jinetero/a: A street hustler or prostitute.

La dolce vita: Pejorative term referring to the lifestyles of corrupt officials and black marketeers.
Latifundia: Large-scale landed estates.
Luchar: To fight or to struggle in order to find the necessities of life.
Maceta: Person engaged in black market activity.
Mensajero: A person who runs errands, including acting as a "*colero,*" for others for a fee.
Mercachifleo: Pejorative term referring to black market activities.
Mercados Agropecuarios: Farmers' markets legalized in 1994 (often referred to simply as "*agros*").
Mercados Libres Campesinos (MLCs): Farmers' markets legalized in 1980 and eliminated in 1986.
Moneda Nacional (CUPs): National peso currency.
Nomenklatura: Pejorative Russian term used in Cuba that refers to privileged government officials.
Oficina Nacional de Estadisticas (ONE): National Statistics Office.
Paladar: A private, home-based restaurant (literally "palate").
Palanca: Literally meaning "lever," used to refer to special relations or "pull" that allow for access to scarce goods and services.
Piquera: A taxi stand.
Por la izquierda: "Under the table" or by an illegal transaction.
Punto fijo: A porch-front cafetaria (also called "*al detalle,*" "*merenderos,*" and "*sombrillitas*").
Resolver: Solving problems of scarcity often by illegal means.
Servicios gastronómicos: The legal designation for private restaurants, or *paladares*.
Socio-lismo: Literally, "associate-ism," a spoof on the official term "*socialismo.*" *Socio-lismo* refers to the exchange of favors, usually for illicit purposes among friends.
Taxi particular: A privately owned car used as a taxi.
Tiendas de los ricos: Government-run parallel markets where goods can be purchased outside of the monthly ration at higher prices.
Tiendas de Recaudación de Divisas (TRDs): Stores for the recovery of hard currency, also referred to as "*tiendas de dólar*" (dollar stores) before 2004 and now often as "*los shopping.*"
Tocar el arpa: Literally "to play the harp" meaning to pilfer or to engage in a similar illegality, also indicated without words by a "riff" of the fingers in the air as if one were playing the harp.
Trabajo por cuenta propia: "Own-account" work or self-employment.

Bibliography

14ymedio. 2014a. "El sector privado en Cuba alcanza en julio los 471.085 cuentapropistas," August 25.
14ymedio. 2014b. "Vuelta de tuerca contra el mercado informal," May 30.
Abd'Allah-Álvarez Ramírez, Sandra. 2013. "Trabajo por cuenta propia revela tensiones de género en Cuba," *Global Voices en Español*, October 14.
AC/COA (Americas Society/Council on the Americas). 2014. "Action Memo to the President: Cuba and Entrepreneurship," Cuba Working Group, April.
Accord #84. 1997. "Regulaciones específicas para el ejercicio del trabajo por cuenta propia en el territorio de la Ciudad de La Habana," p. 490 in Dietmar Dirmoser and Jaime Estay, eds., *Economía y reforma económica en Cuba*. Caracas: Nueva Sociedad.
Acosta, Abel. 2000. "No official market economy for Cuba: Sharp decline in numbers of small entrepreneurs." *Latin American, Caribbean, and Central American Report*, August 22.
Adams, David. 2014. "Open letter to Obama calls for new steps to promote change in Cuba," *Reuters*, May 19.
AFP (Agence France-Presse). 2013. "Cuban merchants defy ban on sale of imported clothes," October 8.
AIN (*Agencia de Información Nacional*). 2014. "Capacita Universidad de La Habana a emprendedores cubanos," *Granma*, March 21.
Alessandrini, Sergio and Bruno Dallago, eds. 1987. *The Unofficial Economy: Consequences and Perspectives in Different Economic Systems*. Aldershot, England: Gower.
Alfonso, Pablo. 2012. "De cómo un idóneo se convierte en disponible," *Martinoticias*, June 11.
Alfonso Torno, Odelin. 2014. "¿Cuentapropistas: desempleados o ilegales?" *Cubanet*, January 30.
Alonso, José. 1993. "An Analysis of Decree 141 Regarding Cuban Small-Scale Enterprises." *La Sociedad Económica Bulletin* 35, September 20.
Alonso González, David. 2013. "Para no fracasar por cuenta propia," *On Cuba*, April 9.
Álvarez, Julio Cesar. 2013a. "Censura en 3D," *Cubanet*, October 29.
Álvarez, Julio Cesar. 2013b. "3D Movie and Video Game Rooms Going Underground," *Translating Cuba*, November 5.
"Ampliación de actividades: Paladares." 1997. Joint Resolution #4, June 8, pp. 485-487 in Dirmoser, Dietmar and Jaime Estay, eds. 1995. *Economía y reforma económica en Cuba*. Caracas: Nueva Sociedad.
Anderson, Jon Lee. 2006. "Castro's Last Battle: Can the Revolution Outlive Its Leader," *The New Yorker*, July 31.
Antúnez Sánchez, Alcides Francisco, Jorge Manuel Martínez Cumbrera, and Jorge Luis Ocaña Báez. 2013. "El trabajo por cuenta propia: Incidencias en el nuevo relanzamiento en la aplicación del modelo económico de Cuba en al siglo XXI." *Nómadas: Revista Crítica de Ciencias Sociales y Jurídicas*, Número Especial: América Latina.

Apuleyo Mendoza, Plinio, Carlos Alberto Montaner, and Alvaro Vargas Llosa. 1996. *Guide to the Perfect Latin American Idiot*. New York: Madison Books.
Armengol, Roberto I. 2013. "Competitive Solidarity and the Political Economy of *Invento*." *Cuba in Transition*, Vol. 23, pp. 205-215, Washington, D.C.: The Association for the Study of the Cuban Economy.
Associated Press. 2011. "List of 178 Cuban private-sector jobs," January 30.
Avendaño, Bárbara. 1997. "Trabajadores por cuenta propia. Incremento de las cuotas fijas mensuales," *Tribuna de La Habana*, May 5, 1996, pp. 496-497 in Dietmar Dirmoser and Jaime Estay, eds., E*conomía y reforma económica en Cuba*. Caracas: Nueva Sociedad.
Ávila, Eliécer. 2012. "¿Por qué fracasan los negocios privados en Cuba?" *Diario de Cuba*, October 2.
Ayala Castro, Héctor. 1982. "Transformación de la propiedad en el período 1964-1980." Mimeo.
Azicri, Max. 2000. *Cuba Today and Tomorrow: Reinventing Socialism*. Gainesville: University Press of Florida.
Azor Hernández, Marlene. 2013. "La prohibición no es la salida," *Cubaencuentro*, November 6.
Baker, Christopher P. 2000. *Cuba: Moon Handbooks*, Second edition. Emeryville, CA: Avalon Travel Publishing.
BBC Mundo. 2005. "Cuba: Sorpresa en las gasolineras," October 17.
BBC Mundo. 2014. "El exorbitante precio de los autos en Cuba: Hasta US$262.000 por un Peugeot," January 3.
Barberia, Lorena. 2004. "The End of Egalitarianism? Economic Inequality and the Future of Social Policy in Cuba," in Jorge Domínguez, et al., editors, *The Cuban Economy at the Start of the Twenty-First Century*. Cambridge: Harvard University Press.
Batista, Carlos. 2011. "'Paladares' brotan como hongos en La Habana," *El Nuevo Herald*, January 11.
Batista Valdés, Pastor. 2014. "Espacio para cuentapropistas en Universidad de Las Tunas," *Granma*, April 1.
Beatón Ruiz, Betty, Iliana Hautrive, and Juanita Perdomo. 2012. "El otro sabor de la gastronomía," *Trabajadores*, July 8.
Bengelsdorf, Carolee. 1994. *The Problem of Democracy in Cuba: Between Vision and Reality*. New York: Oxford University Press.
Benítez, Carlos Alberto. 2013. "Guía Cuba, una aplicación que pretende revolucionar el cuentapropismo," *OnCuba*, July 7.
Boti, Regino and Felipe Pazos. 1958. "Tesis del Movimiento Revolucionario 26 de Julio," *Revista Bimestre Cubana*, July-December.
Brouwer, Maria T. 2002. "Weber, Schumpeter, and Knight on entrepreneurship and economic development." *Journal of Evolutionary Economics* Vol. 12, Issues 1-2, p. 83.
Burki, Shahid Javed and Daniel P. Erikson. 2005. *Transforming Socialist Economies: Lessons for Cuba and Beyond*. New York: Palgrave Macmillan.
Burnett, Victoria. 2013. "Harsh Self-Assessment as Cuba Looks Within," *The New York Times*, July 23.
Cabarrouy, Evaldo. 2000. "Evolución y perspectiva de la pequeña empresa no estatal en Cuba." *Cuba in Transition*, Vol. 10, pp. 54-63. Washington, D.C.: The Association for the Study of the Cuban Economy.
Café Fuerte. 2011. "Transfieren al sector privado varios servicios controlados por el Estado," December 27.

Café Fuerte. 2012. "Cubanos podrán alquilar locales estatales para ofrecer servicios gastronómicos," November 9.
Café Fuerte. 2013a. "Cuba amplía acceso público a internet en moneda convertible," May 28.
Café Fuerte. 2013b. "Cuba: 429,458 cuentapropistas registrados," June 25.
Café Fuerte. 2013c. "Cuentapropistas entran al negocio del turismo," October 17.
Café Fuerte. 2013d. "Gobierno Cubano ordena el cierre innediato de salas privadas 3D," November 2.
Café Fuerte. 2014. "Gobierno cubano aprieta las clavijas al trabajo por cuenta propia," January 15.
Cancio Isla, Wilfredo. 2012. "Cuba anuncia reforma migratoria y elimina el permiso de salida del país," *Café Fuerte*, October 16.
Cancio Isla, Wilfredo. 2013. "Cuba autoriza cuentapropismo para agentes onmobilarias," *Café Fuerte*, September 26.
Cantillion, Richard. 1755. *Essai Sur la Nature du Commerce en General*. London.
Cárdenas Lima, Harold. 2013. "Un paso atrás," *La Joven Cuba*, October 24.
Carranza Valdés, Julio, Luis Gutiérrez, and Pedro Monreal. 1995. *Cuba: La restructuración de la economía*. Havana: Editorial de Ciencias Sociales.
Carrillo Ortega, Venus. 2013. "Self-employment in Cuba: more string to the kite...," *On Cuba*, October 11.
Carrillo Ortega, Venus. 2012. "El 1 de diciembre comenzará en Cuba sistema de arrendamiento de locales estatales para servicios gastronómicos," *Cuba Información*, November 9.
Carrillo Ortega, Venus. 2014. "Sector privado en Cuba se abre espacio tambien en el turismo," *Cuba Contemporánea*, February 26.
Carson, Richard. 1973. *Comparative Economic Systems*. New York: Macmillan.
Carthy Correa, Roberto and María Antonia Núñez Valerino. 2013. "El trabajo por cuenta propia en el marco de la actualización del modelo económico cubano," mimeo., Universidad de Oriente, Santiago de Cuba, June.
Caruso-Cabrera, Michelle. 2013. "Cuba shows beginnings of free enterprise—sort of," *CNBC*, July 12.
Cartaya, Rolando. 2014. "Almost half of small businesses have gone under in Cuba," *Martinoticias*, February 5.
Castellanos, Dimas. 2013. "Raúl Castro's Reforms: Two Steps Forward, One Step Back," pp. 411-422 in *Cuba*, edited by Ted A. Henken, Miriam Celaya, and Dimas Castellanos. Santa Barbara: ABC-CLIO Publishers.
Castellanos, Dimas, Ted A. Henken, and Miriam Celaya. 2013. "History," pp. 21-83 in *Cuba*, edited by Ted A. Henken, Miriam Celaya, and Dimas Castellanos. Santa Barbara: ABC-CLIO Publishers.
Castells, Manuel and Alejandro Portes. 1989. "World Underneath: The Origins, Dynamics, and Effects of the Informal Economy," in *The Informal Economy: Studies in Advanced and Less Developed Countries*, edited by Alejandro Portes, Manuel Castells, and Lauren A. Benton. Baltimore: The Johns Hopkins University Press.
Castro, Fidel. 1968. "Speech of March 13," *Granma*, March 15.
Castro, Fidel. 1970a. "Speech of February 9," *Granma Weekly Review*, February 15.
Castro, Fidel. 1970b. "Speech of July 26," *Granma Weekly Review*, August 9.
Castro, Fidel. 1990. "Castro Gives Speech on 30th CDR Anniversary." (FBIS-LAT-90-190). September 29.
Castro, Fidel. 1993. "Castro Gives Speech at Moncada Barracks Anniversary." (FBIS-LAT-93-142). July 26.

Castro, Fidel. 1995a. "Castro Addresses Session of National Assembly Meeting." (FBIS-LAT-95-250). December 27.
Castro, Fidel. 1995b. "Fidel Castro Speaks at Moncada Ceremony." (FBIS-LAT-95-145). July 26.
Castro, Fidel. 1997. "Discurso en el acto central por el 35 aniversario de la Unión de Jovenes Comunistas," *Juventud Rebelde*, April 4.
Castro, Fidel. 2005a. "Discurso pronunciado por Fidel Castro Ruz en el acto por el aniversario 60 de su ingreso a la universidad," Havana, November 17.
Castro, Fidel. 2005b. Speech delivered during the ceremony comemorating the 60th anniversary of Castro's entry into the University," University of Havana, November 17.
Castro, Fidel. n.d. *History Will Absolve Me*. Havana: Book Institute.
Castro, Raúl. 1996. "Informe," read to the Central Committee of the Communist Party of Cuba, March 23.
Castro, Raúl. 1997. "Si hay comida para el pueblo, no importan los riesgos," *Granma Internacional*, September 28, 1994, pp. 458-467 in Dietmar Dirmoser and Jaime Estay, eds., *Economía y reforma económica en Cuba*. Caracas: Nueva Sociedad.
Castro, Raúl. 2007. Speech of July 26th. Accessed December 19, 2012.
Castro, Raúl. 2008. Speech at the close of the first ordinary of the Seventh legislature of the National Assembly, July 11.
Castro, Raúl. 2009. Speech at the 7th Legislature of the National Assembly of People's Power, August 1.
Castro, Raúl. 2010a. Seventh Legislature of the National People's Power Assembly. December 18.
Castro, Raúl. 2010b. "Speech Given by Cuban President Raúl Castro Ruz at the 5th Ordinary Session of the 7th Legislature of the National Assembly of People's Power (Extract)," *TML Daily*, August 1.
Castro, Raúl. 2011a. Central Report to the 6th Congress of the Communist Party of Cuba, April 16.
Castro, Raúl. 2011b. "Speech delivered during the closing ceremony of the Sixth Session of the Seventh Legislature of the National Assembly of People's Power," *CubaDebate*, December 18.
Castro, Raúl. 2011c. "Closing Remarks by Raúl Castro Ruz, at the 6th Party Congress," *CubaDebate* (English), April 21.
Castro, Raúl. 2013. "Discurso de Raúl Castro del 21 de diciembre, 2013," *Havana Times*, December 22.
Cave, Damien. 2014a. "Cuban Vendors, in Rare Move, Stage a protest," *The New York Times*, January 23, 2014.
Cave, Damien. 2014b. "The Cuban Evolution," *The New York Times*, March 1.
Cave, Damien. 2014c. "As Cuba's Economy Opens a Bit, some Who Fled Castro Return to Help," *The New York Times*, March 4.
Cave, Damien. 2014d. "A Miami Congressman Adamantly Defends Isolating Cuba," *The New York Times*, March 4.
Celaya, Miriam. 2013a. "Cuentapropistas: Contra ellos viejo método de 'premio y castigo'," *Cubanet*, October 1.
Celaya, Miriam. 2013b. "Trapi-shoppings: Cuentapropistas en riesgo," *Penúltimos Días*, October 7.
Centeno, Miguel Angel and Alejandro Portes. 2006. "The Informal Economy in the Shadow of the State," in *Out of the Shadows: Political Action and the Informal Economy in Latin America*, edited by Patricia Fernández-Kelly and Jon Shefner. University Park, PA: The Pennsylvania University Press.

Central Committee of the Communist Party of Cuba. 1996. "Informe." March 23.
CEPAL (Comisión Económica para América Latina y el Caribe). 1997. *La economía cubana: Reformas estructurales y desempeño en los noventa*. México: Fondo de Cultura Económica.
Chomsky, Aviva, Barry Car, and Pamela Maria Smorkaloff, eds. 2004. *The Cuba Reader: History, Culture, Politics*. Durham: Duke University Press.
City of Havana. 2010. "Proceso de reducción de plantillas," Power Point Presentation, August 24.
Ciudad de La Habana. 2010. *Proceso de reducción de plantillas*. (Power point presentation). August 24.
Claudia Ferman, Videorecording, 29:40, USA/Cuba/Argentina.
Cluster, Dick. 2004. "To Live Outside the Law You Must Be Honest: Daily Illegality and Its Effects." Proceedings of the Bildner Center symposium, *Cuba Today: Continuity and Change Since the 'Periodo Especial'*, edited by Mauricio Font with Scott Larson and Danielle Xuereb, October 4-5.
"Código de Etica y Conducta." 1995. In Principales disposiciones lagales e indicaciones para ser utilizadas por los inspectores laborales para el trabajo por cuenta propia, 44, mimeo.
Commission on the Private Sector and Development. 2004. Report to the Secretary-General of the United Nations. "Unleashing Entrepreneurship: Making Business Work for the Poor." New York: United Nations Development Program.
Cooke, Julia. 2014. "In Cuba, Unequal Reform," *The New York Times*, April 1.
Corrales, Javier. 2004. "The Gatekeeper State: Limited Economic Reforms and Regime Survival in Cuba, 1989-2002." *Latin American Research Review* Vol. 39, No. 2, pp. 35-65, June.
Corrales, Javier. 2012. "Cuba's 'Equity Without Growth' Dilemma and the 2011 Lineamientos." *Latin American Politics and Society*, Vol. 54: 3, pp. 157-184, Fall.
Corrales, Javier, Dan Erikson, and Mark Falcoff. 2005. *Cuba, Venezuela, and the Americas: A Changing Landscape*. Cuba Forum Working Paper, Inter-American Dialogue, Washington, D.C., and the Cuban Research Institute, Florida International University, Miami, Florida. December.
"Corruption Revealed." 1999. *Caribbean Update*, p. 7, March.
Crabb, Mary Katherine. 2001. "The Political Economy of Caudillismo." In *Cuban Communism* (10th edition), edited by Irving Louis Horowitz and Jaime Suchlicki, 160-181. New Brunswick: Transaction Publishers.
Cruz, Consuelo, and Anna Seleny. 2002. "Reform and Counterreform: The Path to Market in Hungary and Cuba." *Comparative Politics* Vol. 34, No. 2, pp. 211-231, January.
Cruz Reyes, Jesús. 2014. "Cooperativas en Cuba: Participación y democratización en la dirección." Paper presented at the 32nd International Congress of the Latin American Studies Association, Chicago, Illinois, May 21–23.
Cruz, R. and Villamil, A. 2000. "Sustainable Small Enterprise in a Cuban Transition Economy." *Studies in Comparative International Development*, Vol. 34, pp. 100-122.
Cubadebate. 2012. "Arrendarán locales gastronómicos a sus trabajadores," November 9.
Cubadebate. 2013a. "Crece el empleo no estatal en Cuba," August 18.
Cubadebate. 2013b. "Cómo marcha el experimento de las cooperativas no agropecuarias?" August 21.
Cubadebate. 2013c. "Los cines 3D deben cumplir la política cultural del país, afirma viceministro cubano," October 27.

Cubadebate. 2013d. "Cooperativas no agropecuarias a buen ritmo," November 29.
Cubadebate. 2014a. "Actualizan regulaciones para el trabajo por cuenta propia," January 15.
Cubadebate. 2014b. "Trabajo por cuenta propia crece y se valida como opción de empleo en Cuba," March 19.
Cuba Central Blog. 2013. "The Cuba Central News Blast and A Note to Our Readers," August 30.
Cuba Central Blog. 2014. "State media releases latest self-employment stats; Poor evaluations for almost half of Cuba's state enterprises," March 21.
Cuba Dice. 2013. "Trabajo por cuenta propia," October 9.
CubaEncuentro. 2008. "El gobierno anuncia licencias para taxistas privados," July 9.
CubaEncuentro. 2010a. "Entregan barbarías y peluquerías a los empleados," April 13.
CubaEncuentro. 2010b. "Reabre emblemática paladar habanera," November 18.
CubaEncuentro. 2010c. "Resurgen los 'paladares'," December 15.
CubaEncuentro. 2011a. "El gobierno autoriza más capacidad a las paladares," May 27.
CubaEncuentro. 2011b. "Raúl Castro advierte que resistencia a reformas será inútil," August 2.
CubaEncuentro. 2012. "Locales gastronómicos estatales podrán ser alquilados para la gestión privada," November 9.
Cuba Emprende Foundation. 2014. "What we do, about us, and who we support," *CubaEmprendeFoundation.org*, March 4.
Cuba Libre Digital. 2013. "La burocracia 'socialista' consume a las nuevas cooperativas no agropecuarias," January 10.
Cubanet. 2004. "More that 11,000 boxes of counterfeit cigars confiscated," January 6.
Cubanet. 2005. November 29.
Cubanet. 2012. "El régimen critica cobertura de la prensa sobre cierre de El Cabildo," August 8.
Cubasource. 2005. "Chronicle on Cuba," FOCAL, Ottawa. November.
Cubasource. 2006. "Chronicle on Cuba," FOCAL, Ottawa. April.
Cuesta Morúa, Manuel. 2013. Twitter feed (@Cubaprogresista), April 13.
D'Cubanos. N.d. "Actividades autorizadas para el ejercicio del trabajo por cuenta propia en Cuba." http://www.dcubanos.com/archivospdf/Actividades_trabajo_cuentapropia.pdf
Dámaso, Fernando. 2013a. "More of the Same," *Translating Cuba*, October 9.
Dámaso, Fernando. 2013b. "Self-Employment in the Arena," *Translating Cuba*, October 16.
Dámaso, Fernando. 2013c. "The Return of Illegality," *Translating Cuba*, November 11.
DDC (*Diario de Cuba*). 2010. "Los mariscos y la carne de res ya no estarán prohibidos en las 'paladares'," September 24.
DDC (*Diario de Cuba*). 2012a. "El Gobierno prefiere subvencionar la Ópera de la Calle antes que permitir su gestión privada," August 2.
DDC (*Diario de Cuba*). 2012b. "El Gobierno cierra El Cabildo, mayor negocio privado de La Habana, por 'enriquecimiento'," July 27.
DDC (*Diario de Cuba*). 2012c. "Gobierno: Hay 1,610 'paladares' y 5,207 habitaciones en el sector privado," May 10.
DDC (*Diario de Cuba*). 2012d. "El Gobierno planea crear cooperativas en transporte, gastronomía y otros servicios," July 9.
DDC (*Diario de Cuba*). 2013a. "El régimen impidió la reapertura del restaurante El Cabildo, adonde Beyoncé había solicitado ir," April 11.
DDC (*Diario de Cuba*). 2013b. "El Gobierno autoriza a los cuentapropistas a entrar en el negocio turístico estatal," October 9.

DDC (*Diario de Cuba*). 2014a. "El Gobierno anuncia un paquete de sanciones para los cuentapropistas infractores," January 15.
DDC (*Diario de Cuba*). 2014b. "Más de 407.000 cubanos han visto fracasar sus negocios por cuenta propia," February 1.
DDC (*Diario de Cuba*). 2014c. "Holguín: Testigos de la protesta cuentapropistas narran lo ocurrido," February 10.
DDC (*Diario de Cuba*). 2014d. "Ulises Aquino: 'La UNEAC no funciona como contrapeso entre la aspiraciones de los artistas y las del Estado'," February 9.
De Balboa y Troya de Quesada, Silvestre. 1608. *Espejo de Paciencia, Relacion del caso, en octavas.*
De la Soledad, María. 2006. "In Life, 'There is Little Worth Believing': An Exclusive Interview with Cuban Author Leonardo Padura Fuentes," *Progresso Weekly*, February 2-8.
De Soto, Hernando. 1989. *The Other Path: The Invisible Revolution in the Third World.* NewYork: Harper and Row Publishers.
De Soto, Hernando. 2000. *The Mystery of Capital: Why Capitalism Triumphs in the West and Fails Everywhere Else.* New York: Basic Books.
Decree-Law #141. 1993. "Sobre el trabajo por cuenta propia." *Granma*, September 9.
Decree-Law #174. 1997. "De las contravenciones personales de las regulaciones de trabajo por cuentapropia," *Gaceta Oficial*, June 30.
Decree-Law #302. 2012. "Ley de Migración." *Gaceta Oficial*, October 16.
Decree-Law #305. 2012. "De las cooperativas no agropecuarias." *Gaceta Oficial*, Número 53. December 11.
Decree-Law #309. 2012. Council of Ministers. *Gaceta Oficial*, Número 53. December 11.
Del Valle, Amaury. 2013. "Cuba amplía el servicio público de acceso a Internet," *Juventud Rebelde*, May 27.
Desjardins. 2011. "Cooperatives and Social Economy: Quebec's cooperatives and mutual aid organizations: An undeniable economic force," *Perspective: Economic Analysis Review*, Vol. 21, fall.
Díaz Briquets, Sergio and Jorge Pérez-López. 2006. *Corruption in Cuba: Castro and Beyond.* Austin: University of Texas Press.
Díaz Fernández, Ileana, Héctor Pastori, and Camila Piñeiro Harnecker. 2012. "El trabajo por cuenta propia en Cuba: Lecciones de la experiencia uruguaya." *Boletín Cuatrimestral*, April.
Díaz Rodríguez, Elaine. 2013. "Economía sumergida: de las calles a la web," *On Cuba*, April 16.
Dilla Alfonso, Haroldo. 2012. "¿Recuerdan la ofensiva revolucionaria de 1968?" *Cuba Encuentro*, July 9.
Dirmoser, Dietmar, and Jaime Estay, eds. 1997. *Economía y reforma económica en Cuba.* Caracas: Nueva Sociedad.
Diversent, Laritza. 2010. "Entre no idoneos y disponibles," *Jurisconsultocuba*, October 21.
Diversent, Laritza. 2011a. "Cuentapropistas entre la espada y la pared," *Diario de Cuba*, June 16.
Diversent, Laritza. 2011b. "Lectores de Granma arremeten contra revendedores," *Diario de Cuba*, June 14.
Diversent, Laritza. 2011c. "Cuentapropistas se siente amenazado por lectores de Granma," *Jurisconsulto de Cuba*, June 14.
Diversent, Laritza. 2012. "Readers of *Granma* in an Angry Struggle Against Retailers," *Translating Cuba*, June 25.

Domínguez Cuadriello, Jorge. 2008. "Cuba '68: 40 años después," *Espacio Laical*, Vol., No. 49, November.
Domínguez, Jorge. 2001. "Why the Cuban Regime Has Not Fallen." In *Cuban Communism*, tenth edition, edited by Irving Louis Horowitz and Jaime Suchlicki, 533-5450. New Brunswick: Transaction Publishers.
Domínguez, Jorge. 2012. "Can Cuban Rulers Rule Cuba?" *Cuba in Transition*, Vol. 22, pp. 269-276, Washington, D.C.: The Association for the Study of the Cuban Economy.
Domínguez, Jorge, et al. Editors. 2004. *The Cuban Economy at the Start of the Twenty-First Century*. Cambridge: Harvard University.
Donate, Maida L. 2011. "Oscar Lewis: Proyecto Cuba," *CubaEncuentro*, June 30.
DPPFA (Dirección Provincial de Planificación Física y Arquitectura). 1997. "Diagnóstico de Población," Havana, July.
Duany, Jorge. 2001. "Redes, remesas y paladares: La diáspora cubana desde una perspectiva transnacional." *Neuva Sociedad* 174, pp. 40-51 (July-August).
Dweck, Michael. 2011. *Habana Libre: The Other Side of the Story*. Italy: Damiani Publishers.
Dylan, Bob. 1966. "Absolutely Sweet Marie," *Blonde on Blonde*, Columbia Records.
Eaton, Tracey. 2004. "Cubans 'Resolve' to Make Ends Meet," *The Dallas Morning News*, September 26.
Eckstein, Susan Eva. 1994. *Back from the Future: Cuba Under Castro*. Princeton: Princeton University Press.
Economics Press Service. 2001. "Mercado Negro: Historia de Siglos," *Boletín Quincenal sobre Cuba*, 14:7, April 15.
Economist Intelligence Unit (EIU). 1994. "Cuba Economic and Political Outlook, Country Report Cuba." London.
Economist, The. 2012. Editorial. "Indecision Time: Never rapid, Raúl Castro's reforms seem to be stalling," September 15.
El Nuevo Herald. 2005. November 8.
El Nuevo Herald. 2013a. "Más de 436,000 cubanos en la isla trabajan ya en sector privado, según reporte official," August 17.
El Nuevo Herald. 2013b. "Ministerio de Turismo cubano incluirá oftertas del sector privado en sus paquetes," September 9.
El Universal. 2010a. "Cuba estimula creación de cooperativas para afrontar crisis," September 14.
El Universal. 2010b. "Ruta de reformas propiciada por gobierno cubano," September 20.
El Universal. 2014. "Descontento de trabajadores a cuenta propia provoca manifestación en Cuba," January 24.
Erikson, Daniel P. 2005a. "Cuba's Economic Future: The Search for Models." The Canadian Foundation for the Americas (FOCAL): Ottawa, Ontario, December.
Erikson, Daniel P. 2005b. "Cuba, China, Venezuela: New Developments." *Cuba in Transition* Vol. 15, pp. 410-418, Washington, D.C.: The Association for the Study of the Cuban Economy.
Escobal Rabeiro, Vicente. 2001. "Las pequeñas y medianas empresas en Cuba," Instituto Cubano de Investigaciones Sociolaborales y Económicas Independiente, *CubaNet*.
Espacio Laical. 2013. "La polémica: En torno al cierre de los cines 3D," Volume 4, pp. 128-142.
Espina Prieto, Mayra Paula. 1997. "Transformaciones recientes de la estructura socioclasista cubana." *Papers* 52: pp. 83-99.

Espina Prieto, Mayra, Lucy Martín Posada, and Lilia Núñez Moreno. 1998. "Componentes y tendencias socioestructurales de la sociedad cubana actual—resumen ejecutivo." Havana: Centro de Investigación Psicológica y Sociológica (CIPS), March.
Espinosa Chepe, Óscar. 2011. "Cambios en Cuba: Pocos, Limitados y Tardíos," Havana.
Espinosa Chepe, Óscar, and Ted A. Henken. 2013. "Economics," in *Cuba*, edited by Ted A. Henken, Miriam Celaya, and Dimas Castellanos. Santa Barbara, CA: ABC-CLIO.
Europa. 2013. "Summaries of EU Legislation, Definition of micro, small, and medium-sized enterprises."
Farah, Douglas. 1994. "Speak-Easy Eateries Attract Diners with Dollars in Food-Short Havana," *The Washington Post*, pp. A9, A14, February 16.
Farber, Samuel. 2011. *Cuba Since the Revolution of 1959: A Critical Assessment*. New York: Haymarket Books.
Feige, Edgar L. 1989. *The Underground Economies*. Cambridge: Cambridge University Press.
Feinberg, Richard. 2013. "Soft landing in Cuba? Emerging Entrepreneurs and Middle Classes." Latin America Initiative Working Paper, Brookings Institution, Washington D.C., November.
Ferman, Claudia. 2006. "Misterios Cubanos: Entrevista con Leonardo Padura." A Videovit.
Fernández, Damián. 2000. *Cuba and the Politics of Passion*. Austin: The University of Texas Press.
Fernández, Nadine T. 2010. *Revolutionizing Romance: Interracial Couples in Contemporary Cuba*. New Brunswick: Rutgers University Press.
Fernández-Kelly, Patricia. 2006. "Introduction," in *Out of the Shadows: Political Action and the Informal Economy in Latin America*, edited by Patricia Fernández-Kelly and Jon Shefner. University Park, PA: The Pennsylvania University Press.
Fernández-Kelly, Patricia and Jon Shefner, eds. 2006. *Out of the Shadows: Political Action and the Informal Economy in Latin America*. University Park, PA: The Pennsylvania University Press.
Fernández Peláez, Neili. 2000. *Trabajo por cuenta propia en Cuba: Disarticulación y reacción*. Degree Thesis, Department of Sociology, University of Havana, July.
Fernández Sosa, Ivette. 2011. "Entran en vigor medidas para continuar flexibilizando el trabajo por cuenta propia," *Granma*, September 10.
Fernández Sosa, Ivette. 2012. "More than 385,000 self-employed workers," *Granma International*, July 6.
Ferreira, Rui. 2000. "El Gobierno cubano en plena ofensiva contra los paladares," *El Nuevo Herald*, September 30.
Ferrer, Jorge. 2010. "Las barberías de los Hermanos Castro," *El Tono de la Voz*, April 14.
Fletcher, Pascal. 1995. "Havana permits private restaurants," *Financial Times*, June 15.
Frank, Marc. 2004a. "Cubans purge hotel trade of bad habits: Everyone from the laundry maid to tourism chiefs is vulnerable in a crackdown on a booming sector's 'privileges'," *Financial Times*, January 8.
Frank, Marc. 2004b. "Cuba Plans Crackdown on Army of Self-Employed," *Financial Times*, June 2.
Frank, Marc. 2005. *Financial Times*, June 19.
Frank, Marc. 2010. "Cuba Unveils New Tax Code for Small Business," *Reuters*, October 22.

Frank, Marc. 2011. "Chronology: Raúl Castro's Road to Reform in Cuba," *Reuters*, April 13.
Frank, Marc. 2012a. "In Cuba, an Opera Singer Builds an Empire," *Reuters*, July 11.
Frank, Marc. 2012b. "Opera Shut Down," *Reuters*, August 1.
Frank, Marc. 2012c. "Cuba broadens economic reforms, plans new measures," *Reuters*, July 26.
Frank, Marc. 2013a. "Cuba's non-farm co-ops debut this week amid move toward markets," *Chicago Tribune*, June 30.
Frank, Marc. 2013b. "Cuban state begins to move out of the restaurant business," *Reuters*, August 26.
Frank, Marc. 2013c. "Cuba to open state-run wholesaler for private companies," *Reuters*, March 7.
Frank, Marc. 2013d. "Cuba moves to safeguard monopoly on imported goods," *Reuters*, September 26.
Frank, Marc. 2014. "Cuba continues to trim state payroll, build private sector," *Reuters*, February 24.
Frank, Marc and Rosa Tania Valdés. 2014. "Cuba looks to cooperatives to slow rise of capitalism," *Reuters*, April 13.
Freire Santana, Orlando. 2012. "Comineza el arrendamiento de locales gastronómicos estatales a los trabajadores," *Cuba Verdad*, November 29.
Freire Santana, Orlando. 2014. "Cuentapropistas: No se pasen de la raya," *Cubanet*, January 22.
Gábor, Istaván R. 1989. "Second Economy and Socialism: The Hungarian Experience." In *The Underground Economies*, edited by Edgar L. Feige, pp. 339-360. Cambridge, MA: Cambridge University Press.
Gábor, Istaván R. 1994. "Modernity or a New Kind of Duality? Second Thoughts About the 'Second Economy'." Pp. 3-20, in *Transition to Capitalism? The Communist Legacy in Eastern Europe*, edited by János Kovács. New Brunswick: Transaction Publishers.
Gaceta Oficial de la República de Cuba. 1997. Decreto-Ley No. 174, "De las Contravenciones Personales de las Regulaciones del Trabajo por Cuenta Propia." Number 22, June 30.
Gaceta Oficial de la República de Cuba. 2008. No. 46, Ministry of Transportation, Resolutions #263 and #331, December 22.
Gaceta Oficial de la República de Cuba. 2010a. Ministry of Justice, Special Edition, No. 11, Decree-Laws Nos. 274/10 through 278/10 and Decree 284/10, 17 pp., October 1.
Gaceta Oficial de la República de Cuba. 2010b. Ministry of Justice, Special Edition, No. 12, Resolutions Nos. 32/10–36/10, 98/10, 285/10–289/10, 305/10, 399/10, 750/10, 81 pp., October 8.
Gaceta Oficial de la República de Cuba. 2012. Decree-Law 259.
Gaceta Oficial de la República de Cuba. 2013a. Ministry of Justice, Special Edition, No. 27, Resolution No. 353/2013, Resolution No. 41/2013, and Resolution No. 42/2013, September 26.
Gaceta Oficial de la República de Cuba. 2013b. Ministry of Justice, Special Edition, No. 17, November 2.
Gaceta Oficial de la República de Cuba. 2014a. Ministry of Justice, Special Edition, No. 3, Decree-Law No. 315, 4 pp., January 15.
Gaceta Oficial de la República de Cuba. 2014b. Decree-Law 118/2014, "Ley de la Inversión Extranjera," April 16.
Gálvez Chiú, Karina. 2010. "El trabajo por cuenta propia, ¡otra vez!" *Convivencia*, November 25.

Gálvez Chiú, Karina. 2013. "Trabajo por cuenta propia en Cuba hoy: Trabas y oportunidades." *Cuba in Transition* Vol. 23, pp. 403-407, Washington, D.C.: The Association for the Study of the Cuban Economy.
García, Anne-Marie. 2013. "Cuban Ban On Import Sales Leaves Entrepreneurs With Uncertain Future," *Associated Press*, October 18.
Gettig, Eric. 2013. "Cuba's Economic Changes Reflected in Havana's Transportation Network," *Americas Quarterly Blog*, March 26.
Goldberg, Jeffrey. 2010. "Fidel: 'Cuban Model Doesn't Even Work For Us Anymore'," *The Atlantic*, September 8.
Gómez, Alan. "Voices: In Cuba, entrepreneurial spirits sparkle," *USA Today*, August 28.
González, Luis Jesús. 2012. "The Secrets of La Guarida," *On Cuba*, May 24.
González-Corzo, Mario and Orlando Justo. 2014. "Cuba's Emerging Self-Employed Entrepreneurs: Recent Developments and Prospects for the Future." *Journal of Developmental Entrepreneurship* Vol. 19, No. 3.
González Gutiérrez, Alfredo. 1997. "La economía sumergida en Cuba." In *Economía y reforma económica en Cuba*, edited by Dietmar Dirmoser and Jaime Estay, 239-256. Caracas: Editorial Nueva Sociedad.
González Mirabal, Mayle. 2012. "New policy for renting retail space in Habana Vieja," *On Cuba*, October 27.
Granma. 1968. Pp. 2-7, March 15.
Granma. 1970. September 2.
Granma. 1993. "Sobre el trabajo por cuenta propia," September 9.
Granma. 1994a. September 21.
Granma. 1994b. October 20.
Granma. 1995a. June 13.
Granma. 1995b. July 1.
Granma. 1997a. April 8.
Granma. 1997b. "Establecen procedimiento para el pago del impuesto por el arrendamiento de viviendas, habitaciones o espacios," May 23.
Granma. 1997c. November.
Granma. 2005. "Incremento salarial para los trabajadores de más bajos ingresos del país," April 22.
Granma. 2008. "Decreto Ley No. 259 sobre la entrega de tierras ociosas en usufructo," July 18.
Granma. 2010. "Pronunciamiento de la Central de Trabajadores de Cuba," Septiembre 13.
Granma. 2011. "Continuar el proceso de flexibilización del trabajo por cuenta propia," May 27.
Granma. 2012a. September 11.
Granma. 2012b. September 14.
Granma. 2012c. "Actualiza Cuba su Política Migratoria," October 16.
Granma. 2013. "Nota informative sobre el trabajo por cuenta propia," November 2.
Granma International. 1997. April 23.
Granma Internacional. 2011. "Continuar facilitando el trabajo por cuenta propia," May 27.
Granma Weekly Review. 1968. April 7.
Greene, David. 2014. "Cuba's Black Market Loosens Government Control of Information," *NPR*, June 27.
Greene, David and Jasmine Garsd. 2014. "Cuba's Budding Entepreneurs Travel a Rocky Road Toward Success," *NPR*, June 24.
Grogg, Patricia. 2012. "Q&A: 'Cuba Needs to Be Bold and Creative'—Interview with Ricardo Torres," *Inter Press Service*, October.

Grossman, Gregory. 1977. "The 'Second Economy' of the USSR." *Problems of Communism* 26 (September-October): 25-40.
Grossman, Gregory. 1979. "Notes on the Illegal Private Economy and Corruption." In *Soviet Economy in a Time of Change* Vol. 1, 834-855. Washington, D.C.: U.S. Government Printing Office.
Grossman, Gregory. 1989a. "Informal Personal Incomes and Outlays of the Soviet Urban Population." In *The Informal Economy: Studies in Advanced and Less Developed Countries*, edited by Alejandro Portes, Manuel Castells, and Lauren A. Benton, pp. 150-170. Baltimore: The Johns Hopkins University Press.
Grossman, Gregory. 1989b. "The Second Economy: Boon or Bane for the Reform of the First Economy?" In *Economic Reforms in the Socialist World*, edited by Stanislaw Gomulka, Yong-Chool Ha, and Cae-One Kim, pp. 79-96. Armonk, New York: M.E. Sharpe, Inc.
Grupo Cubano de Investigaciones Económicas. 1963. "Un estudio sobre Cuba; colonia, república, experimento socialista: estructura económica, desarrollo institucional, socialismo y regresión." Miami: University of Miami Press.
Grupo consultor de la sociedad civil cubana. 2013. First quarterly report, October 16.
Grupo consultor de la sociedad civil cubana. 2014. Quarterly report (Oct.-Dec., 2013), January 27.
Guevara, Ernesto. 1968. "On Growth and Imperialism" in John Gerassi, editor, *Venceremos: The Speeches and Writings of Ernesto Che Guevara*. New York: The Macmillan Company.
Guillermoprieto, Alma. 2004. *Dancing with Cuba: A Memoir of the Revolution*. Translated by Esther Allen. New York: Pantheon Books.
Gutiérrez Urdaneta, Luís, Pedro Monreal González, and Julio Carranza Valdés. 1996. "La pequeña y mediana empresa en Cuba: El problema de la propiedad." Mimeo, Havana.
Hagelburg, G.B. 2010. "If It Were Just the Marabu......Cuba's Agriculture 2009-2010." Unpublished Manuscript.
Hakim, Catherine. 1987. *Research Design: Strategies and Choices in the Design of Social Research*. London: Allen and Unwin Publishers.
Hardin, Garrett. 1968. "The Tragedy of the Commons." *Science*, Vol. 162, No. 3859, pp. 1243-1248, December 13.
Hart, Keith. 1971. "Small Scale Entrepreneurs in Ghana and Development Planning." *Journal of Development Studies* 6: 4, pp. 104-120.
Hart, Keith. 1973. "Informal Income Opportunities and Urban Employment in Ghana." *Journal of Modern African Studies* 11:1, pp. 61-89.
Hautrive, Iliana and Francisco Rodríguez Cruz. 2011. "Disminuyen carga impositiva a trabajadores por cuenta propia," *Trabajadores*, December 23.
Havana Times. 2012. "Spaces Rented to Self-Employed Workers in Old Havana," July 17.
Haven, Paul. 2011. "Car Sales Legalized," *Associated Press*, September 28.
Henken, Ted A. 2001. "Che Guevara's 'New Man'," p. 257 in *Che Guevara: Critical Lives* by Eric Luther with Ted Henken. New York: Alpha Books.
Henken, Ted A. 2002a. "Cuba's Experiments with Self-Employment during the Special Period (The Case of the Bed-and-Breakfasts)." *Cuban Studies* Vol. 33, pp. 1-29.
Henken, Ted A. 2002b. "Condemned to Informality: Cuba's Experiments with Self-Employment During the Special Period," Ph.D. Dissertation, Tulane University, Stone Center for Latin American Studies, April.
Henken, Ted A. 2008a. "*Vale Todo*: In Cuba's Paladares, Everything is Prohibited, but Anything Goes." In *A Contemporary Cuba Reader: Reinventing the Revolution*, edited by Phillip Brenner, Marguerite Rose Jimenez, John M. Kirk, and William M. Leo Grande. Lanham, MD: Rowman & Littlefield Publishers.

Henken, Ted A. 2008b. *Cuba: A Global Studies Handbook*. Santa Barbara: ABC-CLIO.
Hernádez, Rafael, and Maby González. 1993. "Cuba: Otros pasos en la apertura económica." In *La despenalización del dolar, trabajo por cuenta propia y coopeerativización en Cuba: Documentos y comentarios*, edited by Caridad Rodríguez and Nelson P. Valdés, 81-82. Dossier No. 3, The Latin American Institute of the University of New Mexico (Albuquerque) and the Centro de Estudios sobre América (Havana).
Herrero, Ric. 2014. "Cuba hardliners suppress free exchange of ideas," *Miami Herald*, May 19.
Holgado Fernández, Isabel. 2000. *No es Fácil! Mujeres cubanas y la crisis revolucionaria*. Barcelona: Icaria Editorial.
Horvath, Branco. 1971. "Yugoslav Economic Policy in the Post-War Period: Problems, Ideas and Institutional Developments." *American Economic Review*. June.
ICA (International Cooperative Alliance). N.d. "What's a Co-op? Co-operative Identity, Values, and Principles." http://ica.coop/en/whats-co-op/co-operative-identity-values-principles
"Indicaciones a los inspectors laborales para el trabajo por cuenta propia." 1995. In Principales disposiciones lagales e indicaciones para ser utilizadas por los inspectores laborales para el trabajo por cuenta propia, 40-43, mimeo, September 7.
International Bank for Reconstruction and Development (IBRD). 1951. *Report on Cuba*. Washington D.C.
International Labour Organization (ILO). 2002. "Women and Men in the Informal Economy: A Statistical Picture," Geneva.
Jackiewicz, Edward L. and Todd Bolster. 2003. "The Working World of the *Paladar*: The Production of Contradictory Space during Cuba's Period of Fragmentation." *Professional Geographer* 55: 3 (August), pp. 372-382.
Jatar-Hausmann, Ana Julia. 1999. *The Cuban Way: Communism, Capitalism, and Confrontation*. West Hartford, CT: Kumarian Press.
Junta Central de Planificacion. 1992. "Situacion Actual de la Economía Cubana." Havana: Instituto de Investigaciones Economicas, March.
Juventud Rebelde. 2011. "Directorio telefónico incluirá anuncios del sector no estatal," December 7.
Juventud Rebelde. 2012. "Debate sobre la nueva ley de cooperativismo: Se buscan socios," December 18.
Juventud Rebelde. 2013. "La vida en 3D?" October 27.
Kelley, Robin D.G. 1994. *Race Rebels: Culture, Politics, and the Black Working Class*. New York: Free Press
Knight, Frank H. 1961 (1921). *Risk, Uncertainty and Profit*. New York: Kelley and Millman, Inc.
Kornai, János. 1989. "The Hungarian Reform Process: Visions, Hopes, and Reality." In *Remaking the Economic Institutions of Socialism: China and Eastern Europe*. Stanford: Stanford University Press.
Kovács, János Mátyás. 1994. "Introduction: Official and Alternative Legacies." In *Transition to Capitalism? The Communist Legacy in Eastern Europe*, edited by János Mátyás Kovács. New Brunswick: Transaction Publishers.
Kozlowska, Hanna. 2013. "Can The Castro Regime Ban 3D Movies… And Survive?" *Passport, Foreign Policy Magazine Blog*, November 13.
Kubalkova, Vendulka. 1994. "The Experience of Eastern Europe: Seven Lessons for Cuba." In *Investing in Cuba: Problems and Prospects*, edited by Jaime Suchlicki and Antonio Jorge. New Brunswick: Transaction Publishers.
La Nación. 2013. "Primeras cooperativas no agropecuarias en Cuba comienzan en una semana," June 23. San José, Costa Rica.

Laffita, Osmar. 2013. "Self-Employment or Private Property," *Translating Cuba*, September 8, 2013; Originally published in *Cubanet*, Aug 30.
LaFranchi, Howard. 1996. "Cuba's Enterprising Cooks Open their Homes: Since Castro's government legalized small, private eateries, 'paladares' keep popping up," *Christian Science Monitor*, May 9.
Lam, Lorenzo and Aleida Fernández. 2002. "El consumo normado en Cuba," Ponencia presentada al VIII Forum de la ANEC, Havana, Cuba.
Latin American, Caribbean, and Central American Report. 2000. "No official market economy for Cuba: Sharp decline in numbers of small entrepreneurs," August 22.
Latin American Herald Tribune. 2013. "Over 436,000 Cubans Work in Private Sector, Official Report Says," August 18.
Lee, Susana. 1996a. "La ayuda familiar y otras respuestas," *Granma*, May 23.
Lee, Susana. 1996b. "Entra hoy en vigor nuevo reglamento del trabajo por cuenta propia," *Granma*, p. 2, June 1.
Lee, Susana. 1996c. "Trabajo por cuenta propia: una reflexión necesaria," *Granma*, p. 4, September 13.
Lee, Susana. 1996d. "Trabajo por cuenta propia: hay que combatir el desorden," *Granma*, p. 4, September 19.
Lee, Susana. 1997a. "La disciplina de pago, sinonimo de orden," *Granma*, March 13.
Lee, Susana. 1997b. "ONAT: De lo actual y próximo en el sistema tributario," *Granma*, March 27.
Lee, Susana. 1997c. "La batalla contra las ilegalidades y las indisciplinas sociales no se ganará sin los CDR," *Granma*, April 25: 3.
Lee, Susana. 1997d. "Cuentapropismo y pago de impuestos en próximas asembleas cederistas," *Granma*, May 15.
Lee, Susana. 1998. "El impuesto de los 'paladares'," *Granma*, p. 2, November 12.
Leibenstein, Harvey. 1968. "Entrepreneurship and Development." *American Economic Review*, Papers and Proceedings, Vol. 58, no. 2 (May), pp. 72-83.
Leiva, Miriam. 2003. "Libertad para ejercer actividades privadas en Cuba," *Cubanet*, February 12.
LeoGrande, William M. and J. M. Thomas. 2002. "Cuba's Quest for Economic Independence." *Journal of Latin American Studies*, 34.
León, Francisco. 1995. "Socialismo y sociolismo: Los actores sociales en la tranción cubana." Paper presented at the conference, "Toward a New Cuba: Legacies of Revolution." Princeton, New Jersey, Princeton University, April 8, mimeo.
León, Luis Leonel. 2013. "Fundador de la Opera de la Calle arremete contra el gobierno cubano," *Café Fuerte*, November 20.
Lewis, Oscar, Ruth E. Lewis, and Susan M. Rigdon. 1977a. *Four Men: Living the Revolution, an Oral History of Contemporary Cuba*. Urbana: University of Illinois Press.
Lewis, Oscar, Ruth E. Lewis, and Susan M. Rigdon. 1977b. *Four Women: Living the Revolution, an Oral History of Contemporary Cuba*. Urbana: University of Illinois Press.
Lewis, Oscar, Ruth E. Lewis, and Susan M. Rigdon. 1978. *Neighbors: Living the Revolution, an Oral History of Contemporary Cuba*. Urbana: University of Illinois Press.
Light, Donald W. 2004. "From Migrant to Mainstream: Reconceptualizing Informal Economic Behavior." *Theory and Society* 33: 6 (December), pp. 705-737.
Linares, Gladys. 2014. "Adios al trabajador por cuenta propia," *Cubanet*, 31 January.
Lineamientos. 2010. "Proyecto de Lineamientos de la Política Económica y Social," Cuban Communist Party, *Cubadebate*, November 9, 2010.

Lineamientos. 2011. "Lineamientos de la Política Económica y Social del Partido y de la Revolución," Sixth Congress of the Cuban Communist Party, *Cubadebate,* April 18.
Long, Wayne. 1983. "The meaning of entrepreneurship." *American Journal of Small Business,* 8: 2, pp. 47-59.
López Corzo, Elizabeth. 2012. "Entrevista con Ulises Aquino: Ópera de la Calle es la luz que necesitábamos," *Cubasí,* August 19.
López Levy, Arturo. 2002. "De caballos y ferias," *CubaEncuentro,* December 20.
Los, Maria. 1987. "The Double Economic Structure of Communist Societies." *Contemporary Crises* 11, pp. 25-58.
Los, Maria. 1990. *The Second Economy in Marxist States.* London: Macmillan.
Losby, Jan L., John F. Else, Marcia E. Kingslow, Elaine L. Edgcomb, Erika T. Malm, and Vivian Kao. 2002. "Informal Economy Literature Review." Newark, DE: ISED Consulting and Research and Washington, DC: The Aspen Institute, December.
Lotti, Alina M. 2012. "Empleo y trabajo por cuenta propia reportan indicadores favorables," *Trabajadores,* March 27.
Manguela, Gabino. 2014. "Trabajo por cuenta propia: Con el pie en el pedal," *Trabajadores,* August 24.
Manguela Dáiaz, Gabino. 2012. "Ejercen trabajo por cuenta propia más de 387 mil 200 cubanos," *Trabajadores,* June 28.
Marshall, Jeffry H. 1998. "The Political Viability of Free Market Experimentation in Cuba: Evidence from *Los Mercados Agropecuarios.*" *World Development* 26:2, pp. 277-288.
Martínez, Silvia. 1995. "Regulan ejercicio de trabajo por cuenta propia," *Granma,* August 17.
Martínez Hernández, Leticia. 2010. "Trabajo por cuenta propia: Mucho más que una alternativa," *Granma,* September 24.
Martinez Hernandez, Leticia. 2014. "Trabajo por cuenta propia. Contravenciones en la mira." *Granma,* January 15.
Martínez Molina, Julio, Juan Morales Agüero, Roberto Díaz Martorell, Haydée León, and Mayte María Jiménez. 2011. "Self-Employment Takes Off in Cuba," *Juventud Rebelde,* March 22.
MartíNoticias. 2013. "Se acerca a los 440.000 cifra de cuentapropistas," August 17.
MartíNoticias. 2014a. "Cuentapropistas bajo fuerte vigilancia," January 22.
MartíNoticias. 2014b. "Padura dice estar asfixiado de Cuba," May 7.
Marx, Gary. 2003. "Cuban lottery as ubiquitous as it is hush-hush," *Chicago Tribune,* February 26.
Mayoral, María Julia. 1996. "Comienza reinscripción de los trabajadores por cuenta propia," *Granma,* p. 2, June 21.
McAuliff, John. 2012. "Opera de la Calle a New Model for Performance (Update, And Controversy)," *Cuba-US People to People Partnership Blog,* July 11.
Mesa-Lago, Carmelo. 1988. "The Cuban Economy in the 1980s: The Return of Ideology." In Sergio Roca, editor, *Socialist Cuba: Past Interpretations and Future Challenges.* Boulder: Westview Press.
Mesa-Lago, Carmelo. 2001. "Assessing Economic and Social Performance in the Cuban Transition of the 1990s." In *Cuban Communism,* tenth edition, edited by Irving Louis Horowitz and Jaime Suchlicki, 119-146. New Brunswick: Transaction Publishers.
Mesa-Lago, Carmelo. 2008. "The Cuban Economy at the Crossroads: Fidel Castro's Legacy, Debate over Change, and Raúl Castro's Options." Working Paper 19/2008, Real Instituto Elcano, Madrid.

Mesa-Lago, Carmelo. 2010. "El desempleo en Cuba: de oculto a visible," *Espacio Laical*, Havana Cuba.
Mesa-Lago, Carmelo. 2013. "Los cambios en la propiedad en las reformas económicas estructurales de Cuba," *Espacio Laical*, Year 9, No. 1.
Mesa-Lago, Carmelo, Alberto Arenas de Mesa, Verónica Montecinos, and Mark Samara. 2000. *Market Socialist and Mixed Economies: Comparative Performance of Chile, Cuba, and Costa Rica.* Baltimore and London: Johns Hopkins University Press.
Mesa-Lago, Carmelo, and Jorge Perez-Lopez. 2005. *Cuba's Aborted Reform: Socioeconomic Effects, International Comparisons, and Transition Policies.* Gainesville: University Press of Florida.
Mesa-Lago, Carmelo, and Jorge Pérez-López. 2013. *Cuba Under Raúl Castro: Assessing the Reforms.* Boulder, CO: Lynne Rienner.
Mesa Redonda, TV Cubana. 2013. August 21.
Mesa Redonda. 2014. "Situación actual del Trabajo por Cuenta Propia," Part 1, March 20 and Part 2, March 21.
Ministerio de Finanzas y Precios. 1996. Instrucción No. 11/96, Declaración Jurada, Divisas.
Ministry of Finance and Prices. 2012. Resolución 427/2012, *Gaceta Oficial de la República de Cuba*, Número 53. December 11.
Ministerio de Trabajo y Seguridad Social y de Finanzas y Precios. 1995. *Resolución Conjunta No. 4/95*, *Granma*, June 14.
Ministerio de Trabajo y Segundad Social and Direccion Provincial de Trabajo y Seguridad Social. 2001. Pp. 1 and 5.
Miroff, Nick. 2009. "Cuba's Craigslist," *Global Post*, July 24.
Miroff, Nick. 2010. "Some Cuban Barbers Unhappy With Their New Cut," *NPR*, May 3.
Miroff, Nick. 2011. "Cuba Issues Thousands Of Self-Employment Licenses," *NPR*, January 18.
Miroff, Nick. 2012a. "Cuba: When bureaucrats attack," *Global Post*, July 31.
Miroff, Nick. 2012b. "Opera Unfolds When A Cuban Cabaret Is Shut Down," *NPR*, July 31.
Miroff, Nick. 2012c. "To Get Rich is Inglorious," *Global Post*, September 4.
Miroff, Nick. 2013. "Cuba's 'resale' economics," *Global Post*, January 23.
Monzó, Rebecca. 2012. "¿A la calle, Opera de la Calle?" *Por el ojo de la aguja*, August 10.
Monzó, Rebecca. 2013. "Small Businesses," *Translating Cuba*, August 22.
Morales, Esteban. 2010a. "Corruption: The True Counterrevolution," *Internal Reform Blog*, April 22.
Morales, Esteban. 2010b. "The Mystery of the Holy Trinity: Corruption, Bureaucracy and Counterrevolution," *Esteban Morales Domínguez Blog*, July 11.
Morales, Esteban. 2013. "How Far Will We Allow Corruption to Spread in Cuba," *Havana Times*, December 16.
Morales, Emilio. 2011. "Cuba: menos impuestos para impulsar el trabajo privado," *Café Fuerte*, June 6.
Morales, Emilio. 2013. "Cuba eleva precios para el mercado mayorista," *Café Fuerte*, March 23.
Morales Dopico, Emilio. 2013. "Reformas en Cuba: ¿La última utopía?" *Cuba in Transition*, Vol. 23, pp. 32-37, Washington, D.C.: The Association for the Study of the Cuban Economy.
Morales, Emilio and Joeseph Scarpaci. 2012. *Advertising without Marketing: Brand Preference and Consumer Choice in Cuba.* New York and London: Routledge.

Mulet Concepción, C. Yailenis. 2013. "Non-agricultural cooperatives in Cuba: A new way to unleash the forces of production?" *From the Island*, Issue No. 22, Miami: Cuba Study Group, November 7.
Municipio de La Habana. 1958. Directorio Comercial. Departmento de Control, Censo Fiscal y Estadisticas. Havana.
Naciones Unidas, CEPAL. 1997. *La Economia Cubana: Reformas estructurales y desempeño en los noventa.* Santiago, Chile, First Edition.
Naciones Unidas, CEPAL. 2000. *La Economia Cubana: Reformas estructurales y desempeño en los noventa.* Santiago, Chile, Second Edition.
Naciones Unidas, CEPAL. 2013. *Balance Preliminar de las Economías de América Latina y el Caribe.* Santiago, Chile.
Nee, Victor and David Stark, eds. 1989. *Remaking the Economic Institutions of Socialism: China and Eastern Europe.* Stanford: Stanford University Press.
Nee, Victor and Peng Lian. 1994. "Sleeping with the Enemy: A Dynamic Model of Declining Political Commitment in State Socialism." *Theory and Society* 23:2 (April): 253-296.
Newman, Lucia. 2001. "Cuba squeezes private business as economy grows," *CNN*, March 12.
Nieves Cárdenas, José Jasán. 2012. "Ópera de la Calle: ¿Un mal ejemplo?," *Radio Ciudad del Mar*, August 1.
Nieves, J.J. 2014a. "Virtual stores in Cuba," *On Cuba*, February 2.
Nieves, J.J. 2014b. "Trading online in an 'offline' country," *On Cuba*, February 19.
Nieves Cárdenas, José Jasán. 2014. "Cuba y cooperativas 'sin papeles'," *Progreso Semanal*, May 20.
Nova González, Armando. 2012. "Agricultura," in Colectivo de Autores de Centro de Estudios sobre la Economia Cbana, *Miradas a la Economia Cubana II*, Havana: Editorial Caminos.
Núñez Moreno, Lilia. 1997. "Más allá del cuentapropismo en Cuba." *Temas* 11: 41-50.
Oficina Nacional de Administración Tributaria (ONAT). 1997. Declaración Jurada, Impuesto sobre Ingresos Personales, Moneda Nacional.
Oficina Nacional de Estadísticas (ONE). *Anuario Estadístico de Cuba (AEC)*, various years.
OnCuba. 2014. "Updated regulations for self-employment implemented in Cuba," January 15.
Opciones. 2012. "Número de cuentapropistas sigue creciendo en La Mayor de las Antillas," April 2.
Open Letter. 2014. "Open Letter to President Obama: Support Cuban Civil Society," May. http://www.supportcubancivilsociety.org/
Ópera de la Calle Blog. 2012a. "You Tube video of opening night."
Ópera de la Calle Blog. 2012b. "Three statements by Ulises Aquino."
Oppmann, Patrick. 2012. "Cuba Shuts Down 'Street Opera'," *CNN*, August 13.
Orozco, Manuel and Katrin Hansing. 2011. "Remittance Recipients and the Present and Future of Micro-enterpreneurship Activities in Cuba," *Cuba in Transition*, Vol. 21, pp. 302-308, Washington, D.C.: The Association for the Study of the Cuban Economy.
Orsi, Peter. 2012. "Havana's historic quarter begins small-biz rentals," *Associated Press*, July 16.
Orsi, Peter. 2013a. "Castro speech scolds islanders for bad behavior," *Associated Press*, July 8.
Orsi, Peter. 2013b. "Cubans heartened by possible reversal of 3D ban," *Associated Press*, November 12.

Orsi, Peter. 2014. "Cubans with money revel in booming social circuit," *Associated Press*, March 24.
Orta Rivera, Yailin and Norge Martínez Montero. 2006a. "La vieja gran estafa," *Juventud Rebelde*, October 1.
Orta Rivera, Yailin and Norge Martínez Montero. 2006b. "Sancionan a taxistas que adulteran precios," *Juventud Rebelde*, October 8.
Orta Rivera, Yailin, Norge Martínez Montero, and Dilbert Reyes Rodríguez. 2006. "El mango de la sartén," *Juventud Rebelde*, October 15.
Orta Rivera, Yailin, Norge Martínez Montero, and Roberto Suárez. 2006. "Iniciarán proyecto investigativo sobre propiedad socialista en Cuba," *Juventud Rebelde*, October 22.
Outcalt, Charles. 2000. "The Notion of Entrepreneurship: Historical and Emerging Issues." CELCEE Kauffman Center for Entrepreneurial Leadership Clearinghouse on Entrepreneurship Education, digest number 00-4, September.
Oxford Analytica. 2012. "Dissident death overshadows slow-motion reforms," August 17.
Padgett, Tim. 2014. "The Cuba Debate: Can Capitalist Rookies Thrive in a Communist Revolution?" *WLRN*, August 19.
Padura Fuentes, Leonardo. 2000. *Pasado perfecto*. Barcelona: Editores Tusquets.
Padura, Leonardo. 2005. *Havana Red* [originally published in 1997 as *Máscaras*]. Translated by Peter Bush. London: Bitter Lemon Press.
Palacios, Daniel. 2013. "Ola de críticas y descontento popular por cierre de cines 3D," *Café Fuerte*, November 7.
Palacios Almarales, Daniel. 2013. "Tensión entre vendedores de ropa importada ante inminente cierre de sus negocios," *Café Fuerte*, October 31.
Palma, Orlando. 2014. "Almacenes de viejos," *14ymedio*, August 11.
Partido Comunista de Cuba. 2010. "Proyecto de Lineamientos de la Política Económica y Social del Partido y la Revolución." Havana, November.
Partido Comunista de Cuba. 2011. VI Congreso. "Lineamientos de la Política Económica y Social del Partido y la Revolución." Havana. April.
Pavón González, Ramiro. 1996. "Estudio diagnóstico sobre el trabajo por cuenta propia en Santiago de Cuba." *Economía y Desarrollo* 120, no. 2, pp. 74 -90, June.
Peláez, Orfilia et al. 2014. "Expectativas por cuenta propia," *Granma*, January 31.
Penúltimos Días. 2009. "Cierra 'La Guarida'," December 24.
Penúltimos Días. 2010. "La reforma que viene," September 14.
Penúltimos Días. 2014. "Emprendedores: Un documental sobre cuentapropistas de Santa Clara," January 21.
Perdomo, Juanita. 2012. "Más ofertas para una major gastronomía," *Trabajadores*, July 27.
Perera, Alina. 2010. "No es cuestión de edad se queda quien mejor trabaje," *Juventud Rebelde*, October 30.
Pérez Izquierdo, Victoria, Fabian Oberto Calderón, and Mayelín González Rodríguez. 2003. "Los trabajadores por cuenta propia en Cuba." *Nodo* 50, Cuba Siglo XXI, October.
Pérez-López, Jorge. 1995a. *Cuba's Second Economy: From Behind the Scenes to Center Stage*. New Brunswick, NJ: Transactions Publishers.
Pérez-López, Jorge. 1995b. "Coveting Beijing, but Imitating Moscow: Cuba's Economic Reforms in Comparative Perspective." *Cuba in Transition* Vol. 5, pp. 11-20, Washington, D.C.: The Association for the Study of the Cuban Economy.
Pérez-López, Jorge. 2004. "Foreign Investment in Cuba." In Archibald R.M. Ritter, editor, *The Cuban Economy*. Pittsburgh: University of Pittsburgh Press.
Pérez Navarro, Lourdes. 2009. "Licencias para transportar pasajeros," *Granma*, July 8.

Pérez Roque, Martha Beatriz. 2002. "Economia Informal en Cuba." Report commissioned by the Center for Migration and Development, Princeton University, May.
Pérez-Stable, Marifeli. 1999. *The Cuban Revolution: Origins, Course, and Legacy.* New York: Oxford University Press.
Pérez, Tómas E. 2013. "Muchísimas preguntas (y casi ninguna respuesta) sobre los cines 3D," *El Colimador*, November 3.
Pérez Villanueva, Omar Everleny. 2009. "The Cuban Economy: A Current Evaluation and Proposals or Necessary Policy Changes," *Discussion Paper No. 217*, Institute of Developing Economies, Tokyo.
Pérez Villanueva, Omar Everleny and Viviana Togores González. 1996. "Las pequeñas empresas in Cuba: Posibilidades." In *Cambios y perspectivas en la economía cubana, 1995*, edited by Elsa Barrera López, pp. 149-153. Dossier No. 10, The Latin American Institute of the University of New Mexico (Albuquerque) and the Centro de Estudios Sobre América (Havana), February.
Peters, Philip. 1997. "Islands of Enterprise: Cuba's Emerging Small Business Sector." Arlington: Alexis de Toqueville Institution.
Peters, Philip. 2006a. "Cuba's Small Entrepreneurs: Down but Not Out." Lexington Institute, September 30.
Peters, Philip. 2006b. "Who's to Blame for Corruption?" *Cuba Policy Report Issue #22*. Lexington Institute, October 27.
Peters, Philip. 2008. "An opening in private transportation (Updated)," *The Cuban Triangle*, July 9.
Peters, Philip. 2009. "More cabs on the way," *The Cuban Triangle*, January 15.
Peters, Philip. 2010a. "Looking Like a Small Business Sector," *The Cuban Triangle*, September 24.
Peters, Philip. 2010b. "The New Tax System," *The Cuban Triangle*, October 22.
Peters, Philip. 2010c. "The state lightens its burden," *The Cuban Triangle*, April 13.
Peters, Philip. 2010d. "Be a Good Communist, Support your Local Entrepreneur," *The Cuban Triangle,* December 20.
Peters, Philip. 2010e. "The Plan for Havana," *The Cuban Triangle*, September 15.
Peters, Philip. 2011a. "Let the private sector do it," *The Cuban Triangle*, December 26.
Peters, Philip. 2011b. "Tax relief for entrepreneurs, and other economic news," *The Cuban Triangle*, December 26.
Peters, Philip. 2011c. "What would you people have done with Frank País?" *The Cuban Triangle*, August 2.
Peters, Philip. 2012a. "A Viewer's Guide to Cuba's Economic Reform." Arlington, VA: Lexington Institute. May.
Peters, Philip. 2012b. "Cuba's Entrepreneurs: Foundation of a New Private Sector." Arlington, VA: Lexington Institute. July 31.
Peters, Philip. 2012c. "Migration Policy Reform: Cuba Gets Started, U.S. Should Follow." Arlington, VA: Lexington Institute. December.
Peters, Philip. 2012d. "Reforming Cuba's Agriculture: Unfinished Business." Arlington, VA: Lexington Institute. October.
Peters, Philip. 2012e. "Pro-growth measures for the private sector," *The Cuban Triangle*, October 12.
Peters, Philip. 2013a. "A Chronology of Cuba's Economic Reform," *Cuban Research Center*, August 19.
Peters, Philip. 2013b. "The Hard Part," *Cuban Research Center*, August 19.
Peters, Philip. 2013c. "A step back, a step forward," *The Cuban Triangle*, October 1.
Peters, Philip. 2014. "Cuba's New Real Estate Market," Latin America Initiative Working Paper, Brookings Institution, Washington D.C., February.

Peters, Philip and Joseph L. Scarpaci. 1998. "Cuba's New Entrepreneurs: Five Years of Small-Scale Capitalism," Arlington: Alexis de Toqueville Institution.

Piñeiro-Harnecker, Camila. 2011. (Compiladora). *Cooperativas y Socialismo: Una Mirada desde Cuba.* Havana: Editorial Caminos.

Piñeiro-Harnecker, Camila. 2012a. "Las cooperativas en el nuevo modelo económico." In Pavel Vidal Alejandro and Omar Everleny Perez Villanueva (Compiladores), *Miradas a la economía cubana: El proceso de actualización.* Havana: Editorial Caminos.

Piñeiro-Harnecker, Camila. 2012b. "Visiones sobre el socialismo que guían los cambios actuales en Cuba." *Revista Temas,* No. 70, April-June.

Piñeiro-Harnecker, Camila. 2012c. "Non-state enterprises in Cuba: Current situation and prospects," Power point presentation, Colloquium on "Economic Transformation in Cuba," Bildner Center, CUNY, May 2012.

Piñeiro-Harnecker, Camila. 2013. *Cooperatives and Socialism: A View from Cuba.* New York: Palgrave Macmillan.

Portes, Alejandro and Wiliam Haller. 2005. "The Informal Economy." In *The Handbook of Economic Sociology,* second edition. Edited by Neil J. Smelser and Richard Swedberg. Princeton: Princeton University Press and New York: Russell Sage Foundation.

Portes, Alejandro and József Böröcz. 1988. "The Informal Sector under Capitalism and State Socialism: A Preliminary Comparison." *Social Justice* 15: 17-28.

Portes, Alejandro and Richard Schauffler. 1993a. "The Informal Economy in Latin America: Definition, Measurement, and Policies." In *Work Without Protections: Case Studies of the Informal Sector in Developing Countries,* edited by Gregory K. Schoepfle and Jorge F. Pérez-López, 3-40. Washington, D.C.: U.S. Government Printing Office.

Portes, Alejandro and Richard Schauffler. 1993b. "Competing Perspectives on the Latin American Informal Sector." *Population and Development Review* 19: 1 (March) 33-60.

Portes, Alejandro, Carlos Dore-Cabral, and Patricia Landolt. 1997. *The Urban Caribbean: Transition to the New Global Economy.* Baltimore: The Johns Hopkins University Press.

Portes, Alejandro, Manuel Castells, and Lauren A. Benton, eds. 1989. *The Informal Economy: Studies in Advanced and Less Developed Countries.* Baltimore: The Johns Hopkins University Press.

Progreso Weekly. 2014. "Cuba: Self-employment rules modified," January 15.

Puig Meneses, Yaima and Leticia Martínez Hernández. 2013. "Updating of Cuban economic model continues to advance," *Granma Internacional,* September 25.

Quintana Mendoza, Didio. 1997. "El sector informal urbano en Cuba: Algunos elementos para su caracterización." *Cuba, investigación económica* 3, no. 2, pp. 101-120, Havana: Instituto Nacional de Investigaciones Economicas, April-June.

Radu, Michael. 1995. "Cuba's Transition: Institutional Lessons from Eastern Europe." *Journal of Inter-American Studies and World Affairs* Vol. 37, No. 2, pp. 83-111 (Summer).

Rainsford, Sarah. 2013. "Tighter rules threaten Cuba's independent clothes sellers," *BBC,* October 12.

Rakowski, Cathy A., editor. 1994. *Contrapunto: The Informal Sector Debate in Latin America.* Albany: State University of New York Press.

Rassí, Reynold. 2004. "Security and Protection of resources: Closing the Doors to Crime," *Granma,* September 21.

Ravsberg, Fernando. 2012a. "Cuba Closes 'Street Opera' Project," *Havana Times,* July 27.

Ravsberg, Fernando. 2012b. "'Opera in the Street' Receives Support," *Havana Times*, July 30.
Ravsberg, Fernando. 2012c. "Cuba Reforms in Search of a Model," *Havana Times*, July 26.
Ravsberg, Fernando. 2012d. "La aduana de Cuba aprieta las tuercas," *Havana Times*, July 18.
Ravsberg, Fernando. 2013a. "Opera de la Calle and a Show for Beyoncé," *Havana Times*, April 12.
Ravsberg, Fernando. 2013b. "Cuba autoriza la venta libre de autos," *BBC Mundo*, December 20.
Ravsberg, Fernando. 2014. "The Causes and Consequences of Cuba's Black Market," *Havana Times*, August 21.
Recio, Milena. 2013. "Self-employment in Cuba (Infographic)," *On Cuba*, May 1.
Rehn, A. and Taalas, S. 2004. "*Blat*, the Soviet Union and mundane entrepreneurship." *Entrepreneurship and Regional Development*, Vol. 16, No. 3, pp. 235-250.
República de Cuba. 1997. Decreto-Ley No. 174, "De las Contravenciones Personales de las Regulaciones del Trabajo por Cuenta Propia," *Gaceta Oficial*, No. 22, June 30.
República de Cuba, Oficina Nacional de Estadisticas (ONE), Anuario Estadistico de Cuba. Various years.
República de Cuba. 2011. *Gaceta Oficial*, No. 11, and *Gaceta Oficial*, No. 12, April.
Resolución No. 270. 2003. "Reglamento sobre el arrendamiento de viviendas, habitaciones o espacios." Instituto Nacioinal de Vivienda, June 5.
Resolución No. 11. 2004. "Reglamento sobre el trabajo por cuenta propia." *Gaceta Oficial*, No. 32, Ministerio de Trabajo y Seguro Social, May 11.
Reyes, Gerardo. 1998. "Home restaurants in Havana keep eye on inspectors," *Miami Herald*, October 12.
Ricardo Luís, Roger. 1993. "Profundo analisis sobre el trabajo por cuenta propia y la situacion de las finanzas internas,"*Granma*, pp. 1, 2-6, December 29.
Rice, John. 1997. "Cuban official signals limits on capitalism," *Miami Herald*, November 28.
Ritter, Archibald R.M. 1974. *The Economic Development of Revolutionary Cuba: Strategy and Performance*. New York: Praeger.
Ritter, Archibald R.M. 1990. "The Cuban Economy in the 1990s: External Challenges and Policy Imperatives." *Journal of Interamerican Studies and World Affairs*, 32:3, Fall.
Ritter, Archibald R.M. 1998. "Entrepreneurship, Microenterprise, and Public Policy in Cuba: Promotion, Containment, or Asphyxiation?" *Journal of Interamerican Studies and World Affairs* 40:2, pp. 63-94 (Summer).
Ritter, Archibald R.M. 2000a. "El regimen impositivo para la microempresa en Cuba." *Revista de la CEPAL* 71, pp. 145-162 (August).
Ritter, Archibald R.M. 2000b. "The Tax Regime for Microenterprise in Cuba." *CEPAL Review*, United Nations: Economic Commission for Latin America and the Caribbean, pp. 139-156 (August).
Ritter, Archibald R. M., editor. 2004. *The Cuban Economy*. Pittsburgh: University of Pittsburgh Press.
Ritter, Archibald R.M. 2005. "Survival Strategies and Economic Illegalities in Cuba." *Cuba in Transition* Vol. 15, pp. 342-359, Washington, D.C.: The Association for the Study of the Cuban Economy.
Ritter, Archibald R.M. 2006. "Cuba's Economic Re-Orientation." Paper presented at the Bildner Center conference, "Cuba: In Transition? Pathways to Renewal, Long-Term Development and Global Reintegration," March 30-31.

Ritter, Archibald R.M. 2010. "State Sector Lay-offs then Private Sector Job Creation: Has Raúl Got the Cart before the Horse?" *The Cuban Economy Blog*, September 22.
Rivera, Mario A. 1998. "The Imperatives of Economic Liberalization and Political Control in the Cuban Transition." In *Handbook of Economic Development*, edited by Kuotsai Tom Liou, pp. 631-647. New York: Marcel Dekker, Inc.
Robles, Frances. 2010. "With beauty shops, Cuba may be inching toward capitalism," *The Miami Herald*, April 14.
Rodríguez, José Luis. 1997. Interview, *El País* (Argentina), January 6.
Rodríguez Aguila, Jorge A. and Juan José Rodríguez Causa. N.d. "Algunas consideraciones del Trabajo de Inspector en el Terreno a Trabajo por Cuenta Propia." Dirección Municipal de Trabajo y Seguridad Social, Departmento de Inspección, mimeo, Havana.
Rodríguez, Alejandro. 2013. "Negocios privados en Cuba: El malestar en la acualización," *On Cuba*, October 1.
Rodríguez, José Alejandro. 2013. "Aumenta el trabajo por cuenta propia," *Juventud Rebelde*, August 16.
Rodríguez Cruz, Francisco. 1996. "El cuenta propia es también cuenta nuestra," *Trabajadores*, June 3.
Rodríguez López, Yusimí. 2013. "Lo que nos ofrece La Buena Vida," *Diario de Cuba*, August 4.
Rodríguez Milán, Yisell. 2013. "3D Dilemmas," *On Cuba*, August 9.
Róna-Tas, Ákos. 1995. "The Second Economy as a Subversive Force." In *The Waning of the Communist State: Economic Origins of Political Decline in China and Hungary*, edited by Andrew G. Walder. Berkeley: University of California Press.
Róna-Tas, Ákos. 1997. *The Great Surprise of the Small Transformation: The Demise of Communism and the Rise of the Private Sector in Hungary*. Ann Arbor: The University of Michigan Press.
Rosenberg, Jonathan. 1992. "Cuba's Free Market Experiment." *Latin American Research Review* 27:3, pp. 51-80.
Sacchetti, Elena. 2011. *Vivir en la cuerda floja: La microempresa en Cuba*. Editorial Académica Española.
Sánchez, Francis. 2011. "Le guerra de las paladares," *Hombre en las nubes*, March 6.
Sánchez Serra, Óscar. 2013a. "Orden y legalidad: Un interés de todos," *Granma*, November 11.
Sánchez Serra, Óscar. 2013b. "La ruta de la indisciplina y las ilegalidades," *Granma*, November 15.
Sánchez, Yoani. 2009. "Feast envy," *Generation Y*, April 8.
Sánchez, Yoani. 2010. "Chaplinesque," *Generation Y*, September 29.
Sánchez, Yoani. 2011a. "Daddy State and His Frightened Children," *Huffington Post*, January 10.
Sánchez, Yoani. 2011b. "Cuba Allows Car Sales: Cars Over 15 Years Old for Us, Newer Cars Only for the Party Faithful," *Huffington Post*, September 30.
Sánchez, Yoani. 2013. Twitter feed. July 27, 10:30 a.m.
Sánchez, Yoani. 2013. "Report to the Inter-American Press Association (SIPIAPA) on Press Freedom in Cuba," October.
Sánchez, Yoani. 2014a. "Ah... tú no sales en 'el paquete'," *Generación Y*, May 17.
Sánchez, Yoani. 2014b. "5 apps de iOS inprescindbiles para Cuba," *Generación Y*, April 11.
Sánchez, Yoani. 2014c. "Las diez Apps de Android más populares en Cuba," *Generación Y*, January 10.

Sánchez, Yoani. 2014d. "*Y tú, hijo, no te destaques*," *Generación Y*, March 26.
Sawyer, Mark Q. *Racial Politics in Post-Revolutionary Cuba*. New York: Cambridge University Press, 2006.
Say, Jean Baptiste. 1847. *A Treatise on Political Economy*. Grigg, Elliot, and Co.
Scarpaci, Joseph L. 1995. "The Emerging Food and *Paladar* Market in Havana," *Cuba in Transition* Vol. 5, pp. 74-84, Washington, D.C.: The Association for the Study of the Cuban Economy.
Scarpaci, Joseph L. 2009. "Fifteen Years of Entrepreneurship in Cuba: Challenges and Opportunities," *Cuba in Transition* Vol. 19, pp. 349-353, Washington, D.C.: The Association for the Study of the Cuban Economy.
Scarpaci, Joseph L. 2014. "Doing the Right Thing: Entrepreneurship, Ethics, and Corporate Social Responsibility in Castro's Cuba and Pinochet's Chile." *Journal of Ethics and Entrepreneurship* Vol. 4, No. 1, pp. 73-94, Spring.
Schneider, Friedrich and Dominik H. Enste. 2002a. "Hiding in the Shadows: The Growth of the Underground Economy." *Economic Issues*, No. 30, International Monetary Fund, March.
Schneider, Friedrich and Dominik H. Enste. 2002b. *The Shadow Economy: An International Survey*. Cambridge: Cambridge University Press.
Schoepfle, Gregory K. and Jorge F. Pérez-López. 1993. *Work Without Protections: Case Studies of the Informal Sector in Developing Countries*. Washington, D.C.: U.S. Government Printing Office.
Schumpeter, Joseph A. 1974. *The Theory of Economic Development*. Oxford: Oxford University Press.
Schwandt, Thomas A. 2001. *Dictionary of Qualitative Inquiry*. Second edition. Thousand Oaks, CA: Sage Publications.
Scott, James C. 1979. *The Moral Economy of the Peasant: Rebellion and Subsistence in Southeast Asia*. New Haven: Yale University Press.
Scott, James C. 1985. *Weapons of the Weak: Everyday Forms of Peasant Resistance*. New Haven: Yale University Press.
Scott, James C. 1990. *Domination and the Arts of Resistance: Hidden Transcripts*. New Haven: Yale University Press.
Segre, Roberto, Mario Coyula, and Joseph L. Scarpaci. 1997. *Havana: Two Faces of the Antillean Metropolis*. Chichester: John Wiley and Sons.
Seleny, Anna. 1995. "Property Rights and Political Power: The Cumulative Process of Political Change in Hungary." In *The Waning of the Communist State: Economic Origins of Political Decline in China and Hungary*, edited by Andrew G. Walder. Berkeley: University of California Press.
Siegelbaum, Portia. 2012. "Contradictory Policy on Paladars: Cuba both fuels, fights new private restaurants," *CBS News*, June 29.
Sik, Endre. 1992. "From the Second to the Informal Economy." *Journal of Public Policy* 12:2, pp. 153-175.
Sosín Martínez, Eileen. 2013. "Paladares, family business," *On Cuba*, December 27.
Smith, Benjamin. 1999. "Self-Employment in Cuba: A Street-Level View." *Cuba in Transition* Vol. 9, pp. 49-59, Washington, DC: The Association for the Study of the Cuban Economy.
Smith, Tony. 2001. "Se cierra el circulo sobre los negocios privados," *Nuevo Herald*, July 9.
Stanley, David. 2000. *Lonely Planet: Cuba*. Second Edition. Melbourne: Lonely Planet Publications.
Stark, David. 1989. "Bending the Bars of the Iron Cage: Bureaucratization and Informalization in Capitalism and Socialism." *Sociological Forum* 4: 4, pp. 637-64.

Stark, David, and Victor Nee. 1989. "Toward an Institutional Analysis of State Socialism." In *Remaking the Economic Institutions of Socialism: China and Eastern Europe*, edited by Victor Nee and David Stark. Stanford: Stanford University Press.

Stein, Stanley J. and Barbara H. Stein. 1970. *The Colonial Heritage of Latin America*. New York: Oxford University Press.

Tamayo, Juan O. 2013. "Periódico Granma reconoce malestar por el cierre de cines y tiendas privadas en Cuba," *El Nuevo Herald*, November 12.

Tamayo, Juan O. 2014a. "Street protest in Cuba draws at least 500, sparks clash with police," *The Miami Herald*, January 22.

Tamayo, Juan O. 2014b. "Cuban women say their businesses are doing well," *Miami Herald*, August 8.

Tamayo Batista, Hilia. 2014. "Continúa organizándose el trabajo por cuenta propia en Cuba," *Radio Rebelde*, February 18.

Togores González, Viviana. N.d. "Consideraciones sobre el sector informal de la economía: Un estudio de su comportamiento en Cuba." Mimeo, Havana.

Togores, Viviana and Anicia García. 2004. "Consumption, Markets and Monetary Duality in Cuba" in Jorge I. Domínguez et al, editors, *The Cuban Economy at the Start of the Twenty-First Century*. Cambridge: Harvard University.

Togores González, Viviana and Omar Everleny Pérez Villanueva. 1996. "Consideraciones sobre la pequeña y mediana empresa en Cuba." Mimeograph provided by authors.

Torres Hernández, Yirmara. 2014. "Mitos y realidades del TPCP en Cuba," *Radio Coco*, January 23.

Trabajadores. 1996. "Sobre el ejercicio del trabajo por cuenta propia." Joint Resolution #1. June 3.

Trabajadores. 2011. December 23.

Trabajadores. 2012a. "Crece el número de trabajadores no estatales," March 2.

Trabajadores. 2012b. "Paladares: tendencia creciente," June 27.

Trabajadores. 2012c. "Alimentos: servicio creciente," July 4.

Trabajadores. 2012d. "Cuba implementará gestión económica no estatal en sector gastronómico," November 9.

Trabajadores. 2012e. "Comenzará en breve arrendamiento de locales gastronómicos estatales," December 1.

Trabajadores. 2012f. "State Gastronomy Premises Will Soon Be in Rent," December 4.

Trabajadores. 2013. "¿Cómo marcha el experimento de las cooperativas no agropecuarias?" August 22.

Triana Cordoví, Juan. 2012. "From the submerged economy to the microenterprise: Are there any guarantees for the future?" *From the Island*, Issue No. 14, Miami: Cuba Study Group, November 15.

Triana Cordoví, Juan. 2013. "Microfinancing and Microloans for Cuba." *From the Island*, Issue No. 18, Miami: Cuba Study Group, July 23.

Trip Advisor. 2013. "La Opera de la Calle Returns," June 17.

Ulloa García, Alejandro. 2013. "Espacios públicos, negocios privados," *On Cuba*, April 23.

United Nations Development Program (UNDP). 2001 and 2009. *Human Development Reports, 2001 and 2009*. New York: Oxford University Press.

United Nations Economic Commission for Latin America and the Caribbean (UNECLAC). 2000. *Preliminary Overview of the Economies of Latin America and the Caribbean*. Santiago, Chile.

United States Census Bureau, International Data Base, Cuba. N.d.
Uno de Guanajay. 2013. "La política cultural del país," October 30.
Usborne, David. 2011. "Chef with a dream bets on Castro's hunger for reform," *The Independent*, March 8.
Valdés, Rosa Tania. 2013. "Conflict brews in Cuba over ban on sales of imported good," *Reuters*, October 3.
Valdés, Rosa Tania and Daniel Trotta. 2014. "Market-style reforms widen racial divide in Cuba," *Reuters*, September 2.
Valdés Hernández, Dagoberto and Paul Echániz. 2004. "Levantar cabeza," *Revista Vitral*, January 19.
Valdés Hernández, Dagoberto. 2013. "Reconciliation in Cuba: Bringing down walls, building a peaceful coexistence," *From the Island*, Issue No. 21, Miami: Cuba Study Group, October 13.
Valdés Vivo, Raúl. 1998. "Cuba will not allow citizens to open businesses." In *Caribbean Update*, p. 6, citing *Granma* article, January.
Vanek, Yaroslav. 1969. "Decentralization under Workers Management: A Theoretical Appraisal." *American Economic Review*, December.
Vega, Verónica. 2014. "La muerte en 3D," *Diario de Cuba*, January 10.
Vicent, Mauricio. 2000. "'Paladares' de La Habana," *El País*, p. 6-7, December 10.
Vidal Alejandro, Pavel. 2009. "Politica Monetaria y Doble Moneda," in Omar Everleny Pérez et al, *Miradas a la Economia Cubana*. Havana: Editorial Caminos.
Vidal Alejandro, Pavel. 2012. "Micro-Finance in Cuba," Center for the Study of the Cuban Economy, University of Havana. Presentation given on May 21 at the Colloquium on Economic Transformation in Cuba, The Cuba Project, Bildner Center for Western Hemisphere Studies.
Vidal Alejandro, Pavel and Omar Everleny Pérez Villanueva. 2010. "Entre al ajuste fiscal y los cambios estructurales: Se extiende el cuentapropismo en Cuba," *Espacio Laical*, No. 112, October.
Vidal Alejandro, Pavel and Omar Everleny Pérez Villanueva. 2012. "Apertura al cuentapropismo y la microempresa, una pieza clave del ajuste estructural," in *Miradas a la economia cubana: El proceso de acualización*. Edited by Pavel Vidal Alejandro and Omar Everleny Pérez Villanueva. Havana: Editorial Caminos.
Vignoli, Gabriel. 2014. "Schizonomics: Remapping La Habana's black market," Ph.D. Dissertation, New School for Social Research, Department of Anthropology, May.
Viño Zimerman, Luis. 2001. "Politica de exterminio de la iniciativa privada," *Cubanet*, No. 32, April 1.
Wald, Karen Lee, Walter Lippmann, and Nelson Valdés. 2004. "Pilfering: A Little Analysis Needed Here." *CubaNews* List, September 25.
Walder, Andrew G. 1994. "The Decline of Communist Power: Elements of a Theory of Institutional Change." *Theory and Soceity* 23:2 (April), pp. 297-324.
Walder, Andrew G. 1995. "The Quiet Revolution from Within: Economic Reform as a Source of Political Decline." In *The Waning of the Communist State: Economic Origins of Political Decline in China and Hungary*, edited by Andrew G. Walder. Berkeley: University of California Press.
Weinreb, Amelia Rosenberg. 2009. *Cuba in the Shadow of Change: Daily Life in the Twilight of the Revolution*. Gainesville: University Press of Florida.
Wessenstein, Michael. 2014. "Cuba Cracks Down on Goods in Flyers' Luggage," *AP*, August 31.
Weissert, Will. 2009. "Calling all cars: Cuba recruits free-market taxis," *Associated Press*, January 12.

Whitefield, Mimi. 1993. "Rapid changes push Cuba into unknown: Will reforms spin out of control?" *Miami Herald*, September 27.
Whitefield, Mimi. 1994a. "Cuban home eateries refuse to close shop: Undeterred by government order," *Miami Herald*, January 7.
Whitefield, Mimi. 1994b. "Cuba Tries to Reign In Market Abuses," *Miami Herald*, January 29.
Whitefield, Mimi. 1996a. "A Taste of Capitalism," *Miami Herald*, May 19.
Whitefield, Mimi. 1996b. "The Taxman Comes to Cuba ," *Miami Herald*, June 9.
Whitefield, Mimi. 2013. "Budding entrepreneurs face obstacles," *Miami Herald*, August 12.
Wilkinson, Stephen. 2006. *Detective Fiction in Cuban Society and Culture*. Bern: Peter Lang.
Wu, Tim. 2011. *The Master Switch: The Rise and Fall of Information Empires*. New York: Vintage.
Xinhua News Agency. 2013. "Prensa official respalda cierre de salas privadas de cine 3D en Cuba," November 11.
Yáñes, Hernán. 2005. "The Cuba-Venezuela Alliance: 'Emancipatory Neo-Bolivarismo' or Totalitarian Expansion?" Occasional Paper Series, Institute for Cuban and Cuban-American Studies, University of Miami, December.
Yhanes, A.S. 2012. "La Ópera que nunca cerró," *La Jiribilla*, August 4-10.
Zimbalist, Andrew and Susan Eckstein. 1987. "Patterns of Cuban Development: The First Twenty-Five Years." In Andrew Zimbalist, editor, *Cuba's Socialist Economy toward the 1990s*. Boulder, CO: Lynne Rienner.
Zimbalist, Andrew. 1987. *Cuba's Socialist Economy toward the 1990s*. Boulder, CO: Lynne Rienner.
Zúñiga, Jesús. 1999. "Paladares amargan la vida de restaurantes estatales," *Cubanet*, September 6.
Zurbano, Roberto. 2013. "For Blacks in Cuba, the Revolution Hasn't Begun," *The New York Times*, March 23.

Index

Absenteeism, 43, 62, 200
Actualización, 2, 140
Adam Smith, 6, 30
Advertising, 226, 267, 282, 288, Cooperatives, 192; Loosening restrictions, 175-177, 180 (n23), 308; prohibition of, 103, 106, 146, 245, 257, 258
Agrarian Reform Law, 55, 56, 57
Agriculture, 3, 9, 55, 57, 61, 209, 322, 323, 325, agricultural markets, 90; agricultural production, 84, 136, 186; agricultural production cooperatives, 67, 159, 185, 186, 187, 194; imports and exports 83, 135, 136 (table); private farmers, 57, 66, 68, 70, 77, 106, 136, 142, 229, 317, 319, 323; property rights, 11, 19, 182, 280
Alarcón, Ricardo, 95, 255
Acopio procurement system, 66, 337
Amiguismo, 74, 75, 210, 337. See also *sociolismo*
Anti-Loafing Law, 44, 48, 64
Aquino, Maestro Ulises, 20, 243, 286-291
Arts and Crafts, 65, 100, 106, 128, 328
Association for the Study of the Cuban Economy, 137, 179
Authoritarian, 5, 43, 48, 237, 261
Automobiles, market for, 162, 175, 231, 325, 326
Barbershops and beauty shops, 87, 88 (table), 142, 143, 190, 235, 280, 284; vignette, 220-221
Battle of Ideas, 117, 213, 233, 301, 322
Bed and Breakfasts, 15, 42, 90, 99, 119, 161, 170, 242, 263, 308. See also *Casa Particular*
Bicitaxi, (pedicab or "bicycle-taxi"), 97, 231, 263, 318
Big Old Swindle, 322, 334
Bisnero, 38
Black market, 10, 129, 204, 205 (table), 303, 317, 328; causal forces, 74-76, 84-85, 149, 165, 182, 206, 209-216, 243, 262, 292, 294 (n11); clandestine enterprises and the black market, 121; developmental consequences, 84-85, 223 (table), 224, 227-230; deterrence, 233, 236, 295 (n19); in state socialist economies generally, 17, 38; expansion after 1959, 40, 41, 57, 60, 64-67; Padura's novel, 243 (n13); *paladares*, 268, 269, 273, 279; prices, 125 (n9), 137, 182, 232, 242 (n6); Rectification Process, 70, 71. See also Underground economy and economic illegalities
Boti, Regino, 54
Brazil, 134, 155, 185, 250, 267
Buen Provecho, paladar, 281-282, 303
Bureaucratic controls. See Regulations
Campaign against illegalities, 17, 228, 229, 230, 295, campaign of October 2005 to March 2006, 206, 207, 230-232
Canada, 27, 185, 193
Cantillion, Richard, 24
Casa de Contratación, 52, 337
Casa particular, 327. See also bed and breakfasts
Castro Ruz, President Fidel: accession to power, 51; "Battle of Ideas," 17, 213, 233, 301, 322, 40; cooperatives, 189; economic illegalities, 203, 210, 217, 230, 231, 320, 322; economic reforms, 55; economic team, 141; illness, 49, 127, 137, 322; "History Will Absolve Me," 54, 342; missile crisis, 316; policy orientation, 54, 61, 137, 276, 307; policy towards small enterprise, 11, 14, 93, 96, 130, 143, 248, 266, 275, 276, 286, 297, 298, 300, 301, 309; quotations, 1, 61, 95, 217, 243, 245, 266, 324; repudiation by brother's policies, 144, 145, 177, 181, 182, 200, 211, 228, 285, 305, 309; "Special Period," 89, 318; sugar sector, 136

365

Castro Ruz, President Raúl: accession to power, 71, 127; agriculture reforms, 186; agricultural markets, 89-90; context for reforms, 130-138; corruption and illegalities, 228, 230; economic reforms, 4, 5, 18, 21, 29, 127-180; egalitarianism, 3, 275; evaluation of reforms, 304-306; first reforms, 2006-2010, 141-142; future approach, 309-312; lay-offs, labor redundancy, 7, 13, 142-144; pragmatism, 14, 29, 177, 195, 220, 285, 286; quotations, 1, 12, 93, 138-141, 245, 267, 276, 297; repudiation of Fidel's policies, 144, 145, 177, 181, 182, 200, 211, 228, 285, 297-298, 305, 309; resistance to reforms, 174, 280, 285-286; small enterprise, approach to, 7, 11, 12, 13, 21, 39, 93, 241; state sector layoffs, private sector job creation, 142-144; views on reform, 138-141, 297, 298; underground economy during Raul's Presidency, 235-239

Casa particular, 337. See also "Bed and Breakfasts"

Center for the Study of the Cuban Economy, 137, 337

Central de Trabajadores de Cuba, 127

Central Planning Board, 56, 61, 83. See also *Junta Central de Planificación (JUCEPLAN)*

Central planning, 51, 54, 60, 61, 236; System, 41-43, 209, 299; Difficulties, 138; Unintended consequences, 73-74, 75, 82, 210

Centro Cultural Padre Félix Varela, 313

Centro de Estudios sobre la Economía Cubana. See Center for the Study of the Cuban Economy

China, 48, 134, 155, 266, 277, 300, 307

Cigars, 52, 74, 82, 85, 168, 206, 213, 217

Civil society, 19, 22, 27, 38, 57, 162, 309, 311

Cold War, 31

Coffee, 66, 82, 135

Collectivization, 54, 55, 57, 64

Colonial period, 27, 31, 37, 51-52, 208, 299

Command economy, 54-58

Committee for the Defense of the Revolution, 76

Common property problem, 210, 236, 242

Communist Party of Cuba, 5, 59, 60, 61, 90, 210, 288; congress, 2, 68, 300, 276, 317; corruption, 228; resistance to policies, 286, 291; role in cooperatives, 197, 200. See Sixth Congress of the Communist Party of Cuba

Competition, 208, 226, 308; effects of microenterprise liberalization, 99, 117, 129, 145, 159, 172; state sector competition with microenterprise, 8, 101, 105, 107, 124, 128, 164; *paladar*, 251, 253, 259, 275; tax regime, 117, 118

Conciencia, 59, 61, 62, 93

Contraband trade, 37, 52, 53, 91, 208, 219, 239, 299

Convertible Cuban peso, 105, 111, 133, 150, 210, 212, 242 (n6)

Cooperatives, non-agricultural, 4, 18, 128, 171, 172, 174, 181-201, 198 (table), 302, 311, 313; "Second degree" cooperatives, 192; advantages, 191-193; agricultural, 64, 185, 193, 301; approval process, 188, 198 (table); Credit and Service Cooperatives, 186; disadvantages or limitations, 193-197; implementation process, 197-199; managerial structure, 189; types of cooperatives, 186 (table), 190

Corruption, 25; campaigns against corruption, 17, 206, 228, 229-232, 295 (n16); high-level, 38, 46; low-level, 40, 41, 69. See also economic illegalities

Council for Mutual Economic Assistance (CMEA), 63

Criminal economy, 33, 34, 205, 223

Critics of government policy, 137, 146, 165, 179, 180, 259, 265, 309, 313

CUC. See Convertible Cuban peso

Cuentapropista. See Small enterprise

Culture of illegality, 7, 8, 30, 73, 123, 124, 203, 207, 240

Cuota fija mensual, 109-110, 118, 156, 337. See also Monthly lump-sum tax

Definitions: cooperative enterprise, 184;

informal sector, 32-34; second economy, 39-44, 241 (n3); self-employment activities, 164, 162, 326, 327-337; small enterprise, microenterprise, and self-employment, 9
De Soto, Hernando, 7, 21, 26, 34, 34-37, 39, 47, 122, 226
Domínguez, Jorge, 76, 251, 280, 285, 286, 311
Downsizing of state sector, 22, 86, 99, 143, 172
Draft Guidelines for Economic and Social Reform for the Party and the Revolution, 2, 147-149, 181, 187, 188, 194, 324
Dual currency and exchange rate system, 134, 177 (n3), . See also Exchange rate system
Eastern Europe, 6, 24-30, 42-46, 49, 299; Economic reforms, 276, 306-307; Economic relations, 79, 81, 83, 316. See also Second economy
Economic assistance (from the Soviet Union to Cuba), 55, 63 (fig.)
Economic crisis, 70; during "Special Period" 79, 81-85, 218, 240, 297
Economic illegalities, 15, 17, 18, 203-243; causal forces, 204, 208-213; character, 204; pre-revolutionary roots, 208; social and economic consequences, 222-228; specific cases, 218-222; varieties of illegalities, 213-218. See also Corruption
Economic liberalization, 81-92, 242
Economic model, 2, 5, 17, 52, 139, 182, 257, 300
Economic melt-down, 2, 133
Economic performance, 70, 72, 131, 191, 235, 353, 359
Economic recovery, 18, 79, 124, 131, 237, 273
Economic reform, 4-6, 13, 16-21, 127-180, 245; context for reform, 1990-1993, 81-92; context for reforms, 2006-2014, 130-137; cooperatives, 181-201; czar Marino Murillo, 182, 198; future reform, 297-312; Presidency or Raúl Castro, 127-180; Revolutionary reforms, 1959-1961, 56 (table); Special Period economic reforms, 79-126; within socialist systems, 40, 44-46, 48 (n2)
El Cabildo, 20, 285-291, 293, 303, 304, 344
El Rinconcito, 252, 256-257, 267, 281-282, 303
Embargo, U.S., 6, 82, 83, 90, 315, 316, 318, 321, 326
Employment. See Labor force and employment
Energy crisis, 83
Entrepreneurship, 17, 209, 223 (table), 226, 249, 273, 277; aptitudes towards, 128, 225, 302; attitudes towards entre-preneurship, 28-30,177, 276, 303; concept, 23-25; egalitarianism, 40; informality and entrepreneurship, 35; underground entrepreneurship. See also Underground economy
Exchange rate system, 83, 198, 319; consequences for incentive structure, 84, 105, 119, 125 (n9), 131, 137, 177 (n3), 235, 242 (n6); consequences for taxation, 111; overvaluation, 134; unification, 148, 150, 241, 238, 241. See Dual currency and exchange rate system
Exports of goods and services. See Trade, foreign
Fidelistas, 309
Food: availability, 84; exports and imports, 84, 130, 136 (fig.), 322; production, 83, 84, 135, 139, 187; rationing, 19, 57, 70, 84, 148, 149, 212
Food service activities, 251, 253, 295. See also *paladar* and Private restaurants
Foreign enterprise, 9, 55, 171, 312; taxation, 117, 143, 155-156, 177
Formal economy, 10, 21, 33, 34, 64, 205. See also Formal sector
Future of small enterprise, 297-313
Gabor, Istaván, 38, 45, 306
Gastronomic services, 87. See also *paladar* and Private restaurants
GDP, 63, 84, 130; GDP per capita, 130, 131 (fig.)
Generación Y, 216, 360
Goldberg Jeffrey, 1, 324
Golden Age of Cuban Socialism, 62-68

368　Index

Guevara, Ernesto "Che," 54, 58, 59, 60, 61, 316
Guia Cuba, 216
Guidelines. See Draft Guidelines
Hairdressers, 65, 190, 220, 235. See also Barbershops and beauty shops
Hart, Keith, 32
Helms-Burton Bill, 83, 319
Household Economy, 34, 204-205
Human rights issues, 321
Imports. See Trade, foreign
Incentives, moral and material, 56, 61, 69
Income distribution. See Income inequalities
Industry, 30, 53, 54, 55, 58, 138, 198, 199, 224
Industrialization, 58, 60, 83
Income inequalities, 12, 29, 93, 224, 294, 300, 306, 308, 312, 322
Informal economy or sector, 11, 23-38, 39, 41, 208, 251, 299
Informality, 5, 7, 16, 21, 22, 23-30
Inspectors of small enterprises, 91, 95, 283; enforcement of microenterprise regulations, 104 (table), 107, 116, 123, 168, 261; further reforms of microenterprise policies, 177; participation in illegal or corrupt practices, 120, 121, 125 (n3), 169, 229, 232, 269, 295 (n20); powers exercised, 261, 266, 271; state enterprises, 234; toleration of infractions, 106-107
Institutional structure, 42, 138, 175, 181, 302
Institutionalization, 316
Intermediaries, 48, 66, 67, 68, 86, 90, 104, 106, 122, 123, 146, 167, 175, 245, 268, 308
International Bank for Reconstruction and Development (World Bank), 208, 351
International Cooperative Alliance, 184, 196, 351
Inventar, 38, 75, 212
Job creation, 6, 142, 174, 308; small enterprise, 142-144, 147, 158; tax on labor, 150, 154, 160
Joint ventures, 38, 80, 212, 302; tax discrimination, 117, 118 (table), 155, 174, 177, 279

José Ramón Machado Ventura, Vice President, 146
JUCEPLAN. See *Junta Central de Planificación*
Junta Central de Planificación, (JUCEPLAN) 56, 83, 351. See also Central Planning Board
La Guarida, 260-261, 267, 271, 279, 286, 293, 303
"*La vieja gran estafa.*" See Big Old Swindle
La Ópera de la Calle, 20, 285, 286, 287, 290, 291, 293
Labor force and employment, 36, 76, 173, 304; by institutional form, 68 (table); China's labor force, 134; Co-operatives, 185, 186 (table), 188, 189, 196; employment, 128; "militarization," 62; self-employment as part of the labor force, 66, 89 (fig.), 170 (fig.), 171; small enterprise sector, 123, 171; state sector employment, 129, 148, 171, 299, 308; Unionization, 169; unregistered, 173, 203-243. See also Job creation, Layoffs, and Redundancy of labor
Latin America, 8-17, 58, 73, 155; experience with the informal sector, 10, 11, 16, 23, 34-38, 42, 298; Cuba's distinct experience with informality, 31, 40, 247, 299; debates over informality, 339, 438; "frustrated or mercantilist" state, 26-30; implications for Cuba, 46, 47
Lay-offs, 141-144, 158. See also Redundancy of labor
Legitimate Underground Economic Activity (LUEA), 15, 18, 29, 34, 204, 240, 247, 293, 302, 304; cases, 217, 218-222; clandestinity, 211, 223, 225-227, 240, 302, 303, 304; costs and benefits, 222-228; origins, 209-213; policies under Raúl Castro's Presidency, 235-239; public policy, 228-232; range and variety, 213-218; schools of entrepreneurship, 225; social and economic consequences, 222-228; tax evasion, 14, 222, 227, 230, 295. See also "Big Old Swindle"
Leibenstein, Harvey, 24, 25

Liberalization, 317; context for liberalization 1990-1993, 81-85; context for liberalization 2006-2014, 130-137; foreign travel, 4, 19; impacts, 128, 238, 242 (n4), 301, 302; policy reversal 1996-2005, 93-122, 207, 250; policy towards microenterprise, 14, 175 (table), 298; reforms of 1992-1996, 86-92; reforms of 2006-2014, 127-160
Licensing of self-employment, 6, 8, 12, 13, 15, 17, 297, 320, 336 (n1); consequences of rejection or restriction, 102, 165, 210, 211, 236, 301, 323; further liberalization, 235, 240, 248, 302, 308; liberalized licensing, 145, 173, 175; licensing fees, 64, 86, 109, 151, 249; process, 96-102, 96 (table)
Lineamientos, 188. See Draft Guidelines
Maceta, 30, 38, 48, 233, 262, 318, 338
Macroeconomic crisis, 83
Manufacturing, 65; before 1959, 52; cooperatives, 190, 192, 194; during "Special Period," 130, 133-134, 167; reforms under Raul Castro, 173, 176, 254
Maravillas de Alicia, 272-273
Marino Murillo. See Murillo Jorge, Marino Alberto
Market for housing, 102, 161, 161, 175, 201, 215, 337
Market socialism, 38, 183, 277, 306, 310
Markets for automobiles. See Automobiles, market for
Marx, Karl, 35, 257
Marxist, 21, 32, 40, 42, 228, 353
Mercados Agropecuarios, 89, 137, 231, 319, 338
Mercados Libres de Campesinos (MLCs), 66
Mercantilism, 32
Micro-credit, 159, 173, 175, 176, 308
Micro-enterprise. See Small enterprise
Mixed Cooperative Market Economy, 310
Moneda Nacional, 83, 105, 112, 177, 212, 224, 319, 338. See also Cuban peso
Monetary system, 83
Moral incentives. See Incentives, moral
Murillo Jorge, Marino Alberto, Minister of the Permanent Commission for the Implementation and Development of the Guidelines, 182, 183, 188, 198
National Assembly: legislation, 90, 138, 323; sessions, 2, 251, 295 (n19), 318; speeches by others, 98, 182, 255, 324; speeches by Raúl Castro at, 1, 12, 29, 142, 185, 285, 324
National Association of Small Farmers (ANAP), 57, 317
Nationalization, 6, 51, 54, 55, 56-57, 59, 72, 209, 297, 299, 315
New Man, 58-62, 189, 350
Nutrition, 83, 90
Oficina Nacional de Administración Tributaria (ONAT), 110
Oscar Espinosa Chepe, 9, 40, 137, 279, 280
Paladar, 20, 49, 90-92, 124, 161, 176, 245-296, 305; *doce sillas*, 246, 253, 267, 269, 272; expansion, 87, 248, 275, 280-285; legalization, 250-252; official criticisms of *paladares*, 29, 95, 270, 275, 285; regulation, 103, 104, 106, 107, 145, 151, 158, 252-263, 270; taxation, 110, 152, 153 (table); vignettes, 91, 246-247, 252, 256-257, 258-259, 260-261, 264-265, 268, 272, 281-283
Pazos, Felipe, 54
Permanent Commission for the Implementation and Development of the Guidelines, 188, 194
Personal Income Tax, 107, 157, 257, 275
Pilferage, 129, 132, 133, 149, 213, 215, 227, 236, 238, 300
Private restaurants, 29, 91, 103, 110, 125, 126, 213, 245-296. See also *Paladar*
Private Sector, 4-9, 15, 41, 44; consequences of expansion, 8, 13, 53; consequences of suppression, 71-76, 96; definition, 48 (fn.1); expansion 1990-1993, 80; farmers' markets, 66, 67, 68; further policy reforms, 173-177, 297-312; job-creation, 142-144, 305; nationalization, 22, 27, 51, 54-57, 56 (table); political implications, 46, 60, 65; regulatory environment, 102-109, 104 (table); President Fidel

Castro's policy approach, 5, 6, 17, 60, 95, 124; President Raúl Castro's policy approach, 138-173; tax regime, 150-157. See also Small enterprise, Economic reforms
Private transportation, 111, 248, 254, 320. See also Taxi
Privatization, 142, 232, 234, 312
Property rights, 11, 19, 182, 280, 284, 309, 311
Rationing, 19, 57, 70,140, 148; rationing system, 73-74, 84, 149, 210, 212, 242
Raulistas, 309
Real wages, 131, 237
Rectification Process (RP), 68-71, 79, 300
Redundancy of labor, 2, 127, 150, 171, 173, 187, 298. See also Layoffs
Regulation, 144-147, 157, 160, 163; complexity, control and evasion, 23-28, 34, 73, 75, 123; culture of illegality or compliance, 128, 176, 238, 306; effective regulation, 37, 124, 232, 306; further changes to regulations, 173-177; impacts on downsizing informal sector, 99, 107, 109, 116, 123; impacts on underground economy, 207, 211, 222, 229, 236, 304; in authoritarian regimes, 21, 22; informal sector, 32, 33, 34, 35, 36, 28, 42, 90; necessity of regulatory framework, 123, 175; *paladares*, 91, 246, 249, 252-263, 278, 320; regulatory environment during the "Special Period," 103-109, 104 (table); relaxation, 144, 145, 157, 158, 160-162, 238; rental regulations, 92, 97, 99; second economy, 41-44, 47
Regulatory capacity, 22, 26 (table), 247
Regulatory system, 90, 124, 127, 227, 230
Remittances, 80, 105, 132, 156, 161, 212, 242, 265, 311
Research methods, 14-16
Resolver, 38, 75, 212, 338
Retail clothing prohibition, 2013, 18, 163-166
Revolico.com, 215, 216, 217
Revolution, major reforms, 1959-1961, 56-57 (table)

Revolutionary Offensive, 6, 51, 52, 58-62, 72, 209, 297, 299
Rodríguez, José Luis, 86, 94
Russia, 8, 81, 102, 300
Salaries. See Wages
Second Economy, 21-23, 203, 207, 210, 240, 276; Cuban context, 47, 48 (n5), 241 (n3), 247, 299, 300, 307; within socialist states, 23, 28, 30-32, 39-47, 299, 306. See also Informal economy, Underground economy and Economic illegalities
Self-employment. See Small enterprise
Simplified tax regime, 150-152
Sixth Congress of the Communist Party of Cuba, 142, 276
Small enterprise, 4-6; advantages and benefits, 7, 8; analytical approaches, 23-30; consequences of suppression, 71-76, 122-124; containment, 93-96; definitions, 9, 47-48 (n1); disadvantages and costs, government perception, 7, 8; future of small enterprise, 297-312; licensing process, 96-102 (table). See also Licensing of self-employment; limitations, 162-169; magnitude and expansion, 80, 89 (fig.), 169-173, 170 (fig.); nationalizations, 54-57, 59-61; professionals, 4, 14, 18, 65, 86, 108, 162, 182, 188, 196, 211, 214, 291, 308, 319, 325; restaurants. See *Paladares*; range of activities or occupations, 88 (table), 254 (table), 327-332; reforms, 86-93, 144-147, 158-162, 175 (table). See Economic reforms; regulations, 103-109, 104 (table), 167-169. See Regulation; small enterprise before 1959, 52-53; stigmatization, 17, 30, 124, 173, 211, 255, 302; taxation, 109-122, 110 (table), 112 (table), 118 (table), 150-157, 153 (table), 157 (table). See also Taxation and Underground economy
Socialismo, 49 (n12), 75, 76 (n5), 77 (n5), 210, 307. See also *Amiguismo*
Soviet Union: economic subsidization, 63 (table), 81; problems of transition, 10, 49 (n11); roots of Cuba's economic melt-down, 6, 70, 79, 81, 318; second or informal economy,

23, 27, 37, 41, 47, 49 (n9), 247; special relationship with Cuba, 55, 58, 63, 69, 79, 300, 316
Special Period in Time of Peace or "Special Period," 1990-2006, 17, 79-125, 318-320, 327; agricultural sector during, 134, 137; consequences of containment of microenterprise, 123-124; containing microenterprise, 1996-2005, 93-122; context for policy liberalization, 81-85; *paladares* during, 250-267; reforms of 1992-1996, 86-93;
State socialism, 39-46, 310; cooperatives, 182; Eastern Europe and the Soviet Union, 30, 306-307; institutional framework, 21, 22, 28, 47; *paladares*, 249, 267; regulation, prohibition, and informality, 27, 28, 31, 233, 240; second economy, 39-44
"Stigmatization" and "de-stigmatization" of self-employment, 17, 30, 124, 173, 211, 255, 302
Street vendors, 57, 68, 72, 145, 170, 254, 257, 265, 283, 295, 321
Structural adjustment, 4, 143
Sugar harvest, 58, 59, 60, 69
Sugar sector: 10 million ton target, 48 (n2), 51, 58, 60, 61, 299, 316; domestic pricing, 125 (n9); exports, 82 (fig.), 135; nationalization, 56, 315; post-1970 development strategies, 69; production collapse, 130, 134, 135 (fig.), 136, 176-177 (n3), 321; rationing system, 212, 242 (n6); Soviet market, 81, 315; U.S. market, 55, 315
Survival strategies: "extra-legal," 205, 227, 245, 250, 253, 307; entrepreneurs and self-employed, 15, 32; families, 85, 119; *paladares*, 125 (n3) 253, 256, 267-273; underground economy, 97, 267-273
System of Economic Direction and Planning, 64
Taxation, 32, 41, 109-122, 110 (table), 112 (table), 118 (table), 153 (table), 157 (table), "10% rule," 110, 112-113, 117-118, 153-154, 238; "bed and breakfasts," 90; *cuota fija mensual*, 109, 337; effective tax rates, 118, 152, 154-157, 175, 308; evasion, 14, 53, 102, 119, 152, 222, 227, 230, 295; foreign investment in joint ventures, 118, 154-157; monthly lump-sum tax, 107, 110, 118, 157; microenterprise or self-employment, 90, 109-122; of *paladares*, 110 (table), 152-153, 249; personal income tax, 65, 98, 107, 110, 112 (table), 142, 145, 147, 157, 161, 177, 249, 257, 275; reforms, 150-151; tax holiday, 118
Taxi particular. See also Taxi
Taxi, 65, 85, 90, 92, 102; cooperative taxis, 198, 200 (n2); illegalities, 214, 225, 269; regulation relaxation, 141-142, 158, 161, 221, 222, 280, 284; vignette, 100-101, 114-115
Tiendas por la recaudación de divisas, 133, 156, 338
Tobacco, 60, 66, 82, 133, 135
Totalitarian, 26-30, 37-38, 43, 48, 228, 264, 172
Trabajo por cuenta propia (TPCP). See self-employment
Trade, foreign, 37, 55, 79, 61, 318; agricultural, 81, 130, 135 (fig.), 136 (fig.), 322; agreements, 63; colonial, 52, 208; contraband, 52, 53, 208; exports, 82 (fig.), 83, 134, 135, 136 (fig.); imports, 81, 83, 84, 119, 122, 130, 162; Soviet Union, 63, 79, 81, 316, 317; Sugar exports, 58; United States, 83, 315, 316
Transition (from central planning), 5, 8, 14, 44, 49, 79, 93, 306, 310
Unemployment and Underemployment, 22, 36, 43, 44, 64, 70, 80, 125, 130, 154, 165, 317
Underground economy, analytical approach, 14, 15, 28, 93, 205 (table); cases, 218-222, 241-242 (n4); control, 116, 120, 123, 124, 145, 168, 309; emergence from, 146, 298, 304, 317; historical roots, 208, 299; magnitude, 64, 171, 300, 302; origins and causes, 9, 17, 64, 85, 97, 102, 119, 203-213, 310; recent policy approach, 10, 229-232, 235-239, 297; social and economic consequences, 7, 71, 73, 222-228, 223 (table); vari-

eties of illegalities, 164, 188, 213-218, 242. See also Economic illegalities and Black market
Unidades Básicas de Producción Cooperativa (UBPC), 185
United States, 14, 26, 208, 219; cooperatives, 185; diplomatic relations, 54, 55, 311, 315; embargo, 83, 90, 315, 316, 318, 321, 326; informal employment, 32, 150; trade, 135, 150, 218
Updating of the Cuban Economy, 2, 5, 32, 140, 162, 307. See also *Actualización*
U.S.S.R. See Soviet Union
Valdés Vivo, Raúl, 93, 94, 320
Vidal Alejandro, Pavel, 22, 132, 176 (n4)
Venezuela, 13, 130, 218, 266

Wage levels, 150, 152, 208, 212, 294 (n7), 300, 322, 323; cooperatives, 188, 189, 191; state sector, 43, 64, 136, 137, 141, 142, 181, 231, 237; real inflation-adjusted wages, 131, 132 (fig.), 138; underground economy, 222, 225
Walmart, 312
Wholesale markets, 4, 6, 146, 149, 160, 174, 175, 176, 177, 198, 278, 279, 308
Workers' democracy, 197
Yoani Sánchez, 48, 215, 216, 270, 294

About the Book

During the presidency of Raúl Castro, Cuba has dramatically reformed its policies toward small private enterprises. Archibald Ritter and Ted Henken consider why—and to what effect.

After reviewing the evolution of policy since 1959, the authors contrast the approaches of Fidel and Raúl Castro and explore in depth the responses of Cuban entrepreneurs to the new environment. Their work, rich in ethnographic research and extensive interviews, provides a revealing analysis of Cuba's fledgling private sector.

Archibald R.M. Ritter is distinguished research professor emeritus of economics and international affairs at Carleton University.

Ted A. Henken is associate professor of sociology and Latin American studies at Baruch College, CUNY.